Everto:

A lifelong Evertonian, James Corbett was born in Liverpool in 1978. He founded and edited the popular *Gwladys Sings The Blues* fanzine between 1994 and 1997, before leaving to study at the London School of Economics and Birkbeck College. He writes for the influential Egyptian newspaper *Al Ahram Weekly*, is married, and lives in London.

JAMES CORBETT

Everton

The School of Science

PAN BOOKS

First published 2003 by Macmillan

This edition published 2004 by Pan Books
an imprint of Pan Macmillan Ltd
Pan Macmillan, 20 New Wharf Road, London N1 9RR
Basingstoke and Oxford
Associated companies throughout the world
www.panmacmillan.com

ISBN 0 330 42006 2

1 3 5 7 9 8 6 4 2

A CIP catalogue record for this book is available from
the British Library.

Typeset by SetSystems Ltd, Saffron Walden, Essex
Printed and bound in Great Britain by
Mackays of Chatham plc, Chatham, Kent

To Dad

for showing me the way

'We owe a great deal to Everton. No matter where they play, and no matter whether they are well or badly placed in the League table, they always manage to serve up football of the highest scientific order. Everton always worship at the shrine of craft and science and never do they forget the standard of play they set out to achieve.'

Steve Bloomer, 1928

Contents

List of Illustrations

Unless otherwise indicated, all photos are courtesy of the *Liverpool Daily Post & Echo*.

Acknowledgements

Completing a work of this size would simply not be possible without the help of many individuals, be they friends, associates, archivists or others. The roles of some may be more apparent than others, but to each and every one of the following I owe a debt of gratitude.

An original draft of this book, infinitely different from that which you read today, was completed six years ago, at the tail end of my three years as editor of *Gwladys Sings the Blues*. David Pearson and Rory O'Keeffe were my team back in those days, and every second spent with them on what was one of the most enjoyable projects I have undertaken was a pleasure. A number of others, Andrew Corbett, Daniel Hignett, Dave Kelly, Stephen Masterson, Rolant Ellis and Claire Redhead, were fundamental at various stages of its three-year life to it being a success. A debt of gratitude is belatedly owed to Graham Ennis, editor of *When Skies Are Grey*, for being generous enough not to slate a bunch of adolescent upstarts, when I'm sure it was deserved on a few occasions. George Orr, who is now editor of the *Blueblood* fanzine, was also a regular contributor and his diaries as an Evertonian (listed in the bibliography) are an excellent account of some of the joy and much of the angst that go with the territory of being born a Toffee.

While *Gwladys Sings the Blues* fashioned many of my ideas of what it means to be an Evertonian and much of my understanding of the history of the club, there were plenty of people who shaped me as a writer. Viv Graver, Mike Rogers, Jim Thompson, Dave Holmes, Dr Kirsten Schulze, Dr Anita Prazmowska, Dr Robert Singh and Professor Mark Mazower all at one time or another proved inspiring teachers. Thank you.

The staff of the British Library, the Newspaper Archive in Colindale and the British Library of Social and Political Science were invariably and unstintingly helpful and patient. Ian Leonard and Tony Hall were particularly helpful in locating some really fantastic photographs: my thanks for your endeavour.

A far more illustrious author than myself once described my agent, Toby Eady, as being 'the best in the world' – I could not agree more.

Equally, his assistant, William Fisher, always provided generous help and support, and kept my chin up when the heat was on.

I was incredibly lucky to find a splinter cell of staunch Evertonians at Macmillan. My publishers David North and Ursula Doyle provided the necessary injection of enthusiasm that has seen this book come into print. Sam Humphreys, working diligently behind the scenes, has been the embodiment of helpfulness and organization, and Hazel Orme did a wonderful job editing the manuscript. Emma Bravo did a great job publicising the book, likewise Tommy Burns, Roger Kenyon and Bryan Snag of Bluenose in Liverpool. Once a Blue . . . Always a Blue. Thank you all.

My dear friend Mukul Devichand has twice provided me with life-changing advice, and in many ways set me back down the path of undertaking such an ambitious project: 'Expect the impossible' is his mantra, and it isn't a bad creed to follow. On a day-to-day basis the acerbic wit of James Macintyre, Daniel Lewis, Stephen Tudhope, David Locke and Stephen Lawson kept me going while I was thundering along to the book's conclusion. Others who have helped keep a smile on my face – even at my most grumpy – have been my brothers Michael and David Corbett, my sister Anna, my mother, Mary, Cath Mills and Ann Wright.

Other members of my family have generously lent their stories and memories of Everton, some of which are recalled in these pages. To my grandfather, Charles Mills, my uncles Charles and Peter Mills and my cousins Tom and Lucy Mills, my thanks. A special debt of gratitude is owed to a great family friend, Dick White, whose wonderful anecdotes, particularly of Dean and Lawton, illuminate several chapters.

A good Evertonian would be nothing without his football widow, or so their wives will tell you. I would not be allowed to get away without mentioning the silent but cheerful suffering of Liz and Sheila Mills, or that of my late grandmother, May Mills, who had to put up with not only fifty-two years of marriage to one of Goodison's most fanatical patrons, but three children and a son-in-law all hooked on the club, plus a dozen grandchildren likewise inclined. My own wonderful wife Catherine – who first met me in the midst of the woeful Smith years – has not only had a glimpse of some of the lows of being a football widow but has also been subjected to my working on this labour of love.

The book is dedicated to my father, who set me down the venerable path of being both an Evertonian and a historian. My deepest thanks.

With such a team of support – and I would rate them with Catterick or Kendall's finest – it seems astonishing that any work could still have shortcomings. Unfortunately it does, and they are mine.

JAMES CORBETT, July 2003

Foreword by Alex Young

I left Everton Football Club in 1968. But I can honestly say that Everton has never left me.

Most professional footballers embrace some sort of superstitions. But I am the sort of person who can walk into a room and immediately sense vibes about a place – and when I first walked into Goodison Park in November 1960 I could feel something almost spiritual.

People may say that that's just so much mumbo jumbo, but I still get that feeling whenever I go back. Everton possesses a kind of magic – and it is a magic generated by the quality of players who have graced the stadium over the past 125 years.

I was fortunate enough to be accepted by the Evertonians when I arrived from Scotland, even though I hardly played for two or three months. Maybe they knew the kind of player I tried to be. I was immediately made aware of players of the calibre of Dixie Dean, Tommy Lawton and Joe Mercer who had already enriched Everton – and the unique philosophy Evertonians revelled in, the almost mystical Soccer School of Science. I later learned that the phrase was first coined by a legendary pre-First World War goalscorer, the great Steve Bloomer.

'Everton always aim to serve at the shrine of craft and science,' he said. 'They always try to serve up football of the highest scientific order.'

Collecting trophies may have been enough for the Manchester Uniteds, Liverpools and Arsenals of the football world; Evertonians wanted their teams to do that, but to do it with a certain artistry, too.

It was a demand that the club managed to live up to in the 1960s, it was there at the start of the 1970s and it was strictly adhered to in the 1980s. It has not been the case since then, and that has niggled me a wee bit. But hopefully with the arrival of a dynamic new manager like David Moyes and a wonderful young talent like Wayne Rooney we could be on the brink of another new era of scientific football.

Even though I left Everton thirty-five years ago – and even though I started my career at Hearts in Scotland, I still regard myself as an Evertonian.

The relegation-haunted seasons of recent memory have left me pacing the floors at night, just as the glory years left me walking on air.

They are all covered in this wonderful new book which I am delighted to endorse, even though the author hadn't even been born by the time I hung up my boots. But then Everton truly is the people's club, spanning all ages, creeds and nationalities.

I am proud to call myself an Evertonian, and have enjoyed reading once again about the club's 125 years of drama, colour, spectacle, history and tradition. I hope you enjoy it just as much, and can share just a little of the very special magic which makes up Everton Football Club – the first and still the only School of Soccer Science.

1

From St Domingo's to the
Football League

IT'S MATCH DAY in Liverpool 4. Even though kick-off is still two hours away, there is already a buzz of excited anticipation. The street sellers are out in force, hoping to do a brisk trade in scarves, hats, badges, shirts, newspapers, fanzines, programmes and burgers. The pubs are filling up too, and although it's late December, patrons are spilling out on to the streets around Goodison. Walking down Goodison Road, I see familiar faces; I don't know these people, but over the years we have shared moments of glory and despair, sung in the same chorus and added our voices to the unmistakable Goodison roar.

At the gates to the Park Stand, a steward is politely telling the ticketless hopefuls that it's a full house. Someone asks: 'Is *he* playing?' The nameless individual could in the past have been a Dean, or a Young, a Latchford or even a Ferguson – the anonymity is not a barrier. He is a hero and the reverence is such that he need not be named. He evokes instant recognition.

'Team's not been announced yet,' replies the steward. 'But I think *he* will.'

The great unnamed of the early twenty-first century is the club's most promising youngster since the war. For the uninitiated, his name is Rooney.

I walk on past more hot-dog sellers and the Megastore, where queues double back round its corner, over Walton Lane and across Stanley Park, alongside a steady stream of fans, mostly wearing blue, although some Christmas Lacoste and Stone Island sweaters are also in evidence. I carry on across the park, in the shadow of the decaying splendour of former merchants' houses and then Liverpool's ground,

Anfield. A bench has been daubed with the words 'SuperKev' in honour of Everton's current number nine.

Stretched out in front of me are the hills of South Lancashire, distant high-rise flats and, nearer, coaches lined up along Priory Road. And football pitches. Row upon row of muddy fields, marked out with white paint and crooked goalposts at either end. Here, on this south-eastern corner of Stanley Park, in the winter of 1878, the parishioners of St Domingo's Methodist Church first began kicking a football around. Then St Domingo's was just eight years old. It was an amalgamation of three Methodist churches – Bevington Hill, Chatham Place and Hotham Street. The prominent families of this new church bore names that would resonate for the first few decades of Everton Football Club's history: the Cuffs, the Mahons and the Wades.

The church was far more than a place of worship – indeed, work began on the building of St Domingo's School in 1869, a full year before it began on the chapel. Parish societies included an athletics club, and later on a cricket team. And in the winter of 1878, the cricketers took up association football.

Although the Football Association had been formed in 1863, and the FA Challenge Cup inaugurated in 1871, the game was still to penetrate Liverpool. Rugby Union was the winter game of choice of the middle-class families who formed the most influential part of St Domingo's congregation – Liverpool Rugby Union Club had been founded in 1862.

St Domingo's Football Club did not play in any organized competition. Instead they took part in exhibition matches against other local parishes. There was no dressing room, no stands and few spectators. There were certainly no gate receipts and any expenses were paid by the members. Early matches, wrote Thomas Keates (1849–1928), the first chronicler of Everton's history, were played in 'a very crude character', the ball being kicked around in an 'every-man-for-himself scramble for possession'. But despite these humble beginnings, the fledgling St Domingo's team began to acquire a reputation as one of the better local sides, poaching a number of players from its rivals and developing a following of fans.

Liverpool then had one of the most reforming and active local corporations of the day, and much of the proud civic architecture that adorns the city dates from the middle fifty years of the nineteenth century, when Liverpool was at the height of its wealth and influence. Stanley Park came at the tail end of this burst of construction. Taking the lead from a host of mid-century governmental investigations into the industrial living conditions and the plight of the urban poor, public parks were increasingly seen as an antidote to the filth and smog of Britain's cities. The country's first – Birkenhead Park – was opened to the public in 1844, and Sefton Park followed at the end of the 1860s. In 1870 the hundred acres of Stanley Park to the north of the city were opened, the land acquired at a cost of £140,000.

Little more than a year after its formation, St Domingo's was attracting a considerable following of 'outsiders', and the decision was taken – in the interests of inclusiveness – to change its name. At a meeting held at the Queen's Head Hotel in November 1879, Everton Football Club was born. (A plaque that today adorns the wall of the Sandon Hotel states that it was the founding place of Everton Football Club. This is incorrect. The Queen's Head was Everton's first headquarters and the site of its renaming. Nevertheless, within three years, the Sandon was adopted as Everton's new base and remained so until 'the Split' of 1892.) A month later, on 23 December 1879, the new club played its first match.

Despite the change of name, ties remained strong with St Domingo's. Arthur Riley Wade, whose father Joseph Wade was one of St Domingo's original trustees and had laid the foundation stone of the chapel in 1870, was an early player and later director of the club. Will Cuff – a key figure in the club's first sixty years as manager-secretary, then chairman – was later both choirmaster and trustee of the church. George Mahon, its organist, was a leading proponent of Everton's move to Goodison. Today, St Domingo's is no more. After celebrating its centenary in 1971 it amalgamated with another local church to form Oakfield Methodist Church. Its site and buildings were sold and the new church moved to the junction of Oakfield Road and Oakfields in Anfield, where it remains. The role of the church in providing the founding stone for Everton Football Club was short but crucial; the influence of its congregation, as we shall see, was to live on.

○

ALTHOUGH THE FOUNDATION of the English football league was still a decade away the Lancashire Football Association was founded in

September 1878. Under the presidency of the Marquess of Harting-
ton, it was characterized by in-fighting and the clashing of vested
interests, but provided an organizational structure of sorts and, in
1879, inaugurated the Lancashire Senior Cup. Shambolic though the
association often was, its founder members, Blackburn Rovers, Bolton
Wanderers and, from 1880, Everton, might not have prospered
without it.

Everton practised the dour tactical orthodoxy of the day, boasting
a 2–2–6 formation, but on the Lancashire stage it yielded them little
success. Their first foray into the Lancashire Senior Cup in 1881 saw
them drawn away at Great Lever, a strong Bolton-based team – the
first time the club travelled by train to an away match. After emerging
from the game with a surprise and highly creditable draw, which
Keates claimed was 'entirely due' to a virtuoso display by the Everton
goalkeeper George Bargery, a local bank clerk, they succumbed to a
heavy defeat in the replay, losing 1–8 at Stanley Park.

Closer to home, Everton were enjoying more success. Victories
over Liverpool (5–0), Birkenhead (7–0) and their greatest and most
formidable rivals Bootle added to the new club's growing reputation.

Off the field, strong leaders were emerging. J. W. Clarke, pro-
prietor of the Queen's Head, was the club's early secretary and
treasurer and proved an energetic, effective presence in securing
fixtures against the region's most illustrious teams, an important role
when most were friendlies and exhibition matches. In 1882 he was
succeeded by Tom Evans, a 'modest, yet enthusiastic and genial'
Derbyshire all-rounder, who was vice-captain of the Everton team
and as renowned for his ability with a cricket bat as he was with a
football.

On the field, the services of Jack McGill, a brilliant forward and
coach, were secured from Glasgow Rangers. He was soon elected
captain by his peers and provided much of the inspiration behind
Everton's performances, which earned him representative honours
for both Lancashire and his native Ayrshire. His presence contributed to an impressive 1881/2 season, which saw Everton's record
standing as follows: played 22, won 15, lost 3, drawn 4; goals for 70,
against 16.

It was the ambition of the club's management that carried Everton
forward though. The limitations of playing on a public park were
clear, and with a burgeoning reputation and following, which usually

numbered between 800 and 1500, the necessity of moving to a private ground where admission fees could be charged became pressing. In March 1882, at a meeting in the Sandon Hotel, soon to become the club's headquarters for the next decade, a Mr Cruitt of Coney Green offered the club the use of a field that adjoined his house off Priory Road, and in 1883 the club moved.

Its time at Priory Road, after four seasons in Stanley Park, was short-lived and unhappy. It was a 'long long walk to Priory Road,' complained Keates, 'and no buses come near it.' In an effort to raise Everton's profile, at a time when newspaper coverage of football matches was almost non-existent, a declaration was circulated among Liverpool's well-to-do:

> Allow us to introduce to your notice the position attained by the above named organization [Everton Football Club] and to solicit your most valued sympathy and support.
>
> Established in 1879, it has gradually improved in strength and importance, until it now occupies a position second to none in the district; nor do its claims to consideration rest here, for as the club has, season by season, grown in strength, its effect upon the public has been both marked and encouraging, so much so, that at any of its important fixtures there are large gatherings of persons numbering 500 to 2,000 seeking the Saturday afternoon's recreation which the public parks are intended to provide for.
>
> In order to popularize the game we are this year playing a number of clubs of considerable renown from long distances.[1]

Despite such hype the first match at Priory Road yielded receipts of just fourteen shillings – not nearly enough to sustain a new ground. Yet the club had a number of benefactors, and money was somehow raised for railings around the playing area, some seats, a small grandstand and dressing room. The Scottish educational pioneer Samuel Crosbie, a leading light in Liverpool's educational and musical establishment, boosted the club's sagging bank account by arranging a benefit concert at the Hand-in-Hand club on Foley Street.

Everton's year-long stay at Priory Road did, however, yield them their first ever trophy, the Liverpool and District Cup, in January 1884. Having beaten St Peters in the first round and seen off

Liverpool Ramblers in the second, they triumphed over Earlestown in the final. At the Sandon Hotel, the players were presented with commemorative silver medals, and the club president, John Houlding, guaranteed the cup's safety. Indeed, Everton were practically its custodians, winning it 17 times over the first 40 years of the competition and sharing it on a further two occasions.

At the General Meeting that followed, Houlding was re-elected president. The 52-year-old landlord of the Sandon Hotel was a prominent local businessman. With only a rudimentary schooling behind him, he had started out as an errand boy in the Custom House, later working as a 'cow keeper' with his father. An outbreak of cattle plague forced another change, and he took a job as foreman in W. Clarkson's brewery, rising to chief brewer before setting out on his own. He later became Lord Mayor of Liverpool. In 1884 he was best known for his role as Everton's fixer-in-chief – 'King John of Everton'.

One man who did not take pleasure in Everton's success was their landlord, Mr Cruitt. Not liking his 'pastoral serenity' disturbed he gave Everton leave of notice to depart his Priory Road field. A new ground, however, was soon discovered.

Just outside the city boundary, on Walton-Le-Hill, there were two fields owned by Orrell Brothers' Brewers. On one, John Orrell had built himself a house fronting Anfield Road, with a cottage and stables at the back. His brother Joseph's field, however, was still undeveloped. He agreed to loan it to the club on the terms 'That we the Everton Football Club, keep the existing walls in good repair, pay the taxes, do not cause ourselves to be a nuisance to Mr Orrell and other tenants adjoining and also pay a small sum as rent, or subscribe a donation each year to the Stanley Hospital in the name of Mr Orrell'.[2] John Houlding arranged to be the club's representative tenant and to collect the annual monies.

Everton looked forward to playing in their new Anfield Road home. It was closer to the Sandon Hotel than Priory Road, where committee meetings were held and the players changed, and, as Keates recalled:

The members and players turned themselves into a gang of labourers, with spades and barrows, boards and hammers and nails. A hoarding of boards was fixed on the walls and rails around the playing pitch. Spectators stood on the intervening sods, a very humble stand crouching on the east side for officials, members, pressmen and affluents.[3]

Everton began their sojourn at Anfield in style. A team captained by Tom Marriott defeated the previous season's Liverpool Cup Final opponents, Earlestown, 5–0, on 28 September 1884 in an exhibition match, but it was the cup contests that still attracted most attention. When Everton met Bootle, at the end of January 1885, they took gate receipts of £39 3s., of which they kept half. By contrast, in the whole year at Priory Road, they had taken just £45.

A contemporary report of the Bootle game gives an idea of the sort of passions football had by this time begun to unleash.

This match will ever be memorable in the annals of the Club. After playing an hour and a half in ding-dong fashion without either side scoring, the referee ordered an extra half-hour to be played. The excitement became intense, especially so when Bootle, after ten minutes' play, scored the first goal. 'There goes the Cup!' gasped a prominent Evertonian Vice-President, and this was the general feeling all round. Upon starting the last quarter of an hour's play, Parry and his team played harder than ever, and when Whittle equalized, the cheering was tremendous – the pent-up feelings of the supporters finding relief in all manner of extravagant antics. But when Parry added another goal, just on the call of half-time, the wildest scene that can be imagined took place. Parry was seized by those who were nearest and carried shoulder high from the field to the Sandon Hotel, and the same treatment would doubtless have been meted out to all the team, had they not hurried away to the hut and waited till the crowd dispersed. It was a glorious victory!

Later, Everton met Earlestown in the Liverpool District Cup Final for the second year running. Here, they believed themselves to have been robbed of an equalizer when the ball seemed to have passed between the posts. Goal nets, to be invented by J. A. Brodie, engineer to the City of Liverpool, were still five years away, and disputes as to whether a ball had gone under or over the bar, or inside or outside the goalpost, were frequent.

Cup Final disappointment aside, Everton's record in their first season at Anfield was a proud one. In 32 matches they won 18, lost

10, drew 4, scoring 80 goals and conceding just 13. Income for the season totalled £200, and even then it was suggested that ineffective gate management had reduced receipts. They were more than ready to take on football's next developments.

○

THE EXPANSION OF football from a contest between public school-boys to a game involving crowds often numbering thousands meant that its progress towards professionalism was inevitable. Its emergence as a genuinely classless sport that transcended economic and social boundaries pushed the case further for professionalism. Clubs with working-class players did not want to see them using up all their physical strength on a dockyard or railway during the week. Although payment beyond compensation for lost wages and expenses was outlawed by the Football Association in 1882, a series of kickbacks undermined the ruling. Players' wives or a nominee often received payment instead; alternatively a footballer was sometimes engaged by a sympathetic fan in a 'job' that did not really exist. The Football Association's refusal to relent led to the widespread phenomenon of 'sham amateurs', discovery of whom in the teams of Preston North End, Great Lever and Burnley in 1884 resulted in their expulsion from the FA. But across the country genuine amateurs were struggling against men whose exclusive occupation was practising, training and playing the game. It was only when the FA was faced with disintegration in 1885, and the northern clubs threatened to break away into a renegade 'British Association', that they relented, and in July of that year professionalism was legalized.

The storm of protest caused by the inclusion of professionals in football teams soon died down. Professionalism raised the standard of play, increased attendances and paved the way for the Football League three years later. Poor clubs were saved from extinction by transfer fees, which enabled them to secure and improve their grounds. Within a few years, those teams that did not embrace professionalism – the likes of Darwen, Earlestown, Bootle and Great Lever – had slipped into obscurity. One needs only to look at the wooden dressing rooms and basic fields in Moor Lane, Crosby, of one of Everton's strongest rivals back then, Liverpool Ramblers, to realize what would have become of the club had they not turned professional.

'Everton,' wrote Keates, 'followed the light.' They signed their first professionals in time for the 1885/6 season. George Dobson came from Bolton Wanderers and Alec Dick, 'a daring, reckless full back', from Kilmarnock. Dobson was quickly elected captain, and along with Dick formed a formidable line of defence, although in its initial stages the partnership was hampered by injury to Dobson and a two-month ban for Dick as a result of violent play – early shades of Pat Van Den Hauwe! They were joined by a third professional, George Farmer from Oswestry, a tricky left-sided forward.

The new professionals earned wages of 30s. per week, while the amateurs received around half that. With the onset of full-blown professionalism and the subsequent increase in crowds, wages advanced. By the 1891/2 season, twelve of Everton's players received three pounds per week, a decent wage when a coal-miner could expect to earn around 30s. and a labourer 13s.

Dick, Dobson and Farmer brought Everton more success. They regained the Liverpool District Cup in 1886, beating Bootle 2–1, and retained it the following season, defeating Oakfield 5–0.

Everton's fledgling professionalism and their dominance of the Liverpool and District Cup saw them enter the FA Cup for the first time in 1886. Their first match in the competition came that autumn, against Glasgow Rangers, but on the arrival of Rangers at Anfield, Everton discovered that they had an ineligible player and forfeited the tie. A friendly was played instead, which they lost 0–1. A year later they tried again. This time they were drawn away at Bolton Wanderers, but what followed epitomized the petty bickering that plagued local football at the time.

On 15 October 1887, Everton travelled to Pikes Lane, Bolton, where they lost 0–1. Afterwards, the Everton secretary Alexander Nisbet wrote to the Football Association complaining bitterly about the credentials of Bolton's best forward, William Struthers. The FA found that he had been registered three days late for the tie and ordered a replay. On 29 October, the two teams met at Anfield in front of a crowd of 5000, who watched a 2–2 draw. The return at Pikes Lane, two weeks later, in front of 6000, ended in 'darkness and a draw.' A week later, at Anfield, Everton finally won 2–1 and went on to play Preston North End on 26 November, succumbing to a 0–6 defeat.

By then Everton, too, were under investigation. Bolton's officials had lodged a protest against J. Weir and R. H. Smalley, and the FA subsequently ruled against the club, declaring that they had registered seven professional players as amateurs. Unable to demand a further rematch, they ordered Anfield to be closed for a month as punishment. And the matter did not end there. In a fit of self-righteousness the Liverpool Football Association withdrew the Liverpool and District Cup. Its chief, Robert Lythgoe, was dispatched to the Sandon Hotel, where, to howls of derision, he seized the trophy.

Although he lost that battle, Nisbet was proving a proficient club secretary and excellent organizer of matches. When the ban expired, Everton played some of the mightier teams of the Midlands, beating Port Vale, drawing with Derby County and West Bromwich Albion, and losing narrowly to Aston Villa in mid-March.

Everton's worthy performance that day may well have attracted the attention of one of Aston Villa's committee members, William McGregor. McGregor, a 41-year-old Scot, was the owner of a Birmingham drapery, with a tidy sideline in the manufacture of football jerseys. Like many of his counterparts at Everton, he was a staunch Methodist, and also a prominent Liberal. Inspired, perhaps, by both his political beliefs and his religious faith, as well as by Birmingham's reputation as the thriving centre of Victorian reform, McGregor was one of the first men to realize the sociological importance of football: it kept men off the streets, enhanced civic prestige and inspired loyalty in the community.

McGregor was aware of the limitations of football's organizational structure. The system was ad hoc and riven by petty arguments, as demonstrated by Everton's experience with Bolton. Games were frequently cancelled when one or other team was lured into a fixture that promised a higher gate. (The 'scratch' teams sometimes sent in their place were often responsible for the rugby-like scorelines of the time.) The disorganization of the fixture list was exacerbated by the interruption of unscheduled cup matches. When a fixture was cancelled, not only did it mean a loss of income but, for less established clubs, a loss of potential support. In the days before professionalism was legalized, players commonly switched allegiance to whoever could offer them a game or financial inducement. Keates was all too aware of the problem: 'The contrast in the attendances at cup ties and ordinary matches, the trifling interest taken in the latter by the public and the insignificance of the takings had long vexed the souls of club managers. How can we vitalize the torpid? That was the question.'[4]

William McGregor had the answer: a regular competitive system of fixtures involving only the top clubs, along the lines of the County Cricket Championship. The season would allow for local cup competitions and the FA Cup, but interest would still be maintained after a team had been knocked out in their early stages.

McGregor toured the country during the 1886/7 season, seeking the support of his colleagues at other clubs. The response he got was not always favourable: concerns were voiced about upsetting the FA, and about the cost of regularized fixtures. McGregor made his first formal move on 2 March 1888, writing to five clubs – Blackburn Rovers, Bolton Wanderers, Preston North End, West Bromwich Albion and Aston Villa – laying out his ideas: a division of 10 or 12 clubs, who would play each other in home and away matches under FA rules, and a formal association to be managed by representatives of each member. He also asked them to suggest additional members. Of the two replies he received, neither advocated Everton's inclusion. And at the end of March, when several representatives from prospective league members met in London prior to the FA Cup Final between West Bromwich Albion and the mighty Preston, Everton were not present. A further meeting was scheduled in Manchester's Royal Hotel in mid-April. Here the Football League was formally created. Its credo, according to McGregor, was:

> The League should never aspire to be a legislating body . . . by the very nature of things the League must be a selfish body. Its interests are wholly bound up in the welfare of its affiliated clubs, and what happens outside is, in a sense, of secondary importance . . . The League has work to do; the Association has its work to do and there need be no clashing.[5]

This time, surprisingly, Alexander Nisbet was present to sign up Everton as a founder member, along with Accrington Stanley, Aston Villa, Blackburn Rovers, Bolton Wanderers, Burnley, Derby County, Notts County, Preston North End, Stoke City, West Bromwich Albion and Wolverhampton Wanderers.

Everton's inclusion at the eleventh hour was a surprise, and the chain of events leading up to it remains a mystery. Certainly they were not there exclusively on merit – in fact, they were considered one of the weaker members. Bootle felt that they had a better case for inclusion than their great rivals, while *Athletic News* noted, sneeringly, that 'Some of the "twelve most prominent" Association clubs, who are to form the new league, have been knocked into smithereens by teams who, so far, have been left out in the cold.' That, perhaps, did not apply in Everton's case, although it is worth noting that two of that season's FA Cup semi-finalists, Crewe Alexander and Derby Junction, were not part of the league.

McGregor's attitude was perhaps the deciding factor. He was interested only in professional clubs and favoured representatives from the major towns and cities (although that did not preclude Accrington Stanley's inclusion), both of which worked in Everton's favour. If it was a race with Bootle, Everton had embraced professionalism more fully and Anfield was closer to the city boundaries, while Marsh Lane was technically in Lancashire. Everton's dominance of the Liverpool and District Cup competition (ironically won by Bootle that year) would also have helped, as would the strong performance against McGregor's Aston Villa, at a time when his plans were taking shape.

But perhaps it was Everton's roots that clinched it. It had, after all, been just 10 years since the cricketers of St Domingo's had begun kicking a ball around Stanley Park during the winter months. Even with a change of name, Everton's ties with the church had remained strong, and McGregor's Methodism underpinned all that he stood for. Maybe, just maybe, St Domingo was smiling down on Everton, as the club that had once borne his name stood on the brink of a new era.

2

The Split

THE ENERGETIC EFFORTS of Everton's members on and off the field had seen the club rise from a church team who played on their local park to one of English football's élite dozen in the space of a decade. Those behind the scenes at Everton were in many respects visionaries: they had recognized the limitations, first, of remaining a church team; second, of playing on municipal grounds; and, latterly, of retaining amateurism. Whenever they had reached a crossroads between consolidation and progress, they had always taken the road forward. The club had a number of benefactors who had bailed it out in its fledgling days with either services or hard cash. Their part in the development of Everton Football Club was crucial, but for the most part they remain anonymous figures, their names lost to the collective memory of the club and fans.

John Houlding is the most conspicuous figure from this time – he 'found' Anfield, he advanced money for the construction of its stands, and it was he, perhaps, who talked Everton into the Football League.

While the credit for gaining the use of Joseph Orrell's field was all Houlding's, it was a situation he quickly turned to his advantage. For a nominal amount Everton had been given almost unencumbered use of Anfield and allowed to maximize their profits – vital at this stage. It was an act of municipal altruism on the part of the Orrell brothers. Houlding's status as 'representative tenant' did not cause any problems during the early days of Everton's Anfield residency, but the onset of league football and the subsequent increase in gate revenues saw him change the rules. He became the club's landlord and began charging rent. From paying £100 annually, Everton found themselves suddenly paying £240 in 1888, and £250 a year later. Their new 'landlord' also insisted on having a nominee on the club's executive.

The executive responded by requesting a lease in July 1888,

adding that work on the construction of new stands would be suspended until the matter was decided. Houlding refused, cheekily adding that as 'landlord' he was taking sole rights for the sale of refreshments to Anfield's patrons. The age of the exploitative football chairman had arrived.

Houlding had Everton over a barrel. As landlord, even though Anfield was sub-let, he could charge whatever he pleased. On the verge of league football and with the costs of professionalism to pay, Everton's resources were overstretched. They needed a new stadium, but the task of finding one was far more formidable than it had been when Houlding had acquired the use of Anfield in 1884, and a field had been turned, almost overnight, into a venue. League football had seen crowds rise fivefold since those early days at their current residence, which had evolved to meet its growing needs. A boycott of the Sandon Hotel was feasible; an embargo on Anfield was not. As Keates put it:

> The constructive responsibility entailed was intimidating; the finding of a new ground, the drudgery and expense of levelling, draining and sodding; the formidable items of stands, offices, dressing rooms etc., and of incalculable (in advance) tons of bricks, woodwork, roofing etc., were enough to scare average men from the undertaking.[1]

Everton's members were furious, but their attention was soon diverted by the start of the Football League. Under the new secretaryship of William Barclay, Everton set out to put together a team capable of challenging for honours in this new competition. Alf Milward, a pacy eighteen-year-old outside left, arrived from Great Marlow. Along with another new arrival, Edgar Chadwick, an inside forward one year his senior, he was to develop a potent left-sided partnership. Chadwick had come from his native Blackburn, having turned out for both Olympic and, latterly, Rovers. He was to put together a prolific decade-long Everton career, which saw more than 300 appearances and 110 goals. He was also to be among Everton's first internationals, earning seven England caps, the most famous of which came against Scotland in 1892 when he turned out in front of a typically hostile Ibrox crowd and silenced the Glaswegian tumult, scoring after a mere 10 seconds – before a Scotland player had even touched the ball – in a famous 4–1 England victory.

Chadwick was preceded on the international stage by Johnny Holt, another arrival who hailed from Blackburn but had found his way to Anfield via Bootle. A fine centre half who stood at just five foot five inches, he earned himself the nickname the 'Little Everton Devil' from the discerning faithful, who quickly adopted him as a favourite. As guardian of Everton's back line, he was known for his ability to outwit and outhead opponents, despite his diminutive frame, and had a knack of securing a last-ditch tackle or block. Keates described him as 'an artist in the perpetuation of clever minor fouls. When they were appealed for, his shocked look of indifference was side-splitting.'

The new signing that attracted the most interest was Nick Ross, a genuine superstar and paid as such, earning the then huge salary of £10 per month. He had risen to fame in Scotland, captaining Heart of Midlothian at the age of just twenty. In 1883 he moved south, finding 'work' as a slater in Preston, home to the mighty North End, England's finest team, which he joined. At Preston he converted from a forward to a defender, and became captain. In his five years at Deepdale, he gained a reputation as the finest defender in the game.

Ross's signing was a genuine coup, but he lasted only a season with Everton. Elected as captain, he played in all but three of the club's league fixtures, turning out in defence and his previous position in attack, which yielded him five goals. But he was underutilized. An anonymous article in the *Liverpool Review* – a weekly politics, news and culture digest – entitled 'Everton Fiascos' bemoaned the fact that although Ross knew more about football than all the members of the committee combined, he had no voice in team selection. If 'Ross had an entirely free hand in the picking and placing of players,' the article said, 'the teams selected for matches would be much more efficient and the combinations much better.'

Everton opened the Football League era on 8 September 1888. Ten thousand people – twice as many as had been expected and the day's biggest crowd – filled Anfield to see Everton play Accrington Stanley. Everton had by now adopted a somewhat more conservative formation – evidently seeing the need to pack the midfield – and lined up 2–3–5: R. H. Smalley in goal; Ross and Alec Dick the backs; George Dobson, Holt and B. Jones half backs; George Farmer, Chadwick, W. Lewis, D. Waugh and G. Fleming the forwards. Everton came into the match off the back of a friendly defeat at

Bootle a week earlier and were desperate to prove themselves to the large crowd.

On a clear late-summer afternoon the visitors won the toss and elected to kick off. It was the home side, though, who made the first attacks, and early on Farmer brought out the best in Accrington's goalkeeper, Horne, then clipped the visitors' crossbar with a header. Despite the fast pace and the shouts of the Anfield crowd, Accrington made a good game of it, and only the timely defending of Dick and Ross repelled their counter-attacks, keeping the score goalless at half-time. With only a five-minute interval to recuperate, Everton came out strongly in the second half and were rewarded on the hour mark with their first-ever league goal. Dobson intercepted a break from Lofthouse and spread the ball to Waugh. He played in Farmer, whose cross-shot was met by the head of Fleming, who scored, reported the *Liverpool Daily Post*, 'amidst tremendous cheering and waving of hats'. Shortly after, Horne left the field with a fractured rib after a collision with Chadwick. He was replaced by Accrington's back, McLellan, and Everton soon took advantage when Fleming swept home Farmer's cross. Accrington launched a late assault and were rewarded with a consolation goal from Holden, but Everton held on for a 2–1 win.

A week later 7000 people turned out to see Everton win 2–1 again, this time against Notts County. By early November they were riding high in the league, sitting in third place, but thereafter their form dried up. Out of their remaining 13 matches they won just three. Of particular contention to the Everton faithful was the lack of consistency in team selection: no fewer than 35 players turned out in a season of just 22 matches. Even in the Premiership era of seasons with sometimes 40-plus league fixtures and five substitutes, it is a record that has been equalled but not exceeded.

Everton finished their début league campaign in a disappointing eighth place, but high enough to avoid applying for re-election. At the season's end Ross returned to Preston, who had earned the tag 'the Invincibles' after romping to a league and FA Cup double without having lost a single match. He went on to win a Championship medal the following season, but tragically he died early in 1894 from pulmonary tuberculosis aged just 31.

Now the Everton board looked to bolster their team, particularly the forward line, which had been weak the previous season. From

Grimsby Town they brought in the whippet-like 21-year-old Fred Geary, and from Dumbarton Athletic the Scottish international Alex Latta. Geary, at just five foot two, made up for his physical limitations with lightning bursts of speed. Indeed, the new centre forward went to great lengths to cultivate his pace, even insisting that his boots had the thinnest possible soles. The mustachioed Latta was tall and stocky, but his size did not impede an impressive turn of pace and mercurial dribbling skills.

Off the field, the battle with Houlding took on new proportions with the arrival of George Mahon and Dr James Baxter on the management board, significantly strengthening the anti-Houlding faction.

George Mahon came late to football, but once he had been introduced to the game by Sam Crosbie – whose concert at the Hand-in-Hand club six years earlier had helped secure Everton's future – he caught the bug and became the staunchest of Evertonians. Perhaps his early reticence was a reflection of his social standing: he was a middle-class member of St Domingo's congregation, an impeccably dapper man who headed a North John Street firm of accountants; some members hoped that his position among Liverpool's élite might 'popularize "the great game" amongst the better classes of the community'.[2] Later he brought his business acumen to the Everton boardroom, and used it to secure the club's position among the English football élite with the finest ground in the country. Back in 1889 he saw immediately that Everton could not prosper in the long term either without their own home or under the profiteering Houlding.

While Mahon was a mainstay of the local Methodist community, Dr James Baxter was similarly revered by the city's Catholics. Educated at St Francis Xavier College, the physician was well known among the local Irish community, who were beginning to form Anfield's core constituency. Like Houlding, he made a name for himself as a local politician, representing the Liberal Party on the City Council from 1906 to 1920, and he became Everton's medical adviser and later director and chairman. His most tangible contribution, however, came when the dispute with Houlding climaxed in 1892.

Soon after Baxter and Mahon's arrival onto the management committee they attempted to form the club into a limited-liability company for the express purpose of acquiring Anfield. Their demand was put in the form of an official resolution at a special committee meeting. The opening shot in the civil war with Houlding had been fired.

○

THE RUMBLINGS OF backroom dissent did little to impair progress on the field, and Geary gave birth to the legend of the Everton centre forward: he scored twice on his début in a 3–2 home victory over Blackburn, and ended the 1889/90 season with 25 goals to his name, from just 20 league and Cup appearances. Alf Milward, who had hardly been given a chance in Everton's first league campaign, struck up a formidable left-wing partnership with Edgar Chadwick that soon came to be regarded as the most electrifying and productive in the country; it provided Anfield, then Goodison, with eight years of excellence. With the arrival from Sunderland in November 1889 of the free-scoring Alex Brady, who complemented Latta on the right, Everton's forward line was the best in the league.

With an 8–0 win over Stoke City in November, a 7–0 win over Aston Villa in early January 1890 and an 11–0 friendly victory over Notts Rangers, one of Geary's old teams, a week later, confidence was booming in Everton's attacking play. A week after their demolition of Notts Rangers, on 18 January 1890 Everton met Derby County in the first round of the FA Cup at Anfield. Derby were no pushover: playing on a sodden pitch they took an early lead through Goodall. After Geary had equalized for Everton, Derby regained the lead when Higgins's shot slipped through Smalley's grasp. The Derby defence clearly had its deficiencies though, and before half-time Milward had put Everton 3–2 in front with a brace. Defensive shortcomings or not, none of the Anfield crowd could have predicted what was to happen after the interval. Derby simply capitulated. Milward scored his third goal, and Geary added a brace to complete his hat-trick. Alex Brady's excellence perpetually confounded the beleaguered Derby defenders, and he added three goals of his own to make a hat-trick of hat-tricks, while Doyle and Kirkwood each added a goal apiece. The 11–2 scoreline that wet January afternoon remains an Everton record.

Yet with the baffling and frustrating inconsistency that will be familiar to many modern-day Evertonians, the team that had scored 30 goals in three January games lost at the start of February in the next round of the FA Cup, 2–4, to Stoke City. Such lapses also cost Everton the Championship. Topping the league in mid-November Everton had met the 'Invincibles' of Preston at Anfield. The encounter drew a crowd of 20,000, who roared Everton to a 1–0 half-time lead, secured by the omnipresent Geary. Yet they could not sustain the momentum in the second half and collapsed, Preston 'making rings around them, point after point, and won in a common canter so to speak'.[3]

Preston North End returned to Lancashire 5–1 victors at the top of the Football League. From then they held on to their lead, and not even a 2–1 Everton win at Deepdale a month later could supplant them. They finished the 1889/90 season top with 33 points to Everton's 31 – but the Invincibles had shown chinks in their armour.

During their first two seasons of league football Everton's main weaknesses had gradually been eradicated. One area for improvement lay in goal, and at the start of the 1890/1 season R. E. Smalley, who had kept goal in 35 of Everton's first 44 league matches, was replaced by J. Angus. Strengthened at the back, the club strode to the top of the league, winning six of their first seven matches and drawing the other. After a mid-season trough, Angus was replaced by Bootle's Lockerbie-born goalkeeper David Jardine. The new goalkeeper combined, wrote *Out of Doors* magazine, 'the mental and muscular qualities which does leave one little cause for wonderment at his popularity'.[4] Inspired by his presence, Everton regained the top spot, with just five matches remaining.

Wins over Burnley (7–3), Aston Villa (5–0) and Notts County (4–2) meant that Everton went into the penultimate match of the season on 29 points. They were playing Preston, in second place on 25, and a draw would be enough to secure them their first League Championship.

Preston, however, were not yet willing to relinquish their crown. In front of a 15,000-strong Anfield crowd, they stole away with a 1–0 victory, leaving them with a glimmer of hope in their own title quest.

There followed a two-month gap in the league programme before the concluding match of the season. Inclement weather and the interruption of the FA Cup meant that it was not until 14 March 1891 – when they played Burnley at Turf Moor – that Everton could finish their season. In the interim, they had embarked on a three-game tour of London, which had been enthusiastically received –

although the capital would not field a top-flight club for a further 14 years.

When the big day came, around 2000 Evertonians made the trip to Lancashire. On a sleety afternoon, kick-off at Turf Moor was delayed until four o'clock because of crowd congestion, but when play got under way, Everton took the game to their hosts, several times going close, and twice hitting the bar. But at half-time the scoreline was still goalless. Then, within five minutes of the onset of the second half, Burnley shocked the visitors: against the run of play, Haresnape gave his team the lead. His goal stunned Everton, but within two minutes they were level when Geary's low shot crashed into the Burnley goal and sent the visiting fans wild. Ten minutes later, a mix-up in the Burnley goalmouth saw McFetteridge turn the ball into his own goal and give Everton the lead. The title was almost theirs.

But – as only Everton can – they contrived to give up that lead with just five minutes remaining when Bowes headed Burnley level. A point would still be enough, but Everton seemed determined to give that up too: the cheering had barely died down when Stewart shot Burnley in front. Everton rallied desperately, and a goalbound shot agonizingly stuck in the mud of the Burnley goalmouth and was hacked clear. Then the referee blew his final whistle, and it was over.

Team and fans trudged despondently back to Merseyside, furious that the title had seemingly been thrown away. It was only later that evening that news came through that Sunderland had defeated Preston, thus securing Everton's two-point margin at the top. Champions for the first time, they had, recorded Keates, 'reached the zenith of football distinction – achieved the ambition of the management and drove its supporters wild with delight!'.

○

OFF THE FIELD, the battle between Houlding and the management committee was about to climax. On 15 September 1891 a General Meeting was held at the Royal Street Hall, close to Everton Valley. Houlding outlined his plans for the formation of a limited-liability company, and produced a prospectus that suggested the purchase of Mr Orrell's and (bizarrely) Mr Houlding's land, plus the stands and offices, for £9237 10s. Mr W. E. Barclay – in the chair – proposed that the scheme be adopted, and was seconded.

George Mahon's moment of destiny had come. He got to his feet and put forward the following amendment:

That the scheme proposed be not entertained, and that the committee have authority from this meeting to negotiate with Mr Houlding as to the renting of such further land as may be required, subject to Mr Houlding's making the necessary arrangements with Mr Orrell.

It was carried. Once more, it was time for Everton to seek pastures new. The crux was, firstly, that Everton had no new venue. Secondly, the forfeiture of the stands was costly enough to be almost unthinkable, yet retention of them was clearly an obstacle.

A Special General Meeting was convened in the college on Shaw Street on 25 January 1892. It started with Houlding's prospectus again being rejected. The loss of Anfield was now virtually a certainty. Mahon took the floor and began to address the need for a new ground. His 'judicial and dignified reasoning' had, until then, wrote Keates, been 'enthusiastically applauded'. But the mention of a new ground caused one heckler to shout, 'Yer can't find one!', to which Mahon responded, 'I've got one in my pocket.'

He was referring to Mere Green Field, an area of land on the other side of Stanley Park on which he had gained an option to lease. Today it is known as Goodison Park.

With his tenants absconding, Houlding attempted to create another Everton Football Club at Anfield Road, even registering a company called 'The Everton Football Club and Athletic Ground Company Limited'. Naturally there could not be two Evertons. The case went to the Football Association for arbitration, and the council ruled against Houlding, adopting the following resolution:

The Council, in accordance with its past decisions, will not accept any membership of any club bearing a name similar to one affiliated with this Association in the name of the Everton club, and will only recognize the action of a majority of its members at a duly constituted meeting.

George Mahon and his supporters had won the day.

At a committee meeting on 15 March 1892, Houlding and Nisbet were ejected from Everton's ruling council, and at the end of the following month, under FA arbitration, it was agreed that the club would receive £250 compensation for the cost of Anfield's stands.

☽

WORK SOON BEGAN on Mere Green Field, which was surrounded by the terraced streets that still stand today. The new ground had to be cleared and levelled, turf laid and a basic drainage system put in place. A Mr Barton was contracted to do this on 29,471 square yards at 4½d. per square yard – 'a formidable initial expenditure'. A Mr J. Prescott was engaged as architect and surveyor, and Kelly Bros, builders, were appointed to erect two uncovered stands to accommodate 4000 each and a covered stand to accommodate 3000 at a cost of £1640, with a penalty clause in the event of non-completion by 31 July. Two weeks later another contract was agreed with Kelly's to erect outside hoardings for £150. Twelve turnstiles were ordered at £7 15s. each. In August a third contract was signed for gates and sheds, to be completed by 20 August at a cost of £132 10s.

The task facing the builders was formidable, but they stuck to their deadlines. Their construction was the finest club stadium in the country and, less than two years later, host of the 1894 FA Cup Final between Notts County and Bolton Wanderers. It opened officially as Goodison Park on 24 August 1892. An inaugural lunch at the Adelphi Hotel, at which the chief guest was Lord Kinnaird, president of the Football Association, was followed by a procession of open carriages to Goodison, the streets lined with flag-waving crowds. The opening ceremony was watched by 12,000 spectators and concluded with a firework display.

On Friday 2 September 1892, Goodison witnessed its first match, a friendly, kicked off by George Mahon, against Bolton Wanderers, ending in a 4–2 win for Everton. The following day Everton met Nottingham Forest in the opening league fixture of the season. Fred Geary and Alf Milward goals secured a 2–2 draw in front of 14,000. Three weeks later, Goodison saw its first league win, a 6–0 trouncing of Newton Heath.

Nevertheless, the fastidious Mahon lived uneasily with the barrenness of the club's bank account after all the outlays on Everton's new home. With little in the way of assets and before transfer fees were generating serious revenue, a bad season could have put Everton's future in doubt. Knowing of these concerns, Mahon's ally, Dr Baxter, stepped in. He advanced the club a £1000 loan, free of interest or security, which established Everton's future.

The decision to buy Mere Green Field was taken three years later at an outlay of £8090; ten years on, the mortgage had been cleared, and Everton's nomadic period was over.

The off-the-field fighting eventually took its toll on the players. In an expanded division that numbered 14 members, Everton slumped to a disappointing fifth place at the end of the 1891/2 season and dropped out of the FA Cup at its first stage. They clearly missed the impish brilliance of Geary, who had been injured for much of the campaign, although the irrepressible Alex Latta shouldered the goal-scoring burden, laying in with an impressive return of 17 goals from 25 starts, including hat-tricks against West Bromwich Albion and Notts County. Further brushes with glory, however, were not far off.

○

JOHN HOULDING, left with an empty football ground, decided to start all over again. With W. E. Barclay, who had been deposed during the divorce proceedings, he made a £500 loan available for the purpose of creating Merseyside's second Football League club, and Liverpool Football Club was born.

Initially, attendances at Anfield Road were meagre. As the *Liverpool Daily Post* pointed out, although it had been the most popular ground in the country, it was not the stadium but 'the high class quality of the football detailed out to the patrons that has made it a favourite rendezvous'.[5] Nevertheless the city soon proved able to support a second team, and under the directorship of John McKenna, Liverpool embarked on a speedy rise to the First Division. During the 1892/3 season he arranged a series of friendlies and entry into minor competitions for the new team before a piece of luck fell Liverpool's way. Accrington Stanley resigned from the league, and Bootle, who could not come to terms with the cost of professionalism, forfeited their place in the year-old Second Division. McKenna applied for the vacant places, and to his surprise, was successful; Liverpool gained entry to the Second Division for the start of the 1893/4 season. In only their first season of league football they won promotion to the top tier of English soccer, alongside Everton.

The first league derby took place on 13 October 1894 at Goodi-son Park. A then record league attendance of 44,000, yielding gate receipts of £1026 12*s.* 10*d.*, assembled at Goodison. It was a gripping spectacle, and the contrasting styles of the two sides – Liverpool 'kick and rush' and renowned for their abrasive tactics; Everton already established as footballing aristocrats – made an intriguing contest. Everton were initially taken aback by Liverpool's confrontational tactics but survived an early onslaught. Foul followed foul until McInnes lifted the hosts above the tumult with a perfectly timed header that soared into the Liverpool net and gave Everton a 1–0 half-time lead. When hostilities resumed after the break, Everton's superiority began to tell, and Latta and Bell increased the margin to 3–0. The return match at Anfield, on 17 November, ended in a 2–2 draw. At the season's end, the gulf in class ultimately showed: Everton finished second, Liverpool bottom.

The Merseyside derby is the oldest top-flight derby in English football and, arguably, the most famously heated of such fixtures. Houlding's bitter creation of Liverpool Football Club has caused Evertonians much anxiety – and, indeed, the team has often directly blocked Everton's path to glory. They have met Everton three times in FA Cup semi-finals, twice in the Final and once in the League Cup Final, and each time Liverpool have emerged victorious.

But the rivalry sparked by the birth of Houlding's monster has perhaps been good for football on Merseyside. Nowhere else do interest and passion for the game run so high. Other cities – Leeds or Newcastle, for instance – are the poorer for not having their football played against such a backdrop of local rivalry. And those who can lay claim to such rivalries – Birmingham, Sheffield, Manchester and (north) London – have seen the intensity of passions and the standard of local derbies diluted by the prolonged mediocrity of one or both teams.

Within a few years the wounds created by 'the split', at least at boardroom level, had healed. Yet the perception that Liverpool had come to exist only off the backs of Everton in unseemly circumstances never went away. They were thought to have tried to buy success in their early years, and their style of football seldom won the same plaudits as Everton's, even when they were winning championships. Their comparatively late arrival on the Merseyside football scene is reflected even now in their local fan base. It has generally been the rule – and not just on Merseyside – that a son's allegiance will follow his father's. In 1892, Everton's crowds already exceeded

20,000, and the club's head start in establishing family traditions was unquestionable. Until 1970 Everton's average attendance was almost always higher than their neighbour's. Then came Liverpool's unprecedented run of domestic and European success. With it the glory-hunters arrived. Suddenly 'the split' no longer mattered. Liverpool became the first team whose constituency extended well outside their locality (and the footballing deserts of North Wales and Ireland). Coachloads of Kent Kopites, Basingstoke Reds and Thames Valley Liverpool supporters' clubs converged on Merseyside. It is a phenomenon that has persisted and grown, and while a contemporary survey of the city's residents would probably reveal a 50/50 split of allegiance, how many of those Liverpool supporters ever attend Anfield is a different matter. A mid-1990s study revealed that Everton had the most localized support in the Premiership, Liverpool one of the least. Apparently the implications of the split live on.

Regardless, Houlding's actions altered the complexion of football on Merseyside for ever.

3

Early Stories, Early Glories

FIFTEEN MILES down-river from Glasgow, on the confluence of the rivers Leven and Clyde, lies the town of Dumbarton. It has a long and rich history that extends back to the eighth century when it was capital of the Celtic kingdom of Strathclyde. The growth of shipbuilding and marine engineering on the banks of the Leven gave a dramatic boost to the town's development, and in the latter years of the nineteenth century it was at its peak – as were its football teams. Its premier club, Dumbarton Athletic, won the two inaugural Scottish League Championships (1890/91, 1891/2), and in the latter two decades of the century made the Scottish FA Cup Final five times, winning it in 1883. Yet as professionalism took hold on the Scottish game, Dumbarton's members were reluctant to embrace it. The club declined, and by the end of the century they had failed to gain re-election to the league.

For Everton, Dumbarton provided a fertile poaching ground. In the Football League's early years, four of their players made the journey south to Liverpool, and a fifth joined after a spell with St Mirren. For more than twenty years these men were to dominate the ranks of Everton Football Club and play telling parts in Goodison Park's early stories and occasional glories.

The first of these Scottish recruits had been Alex Latta in the 1888/89 season and he was followed a year later by Richard Boyle. A cultured half back who had made his name playing for Dumbarton Episcopalians, Dumbarton Union and then Dumbarton Athletic, Boyle was, like Johnny Holt, physically small, but a nevertheless commanding presence on the field of play, and similarly went on to captain Everton. Yet it was to take him until Goodison Park's opening day, in September 1892, to make his debut, although once that first game had been played he was a regular fixture in the Everton line up for the remainder of the decade. Later on that season he was joined at Goodison by two of his townsmen, Abraham Hartley and John Bell. Hartley an inside right and sometime centre forward spent the majority of his Everton career as a reserve, but when called upon proved a highly able, if not prolific, deputy, scoring 28 times in his 61 appearances, which were usually interspersed with lengthy periods in the reserves. Later, in December 1897, he was to cross Stanley park and joined Liverpool.

Bell had been the young star of Dumbarton's 1891/2 Scottish Championship team: a winger of great skill, he made 199 Everton appearances, spanning two spells and 10 years. He scored 70 goals – an impressive haul for a man regarded as a master dribbler rather than a goalscorer. 'One swallow does not make a summer,' noted Keates, 'but one player of outstanding ability in a football team makes a great difference in its aggregate results.' Highly respected by both the footballing establishment – he won 10 Scotland caps – and his peers, Bell was elected chairman of the first attempt to inaugurate a players' union. Remarkable stories of his playing feats abound, but two in particular show what he was made of. Sam Crosbie – he of the Hand-in-Hand concert – wrote: 'At one game we noticed a player circling around as if very dizzy. Jack Bell ran to him, took hold of his head, put his shoulders between his knees, pulled his head with all his might, and in a few minutes the player joined in the game. It turned out he had dislocated his neck, and would have been a dead man in a few minutes had not Jack Bell adjusted the dislocation.' On another occasion Bell was run over by a cab on the Strand in London on the eve of an England–Scotland meeting at the Crystal Palace. He brushed himself down and turned out the next day. Scotland won 2–1.

Goodison's first season saw an expanded First Division of 16 teams, but despite the anticipated dilution in standards, Everton struggled to thrive. An early injury to David Jardine had seen three goalkeepers tried in his place, without much success, before the fourth, Williams, who had occupied the posts before Jardine, had recovered from a long-standing injury. Everton, placed thirteenth on 3 January 1893, suddenly found their form. 'The sun chased the cloud away and smiled sweetly on the depressed team,' wrote Keates. 'Everything had gone wrong, now everything went right.' Of Everton's remaining 12 matches they won 10, to finish the 1892/3 season third, one point behind second-placed Preston, although 12 behind champions Sunderland.

Their good form carried over into the FA Cup. On 21 January 1893, a week after beating West Bromwich Albion with a solitary Geary goal in the league match at Goodison, Everton met them in the first round, once more at home, and cruised past their opponents with a 4–1 victory. Two weeks later they put four past Nottingham Forest to progress to a quarter-final meeting with yet another top-flight team, Sheffield Wednesday. As had happened in the opening round, they met their opponents in the league days before the Cup tie and ran out 2–0 winners. Buoyed by that victory, Everton went one better in the FA Cup and won 3–0.

Victory over Sheffield Wednesday sent Everton back to the Steel City, on 4 March, to meet the mighty Preston in the semi-final at Bramall Lane. In front of 28,000 people, the tie ended in a 2–2 draw with Chadwick and Gordon grabbing the Everton goals. The replayed semi-final – staged in front of 30,000 at Blackburn – ended in a 0–0 draw. Finally, in the third meeting between the Lancastrian rivals on 20 March in Nottingham, Everton won 2–1, courtesy of strikes by Maxwell and Gordon.

The protracted nature of the semi-final meant that Everton had only five days to prepare for its first FA Cup Final against Wolves at Fallowfield, Manchester. Despite such a short period, Everton had every reason to be confident. Just two days before the second replay with Preston, they had gone to Molineux and, fielding a team that included eight reserves, recorded an easy 4–2 victory. For the final Everton were at full strength: six Scots, five English, including six internationals – Kelso and Latta of Scotland, Holt, Howarth, Chadwick and Milward of England.

Yet the afternoon was one of confusion and, ultimately, disappointment for Everton. Fifty thousand people crammed into a ground suitable for no more than 15,000, and several barriers broke, spilling spectators on to the pitch. Many were injured, some seriously. Eventually, with play under way, Everton had an early goal disallowed, and could not subsequently break down the Wolverhampton rearguard. The match was won by a single, fortuitous Wolves goal. The Midlanders' centre half, Harry Allen, let fly with a long, high, seemingly innocuous shot, yet Williams was blinded by the sun and the ball bounced into his goal. Everton battled back, but the Wolves defence were defiant. As the game neared its end, 'The funeral card purveyors did a roaring trade during the closing stages at Fallowfield,' noted the *Wolverhampton Express and Star*. 'Long before the game was over hawkers were pushing the sale of "Everton's Deathcard", one specimen taking the form of a monumental slab, with the words "Departed from this life in the English Cup".' Another recorded: 'In memoriam of Everton Football Team, who departed from the Cup Competition through a severe attack of Wolves, and whose hopes were interred at the Football Cemetery, the same day'. Three verses followed:

> They came in all their glory,
> From that noted Toffy Town,
> To fight the famous 'Wolves',
> A team of English renown.
>
> The 'Toffys' came on boldly,
> Their victory for to seek;
> But now they go home gravely
> O'er their troubles for to weep.
>
> Farewell, farewell, dear old Everton,
> No more for the Pot you will dribble;
> You have lost it to-day through difficult play
> And we'll shout farewell for ever and ever.[1]

o

With the coffers boosted by the FA Cup run – receipts for the 1892/3 season totalled £8815 19s. – the Everton directors embarked on a spending spree. Their main purchase was Blackburn Rovers' England centre forward Jack Southworth for £400. At Ewood Park he had become something of a legend when they won the FA Cup in 1890 and 1891, and over the three years he was in the team Rovers never lost a match, which more than justified his nickname, 'The Luck of the Blue and Whites'. He joined Everton in September 1893 and scored on his début against Derby County. Yet it was on the penultimate day of 1893 that he made history: he became the first player to score a double hat-trick in the Football League. The game, a 7–1 win over West Bromwich Albion, was described by the *Liverpool Daily Courier* as 'exceptionally interesting'. A crowd of 25,000 braved the foggy weather and, within a minute of kick-off, had been whipped

into a frenzy after John Bell had put Everton ahead. By half-time
they were 4–0 up, thanks to Southworth's first hat-trick: Latta
and Bell had combined to give him his first goal; his second came
when Reader, the Albion keeper, failed to hold a shot from Bell,
and Southworth scooped home the rebound; the third came with a
brilliant solo effort. He added his fourth shortly after the break, and
although Albion battled gamely throughout the second half, Southworth was unstoppable. His fifth came after Bell had beaten three
men to set him up, and he finished off the rout after Latta played
him through. His tally might have been as high as seven had not
Latta rushed in and finished Southworth's late goal-bound header –
for which he was ruled offside.

Southworth ended the 1893/4 season with 27 goals from his 22
starts, but Everton finished only sixth, even though they were top
scorers with 90 goals, an average of three per match. For Southworth
it was his only full season at Goodison – although he added another
nine goals in nine matches the next – before injury forced his
premature retirement.

◊

EVERTON BEGAN the 1894/5 season – the first in which Houlding's
Liverpool were in the top flight – in irresistible fashion. They won
their first eight matches and continued to set the pace at the top of
the division. By Christmas they were still top and had only been
defeated once, but thereafter lost their way and finished runners-up
to Sunderland, five points off the pace. Some solace was derived
by the relegation of Houlding's Liverpool, who had rounded off a
miserable season bottom.

Goodison Park was now the finest ground in the country: it had
played host to the FA Cup Final a season earlier and on 6 April 1895
to the England–Scotland match. More than 30,000 spectators – the
biggest-ever attendance for the fixture – roared the home nation to a
3–0 victory.

The remainder of 1895 was plagued by more off-the-field controversy. There was minor uproar when Fred Geary was allowed to join
Liverpool, although through injury and loss of form he never again
scaled the heights of his Everton days. On 5 June, at a stormy Annual
General Meeting at the Picton Lecture Hall, George Mahon spoke
of how the club's balance sheet 'must command respect both in the

sporting and commercial world'. He went on to describe how, in the three years since departing from Anfield, the club had made £6319. Most pleasingly, he added, should any adverse circumstances arise in the future, the club had substantial wherewithal to fall back on before calling upon members or shareholders for their support. He then announced his own resignation as chairman, along with those of four other board members. Keates – who was elected to the Everton board two years later – spoke of an 'acute administrative difference', but the news was still a shock.

Dr Baxter took Mahon's chair 'reluctantly', said Keates, 'but was relieved later on by learning that overpowering manifestations of regret by the shareholders had induced Mr Mahon to promise resumption'. The other vacancies were filled by J. C. Brookes, J. M. Crawshaw, A. Leyland, J. Prescott, Edward Bainbridge – who also served as director of Liverpool – and a further board member joined the team, Will Cuff. The election of Cuff, the most venerable and respected of St Domingans, was to mark the beginning of an administrative association with the club that spanned more than half a century and encompass not only the role of director, but later those of secretary and chairman.

The new board soon got to the bottom of a problem that had been troubling the club for some time. It had long been suspected that there was a not inconsiderable disparity between the crowd numbers estimated by journalists and the official attendance tallied at the turnstiles. 'A vague suspicion developed into a disagreeable conviction of misappropriation by somebody,' commented Keates. Yet the starting numbers on the machines were noted each week by one or more of the directors before the gates were opened, and again at half-time when they were closed. The takings from each turnstile were invariably correct, so any discrepancy between the official attendance and the estimated crowd was surely a trick of the eye.

Or was it? When Everton met Sunderland on 16 November 1895, one of the directors, as usual, accompanied the groundsman on the weekly inspection to note the turnstile numbers half an hour before the gates opened. Then, twenty minutes later, two other directors inspected them. To their consternation they found that at several of the gates the figures had been clocked back by 200 units. Only the groundsman had the key. He was promptly arrested. Seven turnstile men caught wind of what had happened and each brought in £5 more than their turnstiles registered. None could account for the irregularity. They pleaded ignorance and were allowed to go. Meanwhile, police questioning had unmasked a conspiracy. The result was that the following Monday a dozen turnstilemen, the club mechanic and the groundsman appeared in Dale Street Court. All, save for the instigators, were treated leniently by the stipendiary magistrate and new turnstiles were subsequently installed.

The furore over the 'Everton turnstile fraud' had barely died down when another blew up. On 28 December Everton played Small Heath (later Birmingham City) at Goodison. Since Christmas Day heavy rain had fallen and the ground was a swamp; it was still raining on the afternoon of the match, too, and attendance was just a third of its average. But the referee, James West of Lincoln, decided that the pitch was fit to play. After 37 minutes, with Everton leading 1–0, West called the players together and told them that the ground was now unfit for further action. The players protested that they could continue, but West stood firm and the match was abandoned. Then officials of both clubs agreed that play was possible. West consented to a resumption. Now the players protested; many had taken baths and the delay had been such that it was absurd to proceed. While the club management and the players argued, West left without anyone noticing. But the Everton officials were not so fortunate. As Keates recorded:

> Quite a crowd remained, and, recruited by an army of street loafers who had entered, a howling mob fronted the office demanding their money back. The Secretary tried to appease the brawling but in vain and retreated when a stone was hurled at him. George Mahon did manage to get a hearing, and, pointing out that it was impossible to tell who had paid and who had not, a free ticket was offered to all the demonstrators for the re-played match.

They were not appeased: 'The howling intensified, with the clamour for money. Stones were thrown at Mr Mahon, one of them smashing the thick glass of the clock over his head.' As the situation worsened the policemen on duty called for assistance. While they waited for reinforcements to arrive, 'Showers of stones flew about, every pane of glass in the office windows was broken, and the woodwork was smashed and used as weapons. A crowd made for

the grandstand, and a cry of "Fire the stands" was heard . . . Pande-
monium reigned and dreadful damage was imminent.'

Finally two contingents of police arrived. They 'drew their batons
and at once attacked the mob. A momentary show of resistance was
made, but batoned heads and bodies soon affected a panic-stricken
rush to the gates, with a clearance from the ground and its vicinity.'

Keates's account is almost certainly exaggerated. As an upper-
middle-class director, he had a horror of the working-class men who
came in their tens of thousands to support what he had followed as a
church team. Yet the disturbance also shows that football hooliganism
is by no means a modern phenomenon, and in fact such incidents
pepper the history of all major clubs.

Everton had begun 1896 at the top of the league but, as they had
a year earlier, fell off the pace in the latter half of the season and
ended the 1895/6 campaign third, six points behind champions
Aston Villa. That summer they added yet another former Dumbarton
player to the side. Twenty-four-year-old Jack Taylor was signed from
St Mirren, having started out with his home-town club. He became
another early legend at Goodison Park, an archetypal Victorian
sporting hero willing to adapt to any position to benefit the team. His
Everton career lasted 14 years. Keates lavished praise on his 'high
standard code of life, mentality and lingual purity', adding that he
'played anywhere readily, and played well everywhere'. Indeed, 'no
player has left Evertonians a more fragrant memory.'

Yet Everton opened the 1896/7 season inconsistently. Although
they beat Liverpool 2–1 at the start of October, other results were
less favourable and they ended the year in seventh place – the
previous two years had seen them end top. Nevertheless, their
fortunes were about to change. Although by the season's end they
had risen no higher than their New Year position, an epic FA Cup
run had been strung together.

It started with a 5–2 first-round victory over Burton Wanderers
on 30 January 1897, which was followed a fortnight later with a
3–0 win over Bury. Blackburn Rovers were next up, and Everton's
Dumbarton connection came good: Hartley grabbed both Everton
goals in a 2–0 victory, which set up a semi-final meeting with Derby
County at the Victoria Ground, Stoke-on-Trent. Everton went into
the game favourites, and although Derby made a good match of it,
the Everton half-back line took hold of the game and saw the team

through to their second final in four years with a 3–2 win. Chadwick, Hartley and Milward were the Everton goalscorers.

Faltering in the league – they had lost their last six league matches – Everton took off to Lytham St Anne's to prepare for the big day, this time to be staged in London, at the Crystal Palace. In Merseyside wild rumours flew around that the team had vanished. It was left to the *Liverpool Mercury* to calm anxieties: 'Contrary to the original report, it has since been established that Everton arrived safely in the metropolis, and are put up at a quiet resort in the neighbourhood of the Crystal Palace ... They have left their training quarters at Lytham in high spirits and in the pink of condition ...'

65,204 spectators turned out at the Crystal Palace, where the pitch had recently replaced a former lake. It was a new record attendance and those lucky enough to be there witnessed one of the FA Cup's great finals. An end-to-end start set the pattern for the game, with each defence proving resolute enough to prevent either goalkeeper being seriously troubled in the early stages.

Then, on 17 minutes, after some sound Villa build-up play, Athersmith let fly with a shot that flew beyond the reach of Menham in the Everton goal. Everton were shaken, but although they could have slipped further behind they held firm. Then the game turned. Hartley played Bell through, he waltzed past Spencer and, with only Whitehouse to beat, waited for the Villa goalkeeper to advance and struck the ball past him: 1–1. Shortly afterwards Everton took the lead from Boyle's free kick. Ten minutes later Wheldon brought equilibrium for Villa who, inspired by their equalizer, pressed hard and were rewarded when Crabtree headed past Menham to make it 3–2 in the Birmingham club's advantage.

Five goals in the opening 35 minutes: this was football of the highest quality. Though the tempo was maintained and chances continued to fall the way of both sides, no further goals came, and again the FA Cup had eluded Everton.

Great game though it had been, Keates – who was rare to criticize or put the blame at anyone's door – was blunt in his analysis of where the fault lay: 'In the season 1896/7 the club had got together an array of talented players for every position except in goal, and the weak link in the chain cost the side dearly.' He added that Everton had lost the Cup Final 'as was generally admitted, through feeble goalkeeping. The League position, too, was also weakened.'

Indeed Menham played Everton's remaining three games of the season but never again turned out for the club, having been sold to Wigan that summer.

Billy Muir, the Kilmarnock goalkeeper, came in the hapless Menham's place. He was a more suitable choice for director Keates, who described him as 'not a showy, but a most effective custodian'. Yet Muir's arrival did not prevent an inconsistent start to the 1897/8 season and soon the irritated Keates had found a new target to lambast: 'Meehan, the right-back, the best paid man in the team, played wretchedly. In a difficulty, the directors put in his place a not very imposing, but sturdy and resolute local player, W. Balmer, a stranger to First League games.'

Walter Balmer emerged as one of Goodison's finest early footballers and his arrival on the scene marked the start of a family dynasty. Born in West Derby, he had begun his career with South Shore (Blackpool) and was picked up by his home-town club during the summer of 1897. Although he was never the most cultured of full backs, he had, one historian noted, 'the other major pre-requisites of a reliable defender at the turn of the century – powerful shoulder charges, crunching tackles and hefty clearances'.[2] Walter's brother Robert – four years his junior – made his début some five years later on the opposite side of defence and shone in almost two hundred Everton appearances. Later, the Balmer brothers' nephew, Jack, played as an amateur with Everton before attaining fame with Liverpool. Keates was now happier with the state of defence: 'No further trouble was experienced in the full back position. The same half backs maintained their great reputation.' Now he turned on the attackers: 'The forward line failed to work satisfactorily, its personnel being greatly changed.' Hartley had followed Geary to Anfield, and Milward had joined Southampton, thus ending his brilliant 10-year association with Chadwick on the Everton left. John Bell and Ellis Gee, a recruit from Chesterfield, were left to labour on the flanks with weaker colleagues at the heart of the attack. 'Sometimes they played well,' admitted Keates, 'sometimes they were at sea.' Despite the patchy form, though, Everton finished the 1897/8 campaign a creditable fourth, a feat that was repeated in the following season.

But the forward line still laboured to make an impression. Its cause had not been helped by the departure of John Bell to Tottenham Hotspur during the summer of 1898, although he returned three years later for a second spell at Goodison via Glasgow Celtic and New Brighton Tower and made a further fifty appearances for Everton. In the first season without him, the club tried all number of journeymen in his place, yet it was clear that further buys were necessary.

First through the Goodison doors, in April 1899, was Bury's Jimmy Settle. Already a veteran of Bolton Wanderers and Halliwell Rovers, the tough, stocky inside forward was capable of explosive pace and a devastatingly accurate finish. A native of Millom, Cumberland, Settle was a star of the Everton attack for nearly a decade, scoring 97 times in his 269 league and FA Cup appearances and within months of his arrival he made the first of three appearances for England.

Also that summer, came the Sharp brothers from Aston Villa. Jack Sharp was a double international, who represented Everton and England at football throughout the winter, and played cricket for Lancashire during the summer – he made a handful of Test appearances too, most notably against Australia at the Oval in 1909 when he scored 105. Born in Hereford in 1879, he began his footballing career with Hereford Thistle before Aston Villa signed him and brother Bert in 1897. Neither brother settled at Villa and he turned out just 23 times before Everton made a move for both men.

Bert, a full back, was never able to unseat any of the incumbents in Everton's rearguard and moved to Southampton in 1902, after just 10 appearances. Jack, however, was a different proposition: described by one contemporary as a 'pocket Hercules', he had all the attributes found in many a great winger – he was an accurate crosser, speedy, with lightning acceleration, and could cut inside his defender to let loose with a rocket shot. J. T. Howcroft, who spent thirty years refereeing, described him as the best outside right he'd ever seen, better even than Billy Meredith or Stanley Matthews. He represented England twice at football, in 1903 against Ireland and in 1905 against Scotland. He made headlines in 1909 when he was one of the main protagonists behind a threatened strike on the eve of the new season: along with Manchester City's Billy Meredith, he had long been on the back of the FA to lift the maximum wage and had helped Meredith form the Players' Union in 1907.

Walter Abbott, a prolific inside forward, came from Second Division Small Heath for a fee of £250, and expectations were high of the man who had scored 36 goals during the 1898/9 season. However, at Goodison his goalscoring touch seemed to elude him and he was dropped after just three starts, then returned two months later as left half. Suddenly he was transformed and added the sort of bite to the Everton team that had been lacking since the departure of 'Wee Devil' Johnny Holt to Reading three months earlier.

Keates, however, was not wholly convinced by the new arrivals. 'The ability of the first two [Sharp and Abbott] was not perceptible to the Executive in the first season,' he noted. He had good reason to be sceptical: Everton finished the 1899/1900 season eleventh, their worst showing yet. Nevertheless, the two men began to impress in their second season at Goodison and the directors' 'eyes were opened . . . and kept open for many years by the sheer and fascinating merits of both'.

Improvement in the 1900/01 season was undermined by Sharp's absence during part of it through injury, and Everton only managed seventh position at the end. Yet the team indisputably had a more settled look. Seeking to improve it still further, the board brought back Bell during the summer of 1901 and also added Alex 'Sandy' Young. Although Young was a centre forward he could also play outside left. He had begun his career with St Mirren before a spell with Falkirk where his talents were quickly recognized; a move south to Everton soon followed. He made his Everton début on 28 September 1901 against Aston Villa, but it was December before he registered his first goal in a royal blue shirt. Although an avalance of goals did not immediately follow, he was a graceful footballer, not dissimilar to his namesake of the sixties, and much admired by the Goodison faithful.

The addition of Young and Bell helped Everton to their familiar table-topping position at the end of 1901, but they yet again struggled to sustain their form. Jimmy Settle, who had been outstanding in the run-up to Christmas, scoring 16 goals in the first half of the campaign (17 matches), managed just two more thereafter. With the loss of his goalscoring touch, Everton declined and stuttered to the runners-up spot, three points behind champions Sunderland. 'The general play did not come up to the expected standard,' complained Keates. 'One match dazzling, next puzzling, puzzling to the players as well as to the spectators.' His confusion extended into the 1902/03 campaign when Everton finished twelfth – their lowest placing yet – and were put out of the FA Cup in the quarter-final by non-league Millwall Athletic.

With the passing of 1903 the club's fortunes changed. John Bell had now left for good, but Harold Hardman, a diminutive flankster of considerable flair, proved a stylish replacement. He was one of the last gentlemen amateurs to grace top-flight football: a Manchester solicitor, he played for love of the game on Saturdays, turning in five years of fine service at Everton before beginning a 50-year association with Manchester United as player, then administrator and chairman. His amateur status also allowed him to play in the Olympic Games, and he was Goodison's first gold-medal winner (the other was Daniel Amokachi in 1996) after the Great Britain football team's victory in 1908.

The advent of 1904 saw an upturn in results and Everton finished the 1903/04 season third. Their good form carried through into the 1904/05 campaign, and for much of it Everton looked likely to match Preston North End's 1889 league and Cup double, topping the First Division in the spring with a run of form that looked unstoppable.

In the FA Cup Everton were drawn to meet Liverpool at Anfield in the first round on 2 February 1905. To the delight of the 30,000-strong home crowd Liverpool coasted to a 1–0 half-time lead, but Everton battled back after the interval and Parkinson – Liverpool's first-half scorer – undid his earlier good work by bringing down Young in the penalty area. Makepeace made no mistake in bringing the scores level from the spot. Honours even, the two neighbours met at Goodison six days later. Here, McDermott put Everton in front; Goddard equalized; then, with the game heading for a second replay, Hardman cut in from the left five minutes before the end and let fly with the winner. They disposed of Stoke 4–0, at their own ground in the second round, and Settle's hat-trick against Southampton in the quarter-final set Everton up for another 4–0 win.

The semi-final, with Sharp's former employers, Aston Villa, meant a return to Stoke's Victoria Ground. Thirty-five thousand people saw the inside forward score Everton's goal in a 1–1 draw. Four days later, the teams met again, this time at Trent Bridge, Nottingham. Villa were the superior side, running out 2–1 victors, with Sharp grabbing Everton's consolation.

Everton still had the league. Going into April 1905, they had six games remaining, and stood proudly at the top – a position they had held since mid-January. However, their Cup run – not to mention a meeting the previous November at Woolwich Arsenal, which had been abandoned with 15 minutes to go and Everton 3–1 in front – had left a glut of fixtures at the end of the month: three in four days.

Everton began their task with a 1–0 win over Woolwich Arsenal at Goodison, then followed it up with a 2–2 draw at Stoke. They returned to winning ways with a 2–1 victory over Small Heath. Still top, they entered with confidence against Manchester City – who themselves still entertained faint hopes of Championship glory – but slipped up, losing 0–2. After the match they journeyed immediately south for the rearranged fixture with Arsenal. Again, Everton were defeated, and they were left to rue the earlier abandonment while they waited helplessly to see if Newcastle would win their last match of the season against Middlesbrough and pip them to the Championship post. Newcastle emerged 3–0 winners; Everton, who had led the table for the previous three months, fell to the runners-up spot at the last. It had been a double disappointment. 'Shakespeare wrote of "The uncertain glory of April",' quipped Keates, nearly a quarter of a century later. 'This April is remembered as a shocker.'

○

EVERTON'S YO-YOING between the upper echelons of the First Division and mid-table mediocrity continued in the 1905/06 campaign. In an expanded division, now made up of twenty teams, they finished eleventh. Dignity, however, was restored in the FA Cup. To an extent Everton were assisted by the luck of the draw, which, in the opening three rounds, handed them home ties with Second Division opposition: they saw off West Bromwich Albion (2–1), Chesterfield (3–0) and Bradford City (1–0) without too much difficulty. The quarter-final draw again handed Everton a home tie, though this time against their top-flight rivals, Sheffield Wednesday. The latter promised to be sterner contenders and, for a period, challenged eventual champions Liverpool in their pursuit of the title, finishing the 1905/06 season third. Yet by half-time, the match was over: Everton had strode into a 4–1 lead, with goals from Sharp, Taylor, Booth and Bolton. In the second half, they conceded two, but held on to their earlier advantage to ease through to a tantalizing semi-final with Liverpool.

March 31, 1906, saw the city of Birmingham taken over by the blue, red and white ribbons of Everton and Liverpool fans, who had converged to watch their respective teams vie for a place in the Cup Final.

Once hostilities had commenced on the pitch, Liverpool took the early initiative, holding much of the possession and having the best chances. Everton defended doughtily and made occasional counter-attacks, particularly down the right. As the game progressed into the second half, Everton began to come to terms with their opponents and became more confident in their attacks. In one of their forays into the Liverpool half, Walter Abbott let fly with one of his characteristic long shots, which, via the forlorn Liverpool defender Dunlop, crept into the back of the goal. With Liverpool disoriented, Hardman seized the moment. A minute after Everton had gone in front, he took possession of the ball, ran towards goal and shot. Hardy saved his effort, but the ball fell only as far as Sharp. He played it back to Hardman, who tapped home the goal that sent Everton to their third final.

Their opponents were Newcastle United. Between 1905 and 1911 they were three times champions, and on five occasions reached the Crystal Palace for the FA Cup Final. Yet each time they tried to win their first Cup, they failed. In 1910, the year they won it, they had drawn the Crystal Palace meeting 1–1 with Barnsley and only taken the replay 2–0 on the 'lucky' soil of Goodison. In 1906 the Crystal Palace jinx was only a single game old, but after Everton's poor showing in the league that season, Newcastle were strong favourites.

On a bright, breezy April afternoon 75,609 people filled Crystal Palace; many had made the long journey south from Newcastle and Liverpool. In the first half many high hopes were let down by dour play with few chances: Settle had Everton's best chance with a fierce header, Newcastle had two fleeting opportunities of their own, but at the break, the scores were level. It was, noted the *Daily Mirror*, 'the tamest final for many years . . . [Everton] would have done better even had Young, the centre forward, not marred his dashing display with a good many petty tricks, which Mr Kirkham [the referee] generally noticed and always promptly penalized.' The second half was a different matter. Everton came out and controlled the game, and briefly looked to have broken deadlock eight minutes after the restart when Young put the ball in the net after Lawrence in the

Newcastle goal had failed to hold on to a shot. Settle squared the ball and Young turned it home. Alas for Everton, he was judged offside ('He was standing almost under the bar,' said the *Mirror*). Young, however, was indefatigable. With 13 minutes remaining, Taylor – captain, and sole survivor of Everton's last final – found Sharp with a searching pass. He evaded the Newcastle left back Carr, who had not previously given the Everton wideman an inch, then sent a beautifully centred cross, which Young slotted home with ease for Everton's winner.

The Everton team were heroes and rightly fêted as such. 'For the next two days they were the observed of all observers, the cheered idols of everybody wherever they walked, rode or sat,' wrote Keates, who was a member of the party. They enjoyed a victory banquet at the Charterhouse Hotel, visited Hampton Court the following day and, on the Sunday evening, had dinner with the Newcastle team.

On Monday it was back to business, and they journeyed north to Sheffield for a league fixture, which they lost 1–3. It scarcely mattered. Still glowing with the elation of their FA Cup victory they embarked on the home leg of their journey in a 'special train, decorated with flags, blue preponderating to the home-land'.

In Liverpool the festivities outshone anything that had preceded them. As one local reporter noted, it was 'the most remarkable popular demonstration that has ever taken place within the city boundaries'.

Keates wrote:

> Arriving at Central Station, a thunderstorm of cheering greeted Jack Taylor, Cup in hand, and his victorious comrades as they stepped from a saloon carriage. After a preliminary reception, on the platform, by the Lord Mayor, surrounded by football directors of Liverpool as well as Everton, a host of officials of other clubs and local notables, the Lord Mayor ascended a gorgeously carpeted truck, and delivered a neat congratulatory oration that would have swelled the heads of ordinary mortals. But Jack and his comrades were not ordinaries. Conscious, however, that they were having the time of their lives, they were compelled to keep smiling, couldn't help it, if they could. From the station on a four-in-hand (the players outside), Jack Taylor, on the driver's seat, proudly waved the Cup to the cheering thousands that lined the route to Goodison Park, via Church

Street, Whitechapel, Byrom Street and Scotland Road. The enclosure was crammed with enthusiasts. The team (escorted by mounted police) had a great reception. More ceremony, more speeches. Refreshments, a lull; fatigue, dispersal; followed by a welcome rest after a prolonged hour of glorious life.

Everton had won the FA Cup, Liverpool the Championship. With the onset of the 1906/07 season, it looked as if Everton might wrest that accolade from their neighbours, quickly rising to the top of the table. Their results at home were hugely impressive and included a 9–1 thrashing of Meredith's Manchester City – a record league win. In all they won 16 times at Goodison, drawing twice and losing just once, but their away form cost them dear. At the season's end they had managed just four away victories, which cost them the title. Everton finished third, while Newcastle took their revenge for the Cup Final and finished six points clear. For Sandy Young it had been a season of personal triumph: he had ended the campaign as the First Division's top scorer with 28 league goals.

Yet Young did not match those feats in the FA Cup where, for the second season running, Everton reached the final. The Everton striker scored just once in the seven-match path that led Everton to Crystal Palace, where they met the previous year's semi-finalists, Sheffield Wednesday. Everton had only one change in their line-up from a year earlier – Robert Balmer took Crelly's place to start alongside his brother – but there was still consternation on the day of the final when it was revealed that George Wilson, a recruit from Hearts the previous May, had been omitted. Wilson was an artist and brilliant showman who had begun during his début season to edge out Hardman. He was also a temperamental character, and when he vented his feelings to some of the directors, not only did they take exception but, as an additional disciplinary measure, dropped him for the final. In so doing they ensured that Hardman could feature for a second consecutive year.

Everton went into the match as firm favourites, but it was Sheffield Wednesday who began more brightly, testing the Balmer brothers time and again. Everton threatened on the break – Young shot over the bar, Hardman missed an open goal – but Wednesday took the lead on 20 minutes. Everton rallied, and two minutes before half-time, Sharp equalized. In the second half, Everton sporadically seized control, but it was a poor, scrappy match, and they never looked seriously like getting the breakthrough. Six minutes from time, Simpson, against the run of play, struck the winner for Wednesday. It had been a bad game for Everton and a poor advertisement for football. 'I doubt,' the Football League's founding father, William McGregor, commented, 'if we have ever had a final in which there has been more loose play . . . [It was] one of the poorest finals.' He expressed bewilderment at the exclusion of Wilson, 'probably the best forward in either team'.

Four months later, in November 1907, Wilson was sold to Newcastle for £1500, without having played a further game for the Goodison giants, and Everton was approaching a state of flux. As the *Daily Post* had pondered after the Cup Final defeat: 'What the regular Everton team will be in the future must be a puzzling problem for the directors to solve. It looks as if there will be considerable change from the old regime, and if so it will take some time for a new team to work harmoniously.' Over the 1907/08 season that prophecy was lived out: Walter Balmer, Crelly, Booth and Settle were phased out, and at the season's end Hardman left for Manchester United. Various alternatives were tried out during the course of the season and the frequent changes to the team eventually took their toll on results: Everton finished eleventh, having used 32 men in the process, but also progressed to the quarter-finals of the FA Cup.

One man who had attracted the notice of ever-discerning Evertonians was Bertie Freeman. He had been signed from Woolwich Arsenal for £350 towards the end of the 1907/08 season and became a devastatingly successful centre forward, replacing Sandy Young who reverted to inside right. Freeman was a top-drawer goalpoacher, blessed with the knack of being in the right place at the right time. During his full début season, 1908/09, he scored a league record of 38 goals from his 37 First Division appearances. His goals helped Everton to the runners-up spot, but again the Championship proved elusive. A strong start had seen them lead the table (yet again) going into the New Year but, as in several previous campaigns, the latter half of the season had badly let them down, and at its conclusion Everton were again well off the pace set by champions Newcastle.

Freeman was not the only man to attract rave notices during the 1908/09 season. Val Harris, a versatile and fleet-footed wing half, established himself in the first team, impressing with his commitment and skill. For him it was the first campaign of a six-season Everton career, during which he would be capped 20 times by his native Ireland. For his national team he made his début as centre forward and later played at inside forward, wing half and centre back. Everton also utilized his versatility, and during his 214-game spell at Goodison he played in no fewer than six different positions.

Like Harris, John Smith Maconnachie had been signed in the midst of the 1907/08 campaign, but established his reputation in the next. Signed from Hibernian in April 1907, he débuted at centre half, but made his name at left back, playing every game in the 1908/09 season, mostly with the cool, polished authority that was his hallmark during a 13-year Everton career.

The league runners-up began the 1909/10 season in excellent form, winning five of their seven September games, including a 2–1 triumph over reigning champions Newcastle on their home patch, in the process taking top spot. Yet the winter was disastrous: just five wins over the next four months. Their form improved but Everton finished a disappointing tenth. Although they reached the FA Cup semi-final, they lost 0–3 in an Old Trafford replay to Barnsley, when further disasters befell them.

Ten minutes after the start, the ball struck Jack Taylor in the throat. He doubled over in agony and left the field. Medical examinations revealed that he had sustained severe damage to the larynx – an injury of such severity that it ended his playing days at Goodison. Later he moved into amateur football with South Liverpool and from his retirement became a regular at Goodison. He died in 1949, aged 77, after a motoring accident in West Kirkby.

Taylor's untimely departure might have contributed to Jack Sharp's decision to call time on his playing days at the end of the season. He was a shrewd businessman – one of the few sportsmen of his generation to amass a great fortune– and his sports-outfitting store in Whitechapel (where it remains to this day) was taking up more and more of his time. He continued to play cricket for Lancashire until 1925, and in his career he scored over 20,000 runs, including 38 centuries. His scoring record at Everton is equally impressive: 81 goals in 342 matches, and his involvement with the club continued until his death in 1938, in the capacity of director. His son, Major John Sharp, became a director in 1946 and was later made chairman.

Sharp and Taylor's retirements left gaps in the Everton attack so severe that it was in a state of disarray. Twenty different players were tried in the forward line during the 1910/11 season, none with any great distinction. Yet Everton still finished the campaign fourth, a feat largely due to the steely defence, which conceded a measly 36 goals – a record for the expanded First Division that stood until the top flight was enlarged again in 1919. At the season's end Sandy Young departed for Tottenham Hotspur and Freeman to Burnley.

With the benefit of hindsight, Freeman was sold to Burnley well before he had fully peaked. He finished as the league's leading marksman in the 1911/12 and 1912/13 seasons, and rekindled the affections of Evertonians in 1914 when he scored the only goal in the FA Cup Final ... against Liverpool. After the First World War, he turned to non-league football, winding down his distinguished career with Wigan Borough and Kettering Town.

Young's story was not so happy. His move to London did not last long and he returned north to join Burslem Port Vale. On retiring he emigrated to Australia from where two conflicting stories emerged, both announcing his early end. The first said that he had been caught sheep-rustling and later hanged, which seems scarcely credible even given the then rough justice meted out in the Australian outback. The second had it that he was found guilty of the wilful manslaughter of his brother in 1915.

○

WHILE FREEMAN and Young were ending their Everton careers in 1911, three other men, who were to make a notable impact over the following years, were just beginning theirs. Southampton's scheming inside right, Frank Jefferis, had been signed for £750 towards the end of the 1910/11 season. An intelligent footballer, he was not as prolific a scorer as some of his predecessors, but possessed the grace and skill that befitted the School of Science. Toxteth-born Tom Fleetwood came from non-league Rochdale. Like his new team-mate Val Harris, he was as renowned for his versatility as he was for being part of the finest half-back line in the country. He gave more than a decade's worth of excellent service as a player, and, after a spell at Oldham Athletic, returned to Goodison on the coaching staff.

Born in Ellesmere Port in 1893, Sam Chedgzoy was a brilliant outside right who, as a teenager, had made a solid reputation playing for Burnell Ironworks, where he turned out with Joe Mercer, who made his name as a professional with Nottingham Forest and later fathered one of Goodison's most famous sons. He made his Everton début in the 1910/11 season, although it took him until the latter stages of the 1913/14 season to hold down a regular place in the first team. Like a good wine, Chedgzoy improved with age, and he made the first of his eight England appearances in 1920. Later, as a veteran, he nurtured the young Dixie Dean, but it was for an incident four months before the legendary striker's arrival that he is most famous.

A goal scored by Sam Chedgzoy in November 1924 led to a remarkable and almost immediate change in the laws of football. Chedgzoy had been given two pounds by Ernest Edwards, a local sports reporter, to stage an experiment during a home game with Arsenal. When Everton were awarded a first-half corner Chedgzoy placed the ball by the corner flag and waited for the attacking players to line up in anticipation for his cross. It never came. Chedgzoy, to the amazement of his fellow players and fans, proceeded to dribble the ball inside before shooting into the net. The referee's first inclination was to penalize him for his audacity, but at half-time he was persuaded to consult his rule book, which stipulated that it was legal to score directly from a corner. No mention was made of the taker being restricted to one touch of the ball. The referee's error cost Everton the game, but the rule was amended within forty-eight hours.

Chedgzoy's glories were still in front of him, and at the start of his Everton career he was still very much understudy to George Breare. So much so, that the 1911/12 season came and went without his making a single appearance. Everton's strategy then was still built with a firm emphasis on the rearguard action, and despite having one of the most goal-shy attacks in the division, they boasted the best defence. The famous Highbury chant 'One–nil to the Arsenal' might well have had a predecessor: 11 of Everton's 20 victories were secured by that scoreline. Keates was as surprised as anyone by the lofty finish: 'In the face of the many changes made to the forward line, it is astonishing that the second place was secured,' he admitted. 'It was the gratifying consummation.'

But the lack of goals was a problem. Without a Freeman or a Young, Everton failed to build on their runners-up spot, and finished a disappointing eleventh in the 1912/13 season and a near disastrous fifteenth in the next. The Everton directors were acutely aware, however, of where the problems lay and spent heavily during the dismal 1913/14 campaign to redress them. In November 1913 they paid Glasgow Rangers £1500 for their stocky goalpoacher Bobby Parker, and two months later £750 on Blackburn Rovers' inside forward Joe Clennell. Their arrivals, along with Chedgzoy's establishment in the first team at the tail end of the season, gave cause for optimism: Parker scored 17 times in his 24 appearances, Clennell four from 12, yet it was not enough to prevent Everton's worst ever finish to a season in fifteenth.

○

WHEN EVERTON kicked off the 1914/15 campaign (with a 3–1 win at Spurs) the political climate was very different from the one in which they had ended the previous season. At 11.15 a.m. on 28 June 1914, in the Bosnian capital, Sarajevo, Archduke Francis Ferdinand of Austria and his wife Sophie were shot dead by a Bosnian Serb, Gavrilo Princip. The assassinations set in motion a calamitous series of events whereby the treaty system that had maintained the European status quo for nearly fifty years fell apart, precipitating the outbreak on 4 August of the First World War. This brought with it the dilemma as to whether it was appropriate to begin the Football League programme. As Keates put it:

> The situation was bristling with perplexities for everybody. The directors decided to be guided by public opinion, in conjunction with the League and Football Association. To the impulsive, panic-stricken section of the community, the idea of any entertainments, or sporting games being tolerated, was unthinkable. The experienced governing bodies of the country were soon convinced that the wise and sound policy was to carry on, as far as it was possible, as usual. Every suspension would create additional unemployment, undermine the courage of the population, and be commercially and economically disastrous. Diversion and cheering entertainment was found to be the most essential tonic and sustainer for the men at the front as well as for those by the home fires.

Clearly the 'over by Christmas' conviction also prevailed. Yet the decision to continue with football attracted intense controversy. Clubs were accused of 'helping the enemy', and the Dean of Lincoln spoke for many dissenters when he wrote disapprovingly to the Football Association of 'onlookers who, while so many of their fellow men are giving themselves in their country's peril, still go gazing at football'.

Everton did not allow such distractions to get in the way. The lack of goals that had impeded their success in previous seasons was suddenly overcome. Parker finished as the First Division's top league scorer, with 35 goals from 36 matches, just three short of Freeman's record. At Goodison their form was poor: they won just eight times, an abysmal total matched only by relegated Spurs, but away from home they found salvation, winning 11 times. On the penultimate Saturday, a 1–0 win over league leaders Manchester City took Everton to the top of the division for the first time in 32 months. The following Tuesday, Oldham played their game in hand against local rivals Burnley, but lost 1–2. The advantage in the title race had at last fallen into blue hands, and the pressure was now on Oldham. The next Saturday, with Everton playing their last game of the season on the Monday, they played Liverpool in their final game. For once, Everton's neighbours did them a favour and beat Oldham, which secured Everton's title on goal average. On the Monday they drew with Chelsea, pulling a point clear at the top, and collected their second League Championship.

The celebrations were muted. 'Our gratification was chilled by the catastrophe of the Great War,' wrote Keates. For those men who had not heeded Kitchener's call, the suspension that July of the Football League and reorganization into regional competitions restricted a footballer's income to just £2 per week, and many headed for the killing fields of France and Belgium. Conscription came a year later.

This most horrid and pointless of wars was not unduly unkind to the Everton players. Some, such as Jefferis and Clennell, never saw action and continued to turn out weekly in the regional league competitions. When the Football League resumed on 30 August 1919, only Makepeace – who was approaching his fortieth birthday – was missing. Alongside his one-time colleague Sharp, he continued playing cricket for Lancashire and England. As an opening batsman, he scored 117 against Australia at Melbourne in 1921, becoming the oldest player to score a maiden Test century. He continued to play for his county until he was nearly fifty, amassing 499 first-class appearances, 25,745 runs, including 43 centuries, and later served the Lancastrians for a further 20 years as coach.

Nevertheless, the four-year gap took its toll. The side that had won the Championship had been a good but not great one. Now four years older, many men were past their best, and others were waiting to be demobbed. It was a season of transition. In a chaotic 1919/20 season, which ended with Everton sixteenth in a newly expanded division of 22 teams, Clennell, Jefferis, Maconnachie and Thompson were all phased out. In the following campaign, with a more settled line-up, Everton rose to seventh place and made it to the quarter-finals of the FA Cup.

But much of the old magic was missing. In an effort to restore former glories the Everton board set about changing the squad. In the summer of 1921 Bobby Parker was sold, and during the early stages of the 1921/2 season Dunmurry's Irish international centre forward Bobby Irvine was signed. Later he reverted to his favoured inside-right position and provided Goodison with seven years of thrilling service. Airdrieonians' scheming centre back, Hunter Hart, was acquired, another man who became a Goodison stalwart, and also captain. Yet both men's début seasons were miserable: Everton slumped to twentieth, just one place off relegation, and suffered a humiliating FA Cup exit, losing 0–6 at Goodison to Second Division Crystal Palace. Worse still, Liverpool were crowned champions.

Although it lingered on into the opening matches of the 1922/3 season, the depression was brief. Everton's directors were stirred into action. Wilf Chadwick, a Bury-born inside forward, made the step up from the reserves and money was laid out for Manchester United's Neil McBain, Chelsea's Jack Cock and Dundee's Alec Troup. McBain's transfer was the most famous: an elegant wing half (too elegant, some said), the news of his impending departure from Old Trafford precipitated a public meeting to protest at the deal, and more than a thousand angry United fans turned up. It was to no avail, and over the following four years McBain made more than a hundred appearances in Everton's royal blue shirt. Cock, a flamboyant man both on and off the field, provided three years' sturdy service as centre forward, weighing in with an impressive haul of 31 goals from 72 appearances. Troup, a tiny Scottish international winger, was one of the best crossers in the game.

With these men at the fore – along with Chedgzoy, who was now an established England international – Everton rose to finish the 1922/3 season fifth. The next campaign, aided in large part by Chadwick's 28 goals (which made him the First Division's top scorer), Everton finished seventh. It was a creditable enough achievement, but the side was renowned more for its stylish football than for its winning ways. The onset of the 1924/5 season saw Chadwick's goals dry up, those too of Cock, who was dropped. Everton were averaging just one goal per game, and even Chedgzoy's inventive effort in November could not alter that.

Everton were flirting with relegation and it was clear that a new star had to be found to halt the decline. The club's secretary-manager Tom McIntosh cast his net far and wide.

The man he came up with was almost on his doorstep, but no one could have imagined how great a hero he would become.

4

Dixieland

ALTHOUGH THE First World War had resulted in the League Championship trophy residing at Goodison for an inordinately long time, the decade that had kicked off with Everton's 1914/15 title win was one of Merseyside pre-eminence in English football. For seven of those years, the Championship had been held by either Everton or Liverpool, and twice an Everton player had topped the league scoring charts: Bobby Parker with 35 goals in 1915 and Bill Chadwick with 28 nine years later. Neither side had yet made it to the new national stadium at Wembley, which had opened to a fanfare of hype and controversy when an estimated 250,000 witnessed the 1923 FA Cup Final between Bolton and West Ham, but their time – or, at least, Everton's – would come soon enough. Both sides were packed with stars who dominated the ranks of the home nations. In the 1921 Home International Championship, for instance, Everton and Liverpool between them could muster a dozen players. It was a similar story in previous and subsequent seasons.

Come the 1924/5 season, both clubs were flirting with mediocrity. Everton finished in a desperately disappointing seventeenth place, and while Liverpool rose to fourth they never looked like challenging Herbert Chapman's Huddersfield Town, who won the second of their three consecutive league titles. But football on Merseyside was still causing a stir.

For once, though, it came from neither the blue of Everton nor the red of Liverpool, but the 'third side of the Mersey': Tranmere. Here, a teenage striker with a rocket shot and bullet header, boasting the physique, strength and positional sense more commonly associated with older, more experienced men, was causing a sensation. He had opened the season in the reserves, scoring five times in a match, and it was soon impossible for the Tranmere selectors to leave him out of the first team. He responded to the faith shown in him by averaging a goal a game – this for a side who were stuck almost all season long at the foot of the Third Division (North). Unusually for a team at that level, the feats of this young man quickly became known across the country. His name was Dean, and by the season's end he was an Everton player.

William Ralph 'Dixie' Dean was the dominant figure in football at club and international level in the late 1920s and early 1930s. Later, his goalscoring feats became footballing folklore and he has rightly been immortalized as a soccer legend. His famous smile has adorned postage stamps, his waxwork effigy at Madame Tussaud's and a painting of him in the National Portrait Gallery. To Evertonians he was a legend even as a player, and his name stands proudly and pre-eminently in any sweep of the club's history. Even as the generation of fans who can remember his playing days slowly slips away, subsequent generations marvel at the Dean phenomenon.

For 13 years Goodison was 'Dixieland', ruled by his character both on and off the pitch. On it, his goals and role in both spearheading and assisting the attack were dominant features of Everton's play; off it, Dean the man was, as a colleague remembered, 'bigger and better than life', his generosity, humour and extrovert personality a colossal presence among team-mates and supporters. Few individuals have given more to Everton Football Club than Dean, or achieved more.

The Dixie Dean story began on 22 January 1907. He was born at 313 Laird Street, Birkenhead, and he was later fiercely proud of his Wirral roots, frequently reminding people that he was a 'Wacker' and not a 'Scouser'. His background, in which he took equal pride, was working-class: his father – also William – was a railwayman, and his mother, Sarah, ran two local fish-and-chip shops. Like most boys, he was consumed by football, and his loyalties lay on the royal blue side of the Mersey after his father had taken him as a seven-year-old to watch the Everton of Chedgzoy, Makepeace and Parker in their Championship season. His loyalty never wavered, although he never again visited Goodison, because of a combination of war, his father's work obligations and his own playing commitments, until he joined Everton as a player.

From an early age football took all of Dean's spare time, much of which he devoted to practising his heading. 'When I was twelve or thirteen I used to practise by tossing the ball on to a low chapel roof and heading it as it dropped,' he recounted later. 'Once the ball was on the roof it was out of sight and I only had a split second when it came back into vision. I then tried to head the ball in the opposite direction to that which I was running. I got so good that I could hit virtually any square of the net later on!' Practice soon paid off and he was selected for the Laird Street School team, then Birkenhead Boys' First XI. Besides having a brilliant heading ability he had also developed a tremendously hard shot. In a game against Bootle Boys one of his 'bullets' was said to have broken the goalkeeper's arm. Other than his school team and Birkenhead Boys, 'Digsy', as he was known among his friends, also played for Parkside, Birkenhead Melville and occasionally Upton Hamlet and Wirral Railways. He even turned out for the local Borstal.

He left school at 14 and spent two years on the railways as an apprentice fitter. Typically the main criterion in the happy-go-lucky Dean's career choice had been that he 'liked' Wirral Railways' football ground. He often worked night shifts so that he could continue to play football for his local teams.

It was while he was playing for Wirral Railways that he received his first offer to turn professional, from New Brighton. The 15-year-old turned it down; he was not yet ready for league football, he said. The following season he signed for Pensby Institute, his final non-league team, and his childhood nickname transmuted into 'Dixie', after a typing error in a local newspaper report. It was a tag he came to despise: he would respond to those who called him 'Dixie' with either silence or a polite admonishment – 'My name is William, but you can call me Bill.'

His performances fast attracted attention. Tranmere Rovers soon had scouts watching him and following a four-goal rout against one of his old clubs – Upton Hamlet – they snapped him up. Dean made his début for Tranmere Reserves the following Saturday, 1 December 1923, against Whitchurch. Within weeks he was in the first team, playing against New Brighton, the team he had rejected a year earlier, in a Liverpool Senior Cup tie. He scored, in a 4–2 win for Rovers. Three days later he made his league début in a 5–1 mauling at the hands of Rotherham United and was subsequently dropped in favour of the regular inside right, Brown. Back in the reserves his form was irresistible. In one game against Middlewich, which

Tranmere won 7–0, Dixie set an individual scoring record of five goals and was reintroduced to the Rovers' first team for the final match of the 1923/4 season against Wolves, which finished in a goalless draw. The *Birkenhead News* reported: 'Dean found the Wolves centre back too much for him, and for one so young it is not an easy task for him to come in and play for a team of Second Division calibre.'

Although Dean had failed to hit the net in his first three league matches, he had scored 23 goals in 28 reserve-team appearances. It was not, however, enough to stake the 17-year-old a place in the first team at the start of the 1924/5 season, and he began it in the reserves. He opened the Cheshire League season by drawing a blank against Port Vale reserves, but a four against Nantwich and a five against Whitchurch resulted in a clamour for first-team inclusion. It soon came. An injury to the Tranmere centre forward, Stan Sayer, saw him pitched against Doncaster Rovers on 13 September 1924. Tranmere lost 0–2, but Dean kept his place for the meeting with Southport seven days later. Five starts into his Rovers career he scored his first goal. It was the beginning of a 15-year deluge. At Prenton Park, after 27 goals in 27 appearances during the 1924/5 season, Ernest 'Bee' Edwards commented: 'He is to my mind the most promising centre forward I have seen for years.'

Dean's goalscoring feats soon made him one of the most sought-after players in the country. Tranmere's trainer, Bert Cooke, ever mindful of the perennial financial woes that plagued lower-league teams, began to hawk Dean around the big clubs lest his market value slip from its early premium. Liverpool, Manchester United, Aston Villa and Birmingham City were all tracking him. When Tranmere played Ashington in a Third Division (North) fixture, the team had stayed in Newcastle and Dean had been shown around St James's Park but was 'unimpressed'. Arsenal were also said to be interested, and for years its directors were gently mocked by a telegram that adorned the wall of the Everton boardroom. Addressed to Bert Cooke, it read: 'TO COOKE STOP TRANMERE ROVERS STOP NOT INTERESTED IN DEAN STOP HERBERT CHAPMAN STOP ARSENAL STOP.'*

---

* What those Everton directors who would annually cajole their Arsenal counterparts failed to notice was that Chapman did not become Arsenal supremo until a couple of months *after* Dean had left Tranmere.

Finally Everton, the only club Dean had ever wanted to sign for, came in for him. Secretary-manager Tom McIntosh had already seen him perform well across the Mersey. He recognized that his outstanding ability, both in the air and on the ground, fitted in with the club's credo (later professed by Will Cuff) that 'It has always been an unwritten but rigid policy of the board, handed down from one generation of directors to another, that only the classical and stylish type of player should be signed. The kick-and-rush type has never appealed to them.'

It cost the then sizeable sum of £3000 to buy the youngster in March 1925, though few doubted his potential. As the *Daily Post* put it: 'He is a natural footballer with a stout heart, a willing pair of feet and a constitution that will stand him in good stead.' At the time of his transfer Dean had scored 27 of Tranmere's 44 goals that season and they were second-bottom of the Third Division (North).

In the top flight Everton were not faring much better, sitting in twentieth place, a single position over the two relegation spots. At the campaign's conclusion they had scored 40, conceded 60 and finished seventeenth.

The 18-year-old Dean had added two goals to that tally in his seven appearances. His début, a 1–3 defeat at Arsenal on 21 March 1925, passed without him finding the net, though that was soon rectified. A week later he made his Goodison début, with Aston Villa the visitors. He was quick to impress and had an early shot cleared off the line by Talbot when the Villa goalkeeper had been unable to hold on to his snapshot. A goal was not long in coming, though. Shortly after his near miss, Kennedy laid the ball back to Dean and he hammered home the first of his 377 Everton goals, a feat marked by a standing ovation from the Goodison crowd. Reid made it 2–0 in the second half, and ensured that the Goodison career of its finest son got off to a winning start.

At the season's end, the Football Association, always willing to tinker with its code to promote attacking play, changed the offside law. The number of opponents allowed between the attacker and the goal line was now two instead of three. It seemed a minor alteration, but the impact on the goals for the columns in the Football League tables was immediate and dramatic: the number scored rose from 4700 in 1924/5 to 6373 in the following campaign.

As defences struggled to get to grips with the new rule, it was

boom time for strikers. George Camsell was the first major benefi-
ciary, scoring an astonishing 59 goals for Middlesbrough in the
Second Division during the 1926/7 season. Dean thrived also: despite
being in a team that finished a mediocre eleventh in the 1925/6
season and a more perilous twentieth in the next campaign, he scored
32 and 21 times respectively. The goals, however, tell but half of the
story.

Dean began the 1925/6 season in the reserves, missing the initial
four first-team matches of the campaign. For someone who in his
early years constantly needed the reassurance of a first-team place
and, with it, the bulge of the goal net, it was a severe blow to his
confidence. He was helped through this brief period of self-doubt by
Sam Chedgzoy – now, at 35, the elder figure in the Everton line-up.
He 'kept telling me not to worry,' recalled Dean. 'He was a father to
me. I owe a lot to Sammy – he was a great old china, that fella.'[1]
When Dean was handed his chance five games into the new season,
Chedgzoy was the key influence, along with Alec Troup, behind the
young star's success. Chedgzoy was renowned for his dashes to the
touchline before he hit the ball deep into the penalty area for Dean
to head or volley. Operating on the opposite wing, Troup was a
different kind of player: he made the most of Dean's heading ability
by floating crosses teasingly from the left in anticipation of him
outjumping the opposing defenders. Though Dean made the score-
sheet just once in his first six starts of the season, he soon found the
net with the regularity that persisted throughout his Everton days.
His first hat-trick came against Burnley on 17 October 1925 and the
next, at Goodison a week later, against Leeds. Further trebles came
against Newcastle, at St James's Park and on Merseyside. The roar
'Give it to Dixie' was soon reverberating around Goodison whenever
an Everton attacker caught sight of the centre forward. A new star
had been born.

Everton, however, were still battling to combine as a team.
Though they had scored 70 times – up 75 per cent on the previous
campaign – defensive lapses persistently let them down and the
progress made in attack was undone by those at the back, who leaked
70 goals. At the season's end Sam Chedgzoy, a star and a Goodison
hero with exactly 300 league and Cup appearances to his name,
plus eight England caps (all despite the interruption of the war),
announced his retirement and emigrated to Canada.

But Everton still had Dean. Yet the optimism generated by Goodison's new hero was nearly brought to a violent end on 10 June 1926, when he had a dramatic brush with death. He was out with a girlfriend on a Sunday-afternoon motorbike ride in North Wales when a motorcycle combination, dodging in and out of traffic, crashed head on into his machine. The girl walked away with minor injuries but Dean suffered a fractured skull, broken jaw, eye injuries, multiple bruising and concussion. He was unconscious for 36 hours, and although fears that he might die quickly receded, the visiting Dr James Baxter gloomily predicted that he would 'never play again'.

Dean surprised everybody. His recovery was long by his own impatient standards, but from a medical perspective it was exceedingly speedy. He was transferred from the North Wales hospital, to which he had intially been admitted, to a west Derby nursing home where he continued his convalescence. On being allowed to return home the first thing he did was borrow a motorbike. 'It seemed to be playing with fate,' the *Liverpool Echo*'s Stork later recorded, 'but Dean had his own idea about the matter. He simply wanted to test out his nerve. He came through it successfully.'[2]

He returned to action at the start of October and the 1926 season. Goodison had changed markedly in his absence, with the construction of the Archibald Leitch-designed Bullens Road stand, and an incredible 30,000-strong crowd turned out to see his return in the reserve team. (As if to attest to Dean's popularity, a mere 28,000 had watched his home début.) On a sodden pitch with a heavy ball, any fears about the accident's long-term effects were soon forgotten when he powered home a header from a corner. Keates marvelled: 'The romance of Dean's recovery and the amazing increase in his skill are psychological, physiological and supernatural occurrences.' He went on to score a further 23 goals in 30 league and Cup appearances, but once more Everton's woeful defence let them down, conceding 94 goals, and they slumped to twentieth position, a mere place off relegation.

Dean's recovery had undoubtedly been remarkable, but it was not 'supernatural'; neither did it strengthen his extraordinary heading ability, as contemporary legend had it. Dean had had metal plates inserted in his jaw to aid the healing process, but these were removed when the bone had set. Rumours spread nevertheless throughout Liverpool that a metal plate had been put into his skull, and because of this he could now head the ball with increased power. It was nonsense, but given his fearsome power in the air, it was the only logical conclusion for some fans: Dean could head a ball harder than many players could kick it and could and did score from outside the area with his head. In fact, the trick of his trade lay in the way he struck the ball. As he later revealed: 'The secret of heading is to catch it on your forehead. If you get it on top of your head it will knock you dead in no time. I was not as tall as many of the centre halves I have played against, but I never had any difficulty beating them in the air. It wasn't a matter of leaping higher than they could. It was just a matter of going up at the right time.'[3]

Dean's prowess soon attracted the attention of the England selectors. On 12 February 1927 he made his international début, scoring twice in a 3–3 draw with Wales in Wrexham. Two months later he appeared for a second time in the white shirt in front of 140,000 spectators at Hampden. England had been without a win in Scotland since April 1904 when Steve Bloomer had scored the only goal of the game at Parkhead. It was a miserable run that everyone south of Hadrian's Wall was desperate to bring to an end. Tim Paton, the Yorkshire cotton millionaire, had offered each man a £10 bonus if England could overcome the Scots, plus £10 per goal scored. For the England players, who received £6 or a medal for each international appearance, it was a significant amount. Dean, never one to pass up the opportunity of a bonus, silenced the Hampden roar with both of England's goals in a famous 2–1 win. Although they had seen their proud record against the English broken, at the end of the game the Scotland fans gave him a generous, not to mention unprecedented, standing ovation.

Everton finished the 1926/7 campaign poorly, but a couple of important acquisitions had been made to the squad mid-season. The flamboyant Ted Critchley had arrived from Stockport County for a nominal fee in December and proved himself a worthy heir to Chedgzoy on the Everton left. He made his début on Christmas Day 1926 in a 5–4 thriller with Sunderland. The *Liverpool Echo* reported that 'The Stockport boy did well. His one run the full length of the field was something to memorise, but allowing for his over-anxiety, which made him run the ball out, I thought his passes and centres augur well for future days.' Over the next eight years Critchley provided many of the crosses that aided Dean's scoring.

The defence, which had been so shoddy over previous seasons, was bolstered by Warney Cresswell, signed from Sunderland for the vast sum of £7000. Five years earlier he had been the most expensive player in the country when Sunderland had paid South Shields £5500 for the defender. Now 29 and with eight England caps to his name, Cresswell was regarded as one of the country's best defenders. A versatile and, at the time, unorthodox full back, who would astutely close down opponents rather than dive in for possession, his pace, fluent distribution and imperious organizational skills provided the Everton defence with the kind of solidity and maturity it had long lacked. He was later appointed captain and, despite his age, was the mainstay of Everton's rearguard for a decade.

Dean was still unquestionably the star. Even during pre-season, hundreds came to watch him play in celebrity golf tournaments, while caricatures of him appeared in advertisements that promoted everything from football boots to cigarettes. Such endorsements were usually unofficial and Dean never made any personal gain from them, save £50 from J. Wix & Co., the cigarette manufacturers, and some free cartons of cigarettes, which he mostly gave away. This was not an era when footballers were wealthy, and despite his status, Dean did not earn – or expect – a penny more than any of his first-team colleagues, who received just £8 per week. (By comparison Babe Ruth, the US baseball star, who was also then at the height of his powers earned around £40,000 per year – 100 times Dean's salary.)

○

EVERTON OPENED THE 1927/8 season in style, beating Sheffield Wednesday 4–0 at Goodison. In the second match of the season, the previous year's 59-goal hero, Camsell, came up against Dean at Ayresome Park. Later Dean took pains to emphasize that Camsell's own remarkable haul had been attained in the Second Division, but that afternoon it was the Middlesbrough man who came off the winner. He scored all four of his side's goals to Everton's two – from Dean and Critchley.

Dean, however, was about to hit his own remarkable streak of form. By the end of November he had played 15 matches and scored 27 times. His haul included hat-tricks against Portsmouth and Leicester, plus all five goals when Everton beat Manchester United at the start of October. While Critchley was one of his main sources of attacking ammunition, the tantalizing crosses of the more experienced Troup on the opposite wing were what Dean truly prospered from. 'He stood only five foot five, but was full of bravery and skill,' recalled Dean. 'Because of a weak collarbone, which kept slipping out of joint, he had to play with a strapping on his shoulder every game . . . I think we had a perfect understanding and I think I have to thank him more than anyone else for the part he played in scoring the goals I did. I'd rate him as one of the best wingers there's ever been.'[4]

This was no one-man team either. When Dean was missing, playing for England in Belfast on 22 October, his team-mates still managed to put seven past West Ham without reply.

By Christmas 1927 Everton were top of the Football League and Dean started the New Year having scored 35 goals. Nineteen twenty-eight brought him more goals and cause for celebration: two against Blackburn on 2 January; another two versus Camsell's Middlesbrough on the seventh; one in the FA Cup against Preston North End on the fourteenth. On 22 January he celebrated his twenty-first birthday, and a week later he scored another two in the fourth round of the FA Cup against Arsenal, which ended in a 3–4 defeat.

Little did Dean know that his team were in the midst of a victory-free streak that was to span almost two and a half months. Yet still he kept scoring. When Everton met Liverpool at Anfield on 25 February his tally stood at 40 goals. Up against his great friend and rival Elisha Scott in the Liverpool goal, he hit a hat-trick, which pulled him level with Ted Harper's First Division record set two years earlier. In the event Liverpool scored three of their own to share the honours, but the pleasure that came from scoring against his neighbours was unquestionable for Dean. He later said: 'There was nothing like quietening the Kop. When you stuck a goal in there it all went quiet, apart from a bit of choice language aimed in your direction! Scoring there was a delight to me. I just used to turn round to the crowd and bow three times . . . Everton have always been noted for going on the pitch to play football. We got called the "School of Science" quite rightly. The other lot, the Reds . . . well, they were a gang of butchers! . . . They should have been working in the abattoir. McNab, McKinlay, the Wadsworths. God bless my soul. They'd kick an old woman! I had some great fun, though, with the lot of them.'[5]

After pulling level with Harper's record, it took him a further month to beat it with a brace against Derby County on 25 March, which sealed a 2–2 draw. Camsell's record now seemed to be slipping away from Dean. He was left with the stern task of scoring 15 times in just seven games to beat the Middlesbrough man's total. It was an almost impossibly hard challenge, but Dixie was to let down neither himself nor his side.

Everton's winless streak finally came to an end on 31 March with a 2–0 victory at Sunderland, while Dean was absent on international duty. By then Everton had fallen back to second place behind double-chasing Huddersfield. Six days later, Everton faced Blackburn at Goodison. Dean scored twice in a 4–1 win. The next day Bury were the visitors to Goodison, and Dean scored Everton's only goal in a 1–1 draw, which put Everton back to the top on goal average after Liverpool's defeat of Huddersfield the same afternoon. A week later, on 14 April, Dean scored twice in a 3–1 win at Sheffield United, and again in a 3–0 victory over Newcastle the following Wednesday.

That goal brought Dean's total for the season to 51 goals with three games remaining. Nine goals – or, more to the point, a hat-trick in each fixture – were required. It was surely an impossible task that faced the 21-year-old. When Dean could manage 'only' two goals in his next outing at Aston Villa, it seemed that the record was beyond him.

Watching Everton for the first time as Dean neared the magical sixty mark had been a four-year-old boy named Charles Mills. Although Everton were only in their golden jubilee year, his visit to Goodison in April 1928 marked the third generation of Mills Evertonians and the start of an association that is now in its seventy-fifth year. As a young child, he invariably remembered little of the day, but one boy, seven years Charles's senior, who was more aware of the importance of the times Everton were facing was Dick White. He had been introduced to his own lifelong obsession five years earlier by his own father, a Cork-born policeman. Twenty years later he was to begin one of his most enduring friendships, with the youngster making his Goodison debut. Before that though, he was consumed with Everton's striker: 'We knew that we had a legend,' he recalled. 'Everybody was talking about him, his name was on every man's lips, even Liverpudlians. I can remember, I used to go and watch a local team in Clubmoor and they had a centre forward who had shaped himself on the great man, even to the point of his hairstyle – I don't know how he did it – but they used to call him "Dixie". He dominated the scene on Merseyside.'

The penultimate game of the season saw Dean pitted against Burnley's England centre back and captain, Jack Hill, one of the most uncompromising and formidable defenders of his day. When the teams had met the previous December, Hill had marked Dean out of the game (although the defensive frailties of his team-mates were all too frequently exposed – Everton won 4–1). It was another tough task for the Everton striker, but Dean was never one to let a reputation get in the way of a goal. By half-time he had bagged four, but had to limp off in the second half with a sprained leg muscle. Not only was Huddersfield Town's challenge faltering under Eveton's late-season run, but Dean's record was on. Provided he was fit, of course.

Accompanying Dean home after the Burnley game – which Everton had won 5–3 – was the trainer Harry Cooke. Cooke had been an understudy to Jimmy Settle during the victorious FA Cup run of 1906, but had never been more than a peripheral squad member and when his playing days were prematurely ended by injury, he had joined the Goodison backroom team. As trainer, physio, mentor, coach and later scout, he was an integral part of the Everton set-up for half a century. For generations of Everton teams he was, literally, twelfth man and backstage utility player. On match days he was a constant presence, cigarette in hand, bucket and sponge at his feet, and had, in the words of David France, 'developed his own therapeutic massage treatment involving a proprietary blend of iodine and wayward cigarette ash'.

As Merseyside spent a week hypothesizing as to whether Dean would score the magical three goals against Everton's final opponents of the season, Cooke was staying with him at his Claughton home. 'Harry was bandaging and putting plasters on my right leg through the week,' remembered Dean. 'He stuck with me right to the morning of the match and we went across to Goodison together.'[6] They travelled by tram, Dean's usual mode of transport, with his fans.

May 5, 1928, was the day of destiny, and 60,000 Evertonians had crammed into Goodison to watch their heroes collect the Championship trophy – the title had been won three days earlier after Aston Villa's defeat of Huddersfield Town. First, though, Everton had to conclude their triumphant season and the question on everybody's lips – as it had been for months – was, would Dixie do it?

For Dick White, who had been building up to the big day for weeks, it was very nearly a day of disappointment: 'I kept saying to my father, in the week leading up to that game, "Hey, Dad, we're going to have to be up there early." My father was never a man to hurry, though. Although he was no longer a policeman he had that majestic, slow policeman's gait – he walked that pace everywhere. And he always insisted that I went up to the ground with him.'

On the day of the Arsenal match, the youngster was particularly on edge: 'We lived ten, fifteen minutes' walk away from Goodison, but you wouldn't believe, on this particular day, he still left at the same time *and* insisted I was with him in case I got lost! We walked up to the ground, along Walton Lane, up Bullens Road and into Gwladys Street. The old boys' pen was on the Bullens Road, just around the corner of Gwladys Street, and my father always paid his bob [1s., or 5p in today's money] and stood under the clock [on the corner of Gwladys Street and Goodison Road]. We got to the corner, he put his hand in his pocket and produced fourpence, which was what it cost to get in the boys' pen, and said: "Now, at the end of the game, meet me on the corner, by that lamp-post." I said, "Yes, all right, Dad, I'll be there." And off he went and I got in the queue.'

The streets around Goodison were filled with throngs of expectant and excited fans. As three o'clock neared, the long queue to the boys' pen was shortening, but Dick White was still far from the turnstiles. When he was within five boys of the front of the queue, disaster struck. The gates shut. 'I was distraught. I'd been looking forward to this for weeks, months. It was history in the making. I was weeping and all sorts of things were going through my mind. Shall I go home? Or shall I wait until three-quarter time [when they opened the turnstiles]? If Dad comes out and I'm not here, he'll be worried, so I'll have to wait . . .'

Tears streamed down his face. 'Then this gentleman was walking along, and stopped, and looked at me. "What's the matter with you?" he asked. So I unburdened my sorry tale on him. "How much money have you got?" he asked. "Fourpence," I said. "Well, you need a shilling to get in," he told me. "Yes," I said. "I know." And he gave me eightpence! I don't think I even thanked him! I legged it to the nearest turnstile, paid my shilling and fought my way through this mass of people behind the Gwladys Street goal, around to the far side, as near as I could get to the players' subway, and fought my way down, almost to the well.'

He had missed the opening stages of the game. Just three minutes in, the crowd had been silenced when Arsenal took a 1–0 lead. Within two minutes the hush had turned into a roar of elation when Dean equalized with a typically stupendous header. One down, two to go.

Seconds after the restart, Dean was felled in the Arsenal box. Penalty. There was only one taker, and though Dean intended to place it, he mis-hit his shot. Fortune, nevertheless, was on his side and the ball slid through the Arsenal goalkeeper's legs and into the net. Camsell's record had been equalled. One goal left and 83 minutes to go.

During this period Arsenal not only equalized but threatened to take the lead. Few spectators (or, for that matter, Everton players) were concerned with the scoreline as all attention focused on supporting Dean in breaking the 60-goal mark. With time ticking away, the tension became unbearable and the Arsenal defence seemed impregnable. With just seven minutes left Everton were awarded a corner. Alec Troup, who had set up many of Dean's goals during the season, delivered a beautiful out-swinger and Dixie rose above the Arsenal defence to send the ball into the back of the net. 'You talk about explosions and loud applause,' an ageing Thomas Keates recalled. 'We have heard many explosions and much applause in our loud pilgrimage, but, believe us, we have never heard before such a prolonged roar of thundering congratulatory applause as that which ascended to heaven when Dixie broke his record.'

Dean had marked his sixtieth goal with a simple bow, but Goodison went wild. 'Somebody ran on the pitch and stuck his whiskers in my face and tried to kiss me,' he recalled. 'Well! I'd never seen a supporter run on to the pitch until that day.'[7] He was congratulated by the Arsenal players – the first man to shake his hand had been Patterson, the Arsenal goalkeeper. 'I looked at Dean and he seemed shocked,' he remembered. 'I smiled and, God forgive me, I went over and shook hands with him.'

Arsenal equalized in the closing stages but the final minutes of the season were played out amid a flurry of wild cheering for the champions and, of course, Dean. 'It was the signal for the pantomime dames and gentry to take up their stance,' remembered the watching Will Cuff. 'The crowd raced on to the field, the game appeared as if it would never be restarted. Players leapt into the air, nobody cared a brass farthing for the remaining minutes of the match.'[8] With a couple of minutes to go, Dean left the field to avoid being mobbed, but made his return to watch Warney Cresswell lift the Championship trophy from the directors' box.

Afterwards, the players were invited to a celebratory reception in the boardroom. 'Dean's achievement was the dominant theme,' recorded Keates. 'The modest way in which he minimized his own success and insisted on his comrades being entitled to a big share of the praise, was one of the charms of the fraternization.' Dean heaped praise on his team-mates, particularly Troup. 'What an amazing little man he was ... Wee Alec brimmed over with courage and skill ... He and I had an almost perfect liaison. I have to thank Alec as much if not more than anybody else for helping me to score goals.'[9]

Yet despite the high praise from Cuff and Keates – both of whom were directors – Dean never received formal acknowledgement for his achievement from the club, financial or otherwise. Indeed, it was a quarter of a century after he had left Goodison that he received a long-overdue and deserved testimonial.

Dick White, thanks to his Good Samaritan, had seen Dean's last two goals and the record broken, and met his father, as planned, at the lamp-post outside Gwladys Street School: ' "Wonderful to see the great man get his record," he said. "Yes, Dad," I replied. "But I very nearly missed it." So I told him the story and he stopped, and looked at me. "He gave you eightpence?" he said. "Yes." "Eightpence! You know what that would buy? [It would probably have paid for about four pints.] Who was he?" "I don't know, Dad. He just came and saw me." "Did you thank him, then?" "I don't remember." For weeks after, he'd show me to people and tell the story, and he'd always end it with: "And this unknown man gave him eightpence!" '

The following morning the *Sunday Times*, which seldom reported on football, noted: 'Dean, the Everton and England centre forward, attained a record number of goals. His total of 60 in one season sets up a record, which now seems destined to be broken every season.' The newspaper's lack of interest in the sport showed: no one has come near to equalling Dean's record, never mind bettering it. Pongo Waring, a contemporary of Dean at Tranmere, came closest in the top flight with 49 in the 1930/31 season. Post-war it was Jimmy Greaves with 41 in 1960/61. Outside the First Division, Joe Payne scored 55 in the Third Division (South) in 1936/7.

The modern-day arguments about lax defences and (or) their failure to come to terms with the new offside rule hold some credence. Today defences are faster, more disciplined, possess greater numbers, and benefit from superior tactics and a more scientific approach to training. The same, however, could also be said of forward lines and a modern player seldom comes close to hitting even half of Dean's total.

This was also a time of notoriously hard defenders and unscrupulous tactics, which, in his Tranmere days, had cost Dean a testicle. In his career he underwent 15 operations. Harry Cooke preserved bits of Dean's bone in jam-jars and thrust them under the noses of new recruits, saying, 'That's what it takes to be a real player!'

The late twenties were also an era when the centre-back 'stopper' was being pioneered. Herbert Chapman's Huddersfield and Arsenal teams were early exponents of this tactic and, on one occasion, when Everton were playing Arsenal, Dean came up against their rugged centre back Herbie Roberts, who followed him wherever he went. Eventually Dean decided to do something about it. During the second half he asked the referee if he could leave the field. The Arsenal man ran over to him. 'You don't seem to be injured, why are you leaving the field, Bill?' Roberts asked.

'I'm going for a pee, Herbie,' responded Dean. 'Hasn't your manager instructed you to come with me? Come on, you'll get into a row if you don't!'

The red-faced Roberts ran to a position from which he could observe Dean's return.

Stories of Dean's prowess transcended Britain's borders. At the season's end Everton embarked on a Swiss tour. 'Floral tributes and speeches of welcome were showered on the party and the chairman's vocal cords were severely taxed by acknowledgements and responses,' wrote Keates. An agent made an attempt to bring Dean to the United States, which would have more than doubled his salary to £20 per week and given him a handsome £150 signing-on fee, but he rejected it. Herbert Chapman, who had purportedly turned him down while he was at Tranmere, tried to sign him for Arsenal. 'He put an open cheque on the table, but there was nothing doing,' said

Dean. Eight months after he had scored his sixtieth goal Madame Tussaud's unveiled their first wax figure of Dixie.

In all he had scored in 29 of his 39 First Division appearances: eight singles, 14 doubles, five hat-tricks, a four and a five; 29 at home, 31 away; 40 from shots, 20 from headers. Only West Ham and Sunderland escaped his goals and they featured in two of the three games when Dean didn't play. 'People ask me if that sixty-goal record will ever be beaten,' he later reflected. 'I think it will. But there's only one man who'll do it. That's the fella who walks on water. I think he's about the only one.'

o

WHEN DEAN THRIVED Everton prospered; when he struggled with injuries or form, the team faltered. Although he was still only 21, his effervescent personality was an inspiration to his team-mates and to the crowd. He was a talisman, leader and hero, and no Everton team before or since has been so reliant on one individual. Given the international presence in the Everton ranks at the time, this might seem odd, but Dean's two next injury-plagued seasons revealed Everton's dependence on their star.

With Dean's appearances restricted by rheumatism and an ankle operation, Everton finished the 1928/9 season eighteenth, after an alarming run of eight defeats in their last nine games. Despite a stop-start campaign, Dean still managed 26 goals from 29 league appearances. Partnering him up front was a new inside forward – Jimmy Dunn, one of Scotland's Wembley Wizards who had tormented England in their 5–1 drubbing the previous summer. It marked the start of a close and long-standing off-the-field friendship between the two men, and on it a prolific partnership and understanding. Yet Dunn's first two years at Goodison were characterized by inconsistency and many Evertonians wondered whether his Wembley performance had been a mere flash in the pan.

Yet Dean's fortunes mirrored his team-mates' during this time. Nineteen twenty-nine had been a miserable calendar year for Everton, although they had opened it in fourth place after a Dean hat-trick in the 4–0 win over Derby County on New Year's Day. Twelve months and just 10 wins later, it ended with a 0–5 defeat at Bolton, which left them a single point off the bottom. The only bright spots had been the emergence of the Scottish winger Jimmy Stein, in place of the popular Troup; and Tommy White, an occasional deputy for Dean in attack, at centre half. White had joined Everton from Southport for £1000 as an outside right in 1927, but was to spend most of his Everton career alternating between the two central positions in defence and attack. A physically bulky player, he was a versatile, rugged and powerful member of the Everton squad for much of the next decade.

Dean was to continue to be plagued by injury in the 1929/30 season and underwent major operations on chipped ankle bones, and developed the condition known as 'cold muscle'. He was in and out of the team and often played when lacking full fitness, yet still netted 25 goals from 27 league and Cup appearances.

Not that scoring goals was the problem: Everton scored 80 in the league, but conceded a disastrous total of 92. In both meetings with Leicester City, for instance, Everton scored four times, but on each occasion conceded five. It was to be the pattern of the season: as well as the double defeats against the Foxes, Everton scored three times on four occasions but failed to win; twice in seven matches, and still passed up both points. Not even the addition of the brilliant Welsh right back Ben Williams, or the promising young goalkeeper Ted Sagar, could stem the tide of decline.

With just five matches remaining and Dean sidelined for the remainder of the season, Everton were rooted at the bottom of the First Division. When they met Burnley on 18 April 1930, it seemed almost unthinkable that only two years ago to the day, a 3–0 win over Newcastle had lifted them to the top of the First Division. Now they were staring relegation in the face. Yet Everton beat the Lancastrians 3–0, and although they were unable to overcome Manchester United the next day (drawing 3–3 at Old Trafford), wins over Sheffield Wednesday (3–2) and Huddersfield Town (2–1) meant that they went into the last game of the 1929/30 season against Sunderland, though still bottom, with a chance of staying up.

Unfortunately, Everton's fate depended on results other than their own. They lay at the bottom of the table on 33 points; ahead of them with 34 were Burnley and Sheffield United; on 35 were Newcastle and Grimsby. Of the five strugglers, Everton had the best goal average (goals for divided by goals against) save Sheffield United. The situation was fraught with possibilities, but none of it meant anything if the teams ahead of Everton failed to slip up. A crowd of

51,000 – the biggest of the season – filled Goodison to watch Everton do what they could. The tension eased on 23 minutes, when Tommy Johnson scored after Sunderland had failed to clear a free kick properly. The elation was short-lived and six minutes later Clunas equalized. Everton responded immediately when Tommy White put them 2–1 in front, a scoreline they held on to until the interval. At half-time all eyes were fixed on the ABC board, which showed that Burnley were leading, but Grimsby and Newcastle had each failed to score. White made it 3–1 on 65 minutes and soon after completed his hat-trick, but it was to no avail. Goodison filled with a strange hush at the game's end as the day's other results were broadcast. Burnley had beaten Derby 6–2, Sheffield United had emerged 5–1 winners over Manchester United, Newcastle had won 2–1 at home to West Ham United, and Grimsby were victorious over Huddersfield. Everton had finished bottom, just four points behind fourteenth-placed Arsenal. 'Everton relegated! There is a sad ring about those words,' lamented the *Football Echo*.

o

THE PREVIOUS AUTUMN'S stock-market crash on Wall Street had sent the world economy spiralling into a depression that was, by the end of the decade, to lead indirectly to the Second World War. Everton's downturn, however, was brief. In the short term, though, letters piled into the local newspapers bemoaning the indignity of relegation. When the shareholders' AGM came round the unrest increased, after it was revealed that a loss of £12,000 had been posted for the relegation season. Demands were made for Everton to follow the lead of many of their rivals: appoint a manager and sack the board. The directors refused, and survived a vote of confidence by 82 votes to 61.

The players reported for pre-season training on 1 August 1930, and the first to arrive was Dean – an annual custom he had adopted in his first days at the club and maintained throughout his Everton career. It was a sign of intent, and with Everton's maestro seemingly with the worst of his injury problems behind him, few anticipated that the team's stay in football's second tier would be a long one.

Four weeks after their return to training, Everton began their campaign with a 3–2 win over Preston North End. They won their next four matches and stormed to the top, a position they maintained

– save for a week in September and another in October – until the end of the season. Those who attributed Everton's outstanding league form to the lower standard of opposition were silenced when it carried over into their FA Cup campaign. Plymouth Argyle (2–0) and Crystal Palace (6–0) were both dismissed in potentially troublesome away ties in the opening stages, and in the fifth round they saw off Grimsby Town with a 5–3 victory at Goodison. Next up, on 28 February 1931, came Southport in a local derby of sorts, for the quarter-final. On the snow-covered mudbath that was the Goodison pitch Everton ran to a 7–0 half-time lead, eventually settling for a 9–1 win.

Two weeks later, the semi-final was at Old Trafford, against West Bromwich Albion. The Baggies were Everton's only real contenders for the Second Division Championship and interest was intense. Old Trafford was packed with 70,000 fans, resulting in record semi-final receipts of £7629, despite the attendance standing at 3000 below the ground's record. Outside, 20,000 more thronged the Old Trafford concourse and in the ensuing confusion 333 people were injured. Inside, the game was interrupted on several occasions as the crowd spilled on to the pitch.

Everton controlled the match but spurned a clutch of clear opportunities, then gifted the tie to Albion. Billy Coggins, Everton's West Country-born goalkeeper – a competent trier, who was often the butt of Dean and Dunn's dressing-room jokes – misjudged an innocuous centre, which flew into the back of the net. Everton battled back, but an equalizer proved beyond them.

Despite the disappointment of not getting to Wembley, the 1930/31 season was one of personal triumph for Dean. He completed his double century of goals on 8 November 1930 in only his 207th appearance at the age of 23 years, 290 days – exactly the same age as Jimmy Greaves when he completed the same feat more than thirty years later. Government minister Sir Freddie Marquis presented him with a commemorative medal, and the *Daily Post* noted: 'It is a fine record considering his comparatively short career. No footballer in history had a record of such consistency in league soccer, or ever will, perhaps.' Then, little over three months later, after a brace against Barnsley, he was on the verge of the 200-goal mark for Everton. 'Think of it,' the *Liverpool Echo* had written on the eve of Everton's meeting with Nottingham Forest at the end of February, '200 goals

from this still young man in the space of five and a half seasons of
football, some portion of which he spent in hospital with a motor
injury that threatened he would never play again, and some spent
nursing a damaged bone that was operated upon.' In the event it
took Dean a further six weeks to complete his record, but the day
he scored a brace against Bradford City, Everton were guaranteed
promotion back to the top flight.

By then, many people were paying the admission price just to see
him play and it was estimated that Dean was adding around five
thousand to the average gate. It was known that some fans would ask
at the turnstile, 'Is he playing?' If the answer was negative they would
go home.

Everton's sojourn in the Second Division saw some of their
existing and future stars make names for themselves. Jimmy Dunn,
out of sorts for much of his first two years at Goodison, was now one
of the forward line's most prolific and deadly finishers, scoring 14
times in his 28 outings for the first team. Dean, who had recommended his signing to the Everton board after coming up against
him for England, later described him as 'one of the greatest inside
rights I'd ever seen'.[10] The muscular young centre half Charlie Gee
was signed from Stockport County for £3500 and quickly supplanted
the Welsh international Tom Griffiths. Within a year of signing he
had begun his own international career – for England – completing,
in just three years and 50 league appearances, a meteoric rise from
the realms of junior football, where Stockport had originally spotted
him. Tommy Johnson, a dazzling inside left and Manchester City's
greatest ever league scorer (a record that still stands), had joined
Everton's late-season push to avoid the drop a year earlier. He was
second top scorer, after Dean, with 18 league and FA Cup goals,
and became one of the stars of subsequent campaigns. Finally, the
much sought-after half back Cliff Britton had arrived from Bristol
Rovers in 1930, having originally made his name in amateur football.
'He was a very elegant and skilful player,' recalled Charles Mills. 'He
perfected this lob which Dean would head from.' Indeed, Dean
described him as the best crosser of the ball he ever played with, and
claimed that Britton's crosses were so precise that he could flight the
ball so that the lace was turned away from Dean's head at the time
of impact! However, the Everton selectors initially deemed him too

frail for the first team and decided that the best course for Britton's development was to play him as an outside right for the reserve team, so he was restricted to just 10 league appearances.

Despite later successes in the FA Cup and on the international front, Cliff Britton holds a unique – and unfortunate – position in Everton history: he was unlucky enough to be a reserve twice when Everton won the First Division Championship. The emergence of Joe Mercer in the late thirties deprived him of a medal in 1939, but he spent the entire 1931/2 season in the reserves as Everton marched to their fourth championship success.

◊

THE NEW SEASON, 1931/2, opened just a few days after Ramsay MacDonald's coalition government was formed, aimed at redressing Britain's worst ever financial crisis and grappling with unemployment. Everton won their first three matches, and surprisingly, Dean, now captain, was outshone by his team-mates Dunn and White, who each scored hat-tricks in the opening two games, against Birmingham City and Portsmouth. In fact, it was in Everton's sixth fixture of the season that Dean recorded his first goals, but when he did announce his comeback to top-flight football, it was in typically headline-breaking fashion: a hat-trick against Liverpool at Anfield on 19 September 1931. It was the prelude to an astonishing run of form, which saw Everton take the top spot within the month, a position they did not concede in the remaining seven months of the season.

At Goodison, Everton were simply incredible. During October, November and December, their home record stood as follows: played 7, won 7, goals for 46, goals against 11. Dean scored five in the 9–3 win over Sheffield Wednesday on 17 October, and again when Everton beat Chelsea 7–2 on 14 November. Comparisons were quickly made with the previous Championship-winning side and it was widely debated whether Dean could break his own amazing record. By New Year he had 29 goals to his name, but this was a team that shared the goals. In 1928, Alec Troup had come nearest to Dean in the scoring charts with just 10 goals; in 1931/2 Johnson and Dunn both reached that total; White, who spent 19 of his 23 appearances deputizing at inside right for the injured Dunn, scored 18 times; Johnson 22. Dean had to settle for 45 goals from 38 games, and between them Everton scored 116 times, 12 strikes short of the record set a year earlier by Aston Villa.

Everton lost two of their last four games of the season, and drew a third, leaving only two points between them and second-placed Arsenal at the campaign's end. Accepting the Championship trophy after the last match of the season – a 0–1 defeat at home to Portsmouth – Dean told the watching Evertonians, 'After today's performance I'm ashamed to take it!' Later when he was interviewed by Pathé news he was more generous: 'The lads are splendid. This is a triumph for players who at one time found everything going against them. Today we have touched the peak and Arsenal have been put in second place. I want to thank all our players for their brilliant work.'

In an age without European football, in which even international football was seldom played beyond the realms of home internationals, it was difficult for a player to make a name for himself outside his home country, and sometimes even county. English football – although regarded by its public as the best in the world – was introverted by technological handicaps and the reluctance of the Football Association to engage in more ties with 'foreign' nations. Television was still confined to Logie Baird's laboratory, cinema footage to the occasional Pathé news clip, and radio broadcasts were in their infancy. England had famously vetoed the first World Cup, staged in Uruguay in 1930, and would not enter until 1950. Even friendlies against other European nations were a rarity: just six of Dean's 16 England caps came against countries from outside Great Britain. Given all these factors, the chance of a player being well known, much less as a legend, outside his own league was difficult, if not impossible.

Dean was different. His 60-goal haul and feats for Everton and England had brought him not only immortality on Merseyside but worldwide fame. In John Keith's excellent biography of Dean, he recalls an anecdote of the late actor Patrick Connolly (better known by his stage name Bill Dean – taken in honour of his hero – or as *Brookside*'s Harry Cross). During the Second World War Connolly was based in the Western Desert, where he had to take an Italian prisoner. Furious at being captured, the Italian spat into the sand and cursed, 'Fucka ya Weenston Churchill, and fucka ya Deexie Dean!' Even the American baseball legend, Babe Ruth, insisted on meeting Dean while on a visit to London in the late thirties.

Nevertheless, Dean's chances to prove himself beyond the domestic stage were limited to Everton's intermittent overseas tours and his handful of 'foreign' internationals. The last came in December 1931 against Spain at Highbury. Spain's star was their goalkeeper Ricardo Zamora – like Dean, one of the few players of the time who was famous outside his own country. Zamora had been signed by Real Madrid from Barcelona a year earlier for a world record fee (for a goalkeeper) of £6000. He had just received a £3000 benefit from Real, who paid him £40 per week – five times as much as Dean. To much hullabaloo the game was billed as the chance to see the world's greatest goalkeeper against its best striker. Also, it was an opportunity for England to avenge their 1929 meeting, when Spain had been the first 'foreign' team to beat them.

Yet Zamora was a prima donna. He insisted on playing in ridiculous rubber knee-caps and prefaced his appearance with a catalogue of overly theatrical dives. When hostilities opened on the pitch, Dean upstaged him, setting up England's first and scoring the last in a 7–1 thrashing that included two goals by his team-mate Tommy Johnson.

The Spain match was Dean's penultimate international appearance, but six months later he had the opportunity to add to his fame on the continent when Everton embarked on an end-of-season tour of Germany. The Weimar Republic stood on the brink of collapse: it was the eve of Nazi electoral victory and just six months before Hitler took power. Everton kicked off their tour in Dresden, where Hermann Goering sat among the crowd, along with an assemblage of high-ranking Nazi officials. Although this was still four years prior to the infamous Berlin Olympics and six before England's notorious meeting with Germany, when the England players were instructed by the British Ambassador Neville Henderson to give the fascist salute, the Everton team were expected to give the Nazi salute to the watching Goering. They refused. To catcalls and booing they lined up before kick-off and defiantly resisted raising their arms. When one Everton player looked as if he might waver, Dean apparently held him back, which merely served to increase the crowd's antipathy. As if that wasn't enough, Dean further infuriated his hosts by scoring a hat-trick.

Controversy followed the tour party. On another occasion Jimmy Dunn was arrested for causing a disturbance after he had been robbed in a bar and went in pursuit of the thieves. Dean came to the rescue but received two broken fingers and bruises to his head from heavy-handed police officers, plus a night in a cell for his pains. Next day, he appeared in court and was fined the equivalent of £13 10s., which Will Cuff paid to bring an end to the incident.

Back on Merseyside, the onset of the 1932/3 season saw the champions falter. An inconsistent autumn meant that by Christmas Everton was out of the title race. Celtic's Billy Cook replaced Ben Williams on the right of defence and Everton also signed Bradford Park Avenue's boy wonder, Albert Geldard. Geldard held the distinction of being the youngest player ever to appear in a Football League match, in 1929, when he turned out for Park Avenue against Millwall aged just 15 years and 156 days. A superb all-rounder, he could have taken up cricket professionally and later said that not playing county cricket for his beloved Yorkshire was one of his biggest regrets. Within a couple of seasons of his début, he had attracted the attention of a number of top-flight clubs and was signed by Everton in November 1932 for £4000 – a record fee for a teenager. He scored on his début away to Middlesbrough and followed that up with a spectacular solo goal on his Goodison début against Bolton Wanderers.

In the reserves a lanky youngster by the name of Joe Mercer was making a name for himself at half back. In one of his Central League appearances, against Stoke City, Mercer was lining up alongside Warney Cresswell, who spent the first half being given the run-around by an unknown youngster who had been hugging the Stoke City flank. At half-time, a club director happened to be in the dressing room, and Cresswell urged him to snap up his opponent: 'You see this boy. Go and buy him. Sell the Royal Liver Building to get him if you have to – but get him.' The director paid no heed to his advice; the young pretender turned out to be Stanley Matthews.[11]

Solace was found in the FA Cup. For Dean, losing in the 1931 semi-final had been the biggest disappointment of his short but glorious career. With international honours, two League Championship medals and a Second Division title medal, he needed the FA Cup to complete his collection. Nineteen thirty-three was Dean and Everton's year. In the third round against Leicester City, they came back from behind to win 3–2; Everton's goals came from Dean, Stein and Dunn. In the fourth round, Johnson stole the headlines, scoring twice in a 3–1 home victory over Bury, Dean weighing in with his inevitable goal. Next up were Leeds United, again at Goodison. Coming just a week after Everton had been humbled 4–7 at Anfield, any fears that confidence might have been unduly shaken were quickly forgotten, with Dean and Stein the scorers in a 2–0 win. Luton Town of the Third Division (South) were next up at Goodison, and they found Everton irresistible, succumbing to a 0–6 defeat. Everton's scorers were Stein and Johnson – with two apiece – plus Dunn and Dean.

Molineux, Wolverhampton, was the venue for the semi-final on 18 March 1933, West Ham United the opponents. The Eastenders were stuck in the depths of the Second Division, but Everton – mindful that the FA Cup was the greatest of levellers – were under no illusions that this would be a walkover. And so it proved on the day. West Ham's dubious finishing and defending saved Everton's blushes, and though the Londoners cancelled out Dunn's first-half header shortly after the interval, Critchley – only in for the injured Geldard, whose arrival had edged him out of the first team – scrambled a late winner. For the first time Everton were at Wembley. 'We're there – and now we must land that Cup,' said an elated Dean. 'The whole city of Liverpool is behind us.'[12]

Six weeks passed before Everton's visit to north-west London. Interest on Merseyside was phenomenal, and to cope with demand London Midland and Scottish Railways laid on 40 special trains to take fans south, providing a reserved seat for each of the 700 passengers aboard every train. Everton's pre-final base was the Derbyshire spa town of Buxton and they were on £25 a man to win. The speculation leading up to the game was about whether Critchley – the semi-final hero – would be preferred ahead of Geldard. In the end, the youngster won the race for the number-seven shirt, with Everton's selectors apparently acting on the advice of Dean. 'Critch was a good player and to be left out was a big disappointment for him,' Dean later reflected. 'But this lad Geldard was faster. He was just the lad you wanted at Wembley.'[13] A bigger surprise was nearly sprung before kick-off because Billy Cook had been caught drinking the night before the game. Some of the directors – as they had successfully with Wilson 26 years earlier – sought to bar his inclusion in the side and for a while it looked as if Ben Williams might make an unlikely return. Again, Dean intervened and Cook played.

The final was famous for being the first match in which the

players' shirts were officially numbered. Everton, in white shirts and black shorts, wore numbers 1–11 – with Dean at number nine – Manchester City 12–22.

As kick-off approached, the mood in the Everton dressing room was one of high excitement and nerves. Surprisingly for the most experienced man there, it was too much for Warney Cresswell, who had made his five-hundredth league appearance earlier in the season, and he left the room. According to Will Cuff, he asked a police constable if there was a private room where he could smoke before going on to the pitch, 'to settle me nerves, d'ye know, man'. The policeman obliged, Cresswell smoked his pipe and went off to join his team-mates. He put in a performance of typical ice-cool assurance. 'Cresswell was the team's steadying influence,' said Joe Mercer, 'apparently wise and imperturbable as an owl.'[14]

Indeed, Cresswell's effusive performance was matched by each of his team-mates in a match that Everton controlled from the first minute to the last. Stein opened the scoring on 41 minutes, knocking the ball home from close range after Langford in the Manchester City goal had spilled it following pressure from Dean.

Back on Merseyside, those who were not lucky enough to get tickets were able to listen to the match on the radio in one of the first such broadcasts. Dick White, now a teenager, was one of them. To facilitate the audience's understanding, the pitch was divided into a patchwork of squares and the commentator would describe exactly where the ball was. 'When they scored the first goal,' he recalled, 'not everybody in our street had a radio, and you would see people running out of the houses to tell a less fortunate neighbour that they'd scored.'

Everton's number nine was a perennial torment to the City defence, who were unable to come to terms with either his physical presence or his strength on the ball. As Matt Busby, who was in the City half-back line that day, put it: 'To play against Dixie Dean was at once a delight and a nightmare. He was a perfect specimen of an athlete, beautifully proportioned, with immense strength, adept on the ground but with extraordinary skill in the air.' Seven minutes after half-time Dean had made it two, powering both the ball and the hapless Langford into the net after Britton's centre. Ten minutes prior to the end, Dunn made it 3–0, heading in a corner from Geldard and in the process knocking himself out.

It set in motion celebrations back in Liverpool and Charles Mills's father was back home in Middlesex Road, Bootle, by 9.30 p.m. 'In the interim my mother got in touch with the neighbours – they were all women, because all of the fellas had gone down there. They dressed themselves in white skirts and black knickers (like the team) and were waiting for them when they got back – you should have seen my father's face when he saw that lot!'

Of Everton the following Monday's *Manchester Guardian* reported, 'They were romping about and playing their tricks as unconcernedly as though this were almost an exhibition match at familiar Goodison Park.' Bee in the *Liverpool Post and Mercury* wrote: 'Everton won by convincing methods, by their superior craftsmanship, by all-round merit, with hardly a weakness and with a lot of solid work interspersed with the daintier touches of Johnson and Dunn.'

At the age of 25, Dean had now accomplished everything. 'I'll never forget going up to the royal box at Wembley to collect the FA Cup,' he recalled. 'I received it off the Duchess of York [the late Queen Mother]. She congratulated me and said it was a very good game. She really smiled and said she had enjoyed it. That made me feel so proud. I was walking ten feet tall because it meant I had won every honour in the game. That Cup medal completed my collection.'[15] It was his last major honour. Amazingly, Dean's international career had come to an end too, and his last cap had come against Ireland at Blackpool in October the previous year. In all he had scored 18 goals in 16 internationals.

Dean kept finding the net, though, and broke goalscoring records with abandon. He scored in each of Everton's opening six games of the 1933/4 season, in the process registering his three-hundredth league goal. Yet two days after the sixth match – a 3–1 win over Arsenal – he had an operation to take two small pieces of bone from his left ankle. It kept him out for six weeks. On his return he was injured again and this time his cartilage was operated on. In his absence Everton tried, and failed, in an attempt to sign Chelsea's Hughie Gallacher as a replacement.

Without Dean, Everton struggled to progress beyond the realms of mediocrity. In total he played just a dozen times in the 1933/4 campaign, scoring nine goals as his team slumped to fourteenth place and slunk out of the FA Cup at the first hurdle. Tommy White, Jimmy Cunliffe – who had come from non-league Aldington in 1930 after quitting his job as a plater – and Norman Higham, an inside left signed from Barnsley, all deputized for the missing centre forward with varying degrees of success. Alec Stevenson – according to Dean, 'an inside forward of rare skill, a very tricky player who read the game brilliantly' – was signed midway through the season from Glasgow Rangers. Although he was only five foot three he 'would leave towering opponents wrong-footed and helpless with his dribbling skill'.[16] Yet it was indisputable that Everton were not the same without Dean.

Defences who had rested easy in the 1933/4 season might have held hopes that Dean was finished. He was not, and the impact he made on his return was dramatic. Everton's goals for tally shot up from 62 in 1933/4 to 89 for the 1934/5 campaign. Of those Dean scored 26, but again Everton's defence proved porous and conceded 88 goals; the club had slipped to eighth by the season's end.

The 1934/5 season has, however, been remembered for four epic encounters with Sunderland stretched out over five weeks in December and January. For the first, Sunderland visited Goodison on Christmas Day and were seen off with a 6–2 win. Cunliffe (2), Coulter, Dean, Geldard and Stevenson scored Everton's goals. The following day Everton travelled to the north-east for the return match and were thrashed 0–7.

The opportunity to gain revenge was not long in coming. After Everton beat Grimsby Town 6–3 in the opening round of the FA Cup, the two sides were drawn to meet in the fourth round at Roker Park on 26 January 1935. It was a filthy match that was ultimately tied at 1–1, with Everton's goal scored by Cunliffe. Dean left the field a bruised man, having spent the afternoon being battered and manhandled by the Sunderland defence; on one occasion having to leave the field after his shorts had been shredded.

For the replay the following Wednesday afternoon, the FA appointed Ernie Pinkston as referee, a man known as the 'Sergeant Major'. Prior to kick-off he assembled all 22 players in the centre circle and warned them that any foul play would lead to their immediate dismissal. What followed, 'the match of a hundred thrills', was entirely different from the game that had preceded it.

Despite the midweek mid-afternoon kick-off, the ground was so packed that the crowd broke out on to the pitch from the Goodison Road enclosure. Jackie Coulter, an inside left signed from Belfast

Celtic a year earlier, opened the scoring on 14 minutes and made it 2–0 just past the half-hour mark when he crashed home Geldard's cross. David reduced the deficit to 2–1 shortly before half-time. In the second half, Stevenson controlled the show, delighting the home crowd with his trickery and skill, and the Irishman looked to have won it with his close-range effort just fifteen minutes from the end, which brought the scores to 3–1.

Yet Sunderland were not finished. Connor made it 3–2 and inspired his team-mates to pile forward. Then, with practically the last kick of the game, Gurney equalized with a spectacular overhead kick.

As the players regrouped at the end of 90 minutes, Sunderland's manager Johnny Cockrane was ordered off the field for trying to coach his players. Two minutes into extra time Coulter completed his hat-trick, but Connor cancelled that out with his second to make it 4–4.

Both teams seemed to be heading for a second replay when Geldard seized the day. First he tapped home Dean's knock-down from close range; moments later his cross-shot completed the scoring: 6–4. Journalist Ivan Sharpe described it as 'the most spectacular game of my time . . . Like a bombardment was the thud of leather against goal posts and netting. 1–0, 2–0, 2–1, 3–2, 3–3, 4–3, 4–4, 5–4, 6–4! Accompanying it a crescendo of excitement as 60,000 roaring folk were for two hours raised up, cast down and thrilled to the marrow.' Even Dean, who had not scored, described it as the greatest game he had ever played in. Bee wrote: 'Has there ever been a greater game of skill in the mud in any league or Cup match? We keep all our memory cells filled with noteworthy sporting occasions, but this later 6–4 game will top the lot by reason of its two goals in the last two closing minutes, by the ordering off of a manager of the visiting side, and by the multitudinous moments of dramatic skill and art.'

○

THE INTER-WAR YEARS had seen the rise of the modern football manager and the beginning of the end of boardroom interference in playing matters. Herbert Chapman, of Huddersfield Town and Arsenal, was the forerunner of this new breed of soccer boss. During the twenties and thirties he introduced changes in the way his teams approached games and sought to bring to bear his own playing experience on the game. Chapman's biographer, Stephen Studd, described his approach as: 'a reaction to the days when teams took to the field without an overall plan of how they were to set about winning, when the only initiative that came from management was to encourage friendships in the team so that players were more ready to discuss tactics among themselves'.[17]

Chapman said of his own playing days, 'No attempt was made to organize victory. The most that I remember was the occasional chat between, say, two men playing on the same wing.' He developed a tactical framework around which his teams played and developed revolutionary new tactics, such as the Herbie Roberts-type 'stopper'. The board of directors was confined to the administrative running of the club, and the manager to the team, although Chapman's influence was all-pervasive. Indeed, the Arsenal boss was involved in everything from the renaming of the local tube station to the pioneering of floodlights more than two decades before they became the norm.

In the face of these new developments, Everton remained almost defiantly traditional, despite frequent speculation that they would modernize their set-up. They retained the role of secretary-manager, which had been in place since amateur days and was, in the face of the Chapman-inspired revolution, almost an anachronism. The role was part-administrator, part-selector, and middle man between the coach, captain and team, and members of the board, who retained a say in selection. The role of captain – in Everton's case Dean – was more like that of a modern-day international cricket captain. He had a say in selection and match tactics (if there were any – Dean had a notorious aversion to them) and to an extent was responsible for the daily running of the team, in tandem with the coach, Harry Cooke.

Both coach and captain were answerable to the secretary-manager, who in turn was responsible to the board. The directors seldom, if ever, had any direct dealings with the players and conducted their business with the team via the secretary-manager. His job, as Thomas Keates put it, was to act as 'the consultant and father confessor of the players, a redresser (if it is possible) of their grievances, consulting engineer of the captain and trainer, and prudent adviser and information bureau of the directors'.

For years the system worked with cool efficiency and served

Everton well. Their secretary-manager was Tom McIntosh, and like so many of the men who succeeded him – Catterick, Lee and Kendall – a north-easterner. Born in February 1879, he had had a playing career with Doncaster Rovers before becoming their secretary in 1902. Nine years later he became Middlesbrough secretary-manager, and in December 1919 took up the same position at Goodison. He was perhaps most famous for spotting and signing Dean, and was well respected and liked by both board and players. A kind, patient, articulate man, his 'system of management,' wrote Keates in 1928, 'seems to approach the ideal'. On 29 October 1935, Everton mourned Tom McIntosh's death, at 56, from cancer. Dean was devastated. 'He was a great man and when he passed away I was very upset. He was someone you looked up to and respected ... When I was made captain we used to have many a chat about this and that and you never had any trouble talking to Tom. He'd always listen and he'd try to do what was best for all concerned.'[18]

The repercussions of his death, for Dean in particular, were enormous. Theo Kelly came in McIntosh's place. He was already well established in the club's administration and, for him, it was the natural career progression from his previous role as secretary. He was an expert self-publicist and adept at balancing the club's finances, but lacked rapport with the players and even their respect. He was also fiercely ambitious and sought to be Everton's answer to Chapman. Indeed, in his pursuit of the 'official' manager's job Kelly was utterly ruthless.

Not that Dean let any of this affect him, in the short term anyway. Another stop-start season in the 1935/6 campaign still brought him 17 goals from 29 appearances, as Everton sank to a disappointing sixteenth place. Yet the final game of the season, against Preston North End, brought a flurry of interest as attention turned to the possible breaking of another record. A week earlier Dean had scored a hat-trick against Birmingham City, which brought him to within a goal of Steve Bloomer's record of 352 league goals, scored for Derby County and Middlesbrough between 1892 and 1914.

For the Preston match, Bloomer was invited to Goodison as the guest of Bee to see Dean maybe equal or beat his record. When his train arrived in Liverpool, Dean was waiting with the journalist at the station to meet him. Injury had prevented him playing, but the two legends watched Everton beat Preston 5–0. Bloomer later paid tribute to him: 'I reckon Dean is the best centre forward I have ever seen . . . and I saw all the old-time lads. They were good at heart, but Dean had something none of the others ever had. It is his bonny method of getting away from the centre half and his unequalled skill in heading the ball.' A few weeks later Warney Cresswell left, after more than three hundred appearances, to become manager of Port Vale and later Northampton Town.

It was not long before Bloomer's record had been surpassed. On the opening day of the 1936/7 season Dean equalled it in a 2–3 defeat away at Arsenal. Four days later Everton met Sheffield Wednesday at Goodison and he scored the record-breaking goal in a 3–1 victory. It had taken Bloomer 22 seasons of league football to set such a record. Dean took a mere 13 to beat it. He ended the 1936/7 season with 27 league and FA Cup goals and began the tutelage of a brilliant young striker signed from Burnley on the last day of 1936. His name was Lawton.

It was obvious to most people, Dean included, that Tommy Lawton had been bought with a view to replacing him. Although Dean was only 29 when Lawton arrived, the catalogue of injuries and operations over his time at Goodison had taken their toll. He had lost some of his pace and his movement had become restricted, his frame was stockier – some would say too much so – and he had physically aged. Yet he retained his knack as a goalscorer, as his record shows even in the twilight of his Goodison career. As for Lawton, it would have been easy for Dean, for so long the heart and soul of everything connected with Everton, to allow petty jealousies to undermine the youngster's progress at Goodison, but the notion was alien to Dean's generous nature. Instead, he nurtured Lawton, trained and taught him, and encouraged his every move. 'Tommy often came to me for advice and he always took notice,' he said, in old age. 'I liked Tommy very much.'[19]

Off the field, Dean faced more pressures. Since the death of McIntosh, Theo Kelly's stock had risen. As Charles Mills, then a regular, remembered: 'Theo Kelly virtually ran the club. They had a chairman – Cuff – but he was a hands-off chairman, he left it all to Kelly, he was the man who directed operations.'

Dean never liked Kelly, and later described him as both an autocrat and despot. Over the course of the 1936/7 season, the relationship between the two men deteriorated as Dean watched

Kelly's ambitions surface: 'This chap Kelly had no time for the older lads. I just couldn't get on with him. He was secretary but I didn't care what he was. I knew what was happening. He wanted to get rid of me and also one or two other people who looked like being in with a chance of becoming manager one day. I didn't want to leave Everton. But Kelly was the reason I did leave. It wasn't on account of Tommy Lawton arriving – it was nothing to do with that. That fella Kelly just didn't want me there long.'[20]

The general lack of respect for Kelly's footballing acumen did little to alleviate matters. As T. G. Jones, himself a Kelly signing, from Wrexham in March 1936, put it: 'He wasn't a manager, he was a secretary. He couldn't tell Dixie what to do on the field.'[21]

But he could keep him off it. Three games into the 1937/8 season Dean was dropped. He played just twice more for Everton: a 1–2 defeat at Grimsby, and finally on 4 December 1937, against Charlton Athletic at the Valley. Everton lost 1–3 in Dean's 399th appearance for the club. He continued to play for the reserves, eventually winning a Central League Championship medal, but Kelly had cut off any prospect of his returning to the first team: 'Kelly started telling lies about me and things got worse. He wanted to have that manager's job and definitely wanted to get rid of me. I could see that. So I had it out with him and decided to move on.'

Then, on 11 March 1938, the unthinkable happened. Dean was sold to Notts County for £3000. The ever astute Kelly made certain that Everton recouped the money paid out to Tranmere 13 years earlier. Disgracefully, though, Everton's greatest-ever player was allowed to leave without a farewell or thanks. Perhaps understandably, he did not return to Goodison for many years.

Dean's time in Nottingham was brief and not altogether happy, and he moved on after just nine games and three goals. Later, he enjoyed a swansong in Ireland, with Sligo Rovers, where he was deservedly treated like a legend and helped them to a runners-up position in the league and success in the Irish FA Cup Final – for them an unprecedented spell of glory. The outbreak of war in September 1939 ended any prospect of further adventures in Ireland and he eventually enlisted in the Royal Tank Regiment. During the war he made his last league appearance, as a guest for York City in 1941. Naturally, he scored.

Life outside football for Dean was happier than it was for many of his contemporaries. After the war he ran the Dublin Packet pub in Chester until 1961 and John Moores later gave him a job as a security guard. In 1964, he was the first Everton player to benefit from a testimonial, which raised £10,000. He died in 1980, at Goodison Park. His achievements have never been and are never likely to be forgotten. Two incidents have emphasized this over recent years. Firstly, he was voted by the British public to be immortalized on the second-class postage stamp nearly seventy years after his 60-goal haul. Then, during the 1997/8 season the Goodison crowd were presented with a half-time guest. On to the pitch ran a toddler to a round of applause. It was Dean's great-grandson. Even though he had not kicked a ball for 60 years and had been dead since 1980, it was clear that the legend of William Ralph 'Dixie' Dean had lived on throughout generations of Evertonians. His later immortalization in the form of a bronze statue, which stands proudly outside Goodison Park, will ensure that he is, hopefully, never forgotten.

Dean's career had everything: records, fame, domestic success, international recognition, immortality on the blue half of Merseyside and beyond, but above all else it had goals. Yet in spite of his haul – 377 in total for the Blues – it was the pride of playing for Everton and giving pleasure to those who came to see him that stayed with Dean in his latter years: 'I'll never forget the Everton fans for the way they treated me, not only when I was playing but long after I left the club,' he said. 'I felt that these fans belonged to me and I belonged to them. I was born and bred an Evertonian and I knew I would never change.'[22]

5

Sagar, Smiler, the Master's Apprentice and the Uncrowned Prince of Wales

ON NEW YEAR'S DAY 1937, a nervous 17-year-old arrived at Liverpool Exchange station to embark on a career that would elevate him to fortune, success and superstardom. Although he had already made a name for himself in the footballing backwater of Burnley, turning in an impressive 16 goals in his 25 appearances for them, he was still a virtual unknown outside the mill town. That was already changing. Twenty-four hours earlier the sensational news had broken that the Everton and Burnley chairmen Will Cuff and Tom Clegg had agreed a £6500 transfer for his services. The fee wasn't a record, but it was an unprecedented sum for a teenager.

The young man, Tommy Lawton, had been told to report at his new club the next morning to begin training with his team-mates. Despite the fee, nobody from Everton deigned to meet him, and in spite of his burgeoning fame, Lawton was practically an innocent abroad: although he was only 40 miles away from Burnley, and equidistant from his native Farnworth, he had never before travelled so far on his own. He had to ask a porter how to get to Goodison, and was directed to Dale Street where he was told to take a number four tram. Once on it, the conductor recognized him. 'Hey, you're that young Lawton aren't you?' he asked. Lawton told him he was. The conductor stared at him for a moment, then said: 'You'll never be as good as Dixie!' It was an inauspicious start to life on Merseyside.

Tommy Lawton was born in Farnworth, near Bolton, Lancashire, in October 1919. Like Dean, his father was a railwayman, while his mother worked in one of the town's cotton mills. He had a poor but happy upbringing, set against a backdrop of the Depression and

Dixie Dean's unprecedented goalscoring feats. The football-mad youngster soon came to idolize Dean, and although he never witnessed the legendary figure in action until the day he began training with him, he was quickly scoring goals like his hero.

No fewer than 560 strikes in three years of schoolboy football had alerted a succession of Lancastrian clubs, but he plumped for Burnley and made his league bow while still a 16-year-old amateur. He signed professional forms in October 1936 on his seventeenth birthday. Four days later, Burnley came up against Tottenham Hotspur who, even in the Second Division, boasted a glittering array of international stars, including the England centre back Arthur Rowe. Lawton hit a hat-trick. Two months later he was at Goodison.

Lawton later suspected that the deal had long been set up. Eight weeks earlier, the left-wing partnership of Jimmy Stein and Willie 'Dusty' Miller had arrived at Turf Moor on free transfers. Could they have been a down-payment for him, with the cash sum of £6500 coming later? In later years Lawton often pondered whether he had been 'tapped up', though remained unsure to his dying day. What was certain was that both players talked up Everton no end to the youngster at a time when a host of leading First Division clubs were trailing him. Even without the persuasive charm of Stein and Miller, Lawton was already convinced that Everton were the club for him: he wanted to meet and play alongside his hero Dean.

Although he had not previously met the Everton number nine, Lawton had encountered the Goodison Park experience. As a 13-year-old in March 1933 – a month before Dean was to lift the FA Cup – he had played there in a Lancashire Schools Cup match: 22,000 people turned out to watch Liverpool Schools beat Bolton Schools 3–2, with only a parry from Liverpool's George Burnett – later a post-war Everton goalkeeper – preventing Lawton grabbing a hat-trick. It was a portent of things to come.

On arriving back at Goodison nearly four years later, the first new colleague he met was Joe Mercer, who introduced Lawton to his new team-mates, internationals and stars like Sagar, Gee, Cook and Jackie Coulter, but there was only one man Lawton wanted to meet. 'Where's Dixie, then?' he asked Mercer.

At that moment the dressing-room door flew open, almost knocking the new boy over. 'I'm here,' announced an unshaven Dean, who was wearing a pair of carpet slippers. (Towards the end of his Everton

career, Dean lived in one of the club houses near Goodison Park,
where Everton still trained during the week. He was well known for
turning up at the ground straight out of bed, wearing his dressing-
gown.) He marched over to the young striker and shook his hand
vigorously. Then, his arm round Lawton's shoulders, he took him
aside. 'I know you're here to take my place,' he told Lawton.
'Anything I can do to help you I will. I promise, anything at all.'

'He impressed me right away,' Dean said later. 'He was quiet
and listened.'

The master had an apprentice, the novice a living legend. But
just as Dean was no ordinary teacher, Lawton was not the average
pupil. The tough training drill he had undergone as an amateur at
Turf Moor had already aided his development enormously. With
Burnley's trainer Ray Bennion he had practised aiming shots at
the Bs in beer-advertisement hoardings, the start of his journey to
becoming one of the all-time great strikers of the ball – with low
trajectory and perfect accuracy that rarely lifted into the crowd. The
tall, slim, sharp-eyed boy, with black, brilliantined hair, possessed a
lightning-quick loping stride and a powerful hanging leap, which was
honed under the guidance of his new master. Dean insisted that
Lawton was 'the lightest mover of any man who ever played football'.

Lawton was put into Everton's reserve team for six weeks, then
called up to deputize for Dean – who was being rested for the
following week's FA Cup fifth-round tie with Spurs – on 13 February
1937. The opponents, Major Buckley's Wolves, had been a bogey
team to Everton throughout the late thirties and so it proved again,
as they took a 7–2 victory. On a boggy pitch Lawton got on the
scoresheet via the penalty spot, but the way the team had played
hardly augured well.

When the FA Cup tie came round a week later at home to Spurs,
Lawton was back in the reserves, playing Bury at Gigg Lane. At
Goodison, the game had ended in a brawl, Dean missed a penalty
and Coulter salvaged a 1–1 draw with a last-minute equalizer. The
directors (and team selectors) were unimpressed and insisted on
changes for the rematch at White Hart Lane two days later. Torry
Gillick switched wings from right to left in place of the unlucky
Coulter, and Geldard came in on the right. Alex Stevenson was out
with flu so Lawton replaced him at inside left, alongside Dean.

It was the first of nine occasions the two played alongside each other, master and apprentice, with Dean always at centre forward. His pupil took little time to make an impression. With just two minutes gone, he beat the Spurs left half Grice, crossed to the near post, where the ball was half cleared, but only back to Lawton. 'At this stage,' Ernest 'Bee' Edwards reported in the *Liverpool Echo*, 'up stepped Master Lawton to crack a shot so hot and fast, so rushing that the goalkeeper Hall saw nothing of it. It was a crackerjack shot and taken with Lawton's well-known fury of pace.' As the ball hit the back of the net, Dean turned to Joe Mercer and said, 'Well, that's it. That's the swansong, that's the end of it.' The master had seen his successor.

With just 22 minutes to go, Everton had streamed into a 3–1 lead, but somehow contrived to lose 3–4 after a contentious penalty decision had gone against them and extra time. Lawton appeared a further six times that season alongside Dean and three times without. They played twice more together in the 1937/8 season, but in all were together on the winning side only once, a 7–1 victory over Leeds United in which Dean scored twice, Lawton once. It is a curious quirk in the club's history that its two greatest centre forwards never fully hit it off as a partnership.

Lawton had come into a relatively young squad. Dean was unquestionably the most senior and dominant figure, and alongside him five members of the 1933 FA Cup-winning team – Britton, Cook, Geldard, Sagar and Thomson – still figured prominently. After disappointing ends to the season in 1937 and 1938, with finishes of seventeenth and fourteenth respectively, Geldard was sold to Bolton and Britton stepped down into the reserves to concentrate on developing his coaching skills; Dean, of course, was infamously sold to Notts County.

Since winning the 1933 FA Cup, Ted Sagar had continued to grow in stature and fame. He had collected the first of his four England caps against Northern Ireland in 1935 and retained his place in the national side the following year. Although he cut a slender figure for a goalkeeper at a time when it was considered perfectly acceptable for an opposing striker to bundle the goal's custodian into the back of the net, he overcame his shortcomings with superb reflexes and occasionally reckless bravery. Like Gordon West and Neville Southall after him, Sagar was also well known for his vocal contribution to the Everton team. Dick White later recalled an incident that said much about the characters of Sagar and his colleague T. G. Jones: 'We were behind the goal, right behind the net, and Everton were under pressure. The ball kept coming over and getting cleared and Sagar was hopping around like a cat on hot bricks. Then this fella came tearing in and was blocked by TG, who then took the ball. All the while, Sagar's yelling, "Clear it! Clear it!" Then Jones makes this immaculate pass and the pressure's off. Later when things had died down, somebody shouted: "Ain't he bloody marvellous, Ted?" Sagar turned, and yelled back, "He might be bloody marvellous to you, but he's driving me bloody mad!"'

But for hesitancy on the part of Hull City, Sagar would probably never have become an Everton player. He had been spotted playing for Thorne Colliery in the Doncaster Senior League by the East Yorkshire side, but they were slow to offer him a contract and Everton stole in ahead of them. He had made his début on 18 January 1930 in place of the experienced Davies and promptly kept a clean sheet in a 4–0 victory. He played a further eight games during the campaign, but relegation and the signing of Billy Coggins from Bristol City towards the end of that fateful season restricted his chances. Nevertheless, Sagar's quality was obvious to the Everton selectors and he won his place back on the opening day of the 1931/2 season. From then on he never looked back.

The other veterans of 1933, Cook and Thomson, both dominated the left side of the Everton defence, the former at left back, the latter at left half. Both were products of Scottish football, Thomson signing from Dundee for a fee of £3850 in 1930 and Cook from Celtic in 1932 for £3000. Each was a ferocious and resolute tackler, and Thomson's attacking forays were a frequent source of ammunition for Dean and later Lawton. Yet for a while it looked as if Jock Thomson's Everton days were drawing to a close. Supplanted by a promising and graceful youngster, he played just twice in the 1936/7 season and only nine times in the following campaign. Yet a tactical switch opened the way for a triumphant return in the 1938/9 campaign, the year he captained Everton to the title.

The young pretender who almost ended Thomson's days at Goodison was Joe Mercer. He typified a generation of footballers who played with a genuine affection for the club and its fans: from the day he first pulled on an Everton shirt in 1933 until the bitter day he was forced out 13 years later, his famous Cheshire Cat grin never left his face. Born in Ellesmere Port on the eve of the First World War, football was Mercer's destiny. His father, Joe senior, had played alongside Sam Chedgzoy for Ellesmere Port Ironworks, and when the two hopefuls had come to the attention of league scouts, Mercer had gone to Nottingham Forest, Chedgzoy to Everton. Yet it was Chedgzoy rather than his own father (who died when Mercer was only 12) whom the young Mercer had idolized on the football pitch, and with this infatuation were sown the seeds of a lifelong love affair with Everton. (Years later, even when he was Manchester City manager, he would often say that he remained an Evertonian at heart; and he was a man who was able to boast, 'I have five shares . . . which is more than some of the directors have!') Playing as an amateur while working for Shell, he was picked up by Everton as a 15-year-old and eventually blooded a week before the 1933 FA Cup Final. Teased for his skinny bandy legs – Dean used to joke, 'Blimey, his legs wouldn't last him one day on a postman's round!' – he had thickened out by the time he turned out for the first team two years later. In fact, he had improved so much that by October 1935 he'd replaced Thomson in the Blues' line-up at left half. He developed quickly, and by 1938 had graduated to the England team. He later recounted, 'I was brought up to believe that Everton was the best team in the world and nobody was going to beat us,' but the hopes and aspirations hammered into him as a youngster took slightly longer to realize.

If Mercer cut a distinguished figure in the Everton team, the presence of his best friend, Tommy George (TG) Jones, was positively aristocratic. Jones had signed from Wrexham in March 1936, aged 19, for £3000 – then considered a substantial fee, particularly for a man who had made only six appearances for the Welsh club – but had taken nearly two years to establish himself in the side, replacing Charlie Gee. The styles of the two men differed greatly: Gee was a traditional, uncomplicated centre back, Jones a defender with the skill and composure of an inside forward. Cool and relaxed when in possession, few centre halves of his ilk had been seen before. 'What a player,' remembered Charles Mills, who was then a Goodison regular. 'Never made a foul. A strong tackler, but not one to hoof the ball – the way you see now, with endless kicks up the field.'

A forerunner of the legendary Franz Beckenbauer, Jones's forte was dribbling out of his own penalty area and spraying the field with passes. 'He had the great capacity to stroke the ball around,' Tommy Lawton said later. 'He also had the best right foot in the business and so complete was his positioning and balance that he always seemed to receive the ball on his right foot.' He had his party pieces too: on one occasion he dribbled along his own goal-line before calmly clearing to safety; another was running towards the ball, then letting it roll between his legs, knowing that a team-mate would be in a position to take it. Yet he was never careless, never a show-off, just a virtuoso, possibly a footballing genius, who later doubted that his considerable talents could be utilized in the modern game. 'Don't get me wrong, I'd like to play today, but I have no idea what position I'd play.'[1] He soon acquired the tag 'the Uncrowned Prince of Wales', and his reputation endured even long after he had left Everton, when Dean, Lawton, Mercer and Stanley Matthews each cited him as the greatest player they had ever seen.

Dean started the 1937/8 season as Everton's centre forward, but three games in – all defeats – Lawton was given his chance. He seized the moment with gusto, finishing the season top league scorer with 28 goals. 'If Lawton is not the best centre forward playing today,' wrote the *Sporting Star* at the end of the season, 'I have yet to see one better . . . he is not merely a proposition, but a ready-made player, and I have never seen anyone, including Drake, hit the ball so swiftly and accurately on the turn.' Lawton claimed that his weekend was ruined if he didn't score and he loved to see the back of the net rise more than anything. Evertonians shared such sentiments.

Yet at 18, he was still not the finished article and his footballing education continued under Dean's tutelage. While the master was more than happy to teach Lawton the tricks that had made him a legend – even while he was keeping him out of the side – he would not tolerate watching the prodigy becoming bigger than the team. Dean, of course, at his peak, had earned just eight pounds per week – the same as all his first-team colleagues – and had rejected endorsements if they did not benefit his team-mates; even when the Arsenal net had lifted with his sixtieth goal a decade earlier, he had played down his stupendous personal achievement. He was nothing if not a great leveller.

After Lawton's goal against Leeds United on 16 October 1937 – the fifth time the 18-year-old had struck in eight matches – he walked into Goodison on the Monday morning, whistling, smiling and understandably feeling pleased with himself. As he entered the dressing room, he called, 'Morning, boys!' to his team-mates, but was met with silence. He asked what was wrong. Still silence. Finally Dean spoke up: 'Who the hell do you think you are with your "Morning, boys"? Who're you calling "boys"?' Dean asked all the internationals in the room to stand up and went around: 'Stevie's got fifteen caps, Ted's twelve, Billy fourteen, I've got sixteen – and how many have you got?'

It was a timely reminder of Lawton's inexperience, despite his potential.

The next morning when Lawton went into the dressing room, he said nothing, and kept his head down. Dean started on him again. 'Not good enough for you today, then?' he gibed.

'I just exploded,' recalled Lawton. ' "What the hell do you want me to do?" And I told them all where to get off and leave me alone. Next, they'd grabbed me and thrown me up in the air. My behind hit the ceiling, I came down in about four feet of cold water. "Now you're initiated." They laughed. "Now you're a true Evertonian!" I soon learned what I could say and what I couldn't, to have respect for the top players in the game and not fancy myself too much.'[2]

The reminder of his own fallibility did nothing to knock Lawton's cocksure presence on the pitch, but the team struggled. Although they finished the 1937/8 season second-highest scorers and in the seeming security of a mid-table place, Everton were just three points off relegation in a division where Arsenal at the top and West Bromwich Albion at the bottom were divided by a mere 16 points. In the FA Cup, Everton – after an opening-round win over Chelsea – had met their old rivals and current holders, Sunderland, in the fourth round: 68,158 packed Goodison to watch Bobby Gurney score the only goal of the game in the first half, as the Mackems gained revenge for the 6–4 spectacular at the same stage four years earlier.

Less than two months later, on 11 March 1938, Dean was transferred to Notts County, safe in the knowledge that a rightful heir had been found for his number-nine shirt. 'He helped me a lot when I first joined the club,' Lawton later said. 'He had his faults, he was a boisterous character, but everyone liked him. He was often black and blue from the harsh treatments handed out by unscrupulous defenders, but he used to take it and never complained.'[3]

Top league scorer though Lawton emphatically was, his goals

had not been enough to gain him selection for the England tour of Germany, Switzerland and France at the season's end. Instead he travelled to Scotland with the Everton squad to play in an end-of-season tournament to mark the Glasgow Empire exhibition at Ibrox Park. Three other English clubs took part –Brentford, Chelsea and Sunderland – and four Scottish clubs, Celtic, Rangers, Hearts and Aberdeen. The draw was set up for an Old Firm Final, but Everton ruined any such hopes when they knocked out Rangers in the first match, beating them 2–0. In the semi-final Lawton scored the goal that beat Aberdeen 3–2 to set up a final with Celtic at Ibrox. On a balmy June evening in front of an 82,000-strong crowd, Celtic edged the match 1–0 in extra time. Everton were unlucky and valiant losers, playing much of the game with 10 men after Nat Cunliffe had limped off injured, then seeing an Alex Stevenson goal judged offside.

○

THE VALIANTLY FOUGHT Scottish tournament served as a valuable precursor to Everton's Championship season of 1938/9. It had involved a month-long stay in the west-coast holiday town of Largs and was the point at which a young struggling side with lots of potential became a great one. 'The reason was that we began to know each other as people, not just players,' reflected Lawton. 'People with different personalities, faults, varying moods, likes and dislikes . . . a wonderful blend developed between the players, which resulted in a far closer team spirit.'[4] When the players reported back to training seven weeks later, with the Sudeten crisis dominating the news, it was the first time in 13 years that they weren't greeted by the smiling, tanned face of Dean.

Geldard wasn't there either. Although he had kept Stanley Matthews out of the England team, the Everton board had deemed him surplus to requirements and sold him to Bolton for £7000. He had not always been a crowd favourite: as Charles Mills put it, 'He was very fast, but, as my father used to say, "Half the time he doesn't take the ball with him!"' His departure meant that a first-team place for Everton's supreme artist and showman, Torry Gillick, was secured. He had joined Everton from Glasgow Rangers in December 1935, having played in every forward position for the Scottish club. He spent most of his time at Goodison out on the right wing, occasionally switching to the left to accommodate Geldard. No matter where he played he rarely failed to do what he did best: entertain. Gillick was a natural entertainer and could, at will, waltz effortlessly past defenders with some of the most flamboyant trickery Evertonians have ever seen. While his pace made him an exhilarating sight when he was in full flight down the flank, his major shortcoming seemed to be his outlook on the game: Gillick, to the annoyance of some of his team-mates, played for laughs. At times he could be entirely ineffective, as if his mind was elsewhere, yet in a moment of genius he could still turn a game with a sublime piece of skill.

Gillick's form was greatly helped by the introduction of the dogged inside right Stan Bentham to first-team affairs on a regular basis at the start of the 1938/9 season. Bentham provided Gillick with an even more regular supply of the ball and the two men proved stars of a Championship-winning side. 'As far as I'm concerned,' Bentham later revealed, 'Torry just stayed on the wing, not interested. But suddenly he'd tune in and go past three or four blokes as easy as anything, and either score, or put over a great cross.'

Stan Bentham enjoyed the best part of 30 years with Everton, first as a player, then as a member of the coaching staff. An inside right by number, he was actually a pioneer of the roving midfield role, becoming the 'extra man' in the middle of the team, at hand whenever Everton were on the attack, but always ready to drop back when the defence needed assistance. He had learned his football with his church team, Lowton St Mary's, in the Leigh and District Sunday League and had had a series of trials with Bolton before signing professional forms with Wigan Athletic in December 1933. Within a matter of months he found himself the target of many top clubs and he moved to Everton, along with Springfield Park team-mate Terry Kavanagh, in February 1934. Kavanagh never made the Goodison grade, but after working his way up through the youth and reserve sides, Bentham made his début in November 1935. He could not have dreamed of a better start, scoring twice in a 4–0 away victory against Grimsby. Despite the dream début it took him another three years to establish a regular niche in the Everton starting line-up, but when he did his influence was considerable.

Another man who had progressed from non-league ranks was Tommy 'Gordon' Watson. He had arrived from Blyth Spartans in January 1933 and became one of Goodison's outstanding servants with an association that extended some 70 years, and encompassed virtually every available role on the field – and many off it. He was essentially a utility player, whose presence as twelfth man was so frequent that his team-mates clubbed together to buy him a special cushion so that he had a comfortable seat on the trainer's bench. The role of twelfth man is frequently, often unfairly, overlooked and none of Everton's great sides would have managed, at times, without the likes of Watson or, later, Sandy Brown and Alan Harper to deputize in all manner of unusual circumstances. 'He was never going to be a star,' recalled Charles Mills, 'but what a capable person both on and off the field.' Watson's contribution was never more crucial than in the glorious 1938/9 season, when he made 16 appearances.

The team retained its young, if not an even younger, complexion. Cliff Britton was now a reserve, paying more attention to the training side and taking the first steps that would launch him into a managerial career.

Everton began the new season in blistering form, winning their first four matches. In the fifth, on 10 September 1938, they came up against Arsenal. If Everton had had the greatest player of the generation in Dean, Arsenal had the best team. In the thirties alone they had won the Championship five times and the FA Cup twice. Everton travelled to London in their own first-class rail coach, used exclusively by the team and officials and between times stationed in sidings at Edge Hill, emblazoned with the club logo at each end.

The benefit of such luxuries evidently paid off. At Highbury, Everton dominated the first half and went in at the break with a deserved 2–0 lead. On 15 minutes, Lawton had shielded the ball and released Alex Stevenson. The Irishman left his markers floundering, lured Swindin – in the Arsenal goal – off his line and tucked the ball beyond his reach and into the corner of the net. Seven minutes from the interval Gillick switched the ball from the right to Lawton. With the path to the goal in front of him blocked, Lawton ran to the left wing before turning and – to the surprise of everybody – hitting the ball first time into the Arsenal net.

Lawton's goal was as magnificent as Everton's all-round first-half performance had been. They had handled the ball, according to the *Daily Express*, 'like a weakly child – wheedled, guided, fed and occasionally bullied'. Arsenal struck back in the second half through their £14,500 man, Bryn Jones, but Everton's defence was resolute enough to hold on for a famous win.

Buoyed by their Highbury triumph, Everton won their sixth consecutive match, thrashing Portsmouth 5–1 at Goodison, but fell a week later, losing 0–3 to Huddersfield.

In Europe, however, events were taking on a much darker complexion. Adolf Hitler had completed Germany's *Anschluss* with Austria in March and all summer long had been making hostile noises about what he styled 'Czech persecutions' of the increasingly militant German minority in the Sudetenland of Czechoslovakia. The implication was clear: Czechoslovakia was Nazi Germany's next target. Britain's Prime Minister Neville Chamberlain searched desperately for a way to maintain peace, even if it meant the transferral of the Czech borderlands to Germany. Czechoslovakia had a military alliance with France, and war would surely result if it resisted the Germans and called upon French aid. In one last burst of shuttle diplomacy between 15 and 29 September Chamberlain travelled to Germany three times to meet Hitler. From the last meeting, held at Munich on 30 September, he took back what he believed to be an agreement that the German portions of Czechoslovakia constituted Hitler's last territorial claim in Europe and that Germany, as well as Britain, would renounce war as a means of settling international claims. He had, he said with some pride, brought 'peace for our time'.

Britain, with the appalling memories of the First World War still fresh, breathed a sigh of relief. In Liverpool an official service of thanksgiving was staged at St Nicholas Church, Pier Head. The Lord Mayor of Liverpool, Alderman M. Cory-Dixon, sent a telegram to Chamberlain on behalf of the people of the city, offering their 'grateful thanks for your heroic efforts in the cause of peace, and their heartiest congratulations on the success which has attended them'. Little did they realize how empty Hitler's pledge was.

The day after Chamberlain's announcement, 65,076 turned out to watch Everton play Liverpool. The national anthem was sung prior to kick-off and Bentham and Boyes' goals propelled Everton into a 2–1 half-time lead. In the second half Everton's dominance was such that Liverpool did not venture past the half-way line on more than three occasions. 'It was rather too one-sided at this point to be interesting,' noted Stork in the *Football Echo*. Gillick, Bentham and Boyes each went close twice, but the scoreline remained the same, and Evertonians spent the night celebrating both peace and victory.

A week later Everton met their bogey team, Wolves. In a hard-fought game, which saw the two Stans – Everton's Bentham and Wolves' Cullis – carried off with injury, Lawton's twenty-eighth-minute goal was all that separated the two sides. After the match, the leading football journalist, Charlie Buchan championed the young striker's inclusion in the England team. 'Lawton is undoubtedly England's centre forward,' he wrote in the *News Chronicle*. 'His great headwork, moulded on the pattern of Dixie Dean, and his clever footwork, stamps him as England's leader for many years to come.'

Within a month he was lining up for England against Wales at Ninian Park, Cardiff. Lawton got a goal from the penalty spot – as he had on his Everton début – but was otherwise marked out by his Everton team-mate and friend T. G. Jones. Nevertheless Lawton clearly had a fan in Buchan, who noted that he had played with the 'assurance and thoughtfulness of an old campaigner'. A month later Joe Mercer followed him into the national team, making his England bow in a 7–0 thumping of Ireland at Old Trafford. Lawton and Mercer were joined in the England team by Everton's diminutive flanker, Wally Boyes, who made his début alongside Lawton in Cardiff. A clever – perhaps too clever – winger, who stood just five foot three, with one leg shorter than the other, he had come to Everton from West Bromwich Albion the previous February. Like Gillick and Stevenson he thrilled and delighted, serving chance after chance for the brilliant Lawton.

The teenage star continued to shine. Not even Dean's staunchest admirer, as Lawton himself had once been, could doubt that he was the new master. Although Everton briefly conceded the First Division lead over Christmas, a Lawton brace and an effort from Bentham beat Liverpool at the start of February and restored them to the top. It was an advantage they never looked like losing, and indeed never did.

In Europe, though, the situation was worsening. On 15 March 1939, the German army, virtually without warning, occupied the rest of Czechoslovakia. In the following weeks Britain signed a military alliance with Poland, and began to prepare for war.

Everton did not let geopolitics distract them. Their 6–2 win at home to Sunderland on 10 April put them ten points clear at the top of the First Division. This virtually assured them of the title, and for Bentham, who had scored a hat-trick, it marked his finest hour. The following day the *Liverpool Echo* ran a cartoon singing his praises: 'Bentham had a plaster on his head, a cut over his eye and was kicked in the ribs, yet he scored 3 goals . . . As Bentham seems to thrive on injuries there is no knowing how many he would have scored if he had received a few more bumps!'

Yet the Championship eluded Everton for a further 12 days. The following Saturday – 15 April – they were unable to break the deadlock against Preston North End and the match ended in a goalless stalemate. They had been without Mercer and Lawton, who were playing in front of 145,000 for England against Scotland at Hampden. England had been without a win north of the border since Dean's famous double in 1927 and, in a virtual repeat of what had happened then, Lawton scored two minutes from time to give England a 2–1 victory. The silence was said to be deathly. For once it was not the teenager who grabbed all the plaudits: his Everton team-mate Mercer, who won the man-of-the-match award. 'Mercer was ever in the thick of the throbbing battle,' eulogized the *Daily Express*. 'With the wind and pitiless, ceaseless rain, it provided the severest of all tests of skill, stamina, and heart. Mercer had them all.'

Back in the royal blue of Everton, though, their attention returned to the title. But not even the return of Everton's two England stars was enough for them to beat Charlton the following week and they fell 1–2 at the Valley. It did not matter. Wolves' draw at Bolton brought the Championship crown back to Goodison. 'Everton have only got their deserts,' concluded Stork, in the *Liverpool Echo*. 'They have thrown off challenger after challenger and in Derby County and Wolverhampton they have had two strong rivals.' Everton's side was instantly regarded as one of the greatest ever witnessed in English football. 'They were a bloody good side,' Lawton later said, 'and the next year we should have won the League again, the FA Cup and the bloody Boat Race if they'd put us in it.'

History, however, stood in Everton's way. As Europe stood agape at the Nazi–Soviet non-aggression pact, the 1939/40 season got under way on 26 August with a 1–1 draw at home to Brentford. Lawton was Everton's scorer. On the eve of the match Chamberlain had reiterated Britain's guarantee to Poland, not that anyone in Berlin was listening.

Football carried on and on 28 August Everton beat Aston Villa 2–1 at Villa Park. Bentham and Lawton scored Everton's goals.

Three days later, at 6.30 a.m. on 1 September, the German invasion of Poland began, under the pretext that the Poles had attacked a German radio station. In fact, the aggressors were Nazis, dressed in Polish uniforms. The following day, Saturday 2 September, Britain issued an ultimatum to Germany. That same afternoon Tommy Lawton scored twice to earn Everton a 2–2 draw at Blackburn.

At eleven o'clock the following morning the ultimatum expired and Neville Chamberlain's voice was heard on wireless sets across the nation: 'This morning, the British ambassador in Berlin handed the German government a final note stating that, unless we heard from them by eleven o'clock that they were prepared at once to withdraw their troops from Poland, a state of war would exist between us. I have to tell you now that no such undertaking has been received, and that consequently this country is at war with Germany.'

0

FOR THE SECOND TIME in Everton's history, war changed everything. The assembly of crowds was banned, and the FA and the Football League cancelled the remainder of the season. All players' contracts were suspended. In a fair-minded gesture, which went unmatched almost anywhere else, the Everton directors paid every member of the playing staff their accrued share of the 'benefit'; Lawton collected £300, Charlie Gee the maximum of £650. The redundant players took on civilian jobs. Joe Mercer went to work at Cammell Laird, T. G. Jones to an aircraft factory, and Dixie Dean – now returned from Ireland – to an abattoir. The restrictions on organized games were soon relaxed and regional leagues within a 50-mile radius allowed. Yet crowds were restricted to 15,000 all-ticket affairs in larger grounds, and 8000 or half the capacity, whichever was smaller, elsewhere. Stanley Rous, the FA secretary, urged players to sign up for the Army Physical Training Corps with the promise that they would become sergeant instructors. Joe Mercer was among the first to be recruited, and Lawton, in January 1940, the last.

For the fans too, of course, war brought huge disruption. Charles Mills joined the RAF as a navigator, and later served in the Middle and Far East. Dick White was in the special forces, and spent much of the war training for operations in the north of Scotland. Of wartime football he said, 'There was no enjoyment out of it. We used to dream of the war ending, because we were still living in the shadow of the 1938/9 season. It never crossed my mind that six years of war would pass. It decimated the team.'

Players turned out for their clubs when they could, but it invariably depended upon where they were stationed and when they could get leave. The competitive nature of football was fundamentally altered and fans realized that what they saw was often a mere sop.

The one exception was wartime internationals, where attendance restrictions were not so severe. England played Scotland no fewer than 16 times during the war years and such fixtures provided some sort of antidote to regional matches played with patched-together sides. Moreover, the internationals provided an important morale boost for the troops, who would keep up with results from afar. The playing career of Cliff Britton enjoyed a renaissance, and he formed a famous England half-back line with Stan Cullis and Joe Mercer, who was now England captain.

Given Goodison's proximity to Liverpool's docklands and the terrible damage suffered in its environs, it was remarkably lucky to survive the worst of the German bombing raids. For the damage it did suffer, the club received £5,000 from the War Damage Commission for essential repair work.

Two Everton players lost their lives in the fighting: William Summer, who had got through into the first team after war broke out and made a handful of wartime appearances; and Brian Atkins, who never had the chance to make such a progression. Again, Everton escaped relatively lightly: Arsenal lost nine men, including Herbie Roberts, who had once been so flummoxed when marking Dean.

One man had a 'good war', making the breakthrough to the Everton first team. He was a young striker by the name of Harry Catterick, and signed in April 1937 as a part-time professional while he continued his apprenticeship as a marine engineer. He played a few reserve games alongside Dean, but with the likes of Tommy Lawton and 'Bunny' Bell ahead of him he had to wait until after the war to make his league début in an Everton shirt. He made 73 wartime appearances, scoring 56 times. After the war, although no less accomplished than many of his contemporaries, he struggled to claim the number-nine shirt regularly. He did, however, have his occasional moments of glory such as a hat-trick scored in a 5–1 away thrashing of Fulham in the 1950/51 season. At the end of that campaign he moved into management with Crewe Alexandra. True Goodison glory came his way a generation later.

○

IT WAS MORE THAN a year after hostilities had ceased before the Football League programme fully recommenced. When it did, the all-conquering team of 1939 seemed virtually intact. Of the side that had drawn with Blackburn the day before war had broken out seven years earlier, Bentham, Boyes, Greenhalgh, Jones, Mercer, Sagar, Stevenson and Watson remained. Billy Cook had been transferred to Wrexham for a brief spell before he embarked on a managerial career that took him to Peru and Norway before he settled with Wigan in 1966. Torry Gillick had rejoined Rangers the previous November and lived out his days in the Govan district of Glasgow, where he ran the dog track next to Ibrox.

The most infamous departure was Lawton's. While Gillick and Cook were both in their thirties, Lawton should have been in his prime, aged just 26 when the 1946/7 season kicked off. Amazingly he had been allowed to join Chelsea the previous November. Mystery surrounded the transfer until Lawton's final years but in 1945 the press corps speculated vainly on it. Lawton gave them the rather dubious reason that his wife was ill and he had to 'move south'.

His excuse was half true. Rosaleen Lawton had been the cause of his leaving Merseyside, but when he departed for the bracing (smog-filled) air of London and the therapeutic (putrid) waters of the Thames, she was not with him. In fact, Lawton had run away from Liverpool to escape her.

The 1941 union of Everton's star to a local girl had been problematic from the start. 'The marriage just wasn't working out, in fact it was purgatory,' he said later. 'Home was hell, something had to be done.' When the war ended and he was about to be demobbed, Lawton asked for a transfer. Theo Kelly summoned him to his office. 'You want a transfer, do you, Lawton? Well, let me tell you, we've been trying to give you away for four months and nobody wants you.

There's the door, go out and get your training done and stop wasting my time.' It was vintage Kelly, but he could not sustain the facade of a Dickensian factory owner. Although he was manager of perhaps the biggest football club in England he was dealing with the best centre forward in the world and Lawton could not be duped for long. A second transfer request was accepted and he was sold to Chelsea for £11,500.

For the rest of his life Lawton regretted the move. He never won another trophy, and although he continued to represent England, his domestic career was a pale imitation of what it had been. 'On reflection,' he later admitted, 'I should have stayed and transferred the wife.'

Soon Joe Mercer had followed him out of the Goodison door. In an England versus Scotland international in April 1946, Willie Waddell of Rangers inadvertently landed on Mercer's leg during a challenge. Mercer struggled on gamely, though the injury stunted his efforts. Amazingly, after the game he was accused of not trying. The dispute that ensued ended the international career of England's captain – a man with five full and 26 wartime and 'victory' caps.

Mercer had been hurt by the charge, but even more by the fact that the Everton management seemed to believe it. They were convinced that Mercer was merely making excuses for poor performances in both England and Everton shirts – a line of attack that the devastated Mercer sought to prove wrong. He consulted an orthopaedic surgeon, who recommended a cartilage operation, but even then Everton – with whom his association spanned 17 years – refused to accept the truth and, unbelievably, Mercer had to pay for the surgery.

Theo Kelly was at the heart of the dispute. When the 1946/7 season reopened Mercer was still struggling for fitness and the suggestion that he wasn't trying resurfaced. Everton's manager offered no support and the relationship between the two men broke down and then, as with Dean, became openly hostile.

Four games into the 1946/7 season, Everton played Arsenal at Goodison and, to some surprise, won 3–2. After the game Mercer paid a visit to the Arsenal dressing room where he asked the visitors' physiotherapist, Tom Whittaker, whom he knew from his England days, to inspect his bad leg. Whittaker was shocked by what he saw:

the muscles around Mercer's knee were wasted and the knee severely swollen. He turned to the Arsenal players: 'Look at this, lads – you've been playing against only ten men,' he said.

Mercer persevered, but things got no better. His injury had cost him his fitness and, sapped of his stamina, he had lost the attacking part of his game. Kelly's unremitting hostility persisted, so Mercer went to see Cyril Baxter – son of Dr James Baxter and himself now chairman – and asked for a transfer; he said he would quit football altogether if he was not allowed to leave.

Days later Joe Mercer, who six months earlier had captained his country, was serving customers in the grocery wholesaler's he co-owned with his father-in-law. The impasse lasted three weeks. Then Kelly summoned him to the Adelphi Hotel, where he met Arsenal's manager George Allison. A transfer was agreed, and he joined the Gunners for £7000. 'It was a terrible blow for me to go,' Mercer said later, 'because I was so crazy about Everton.' In a final snub, Kelly brought his boots to the Adelphi, which prevented Mercer returning to Goodison to say farewell.

Without Lawton and Mercer, Everton struggled. The average age of the brilliant young pre-war team had increased considerably and it was now full of grizzled, if not sometimes adept, experience. Stevenson was 35, Sagar 36, Jones approaching 30.

A new school of players had emerged who would figure prominently – although not always with the same distinction as some of their predecessors – over the following decade. Peter Farrell and Tommy Eglington had first come to Goodison in August 1946 in a £10,000 double deal; between them they made more than 850 appearances. Farrell quickly established himself as a sturdy wing half, whose steely tackling served as an inspiration to his team-mates; he was later appointed captain. Eglington came to be regarded as one of the finest left wingers of his era and his talents earned him 24 Eire caps and six Northern Ireland caps at a time when the province could select Eire-born players for the Home International Championship. Stevenson, Everton's Celtic sorcerer of the 1930s, continued to shine. He represented both Everton and Ireland until 1949 – 17 years since he had first appeared for his country and 15 for his club.

The post-war years were a boom time for football attendances. In a country where rationing and austerity were a way of life, football provided an element of escapism. 'It was what you looked forward to all week,' recalled Charles Mills, who had then just returned from national service in Palestine. 'People were glad of the entertainment.' Indeed, football provided a diversion: the harshness of daily life could be forgotten for 90 minutes while the energy and skill of the team would consume every thought and emotion. Well, that was the idea anyway.

Everton seldom provided much cause for cheer in an era characterized by mediocrity. They finished the 1946/7 season tenth; 1947/8 fourteenth and the following two campaigns eighteenth. 'From being at the heights,' remembered Mills, 'we plunged to the depths.'

Still, the crowds flocked. On 18 September 1948, a record attendance of 78,299 turned out to see bottom-placed Everton draw 1–1 with Liverpool. The *Liverpool Echo* reported swaying in parts of the paddock as well as 'many casualties'. The following Monday, Theo Kelly reverted to his old role of secretary and Cliff Britton was appointed manager. After the war Britton had gone into management with Burnley, leading them to promotion from the Second Division in the 1946/7 season and also to the FA Cup Final, which they lost 0–1 to Charlton. It was a promising start, but he was unable to stop the rot at Everton.

Amid all the mediocrity T. G. Jones continued to illuminate Goodison. In 1947 Ernest 'Bee' Edwards – now in retirement – had written of the curly-haired defender: 'Jones is the finest centre playing football today. He is a class by himself. Everything he does has the hallmark of a consummate artist. He is the essence of style, neatness and precision, and a gentleman on and off the field. I have never seen him guilty of shady action. He is a credit as well as an ornament to the game.'

Not everyone agreed. Everton's best player made few more than a dozen appearances in that calendar year, the bulk coming at its end. Given the reluctance to use him, in March Jones had asked for a transfer, but Everton refused to let him go. On four more occasions during 1947 he asked to leave, and each time met the same negative response. The spat with the management then broke out into a public argument – then unprecedented – between Jones and the club. 'Could it be,' asked Jones, in the local press, 'that having lost Tommy and Joe, when both might have been kept if different methods had been adopted, they are frightened of public opinion if they let me go?'

Jones's disillusionment with the Everton hierarchy was long-standing. It dated back to a Lancashire Cup tie on 22 April 1944 with Liverpool at Anfield. It was the third time in 10 days they had met to try to resolve a stalemate, when Jones, already on the scoresheet, was stretchered off injured to the dressing room. The defender was in agony, when an Everton director – who has always remained nameless – came in and had the audacity to disparage the injury. An argument erupted when Jones refused to play on and his anger became incandescent when nobody from the club would help him back to his RAF unit. It emerged that the injury – which the director had pooh-poohed – was severe enough to put Jones into a hospital bed for four months and he was unable to kick a ball for six.

Nineteen forty-eight saw Jones back in the first team and the arrival of Britton as manager. Kelly's move upstairs seemed to coincide with better times for the Welsh Prince. Then, the Italian giants AS Roma came in with a £15,500 offer for his services. It was a sensational development. They offered Jones a lump sum in advance, a contract for from two to four years, depending on his wishes, a wage of £25 per week, which was double his Everton salary, plus bonuses and a house in the best part of Rome. He was even offered a coaching job on retirement from playing. Jones agreed verbally and the FA gave its approval. It looked as if an Everton great was finally finding a more suitable stage than Goodison Park, whose name was now synonymous with mediocrity and where Jones was unappreciated by an ungrateful management. Then, at the eleventh hour, the deal collapsed over 'currency details'. TG was still an Everton player.

Yet by August 1949, it looked as if the disagreements had been consigned to the past. Jones was reinstated as captain in place of Peter Farrell, and looking good at the heart of defence. A handful of games in, he lost his place to Jack Humphreys and then to Dick Falder. The situation got so bad that at times he was unable even to make the reserve side and would turn out secretly for Havarden Grammar Old Boys. Finally, on 26 January 1950, he asked for his release, which was agreed. It was a sad and inauspicious end to the career of the man of whom Dean once said, 'He had everything. No coach could ever coach him or teach him anything. Tommy was the best all-round player I've ever seen.'

T. G. Jones's departure left Ted Sagar as the sole survivor of

1939. During the war he had appeared for Northern Ireland in an international, giving him the unique distinction of playing both for and against the Ulstermen. On returning to Everton he had seen off the challenge to his green jersey from George Burnett and now, aged 40, was holding his own against another young hopeful by the name of Jimmy O'Neill. Finally, in 1953, after nearly five hundred league and FA Cup appearances, he announced his retirement. His Everton career had spanned an incredible 24 years and one month, the longest spell a player has ever spent professionally with one Football League club. During that time he clocked up two League Championships, an FA Cup and four England caps, making him one of the most decorated players in Everton's history. He retired to follow the course of many old professionals: he became an Aintree publican. Even today, after all these years, Ted Sagar retains a presence in the Everton goal: his ashes were scattered between the Gwladys Street posts!

While Sagar built a life for himself outside football, Lawton, Jones and Mercer each remained in the game with varying degrees of success.

Lawton stayed with Chelsea for one full season before Notts County paid £20,000 to take him to the Third Division (South). Stepping down from top-flight football was a staggering departure and another move he lived to regret, but his presence helped County win the division in the 1949/50 season and attendances rose from 9000 to 35,000. He moved later to Brentford for £12,000, had a brief spell as their manager, then reverted to playing, which resulted in Arsenal bringing him back to the First Division at the age of 34, where he was reunited with Mercer. On leaving Highbury three years later, Lawton struggled to find a life outside football. His intermittent spells in charge of Notts County and Kettering were interspersed with unemployment, debts, depression, drink problems and petty crime. He contemplated suicide, the course taken by his contemporary Hughie Gallacher in 1957. Mercer eased some of his friend's financial worries by arranging his testimonial in 1972, only the second such match Everton had given a former player. Eventually he found his niche writing a twice-weekly column for the *Nottingham Evening Post* until his death in November 1996.

T. G. Jones's story was low-key in comparison, but sprinkled with glories. After walking out on Everton he managed Pwllheli part-time and ran a hotel in the same town too. Later, his name was in the headlines when, as Bangor City manager, he masterminded one of the most famous acts of giant-killing ever seen. In 1962 Bangor – under TG's guidance – won the Welsh Cup for the third time, and ventured into the European Cup Winners' Cup. They were drawn with Italian giants Napoli, and amazingly won the home leg 2–0. Sadly they lost 3–1 in Italy and as there was no away-goal rule then, a replay was required. At Highbury, Bangor fought gallantly, but the Italians triumphed 3–1. Like Lawton, nevertheless, his greatest achievements came when he was a young man.

Joe Mercer was the one man who triumphed over Kelly. After his sale to Arsenal he continued to live on Merseyside, training at Anfield and commuting to London for matches. Despite his loss of pace, he modified his game, rarely straying beyond the half-way line, but his vision, passing and experience of the game were utilized to the full. He became captain of the side and served them with distinction for nine years, winning the Championship in 1948, the FA Cup in 1950, narrowly missing on the double in 1952 and again topping the league in 1953. In that time he never once appeared on the losing side against either Kelly's or Britton's Everton.

His playing career ended when he broke his leg against Liverpool in 1954. Retirement saw a brief return to the grocery business, which he gave up when the chance arose to manage Sheffield United. He went on to manage Aston Villa and Manchester City, whom he led to the Second Division Championship, First Division Championship, the FA Cup and the European Cup Winners' Cup. After leaving Maine Road he was general manager of Coventry City and brought a smile back to the England team when he took over as temporary manager between the sacking of Sir Alf Ramsey and the appointment of Don Revie in 1973.

Mercer died in August 1990, but the memory of the man who played with a smile lives on. 'We always had fun,' he once said. 'I probably learned more about the game at Arsenal, but I learned how to laugh at Everton.'

6

Hard Times

T. G. JONES'S DEPARTURE in January 1950 had not only deprived Goodison of one of its greatest sons, but left Evertonians without any genuine stars to celebrate. Behind him, he left the Irishmen Eglington and Farrell, and also their compatriot Jackie Grant who, after years of flitting in and out of the first team, was finally holding down a regular place at half back. The Irish contingent was strengthened later that year when a pair of Dubliners, the rugged full back Tommy Clinton and goalkeeper Jimmy O'Neill, also began to establish themselves in the first team. The connection with the Emerald Isle popularized Everton in the Irish Republic and led to large numbers of fans crossing the Irish Sea to watch their fellow countrymen. Farrell, Eglington and company were popular on Merseyside too, although that might have had as much to do with the city's Irish heritage, and the players' readiness to socialize with the fans, as their ability on the pitch.

Alongside Everton's Irish delegation there was a ragbag army of English players. An ageing and ailing Ted Sagar spent his final four years at Goodison in and out of the first team, and Harry Catterick, approaching his thirties, was troubled by injury during the latter stages of his playing career. Cyril Lello, who had originally signed from Shrewsbury Town as an inside forward in September 1947, made his name as a right half and was one of the most consistent performers in a Goodison career that lasted over nine years. Indeed, his reliability when coming up against some of the great inside forwards of the day – the likes of George Robledo of Newcastle, Wilf Mannion of Middlesbrough and Derby County's Raich Carter – brought him to the verge of an England call-up. Alfred Walter Fielding, better known as 'Wally' or 'Nobby', had been spotted during the war by Jack Sharp junior while stationed in Italy with the Royal Ordnance Corps, and was signed after being demobbed in 1946. A brilliant strategist and ball-player, he was at the centre of many creative moves in a lacklustre side in a 13-year Everton career that extended almost until his fortieth birthday. He was a master at floating past defenders with a deceptive swerve of the body, and even as age diminished his pace, his considerable skill shone through. Ted Buckle, a bold and brazen winger, had been acquired from Manchester United in November 1949, but lacked the consistency or quality partnering him in attack ever to prosper fully. Like Buckle, Southport-born inside right Eddie Wainwright lacked the sort of team-mates who would elevate him to being a top-class footballer. In his 12-year Goodison career he was a diligent, committed player, scoring 76 goals in 228 appearances, though without the extra sparkle that would have seen his name added to the pantheon of Everton greats.

It was an honest, dedicated Everton squad, never lacking in effort or will to win, but never looking as if they ever would win anything, or indeed *be* anything other than perennial strugglers. When Jones left, Everton had stood in eighteenth place, the same position they would hold at the end of the 1949/50 season. The best avenue to success seemed to be the FA Cup, and so it was to prove in that humdrum year of 1950. Victories in the early rounds over Queens Park Rangers (2–0), West Ham United (2–1) and Tottenham Hotspur (1–0) handed Everton an enticing quarter-final tie with Derby County. Despite going a goal down, Wainwright and Buckle both scored to give Everton a 2–1 win. 'There are no personalities in the present-day Everton,' noted the *Liverpool Echo*'s correspondent 'Ranger'. They did, however, possess 'a do-or-die spirit which is overcoming teams chock full of personality'.

Victory over Derby County handed Everton a semi-final meeting with Liverpool on 25 March 1950. It was Everton's eleventh semi-final, Liverpool's sixth. But for the Evertonian half of the 73,000-strong Maine Road crowd it was yet another afternoon of disappointment as Billy Liddell scored in each half to give Liverpool a 2–0 win. Some consolation was derived a month later when one of Goodison's departed heroes, Joe Mercer, captained Arsenal to victory over Liverpool in the final, but that was a solitary glimmer in a dismal year.

Indeed, things continued to deteriorate as 1950 progressed. The 1950/51 season had got off to a poor start, which worsened with a run of 11 defeats over September, October and November that left Everton at the bottom going into December. Injury had all but ended Catterick's playing days and James McIntosh was not an altogether successful replacement, even for a player as ordinary as his predecessor. In an effort to aid the faltering forward line, Cliff Britton went to his former club, Burnley, and paid the extraordinary sum of £20,000 for their inside right, Harry Potts. Potts, like so many of his new colleagues at Goodison, was a proficient, able player but no star, and was not worth such a fee (Everton could have re-signed Lawton for less), and, moreover, was not the answer. Everton already had an established inside right in Fielding and needed a new centre forward. Desperately.

Results, nevertheless, improved. A series of wins over Christmas and New Year hoisted Everton from the perils of an exit to the Second Division. Even a six-match run without a goal over March 1951 did not put them in any imminent danger of relegation. When that run was ended with a 1–1 draw at home to Wolves on 7 April Everton were six points clear of Chelsea and Sheffield Wednesday, who were in the two relegation spots, although Chelsea had played two games fewer, Wednesday one. With four games still to play it would take a hopeless team and an appalling run of form to go down.

Everton, however, were not only hopeless, they were about to hit such a trough. A 0–4 defeat at Sunderland on 14 April and a 1–2 loss at home to Aston Villa a week later combined with an upturn in form from Sheffield Wednesday to put Everton in one of the two relegation spots for the first time since Christmas. For the penultimate game of the season they travelled to Derby, where they had not won in the league for 23 years. Encouraged, perhaps, by their success in the FA Cup there 12 months earlier, Everton won 1–0 thanks to Potts's sixty-second-minute goal.

Everton went into their last game of the 1950/51 season against Sheffield Wednesday looking as if they could assure themselves of safety. They were on 32 points while Wednesday, bottom and all but doomed, were level with Chelsea on 30. Everton's goal average was the worst in the division: they had scored fewer goals and conceded more, save for Huddersfield, than anyone else. A point, however, would be enough.

Everton began the match attacking relentlessly and tackling ruthlessly. For 25 minutes they held their own. Then a slip by T. E.

Jones let in Woodhead, and he made it 1–0. A second defensive error on 30 minutes, when Burnett failed to collect an easy cross, allowed Woodhead to make it 2–0. Three minutes later Woodhead turned provider and Sewell made it 3–0. After the interval Woodhead missed the chance to complete his hat-trick when Burnett saved his penalty, but hopes that that would prompt an Everton revival were immediately extinguished when Finney made it four a couple of minutes later. Froggatt made it five on 63 minutes and Sewell rounded off a miserable day with his second and Wednesday's sixth three minutes from time.

'1–2–3–4–5–6 . . . OUT!' ran the *Liverpool Echo* headline. 'Everton run into a Goal "Blitz".' Everton finished bottom, with Wednesday, also relegated, a place ahead of them.

It was a pathetic end to a truly miserable season. Everton had, of course, been relegated before, but that had been an aberration. The brilliant players who did battle in the Second Division then included Cresswell, Dean, Dunn, Hart, Stein, Thomson, Williams and White. In 1951 Everton had, with all due respect, an ageing and injured Catterick, Ted Sagar, who was past his best, and an assortment of noble but ordinary Irish players.

◊

DURING THE SUMMER of 1951 the Everton board refused to make money available for new players and, come the start of the 1951/2 season, which kicked off with a 0–1 defeat at Southampton, the lack of investment was plain for all to see. Even in the Second Division it did not seem that Everton could be anything but an ordinary team. The Goodison crowd stayed loyal, but their beloved team looked, in the early stages of the new season, as if it might succumb to the unthinkable: relegation to the Third Division.

On Saturday 20 March 1951, Tommy Lawton made his return to Goodison. Fifty thousand people turned up to see him, and even at the age of 32, he possessed all the grace and finesse that had so thrilled Evertonians before the war. But no sentiment existed for him when play got under way: he inspired Notts County to a 5–1 victory, which sank Everton to eighteenth.

The following Monday Ranger used the pages of the *Liverpool Echo* to write an open letter to the Everton board. It was a blistering attack:

Gentlemen, in saying that the prestige of your club today is lower than ever before, and that unless something is done quickly you are going to have difficulty keeping out of the Third Division, none can accuse me of exaggerating the seriousness of the position. It is nothing but the unpleasant truth. At the beginning of this season I wrote that the best I could see this side doing, unless there were several strengthening signings, was to keep a place around the middle of the table. I said that to be charitable. Privately, I had grave fears that you might be where you find yourselves today, but I felt it unfair, on the threshold of a new season, to express too pessimistic a view publicly. Perhaps it would have been better had I done so.

For a club of Everton's traditions and wealth you are in a most humiliating position. I wish you could see some of the letters I have from Evertonians of lifelong standing. Many of your supporters seem almost heartbroken. I have refrained from publishing these letters in order not to embarrass the club so long as there seemed a chance that a realistic attitude would be adopted to tackle an increasingly desperate situation. So far as I can see, there is still no sign of that.

The board still seems to be burying its head in the sand. There has been far too much wishful thinking in the past. Too much hope has been placed in young players who lack experience. Many of these would do well if introduced into a winning side ... Also players who have previously proved not good enough have been recalled too often, some of them even after the club has indicated its willingness to part.

Finally he issued a challenge:

For the past few weeks unthinking folk have been joking about the possibility of 'Derby' games against Tranmere Rovers, Southport and Chester at Goodison Park next season. It is no joke. It is a tragic possibility. It is up to you, gentlemen. The ultimate responsibility for the club rests on your shoulders. What are you going to do about it?[1]

The answer was nothing. Everton's board of directors remained obstinately, even defiantly, silent. For months Ranger tried to goad them out of their inertia, but without success.

Their stated aim had been to see young players develop through the Goodison ranks, although they were less open about their other policy, namely the acquisition of players on the cheap from lower league and Irish teams. Yet, in fairness, both official and unofficial strategies had begun to pay – limited – dividends.

When the great T. G. Jones had left Everton, his natural successor seemed to be his namesake, Tommy Edwin Jones. Although the two players shared a name and a position, the difference in their styles was immense. Whereas TG played as a Continental-style sweeper, TE was a more traditional and towering centre back, a competent man-marker, but maybe lacking some of the finesse of his predecessor. He had signed professional terms in 1948, aged 18, but had to wait a further two years before making his début against Arsenal in September 1950. He established himself in the first team as Everton were succumbing to relegation, an experience he later said strengthened him as an individual and player. In the Second Division, he began slowly to shine and was one of the key individuals behind Everton's later renaissance.

In attack, there was also cause for optimism. Ever since Lawton had departed in 1945, Evertonians had waited in vain for another centre forward whom they could idolize. Catterick, McIntosh and Dodds had each been tried – among others – but none had captured the imagination or the affection of the fans in the way their predecessor had done. Then, with the onset of the 1950/51 season, two came along together.

John Willie Parker had been acquired as a hopeful amateur from the anonymity of St Lawrence CYMS in 1948. An inside left, he could also spearhead the attack as centre forward, and in either position was a clinical finisher and prolific goalscorer. As Ranger wrote of him, 'His deceptively lazy and nonchalant style lulls defenders into a false sense of security. By the time they wake up to it it is usually too late.' Like T. E. Jones, he made his bow in the relegation campaign – a league débutant at 26 no less – although it was not until the onset of life in the Second Division that he staked his claim to the first team, eventually concluding the 1951/2 season as Everton's top scorer with 15 goals.

However, great goalscorer though John Willie Parker undoubtedly was over the subsequent four seasons, if you ask any Evertonian who grew up during the 1950s the name of their hero they will almost invariably tell you, 'Dave Hickson.' He is the only man ever to turn out for all three Merseyside teams. Yet despite being idolized from all three sides of the Mersey, scoring a grand total of 169 goals to the delight of the masses at Anfield, Prenton and Goodison, he never won a trophy or international honours.

However, at Goodison his swashbuckling style and fearless bravery thrilled Evertonians and few have since been so idolized. He had first been spotted playing non-league football for Ellesmere Port by Cliff Britton in 1948 and was duly signed by the Everton manager. Hickson had been brought up in Salford and even confessed a youthful leaning towards Manchester United, but any doubts that the 19-year-old might have had about joining United's north-west rivals were soon dispelled when he was called up for national service shortly after signing for Everton. Here, he found himself playing under the astute management of no less a figure than Dixie Dean, who was in charge of the Cheshire Army Cadets football team. Hickson claimed later it was thanks to Dean that he honed his famous heading ability, though not even Dean could claim to rival some of Hickson's extraordinarily courageous play, which would often see him put his head into places where lesser – saner – men would balk at putting their feet.

On his return from national service he scored five in a reserve game against Sheffield Wednesday and travelled with the first team as twelfth man on a number of occasions during the 1950/51 season. Although Everton were playing some of the worst football in their history it was not until five games into the Second Division campaign that Hickson was given the chance to play for the first team. He made his début against Leeds United on 1 September 1951, when he took the place of Harry Catterick, and scored his first goal in a 3–3 home draw with Rotherham a week later, eventually plundering a further 13 that season.

Everton went on to finish the 1951/2 campaign a disappointing seventh. Worse was to come. A slow start to the 1952/3 campaign saw them bottom for a period, and although relegation concerns were brief, hopes of promotion were extinguished by Christmas.

Again, this left the FA Cup as the sole way to salvage another wretched season. To the surprise and delight of everyone associated with the club, Everton confounded the form book. Ipswich Town (3–2) and Nottingham Forest (4–1) were seen off in the opening rounds to set up a fifth-round tie with league champions Manchester United on Valentine's Day 1953.

It has gone down as one of Goodison's most famous Cup ties and marked the day when Hickson acquired the status of an Everton legend. The day ended in glory, but Manchester United took the lead on 27 minutes from Rowley. It was a short-lived advantage. Seven minutes later, Hickson played in Eglington, who rounded Aston and let fly with a scorching right-footed shot that flew into the back of the United net. It was the Irishman's fifth goal in as many matches. Five minutes from the interval, Hickson dived in like a battering-ram to try to connect with Jack Lindsay's cross, but in doing so caught a defender's boot and had to leave the field with blood streaming from his eye. Half-time came and went without Hickson emerging. A minute into the second half he returned, to cheers, with a handkerchief, with which he occasionally dabbed his wound.

Shortly after his return, he headed against the upright from a corner, which opened the wound again. At this point Mr Beacock of Scunthorpe, the match-day referee, said to the Everton captain Farrell, 'He'll have to go off. He can't go on with an eye like that. He's not normal.'

Hickson, however, who had previously been trying to avoid the referee's notice, had edged over to where he and the captain were talking, and heard him. 'I heard that, Ref, I *am* normal,' he protested. 'Tell him I'm normal, Peter, tell him!'

'Of course you are, Dave,' said Farrell, turning to calm him.

'There you are, Ref!' said Hickson. 'I'm staying!'[2]

Everton were well on top and the blood-splattered Hickson twice linked up with Buckle to go close with angled shots, while Buckle himself was unlucky not to win a penalty when he was tripped by the United goalkeeper, Wood.

Then, on 63 minutes, Everton took the lead. Hickson, who had been playing a hero's role all afternoon, chased Eglington's ball, beat one man, sidestepped another and thundered a right-footed shot beyond the reach of Wood and into the United net. It was a worthy winner from the man who was the hero of a famous victory. 'Not only did he get the winning goal by sheer persistence,' wrote Ranger, 'but, with blood streaming down his face throughout the second half from a cut above his eye, gave a wonderful show of courage and fighting spirit.'

The quarter-final saw Everton visit Villa Park to meet its residents. Again, Hickson upset his opponents. Fifteen minutes from time, a scrum of play in the Everton goalmouth saw the ball hacked clear to Hickson, who was near the touchline, just inside his own half. He switched play to Buckle – who was in the outside-left position – and sprinted forward to take the return pass. Then, holding off the challenge of a Villa defender, he rammed the ball home for the only goal of the game. With the sound of the final whistle, 200 jubilant Evertonians ran on to the pitch and lifted their hero into the air, carrying him off the field in a throne of hands and arms.

Victory over Aston Villa gave Everton their second semi-final in the space of three years, this time against Bolton Wanderers at Maine Road. Three times in the past, Everton had travelled to Manchester to contest the penultimate stage of the FA Cup, and each time they had returned disappointed. Nineteen fifty-three, however, was meant to be different. Brimming with confidence after their earlier victories, Everton entered the game expecting to dispose of a workmanlike, if not ordinary, Bolton side.

The sole exception, however, was their 'Lion of Vienna', the England centre forward Nat Lofthouse. To the eternal misfortune of Everton, he was in mesmerizing form when the two teams met. So much so that when they trooped in at half-time, Lofthouse had inspired Bolton to a 4–0 lead, scoring twice himself. Everton's problems had been compounded by Hickson's absence because of another head injury and Clinton's missed penalty on the stroke of half-time. Despite the repeated setbacks, Everton came out in the second half and took the game to Bolton with gusto and were rewarded on 47 minutes when Parker headed home Buckle's corner. Half an hour later, Farrell's twice-taken free kick brought the score to 2–4. Everton pressed forward and with six minutes remaining their flicker of hope was fanned when Parker headed home his second and Everton's third. In the closing stages they laid siege to the Bolton goal but, despite going close, could not complete their epic recovery.

The valiant efforts against Bolton did not, however, inspire confidence in Everton's remaining 10 league games and they finished the 1952/3 season sixteenth, behind such luminaries as Lincoln City, Doncaster Rovers and Rotherham.

Yet the indignity of life in the Second Division did not plague Everton for much longer. Entering the 1953/4 season, the team indisputably had a more settled look. Although there had been no new additions to the squad, by Christmas they were second. February saw a run of results more reminiscent of the Dean era (6–2, 6–1, 8–4), which kept them on the brink of the Second Division summit. Asked if Everton could gain promotion, Peter Farrell showed all the evasiveness of a silver-tongued politician: 'I am no prophet, and I have been too long in the football game to stick my neck out when so many fixtures yet remain to be played. I think I hardly need say that promotion is the outstanding desire of every player on Everton's books, and if hard and genuine effort can bring about that happy culmination then, to put it no more strongly, I think our chances are very bright.'[3]

If Farrell was not explicitly clear about his hopes, John Willie Parker was. On 13 March 1954 his hat-trick in the last 15 minutes saw off Rotherham in front of a Goodison crowd of 52,000. That 3–0 victory left Everton top with just nine games left.

A week later, they travelled to second-placed Leicester City and came back from 2–1 down at half-time to draw 2–2. Hickson scored both of Everton's goals.

Nevertheless, this Everton team was not well known for its ability to make life easy for itself. The following week they slipped up versus West Ham (1–2), and then, after losing to a John Charles-inspired Leeds (1–3), fell to third with six games left. Three draws in their next four matches left Everton behind Leicester on 56 points and Blackburn Rovers on 55. With both those sides having completed their programme of fixtures, it meant that Everton needed a win against bottom-placed (and relegated) Oldham at Boundary Park the following Thursday, 29 April, to pull level with Leicester and pip Blackburn to promotion. If they scored six, they would be crowned champions.

Interest was feverish and it was expected that Oldham's record attendance of 47,000 would be smashed. In the event, so many people made the journey from Merseyside, and the streets surrounding Boundary Park became so busy, that the gates were opened and thousands of people flooded in without paying. The crowd was estimated to be 70,000, a frightening number given the Oldham ground's limitations, but testament to the enthusiasm that this Everton side had come to inspire. Those who had made the trip saw Everton streak into an early lead. In the seventh minute Hickson squared unselfishly with his head and Parker gleefully headed his pass home. Everton's former keeper, George Burnett, kept goal for Oldham, and just as his errors against Sheffield Wednesday three years earlier had helped seal Everton's demise, so too did his mistakes for Oldham inspire their renaissance. T. E. Jones scored with a 55-yard shot from his own half after Burnett failed to palm the ball away, and Parker got his second when Burnett failed to keep hold of an Eglington shot. Hickson scored the fourth on 36 minutes after running half the length of the field. Could Everton be champions? No. Further goals were beyond them and the game descended into a second-half battle, with players brawling and bottles thrown on to the pitch. It had been enough, though. 'We have no "star" men,' said an elated Farrell of their promotion. 'Our success has been due to our all-round work as a team and with such a great bunch of players my job as captain has been easy.'

In fact, Farrell had understated the roles played by Hickson and Parker. Between them they had managed 56 goals – Parker 31, Hickson 25 – without which Everton would not have been promoted. Their partnership made a promising start to life back in the top flight, and with 10 games left in the 1954/5 season, Everton moved up to fourth, four points behind league leaders Chelsea, and with three games in hand. Could this most ordinary of Everton teams put together the most unlikely of title challenges? Their lack of quality shone through: Everton lost seven, drew two and won just once, finishing the season eleventh.

Eleventh place was, perhaps, an unfair reflection of Everton's fortunes in the 1954/5 campaign. Save for the season's end and a fortnight in November they had figured in the top 10, and Hickson had scored 12 goals, Parker 19. However, while the refusal of the board to invest in the team seemed to consign Everton to a perpetual place in the mid-table, some of the managerial decisions taken by Cliff Britton also seemed questionable. Two games into the 1955/6 season he dropped Parker and Hickson.

'The Cannonball Kid', as Hickson had come to be known, did not take kindly to his omission and requested a transfer. Within a fortnight he was at Aston Villa, sold for £19,500. 'He should do his new club the power of good and if he can finally conquer his rather pugnacious temperament – which he genuinely tried to do all last season – he has it in him to finally become one of the best centre forwards in the country . . .' wrote the *Liverpool Echo*. 'Hickson always gave his last ounce of endeavour to the Everton cause. Many a time his great fighting spirit and sheer determination helped to achieve victory in a game which had seemed to be irretrievably lost.' It was not a happy experience and after netting just once in 12 Villa Park appearances, he was sold to Bill Shankly's Huddersfield Town two months later. Goodison, however, had still to see the last of him.

The man who replaced Hickson was a 22-year-old by the name of Jimmy Harris. To step in for the Goodison idol was a tough challenge for the Birkenhead-born novice but, as the possessor of good pace and control as well as an eye for goal, he justified Britton's faith, scoring 21 times in the League and FA Cup. But Everton as a team again failed to combine and could do no better than finish the 1955/6 season fifteenth, although there was a brief flurry of excitement when they progressed to the quarter-final stage of the FA Cup at Manchester City. Again the Maine Road curse struck, and with City's German goalkeeper Bert Trautmann in superb form, Everton exited the competition after a 1–2 defeat.

At the end of the season a behind-the-scenes argument led to the resignation of Cliff Britton. Apparently the board had wanted to appoint an acting manager while he was abroad with the team, though later evidence showed that they might have been interfering with other aspects of his job. Tellingly, he left, saying, 'I want managers to have the freedom to do the job for which they were appointed, which is to manage their clubs.' His days as Goodison supremo had been tinged with mediocrity from start to finish – despite flirtations with FA Cup glory – and although his hands were tied by lack of funds, the forays he did make into the transfer market, most notably the expensive acquisition of Potts, were poor. His disciplinarian approach to the job also proved unpopular with many of his players, one of whom complained that Britton's ideal team would be comprised of 11 teetotallers. Today that might be regarded as the norm, but in the fifties it was seen as teetering on totalitarianism. He was later in charge of Preston before moving on to Hull City, where he became famous as the manager with a 10-year contract. Evertonians, however, prefer to dwell on his greatness as a player than his mediocrity as a manager. After all, in the words of Dixie Dean, he was 'one of the finest half backs in the history of the game'.

In the short term he was replaced by a committee of three – Tom

Nuttall, Fred Micklesfield and Cyril Balmforth – until, two months later, Ian Buchan, a former lecturer at Loughborough College and a Scottish amateur international, became 'chief coach'. Whether this role encompassed full responsibility for team selection and purchases is unsure, but it is certain that the standard of football in the two austere years he was in charge was unquestionably poor. Everton finished the 1956/7 season fifteenth and the 1957/8 campaign sixteenth, progressing no further than the fifth round of the FA Cup in 1957 and the fourth a year later.

Again, no major signings were made although, to widespread delight, Hickson returned from Huddersfield for £6500 on the eve of the 1957/8 season. The emphasis was, nevertheless, still firmly on youth development and during the year of the Cannonball Kid's return two future Everton stars made their breakthroughs to the first team.

Although initially bought as a winger from non-league Port Sunlight in January 1954, Brian Harris proved a tremendously versatile servant to the club and occupied every outfield position in an Everton career that spanned more than a decade. Indeed, he was one of Goodison's most loyal sons, and even when he lost his place to the expensively acquired Tony Kay during the 1962/3 season, he stayed at the club when many others might have demanded a transfer. His loyalty eventually paid off when Kay was banned for his part in a bribery scandal and Harris reclaimed his place. He made his Everton début in August 1955 on the same day that his namesake, Jimmy, also stepped up to the first team for the first time, and went on to make a further 23 league and Cup appearances that season, but was unable to hold down a regular berth during the following campaign.

Derek Temple had first broken into the Everton team at the end of the 1956/7 season and played in each of the final seven games, scoring three times. In the following campaign he established himself in the first team as a speedy inside right, partnering the irrepressible Dave Hickson for most of the first half of the season before national service halted his progress. He joined the King's Liverpool Regiment because their headquarters were in Formby; they assured him that his Everton career would not be unduly hampered. He ended up in Kenya! He emerged from the depths of East Africa in 1960, but found that after playing at 7000 feet above sea level and at a considerably lower standard, he had lost some of his hallmark pace. Consequently he had to work hard to re-establish himself in the Everton team and, once again, work his way back through the ranks.

At the same time the Irish contingent were being edged out. Farrell and Eglington joined Tranmere Rovers, Grant went to Rochdale, and Don Donovan to Grimsby Town. Wally Fielding was also a departure, sold to Southport in January 1959.

Transition period or not, Everton were now in as poor a state as ever. Mercifully, a benefactor had emerged.

It was during the Second World War that John Moores's financial association with Everton had begun. His friend Dick Searle, then majority shareholder at Goodison and later chairman, had encountered financial difficulties and offered Moores half of his shares. 'It was on the understanding that I always voted with him,' Moores revealed later. 'I agreed to vote with him as long as I didn't think it was against the interests of the club – I reserved that right. So I took half his shares, and he gave me an option to buy the remainder in the event of his death.'

Born in Eccles, Manchester, he had been taken as a youngster to see Manchester United, but switched allegiance to Everton on moving to Merseyside as a teenager, where he became a telegraph boy. His association with the club was rooted in the second decade of the twentieth century, when he stood on the terraces, and he was present on the day when Dixie Dean completed his 60-goal haul. Moores played at amateur level, but his pools business, started as a sideline, slowly began to dominate his life, and he quit playing before he had progressed to a higher level. With Colin Littlewood-Askham he formed the Littlewoods Organization, whose interests became as diverse as home-shopping and supermarkets.

Moores had initially lent his business expertise to the club (though during the early 1950s this was seldom evident), and later, when there was a credit squeeze, his money. First, in 1957, he lent funds for the new floodlights, and over the summer of the following year he nudged the perennially frugal board towards opening the club's coffers. Their first major signings for years were the Falkirk duo, Eddie O'Hara and Alex Parker. Both men had helped the Brockville Park club to win the Scottish FA Cup a year earlier, and although national service initially prevented Parker making his Everton début until November 1958, it was he, rather than outside left O'Hara, who fully established himself at Goodison, serving Everton for six years, making more than two hundred appearances and winning a Championship medal in 1963.

Although he was slightly lacking in pace, Parker had an impeccable sense of timing when entering a tackle. He mastered the art of defending to such an extent that it was once said he had 'elevated the sliding tackle into an art form'. It was not just his part in the occasionally wayward Everton back four that endeared him to the Goodison faithful: Alex Parker was always more than just a defender. Although stockily built he possessed the skill and poise of a winger and his first-rate distribution was later of particular benefit to the likes of Billy Bingham and Alex Scott. Although an early exponent of the overlapping full-back role, he scored just five goals in his Everton career, but when they came, they were spectacular.

The other acquisition was Peter Harburn, a centre forward bought from Brighton and Hove Albion who, to the surprise of everyone, replaced Hickson in the opening fixture of the 1958/9 campaign with Leicester City. Everton were crushed at Filbert Street. 'Two goals to nil Everton lost at Leicester,' reported the *Football Echo*. 'But the margin may well have been heavier and that is making allowance for the desperation of a hard-worked defence.' Débutant Harburn was 'quite at sea'. Four days later they lost 1–4 at Goodison to Preston North End. The next Saturday, 30 August 1958, Newcastle inflicted a 0–2 home defeat, which was greeted with slow handclapping and angry shouts.

Soon letters were flooding into the local newspapers. 'It is perfectly obvious that there is something wrong at Goodison. Despite the accent on youth they have produced nothing worth bragging about. When Mr Buchan came to Goodison he was quoted as saying that Everton were playing a negative type of football. I don't know what he calls the type they're dishing up now. If it were any more negative it would be non-existent,' wrote T. Bartley of Little Crosby. 'We have read about weight-lifting but never anything about heading, trapping and passing the ball in which the team are so poor. They are also slow to make up their minds in going for the ball and also moving into open spaces for a pass,' complained R. J. Darwin of Aughton.

Preston inflicted a fourth straight defeat (1–3) in the return at Deepdale before Arsenal visited Goodison on 6 September. Hopes that the miserable start would come to an end were quickly confounded. Everton were thrashed 1–6. 'This was a massacre at Goodison,' wrote Michael Charters, in the *Football Echo*. 'Everton were completely outplayed at every point by a brilliant Arsenal team who gave them a footballing lesson, plus goals.' Only Temple's consolation five minutes from the end prevented the record 0–6 Goodison defeats of 1912 and 1922 being equalled.

The following Monday the board met to decide Buchan's fate. Earlier claims that Everton had been the fittest team in the division were dismissed by the chairman, Dick Searle, who stoked controversy when he said: 'Everton are three yards slower than opponents they have met this season.' Yet for three days – which saw Everton's sixth straight defeat (1–3) at Burnley – there was silence. Then, in quick succession, they announced three surprises.

First, Harry Wright, Buchan's first-team trainer, was sacked, and Gordon Watson stepped up to take over.

Then Celtic's Bobby Collins was signed for £24,000. He was five foot four inches of tenacious skill, biting aggression and impish brilliance, and his arrival made front-page news on Merseyside. Despite the abysmal start to the season, the *Liverpool Echo*'s Leslie Edwards was optimistic that the new signing could help Everton rise from the depths of the First Division: 'Everton will find that the £24,000 they have spent will be repaid fully by a player Scotland will be sorry to lose.' Twenty-four hours later, Collins had inspired Everton to their first win of the season: a 3–1 victory over Manchester City, and Edwards was singing the new boy's praises in the *Football Echo*. 'First appearances suggest that Collins will be well worth every penny of his transfer fee and although one man may not be the complete answer to Everton's troubles, he can go a great part of the way to restoring Everton's glamour.' Two minutes before the end of the game Collins had produced a 'story-book finale', with a shot so powerful it slipped through the goalkeeper's grasp and into the net to make the score 3–1 in Everton's advantage.

At last Evertonians had another hero to line up alongside the Cannonball Kid. Indeed, Collins's scoring record for an inside right was one of which many an out-and-out forward would have been proud. A prolific goalscorer, too, he finished the 1959/60 season as top scorer with 14, a total he bettered by three goals the following year. Ironically, Collins could have been an Everton player as early as 1947. He came to Goodison from the Scottish junior side, Pollock, as a raw 16-year-old but left after a few weeks because he was homesick. Upset at losing such a promising young star, Everton complained to the Scottish FA and Collins had to serve a six-week ban. Back in Scotland he joined Celtic and won numerous trophies for the team he had idolized as a boy.

His influence at Goodison rallied his team-mates and they began to pick up valuable points. A ferocious tackler, Collins earned the nicknames the 'Little General' and 'Pocket Napoleon' and was more than capable of rattling the bones of any giant who got in his way. Not only were his goals and tackling vital to the team, but he was at the creative heart of an inconsistent Everton side. He could pass with deadly accuracy to colleagues in dangerous positions and such was his influence that, more than 35 years after his departure, Brian Labone still had cause to present him to a half-time Goodison crowd as 'the man who single-handedly saved Everton from relegation – twice'.

Days after the Manchester City win, it was revealed that Blackburn Rovers' manager, Johnny Carey, was to be appointed Everton boss. Carey, a soft-spoken Dubliner, had captained Manchester United's post-war side, helping them to league runners-up in three consecutive seasons and also to the FA Cup Final, which they won in 1948. His first taste of management was at Ewood Park where he led Blackburn to the top flight in the 1957/8 season, and he was seen by the Everton directors as the ideal successor to Ian Buchan. Carey immediately put his free-flowing football principles into practice at Goodison, his motto being 'Only the keeper stops the ball.'

However, it was four weeks before he could take up the managerial reins: he had agreed – always a man of honour – to serve out a four-week notice period at Ewood Park. Before that time could elapse, Everton had suffered their record defeat on 11 October 1958 to Tottenham Hotspur: 1–6 down at half-time, they went on to lose 4–10, even though Jimmy Harris scored a hat-trick. The last time 14 goals had been scored in a top-flight match was in 1892 when Aston Villa beat Accrington Stanley 12–2. 'Comment is superfluous,' wrote the *Football Echo*.

Following his October arrival, Carey steadied the ship, leading

Everton from the relegation spots to the relative respectability of sixteenth. Although Everton had scored 71 goals, their defence let them down, conceding 87. It was the pattern of things to come.

○

THE NEW MANAGER's side kicked off the 1959/60 season with his faith invested in Parker, Collins, O'Hara, Hickson and the promising bunch of youngsters who had emerged in previous seasons, including Brian Labone, a young centre back. It was not enough. Yet again Everton began the season poorly, and after just four wins in the opening three months they were once more staring at the prospect of relegation.

At the start of November, Carey decided to rejig the side. The first step he took was drastic, controversial and traumatic. He sold Dave Hickson for £12,500. To Liverpool.

'I protest at the abominable treatment afforded Dave Hickson. Everton supporters know that Hickson is not the best centre forward in football, but of the centre forwards on Everton's books he is by far the best,' wrote J. D. Pierce of Liverpool 11 to the *Football Echo*. 'It seems ridiculous that other players in the team can play badly and still retain their places while Hickson, who has played his heart out (and, incidentally, is leading goalscorer), should be dropped.'

'Is Mr Carey using Hickson to cover mistakes by rash buying?' pondered C. Purvis of Liverpool 24.

Yet it was not just Evertonians who were outraged at the deal. 'Whether Hickson joins Liverpool or not, I want to express the disgust of some Liverpool supporters of 30 years' standing that the club should even consider a player who has been discarded by Everton Football Club (twice), Aston Villa and Huddersfield,' complained W. Parker of Liverpool 8. 'After talking grandly of Clough, Baker and Holton, Liverpool have come down to this,' moaned A. Alan of Liverpool 18. 'Everton will never be the same without Davy, and if he goes to Liverpool I, and I am sure many more, will willingly pay 2s. to Liverpool just to watch him,' averred A. A. Drury of Liverpool 4.

Indeed, many supporters did. Yet within a couple of months his much-mourned departure, if not forgotten, was made less traumatic as the millions of John Moores began to filter through. The abundant funds he invested allowed Carey to compete with the best in the transfer market and transform his team of valiant no-hopers.

First in was Tommy Ring. Carey bought the one-time Scottish international winger in January 1960 to add fresh impetus to his side, which was still hovering perilously close to the relegation zone. The impact he made was immediate, and Everton beat Nottingham Forest 6–1 on his début. Horrace Yates in the *Daily Post* wrote, 'If one signing, that of Tommy Ring from Clyde, can convert a team of non-scorers in 4 successive matches into a side which can take six goals, with at least as many opportunities wasted in one game, what sort of transformation can be expected when Johnny Carey completes the first instalment in his reconstruction programme with the 2 or 3 captures which are necessary?' Ring became an instant crowd favourite. His dazzling runs past defenders and changes of pace were his most potent weapons, although he was not averse to scoring goals. 'Ring is the most complete outside left I have seen at Goodison in a royal blue jersey since Eglington's brightest days,' Yates later wrote. 'He beats an opponent effortlessly, inside or outside, and having done that centres the ball with an accuracy which is an open scoring invitation to forwards with any competence for their job.'

His time at Goodison was brief, though: that October a sickening collision with the Chelsea goalkeeper, Reg Matthews, resulted in a broken leg and his Everton days were effectively ended. By the time he had recovered, he was in his early thirties and was sold to Barnsley in November 1961 where he played a handful of games before retiring.

Next came Roy Vernon. 'He was about ten stone wet through and looked about as athletic as Pinocchio,' was the image Brian Labone later conjured up of Everton's new playboy striker. Perhaps it was justified: Vernon was once accused by a fan of smoking on the pitch – he was actually inhaling an ammonia capsule – he rarely trained, and, on another occasion, was sent home from a tour of America for breaking a curfew. Yet his off-the-pitch antics and slight build in no way detracted from his superb goalscoring prowess and Labone conceded that he was a 'brilliant player'. In five years at Goodison he scored 110 league and Cup goals in 199 games and captained Everton to their first post-war league Championship.

Like Collins, he had turned down the chance of joining Everton as a schoolboy, preferring instead to sign professional terms with Blackburn Rovers where he first became acquainted with Johnny Carey. When Carey became Everton manager and heard that the striker was available in February 1960, he immediately shelled out £27,000 plus Eddie Thomas – an inside forward – for his services. By then Vernon had already been capped by Wales and had taken part in the 1958 World Cup Finals in Sweden. He went on to make 32 appearances for his country in an international career that spanned a decade.

Although neither Carey nor Catterick could curb the errant Welshman's off-the-pitch behaviour (it was said Vernon could hold a cigarette at such an angle that he could smoke in the shower), both took advantage of his skills on the pitch to transform him into one of the club's most prolific ever strikers. Primarily a penalty-area player, his shot was one of immense power and accuracy and his impact on Carey's struggling side was immediate, reaping six goals in his first five games.

That same month, 19-year-old Jimmy Gabriel was signed for £30,000 from Dundee. At Dens Park his exploits had earned him comparison with his countryman Dave MacKay, who had moved south to Spurs, a year earlier, where he had been showered with acclaim. Indeed, it was only MacKay's excellence at right half that restricted Gabriel to just two Scotland caps, the first coming in 1961 against Wales, the second as a substitute against Norway three years later. At Goodison, Gabriel forged a strong midfield partnership first with Brian Harris, then Tony Kay, and won widespread admiration from fans and fellow players alike. Alex Young described his bravery: 'Jimmy would run through a brick wall and just blink.' Yet there was much more to Gabriel's game than raw aggression: he added grit and skill to the Everton midfield but also possessed the maturity – despite his youth – to act as 'minder' to the younger squad members and improve his own blossoming game. Just three matches into his Everton career, when he was given the run-around by West Bromwich Albion's Derek Kevan, who scored five times in a thrashing at the Hawthorns, he had the resilience to pick himself up and react positively to the humiliation.

Between them this exciting and expensive bunch of stars pulled Everton from the relegation spots to the relative respectability (and safety) of sixteenth place. They were further strengthened in the early stages of the 1960/61 season, by the addition of the Northern Irish winger Billy Bingham. His playing career had begun with Glenavon in the late 1940s and his exploits on the wing soon won him widespread plaudits. By October 1950 he had been selected to play for a representative side of the Irish League and an £8000 move to Sunderland followed shortly after. After seven years with the Roker Park club he was sold to Luton Town and, after starring in the 1958 World Cup in Sweden, he helped Luton to the most successful season in their history. For a short time they topped the First Division and finished FA Cup runners-up to Nottingham Forest, after Bingham had scored in every round leading up to the final. His second season with the Hatters was not so happy: Luton were relegated and, after a contractual argument, he asked for a transfer. When negotiations with Arsenal broke down, Johnny Carey made a £15,000 move for him and he became an Everton player in time for the start of the 1960/61 season. To facilitate his arrival, Carey switched Mickey Lill, Everton's joint top scorer in the previous campaign, to the other wing and Bingham soon built up a keen understanding with the Scottish international full back Alex Parker. Horrace Yates wrote in the *Daily Post*, 'Everton now possess the most goalworthy pair of wingers they have had for many a year.' Parker was equally enthusiastic about his new team-mate: 'He's probably the best winger I've played with. He can read me and I can read him and that's why we play so well together.' The admiration was mutual and Bingham later returned the compliment, stating that Parker was the finest full back he had ever played alongside.

Developments were also taking place off the field during the summer of 1960. At the Annual General Meeting on 23 June, the chairman, Fred Micklesfield, revealed that John Moores had offered £56,000 to the club, free of interest, 'to enable star players to be secured'. Micklesfield offered words of confidence with regard to the club's future before he retired from the chair, to which Moores was elected.

By Christmas 1960, Everton were third and being talked of as genuine title challengers. It was a stark contrast to any season in the 13 that had passed since the war, but Carey's side were entertainers, not winners. They were the sort of side who could thrill with a 3–1 win at Burnley on Boxing Day 1960, then lose miserably (0–3) to the same side in the return fixture at Goodison just 24 hours later. Indeed that same defeat marked the onset of a run of 10 losses in 13 games. It was not catastrophic and Everton fell only as far as sixth, but it was enough to convince Moores that Carey would never be a winner. He recognized that Carey's team often lacked discipline or the killer touch.

When the end of March came, speculation was rife about Carey's future. It intensified when Harry Catterick, now manager of Sheffield Wednesday but rumoured to be of interest to the Everton board, resigned unexpectedly. Wednesday were in second place.

Then, on Friday 14 April 1961, Carey and Moores travelled to London for an FA meeting. Even though Everton had beaten Newcastle United 4–0 at St James's Park the previous Saturday, speculation was more intense than ever about Carey's future. Wanting clarification, he demanded a meeting with his chairman. Moores suggested that they reconvene and the two men took a taxi to the Grosvenor House Hotel. During that journey, Carey repeated his request for clarification on his future. Moores, always a man of principle, went straight to the point. He told Carey that he was being replaced.

The phrase 'taking a taxi' was born, and with it Everton's hard times had ended. A golden era lay ahead.

7

The Golden Vision

CAREY'S SACKING WAS small news that tumultuous week in April 1961. During those seven days the Soviet cosmonaut, Yuri Gagarin, was blasted into space and became the first man to orbit earth, and in Israel the Eichmann trial began, which concluded with the hanging of the Nazi butcher. Even in football, it was not the main story: football's maximum wage had been scrapped.

The clearing of Carey's desk did not take place immediately. The affable Irishman was left in charge for one more game – a home match with Cardiff City on 15 April 1961. With typical diplomacy and a loyalty that the Everton board did not deserve, he would only answer questions about his departure with the quip that he 'must be the most successful failure in the business'.

When Saturday came, Goodison's atmosphere was strangely subdued. Moores's appearance in the directors' box shortly before kick-off was greeted with boos, slow handclapping and chants of 'We want Carey.' Just before the team left the dressing room to come on to the pitch, the captain Bobby Collins made a speech thanking him on behalf of the players and expressing their regret at his departure. Once out there, they let down neither Carey nor the restless crowd. Cardiff were seen off, 5–1, thanks to a captain's hat-trick and a brace by Alex Young. After the game, several fans waited around Carey's car to thank him for everything he had done for the club. 'That touched me very much,' he said, 'and so did the players' little speech before a match which was, for me, one of the greatest and yet one of the saddest of my career.'

Over the weekend, speculation about Harry Catterick continued to mount, until at 6.45 p.m. on the Monday evening it was announced that Everton's former centre forward was to be the club's fifth manager. 'I am delighted to have the opportunity to work again with my old club,' said Catterick. 'I should be anxious to succeed wherever I went but because Everton are my old team I am doubly keen on putting them at the top.'

John Moores was happy to have got his man: 'We want success and I think Mr Catterick will get it for us. As I was responsible for bringing him here I am naturally going to give him all the support I can. He has a big opportunity, the ball's at his feet.'

The inspirational figure behind Everton's 5–1 win over Cardiff City had been Alex Young. From the outset he had run the Welshmen ragged and as early as the third minute was in the thick of things, setting up Collins's opener. Labone had played a perfect crossfield pass to Collins, who pushed the ball through to Young. He held off Molloy's challenge and slipped the ball back to the Scot, who rammed a left-footed shot hard and low into the corner of the net. Collins made it two from the penalty spot on 28 minutes. Seven minutes later Collins made a 30-yard run before passing to Fell. He cut inside, flicked the ball to Vernon, who played in Young. He stepped around the goalkeeper and calmly slotted the ball into the empty net. Immediately after the interval Young had repaid the compliment, but Fell's shot was blocked. Young, however, was on hand to hit the ball into the empty net for Everton's fourth. The rout was completed when Collins headed home a Bingham cross to make it five.

Alex Young had been one of Carey's last signings for Everton and proved to be his most enduring legacy to the club. Born in the Midlothian mining village of Loanhead in 1937, he had played as a boy for the Edinburgh junior side, Newtongate Star, before signing for Hearts. In five seasons for Hearts he scored 77 goals, including 20 in their successful Championship campaign of 1957/8 and 23 when they regained supremacy in 1959/60, also winning the first six of his eight Scotland caps.

Soon an ensemble of English clubs was tracking the blond striker, but it was Everton and Preston who backed up their initial interest with firm bids for his services. Carey had long been in the hunt for a forward partner for Vernon and had already been frustrated in a bid to sign Middlesbrough's Brian Clough and Joe Baker of Hibernian. Early on in the battle for his signature, it looked as if Preston was going to win the deal as their manager, Cliff Britton, the ex-Everton boss, had offered the higher signing-on fee. Carey and Britton had travelled to Scotland on the same day to try to sign Young, even sharing lunch on the train up to Edinburgh. Eventually a boardroom disagreement at Preston over the size of Young's proposed signing-on fee, coupled with the advice of Hearts manager Tommy Walker – who had once played for Chelsea and advised the Scot to sign for a bigger club like Everton – paved the way for his move to Goodison Park.

In total the transfer was worth £55,000 and also brought the full back George Thomson to Everton. Thomson's Everton career lasted three years, during which he made 77 appearances, without ever really settling; a combination of over-elaboration and lack of pace saw him replaced by the more reliable Mick Meagan, paving the way for a transfer to Brentford after he had won a Championship medal in 1963. Young represented £42,000 worth of the deal – at the time a record fee for a player coming out of Scotland – which was criticized by some pundits north of the border who claimed that Hearts had overvalued him.

Young arrived at Goodison with his leg in plaster, having sustained a knee injury while playing for the British Army against Aberdeen. It was nearly four weeks before he made his début, against Spurs, at Goodison on 17 December 1960, a 1–3 defeat that passed without him making any great impression. He stepped down subsequently from first-team action, because of further injury, for another seven weeks. His return – a 1–2 home defeat to Bolton on 4 February 1961 – came in the midst of a miserable run of form, which had seen Everton drop from third to fifth and go out of the FA Cup in the third round against Sheffield United.

Gradually, though, Young began to prosper, and his first league goals came in the 3–1 win over Blackburn Rovers at the end of March. His performance left watching journalists eulogizing:

> Young's continued improvement is the brightest thing on the Everton horizon [opined the *Liverpool Echo*]. The spectators now know him for what he is – one of the most able artists with a ball in Britain. Art conceals art and none conceals this better than Young with his quiet drift to the right or left and the ball taken with head, chest or foot as though killing a fast pass were the easiest of tasks and not one of the most difficult.[1]

Derek Potter of the *Daily Express* continued the praise: 'Young was able to live up to the adoration that would have overwhelmed lesser men. They expected him to walk across the Mersey. He was never vain enough to try. Besides, he had such bad feet!'

None of this, however, had saved the man who had brought him to the club. Later Young admitted feeling a sense of culpability at Johnny Carey's departure. 'If I had been properly fit when he signed me, I don't think Carey would have lost his job,' he confessed. 'I had been in tremendous form for Hearts and if I'd been able to reproduce that straight away with Everton, I don't think we would have lost so many games. In a way, Johnny Carey paid heavily for my injury.'[2]

Catterick, who had succeeded Carey, had seen his stock in the football world rise dramatically after his entry into management with Crewe and then with Rochdale. As a player with Everton his career had been stalled by the war, and he had then had the impossibly hard job of living up to the standards set by Dean and Lawton. Management gave him the chance to shine, and modest success at Gresty Road and Spotland elevated him to the higher stage of Hillsborough. At Sheffield Wednesday he revived fortunes, leading them to the Second Division title in 1959, fifth place and an FA Cup semi-final in their first season back in the top flight, then league runners-up to double winners Spurs prior to his resignation. He had a reputation as a task master and disciplinarian, for ruthlessness and winning football. He 'had the drive we needed,' Moores said later. 'I told him to aim for a place in the top six by playing good football, and by doing that I was sure that success would come.'

There was a sense, though, that Johnny Carey had been unlucky. Dick White, like Charles Mills, now married and carrying on the Everton tradition with his children, remembered: 'He spent extremely wisely and bought well, but he did not have the dynamism, perhaps, or the forcefulness with the players that Moores wanted and would have expected from his own Littlewoods Organization. But the football of that team was absolutely superb. They were great at home, but could not travel.'

The contrast between the new manager and the smiling Carey – whose credo, he once revealed, was 'to give Everton entertaining and, if possible, winning football' – could not have been greater. Catterick had come to win and, if he could, entertain. Over the next dozen years in the Goodison hot-seat, he did just that.

Catterick's first match in charge saw him pitted against his old club, Sheffield Wednesday, at Hillsborough. Everton breezed through with a 2–1 victory, and also won the season's final match against Arsenal at Goodison 4–1. They finished the season fifth. Within days of the end of the 1960/61 season they had travelled to the US for an end-of-season tour. If any of the players had doubts about the nature of the new managerial regime, they need not have: Roy Vernon – club captain, no less – was sent home in disgrace, having broken a curfew.

Back in England, the new manager made no major additions to the impressive squad he had inherited. Everton opened the 1961/2 season against Aston Villa with a 2–0 victory through Young and Bingham goals, but went on to lose five of their next six matches, although the run occurred over less than three calendar weeks in late August and early September. It proved a minor aberration, and Everton were soon back on track with impressive wins over eventual champions Ipswich Town, Manchester City and Arsenal. Young was quickly emerging as a favourite at Goodison, wowing the crowd with his delicate flashes of genius. His 'effect on the team was enormous,' Labone claimed later, 'particularly on the defence. We felt that here was a man you could give the ball to in any situation. He could give us a breather by keeping the ball up there, occupying all the attention of the opposition, giving us time to regroup.'[3] Impressive though he undoubtedly was, Young still had to stake his claim for immortality. It wasn't long in coming.

At the end of the first week of October 1961 tenth-placed Everton played Nottingham Forest, who held fourth position. Though Everton had won the same fixture 6–1 less than two years earlier, few Evertonians could have anticipated a repeat of that hiding, or the way in which Young dominated events from start to finish. Jimmy Gabriel scored first, running on to Young's sideward header and steering the ball past Grummitt for his second goal in successive matches. Vernon added a second on 33 minutes. Young raced down the wing and into the Forest penalty area. His perfectly calculated pass was controlled by the unmarked Welshman, who lashed the ball home. Then, Young's well-directed header from Fell's cross made it 3–0 a minute after half-time, and he returned the compliment 10 minutes later, playing in Fell for the first goal of his Everton career.

Young was now on fire and the Forest defence were finding it impossible to check the Scot's brilliance. He was inspiring Everton to exhibition-like football and started the move for Everton's fifth goal.

Picking up the ball by the half-way line he swerved past a Forest defender and dribbled down the right before flicking the ball to Bingham. His cross was accepted by Collins on the penalty spot and he controlled the ball, then impetuously back-heeled it into the path of Fell, who tapped home his second from four yards. Then, on 76 minutes, Young lobbed the ball in for Bingham at the far post. He headed across the goal and Vernon side-footed home his second and Everton's sixth.

It was, noted one observer, 'The finest exhibition of centre forward play since the days of Dixie Dean and Tommy Lawton – that is how I rate the performance of Alex Young . . . His trademark was on all six goals and it was not his fault there were not three or four others.' The *Liverpool Echo*'s Leslie Edwards said of Young: 'It is not necessary for a player with his extraordinary gifts to play a blood and guts centre forward game. With a slight feint of the shoulders he gets them going the wrong way. Then he drifts past them almost lazily. Like Matthews and other men of football genius he always seems to have time to think and space in which to move. He won't get a packet of goals, but he'll make hundreds of others.'[4]

A few days later Everton met Liverpool at Goodison in a Floodlit Cup fixture. Although few people placed any importance on the competition, the ever partisan Merseyside public – deprived of a competitive derby for a decade – turned out in droves. The match ended in a 2–2 draw, with Collins putting Everton in front on 23 minutes, Roger Hunt scoring on each side of half-time, then Vernon bringing equality from the penalty spot. 'What more could be asked?' pondered Leslie Edwards. 'Both sides led; both were one down; both scored twice, both sent their following home satisfied. Perfectly simple and simply perfect.'

Everton's progress under Catterick continued with some stunning performances. Double-holders Spurs were seen off with a 3–0 win at the start of November, and when Matt Busby's Manchester United visited Goodison at the beginning of the following month Everton had risen as high as third. In Brian Labone's hundredth league appearance, Everton thrashed United 5–1, with all the goals coming in the first half. Collins opened the scoring on nine minutes with a shot from 18 yards for his first goal of the season. Two minutes later Vernon lobbed Gaskell to make it two. Then, on 15 minutes, after Gaskell had saved from Vernon and then Parker, Fell hit home the second rebound. Just after the half-hour mark Vernon scored the pick of the bunch. Turning Nicholson, he broke clear down the centre of the pitch, hitting the ball home from 15 yards past Gaskell. Five minutes later Vernon ran through the heart of the United defence again, but his shot was parried into the path of Young who lifted the ball over the forlorn Gaskell to make it five. In the second half, Everton eased up, but the team's quality had been evident.

Catterick was still to make his first major foray into the transfer market, but when it came – the following March – it was as surprising as it was initially unpopular. Bobby Collins, who had been the central and dominant figure in the revival under Carey, was allowed to join Leeds United in a £30,000 deal, and in his place came Bolton Wanderers' Dennis Stevens. Catterick's new signing found his early days at the club marred by a vociferous faction of the Everton support who wrongly – not to mention unfairly – blamed him for Collins's departure. 'We thought, "What have we signed him for? He's just a thug,"' reminisced Dick White, 'but he was the lynchpin, the Bentham of the age. He did all the grafting and teed it up for Young.' Although lacking in some of the finesse and star quality of his illustrious predecessor, Stevens was a tireless runner and always willing to assist in both attacking and defensive duties. Evertonians soon warmed to his energy and work rate, and he emerged as the unsung hero of the following season's Championship-winning side.

Nevertheless, there was an indisputable sense that Collins had been sold too early, despite having passed his thirty-first birthday a month before his Goodison exit. The gut feeling of Collins worshippers was to be vindicated. At Elland Road he helped transform a side that was hovering perilously close to relegation into the Third Division, into one that was unlucky to miss out on a league and Cup double in 1965 (he picked up the PFA Player of the Year award the same year, aged 34). He left Leeds to join Bury on a free transfer in 1967, and later played for Morton and Oldham Athletic before finally hanging up his boots at the grand old age of 42. His pedigree on the football field was unfortunately not matched with an adeptness in the world of management, and his appointments at Huddersfield, Hull and Barnsley all ended in failure. Despite such all-round brilliance in a playing career that spanned nearly 25 years and more than 600 games, his football philosophy remained simple: 'I went out and tried to be the best,' he once said. And, more often than not, he achieved just that.

The same month Harry Catterick signed Blackpool's teenager Gordon West for a then record fee for a goalkeeper of £27,500. What was most surprising about the deal was that West had been playing in goal for only a year.

His meteoric rise from centre half for Don & Dearne Boys in his native Barnsley to goalkeeper for the Football League Championship winners within a few years is a story that has a hint of schoolboy fantasy about it. He had been playing, without the outstanding ability that is so often the hallmark of a future professional, as the lynchpin of his Sunday league side's defence when a team-mate, Kevin Renie, was invited to Blackpool for a trial and told to bring a friend. 'What position shall I tell Blackpool you play?' Renie asked West. 'Goalkeeper,' West inexplicably replied. Later he revealed a long-standing ambition to become a goalkeeper despite never having played there previously. Little did West know that this was the beginning of a career that would eventually see him challenge Gordon Banks for his England jersey.

A matter of months after his successful trial he had replaced the England international Tony Waiters between the Bloomfield Road goalposts. Indeed, it was the excellence of the more senior professional that had made it easier for Everton to prise the youngster away.

It was the start of an eventful 11-year Everton career, which concluded with West as one of the most decorated players in the club's history. It did not always run smoothly, though. Despite Catterick's early faith in West, he was quick to pick up on flaws in his technique and dropped him on several occasions in the two seasons following the 1962/3 Championship triumph before giving him the chance to re-establish himself as first choice ahead of Andy Rankin. The latter took over the quite considerable berth in Everton's goal when West again fell out of favour with Catterick in the early seventies. His size and hefty figure often led to criticism. Stewart Imlach, who was on Catterick's backroom staff, recalled Fridays at the club when each player was weighed: if they were caught overweight they were sent back for an afternoon training session. 'Westy was always overweight,' recalled Imlach, 'and he'd come into the room and take all the plasters off his leg. Then he'd go into the medical room and shave his legs. There was a little table just by where they were weighed, and Westy used to stand by this and he'd be pushing his hand on the table to take half a stone off!'[5]

Yet West's main critic was not Catterick but himself. He admitted later that he often cringed when he looked back at previous mistakes. 'I have gone home and cried after defeat,' he said. 'It was all immaturity, I suppose.' He also put down to immaturity his compulsive vomiting prior to kick-off. 'Nine times out of ten he used to go and be sick before the game,' said John Hurst. 'It was just his nerves because the tension used to get to him.'

Everton finished the 1961/2 season in fourth place, five points behind champions Ipswich. Poor away form and injuries to several key players cost them a serious stab at taking Championship glory, but the improvement was more evident than the single place they had risen under Catterick. There was more steel and resolve in the team; a winning mentality had developed; and in Young and Vernon a top-flight forward partnership had built up of a calibre not seen at Goodison since Everton had last won the title in 1939. 'It could be said that Vernon made Alex Young, rather than the other way around,' said Charles Mills. 'I rather think he made Vernon: he provided the flicks and the through balls and Vernon was, of course, dynamite anywhere in the penalty area.'

The 1962/3 season began with a tough visit to Burnley, the previous season's league and FA Cup runners-up. Sporting the hoop-necked shirt – which became synonymous with Catterick's Everton – for the first time, they put in a hugely impressive performance, seeing off their opponents with a 3–1 victory. Four days later Everton met Manchester United at Goodison, with 70,000 spectators to watch the spectacle. Again, the genius of Young was the dominant influence, with two goals – including the pick of the bunch: he headed the ball upwards over a United defender and, when it fell, hit the resulting volley into the back of the United net – and Parker adding a third in a 3–1 win.

Again, Catterick had not made any pre-season signings, but on the day of the United match he had signed Johnny Morrissey from Liverpool for £10,000. The deal was met with surprise on either side of Stanley Park: not only was Morrissey just the fourth player ever to move from Anfield to Goodison but he was also a devout Red, whose boyhood had centred on Billy Liddell. With Harry Catterick supposedly building up a side to challenge for honours why, asked many fans, was he spending £10,000 on a man who was essentially a Liverpool reserve having been edged out of contention at the season's start by Alan A'Court? They soon had the answer.

While Young seized all the plaudits against United, when Everton met Catterick's old club, Sheffield Wednesday, in the next match, it was his strike partner Vernon who captured the applause, inspiring Everton to a 4–1 win. The following Wednesday, 29 August, Everton travelled to Old Trafford for the return match against United. In a thrilling end-to-end game, in which the safe hands of West kept United at bay, and only the cross-bar denied Gabriel and Vernon at the other end, a single goal decided it. It came on 78 minutes. Morrissey was fouled by Brennan, and Vernon converted the resulting spot kick to seize a 1–0 victory and maintain Everton's 100 per cent record.

Throughout September 1962 Everton continued to impress, although defeats at Fulham and Leyton Orient cost them the top spot. At the end of the month, they met Liverpool for the first league derby since their 2–0 win in January 1951. If interest had been great when the two sides had met in the Floodlit Cup a year earlier, it was nothing compared to their league reunion: 73,000 crammed into Goodison to see a fixture packed with skill, commitment and high drama. Vernon's first-half penalty – his fifth of the season – was cancelled out by Lewis's far post shot. Everton looked to be heading for victory when Morrissey, in an instant, quelled the doubters with his first goal for the club. A fumble by the Liverpool goalkeeper, Jim Furnell, had allowed Morrissey to gain possession and strike the ball between Ron Yeats and Gordon Milne, and although Ronnie Moran managed to prevent the ball hitting the back of the net, the referee judged it to have gone over the line.

As the countdown of minutes turned to seconds, Evertonians began to celebrate a long-awaited victory. Then, at the very death, A'Court – the man who had edged out Morrissey at Anfield – hoisted a hopeful centre. Lewis got his head to the ball in front of Labone, and Hunt knocked home the loose ball for Liverpool's equalizer: 2–2. Everton remained a place off the top, Liverpool in the division's nether regions.

Everton were soon back at the top, and the Young and Vernon partnership continued to bedevil defences. 'In a sense he was an oddity as a centre forward,' recalled Charles Mills. 'You don't get many centre forwards like Alex Young.'

'Without indulging in any of the histrionics normally associated with star players,' wrote J. C. Fisher of Childwall in a letter to the *Liverpool Echo*, 'Alex Young is providing Goodison Park fans with the most superb exhibitions of the soccer arts. Certainly in my lifetime, I have never seen his superior as a footballer. I believe he is one of the rare players who knows that his function is to entertain, and that he sets out to do just that, detaching himself with contempt from the doubtful tactics and gamesmanship prevalent today.'[6] Maybe so, but when Everton met Young's countrymen, Dunfermline Athletic, for their first ever European tie, in the Inter-City Fairs Cup, he was found wanting.

Both ties were played against a tense political situation, with the Cold War reaching its chilling climax over the Cuban missile crisis. At Goodison, on 24 October, more than 40,000 fans watched a scrappy, defensive game, riddled with fouls and settled by Stevens's contentious goal, which gave Everton a 1–0 advantage for the return at East End Park. Back in Scotland a week later, Everton were overcome by a 0–2 scoreline.

In the league, Everton continued to hover around the top spot and a goalless away draw with their main title rivals Tottenham Hotspur on 1 December 1962 saw them regain it. Britain, however, was about to enter its most bitterly cold winter of the century. Blizzards and frost thrust the country back into an ice age, killing hundreds of people and animals, devastating crops and crippling air, road and rail transport. Everton were left without a league fixture between 22 December and 12 February, although they played two FA Cup ties, away at Barnsley and Swindon.

Catterick put the gap to good use. First he went back to his old club, Sheffield Wednesday, and signed Tony Kay, the man he had made Hillsborough captain, for £55,000 – a record fee for a half back. When Catterick had become Everton boss in April 1961 many had expected Kay to follow him immediately from South Yorkshire. That it took 18 months for the move to happen was largely down to Wednesday's reluctance to allow such a prized asset to leave. Although Brian Harris was desperately unlucky to lose his place to the new boy, the powerful redhead possessed more finesse and style in his performance, and his excellent distribution of the ball could help turn defence into attack in an instant. When Roy Vernon relinquished the club captaincy in the summer of 1963 Kay – by then a full England international – was named as his successor after less than a year with the club. Yet before he had the chance to inspire Everton to more success and further his international career, everything went horribly wrong.

The other acquisition the ever wily Catterick made was Rangers winger Alex Scott. Catterick's eleventh-hour rendezvous in February secured Scott's services from under the noses of Spurs for £40,000, a winning conclusion to one of the fiercest, most closely fought transfer battles of the decade. The chubby winger's ability to demolish an opposing defence with his direct running and deadly accurate crosses soon made him a favourite with the Goodison terraces and earned him the nickname 'Chico' – from a TV company who were screening a promotion that starred a cut-out figure of a Mexican Indian. On match days many Chico cut-outs found their way to Goodison. In his five-year Everton career, Scott tormented opposing full backs with abandon: if they marked him tightly, he would knock the ball past them and run on to it; if they stood back, he would cut inside and run through the available space. Scott exploited indecision mercilessly and had a degree of consistency almost unparalleled among widemen.

When 'the freeze' ended, Everton had slipped down behind Spurs and Leicester, though they had games in hand. A 2–0 win over Nottingham Forest on 9 March 1963 kept the ball rolling, and the disappointment of going out in the fifth round of the FA Cup to West Ham a week later was overcome with a 3–0 win over Ipswich Town, who were now occupying a relegation spot. After that, Young was buoyant: 'It reminded Tottenham and Leicester that Everton are far from finished as far as this season's League Championship is concerned. I think our chances of lifting the First Division title are extremely good.'[7] A 2–1 victory at Blackpool on 6 April brought Everton up to 47 points, with Leicester and Spurs ahead of them on 48, although Everton had a game in hand on both. A draw and then a win, with Birmingham on Easter Monday and the day after, maintained the tempo, bringing Everton level with Spurs on points and games played, and one behind Leicester's tally of 51, when Everton met Spurs on 20 April 1963.

Sixty-seven and a half thousand people packed into Goodison to watch this tense, tightly balanced contest. The two sides had drawn 0–0 at White Hart Lane in December, but this game was more open than the eventual scoreline suggests. Gabriel shadowed Greaves wherever the England man went, and the striker escaped the attention of the Scot just once, early on, when with only West to beat, he shot tamely wide to cheers of relief and derision.

Moments later, Meagan cleared down the left to Kay. He played the ball down the wing to Vernon, who centred a cross for Young, and he rose above Smith to put Everton in front. More than thirty years later, lifelong Blue George Orr published his experiences as an Evertonian. He was watching from the Bullens Road paddock, but later discovered that the roar was heard as far away as his home in Hertford Road, Bootle. 'My brother, who is a Kopite, was sitting on the front step outside our house,' he recalled. 'He said he heard the noise and was sick because he knew what it meant: it meant that we were on our way to becoming champions.'[8]

Young almost added to his tally twice: first, when his delicate lob towards the far post was expertly tipped over by the back-pedalling Brown; next, when he hit the ball over from six yards. Morrissey's shot beat Brown and hit the inside of the Tottenham post and he had to watch as Stevens hit the rebound on to the opposite upright.

Kay was having a superb match, orchestrating the Everton attacks from deep and breaking up Tottenham's forays into the Everton half. Shortly after half-time, he sent Vernon clear and his pass across the mouth of the gaping goal evaded Young's boot by inches. Everton's forwards were missing chances as quickly as they were being manufactured, yet they held on to the single-goal lead, and returned to the top of the Football League for the first time since the freeze.

A midweek draw with Arsenal – in which West suffered a shoulder injury that was to keep him out for the remaining four games of the season (although he played gamely on against the Gunners) – extended their lead at the top by a further point. West Ham were the next opponents, and with Everton seeking to atone for the FA Cup disappointment, they got off to the worst possible start when Meagan put Everton behind with an own goal on 20 minutes. This was the cue for inspiration from Young. Twelve minutes after going behind, Young flicked the ball on to Vernon who controlled and shot past Standon in one movement to bring the scores level. Just before half-time, Temple – playing only his second game of the season – put Everton in front. Young had back-heeled Kay's pass to Scott and he shot so powerfully that Standon was unable to hold on to the ball and Temple gleefully swept it home. Everton weathered a West Ham onslaught in the second half with cool efficiency, marshalled brilliantly by Kay. 'He was dynamic in everything he did,' raved the *Liverpool Echo*. 'His passes were accurate and to his great credit not once did he show dissent, either by gesture or action, when there were occasional provocative moments.'

On 4 May a single Vernon goal against Bolton beat the Trotters 1–0 and kept Everton three points clear of Spurs. Leicester were now all but out of the title race after a 1–2 defeat at West Bromwich Albion. Everton, however, made no such slip-up when they visited the Hawthorns three days later: they thrashed West Brom 4–0.

It still meant that Everton went into their final match, at home to Fulham on 11 May 1963, knowing that they needed a win to secure their first title in 24 years. In a match that they dominated from the opening kick to the final blow of the referee's whistle, Everton won 4–1, Vernon scoring a hat-trick and Scott adding another; 60,578 fans roared the champions to the final whistle with a chorus that could be heard at the Pier Head, some three miles away. 'Never shall I forget those final five minutes of the Fulham match,' said Young, 'when the crowd was stamping and shouting so much that my head was reeling with the noise and it seemed we could feel the playing pitch vibrating under our feet.'

After the final whistle the players completed a lap of honour and when they left the field fans turned to the directors' box with chants of adulation for Moores, the man they had berated two years earlier. The chairman described it as 'the happiest day of my life'. The players then returned: Vernon with a bottle of champagne, Kay chomping on an enormous Cuban cigar. 'This is the greatest thing that has happened to me in football so far,' said a thrilled Young, 'and I was every bit as excited as the sixty thousand fans who cheered their heads off last Saturday.'

Catterick had guided Everton to the title with a squad virtually identical to that which he had inherited. The few signings he had made had been as consistently excellent – Stevens was one of only two ever-presents – as they were timely. Moreover, he had strengthened the players' desire to succeed and overseen their transition from promising hopefuls to top-grade stars. West, Gabriel and Morrissey were the most obvious examples, but Brian Labone went a step further: he became the first Everton player since the war to be capped for England. Kay followed in his footsteps a month after the end of the season, collecting his solitary international honour against Switzerland.

Championship won, Catterick gave his men the double goal of retaining it the following season *and* winning the European Cup. Once more the summer was conspicuous for its lack of transfer activity, and again Catterick made a new signing during the first week of the new campaign, paying Partick Thistle £38,000 for their defender Alexander 'Sandy' Brown. He provided Goodison with eight years of loyal, reliable, if unspectacular service, filling a variety of roles in the Everton defence without ever making one position his own, something that was more down to the excellence of his team-mates than any fundamental flaw in his play. Indeed, Brown would probably have walked into most other First Division sides in his favoured role of overlapping full back. He was a popular character, both on the terraces and in the dressing room, even if his name later became best known for a moment of madness in the cauldron of a derby encounter.

However, Brown had a nightmare début, at home to Burnley on 7 September 1963. The Clarets streamed to a 4–1 half-time lead, eventually holding out for a 4–3 win and inflicting Catterick's first home defeat in two years. It was characteristic of some of the inconsistencies that plagued Everton's league form during the first half of the 1963/4 season. The campaign had opened with the Charity Shield and a 4–0 thrashing of FA Cup winners Manchester United. Ten days later Everton had travelled to Old Trafford in the league and been mauled 5–1. In December Manchester United came to Goodison for the return fixture – just a week after Everton had been hammered 0–6 by Arsenal – and went away beaten 4–0 by the School of Science. It gave Everton a Christmas position of sixth, creditable enough but a far cry from the lofty heights of the previous year.

By then Everton had had their first taste of European football's most glittering prize, the Champions' Cup. Progress was always likely to be difficult when they had the misfortune of being drawn to play Italian giants, Inter Milan. Nevertheless, there was an element of optimism going into the first leg of the tie at Goodison that the

Italians could somehow be upset, but everyone saw the necessity of scoring before they went to Italy. 'We need to build up at least a two-goal lead to give us a chance in the second leg,' said Young. 'This will not be easy for we all know that, if the trend for European competition in recent years is any guide, Milan will arrive here in a defensive frame of mind.'

The build-up to the home leg on 18 September was one of high excitement. The Lord Mayor of Liverpool held a civic reception for the visitors; the *Echo* published a souvenir edition of the paper; and thousands of Liverpool fans promised to turn up. Helenio Herrera, Inter's famous Argentinian-born manager, had visited Goodison for the Burnley match, and paid tribute to the crowd – Everton's 'magnificent twelfth man' – adding that Inter would play for the draw.

Herrera's promise for a defensive game was kidology. While the Italians gave a superb performance at the back, all but blanking out Vernon and Young, cutting off the supply from Temple and Scott, they were lightning quick on the break and their Brazilian winger, Jair, provided a constant threat. Three times he went close, and on a fourth occasion, following a superb 40-yard shot from Suarez, only Harris's last-ditch interception prevented a goal. With 10 minutes to go Vernon gave a brief rush of excitement to the 62,000-strong Everton crowd when his shot hit the back of the Inter net, but he was judged offside and the game ended deadlocked.

A week later the Everton team flew to Milan, accompanied by 130 fans who had each paid £26 for a charter flight from Speke airport, hotel accommodation and a match ticket. A storm delayed take-off and they did not arrive in Italy until 4.32 a.m. Catterick brought 15 players, including full back Roy Parnell, utility man Barry Rees, and Colin Harvey, an 18-year-old inside forward whom even 'fans of the club have scarcely heard of', noted the *Liverpool Echo*.

Herrera had confidently told journalists at Goodison that the match would be a walkover when Everton played on Italian soil, a suggestion that irked Catterick. 'Herrera is entitled to dismiss us as nothing,' he said, 'but I have my own opinion and it is that we are a good side and will be hard to beat. I am not despondent.' To widespread surprise, Catterick included the unknown Harvey – who had travelled to Milan believing that he would merely be helping with the luggage – in his starting line-up. It turned out to be a tightly fought, rough-and-tumble match with Inter emerging as narrow winners. Jair, who had caused so much trouble with his pace at Goodison, scored the only goal after 46 minutes to knock Everton out. However, Catterick's side emerged with a good deal of credit, and Scott and Harvey each went close with chances: Scott after running through the Inter defence on a 40-yard dribble but failing to match his brilliance in running with a finish of similar calibre; Harvey – who, the *Echo* reported, 'could look back upon his first senior game with some pride since he fought hard [and] played at times with veteran coolness' – twice went close with overhead kicks. Even Herrera admitted his team had faced a tough test. 'Everton were bound to play this game defensively as we did at Goodison Park, and until the interval I wasn't sure whether they were going to succeed or not.'

Out of the European Cup, Everton had the opportunity a month later to prove that they were Britain's finest when they met Glasgow Rangers in the two-legged British Championship match. The tie was taken rather less seriously in Liverpool than it was north of the border, where it was assumed that the English would be shown a footballing lesson. Everton arrived at Ibrox on 27 November 1963 to chants of 'Easy, easy, easy,' from the Rangers fans. Defending tightly, they punished the Glaswegians on the break, with efforts by Scott and Young silencing their over-confident compatriots and sandwiching a goal by Temple. Everton left Ibrox 3–1 victors. The return at Goodison was marred by crowd violence. Scottish fans in the Upper Bullens stand rained bottles and other ammunition on to those unfortunate enough to be in the paddock, and on to the pitch. Everton drew 1–1 through a Young goal to take the contest 4–2 on aggregate.

With the arrival of 1964 Everton made fitful progress to the upper echelons of the First Division. It was not, however, without some unpopular decisions by Catterick. Young had missed half a dozen games during January and February through injury and Catterick had experimented with Temple, Gabriel and the rookie Barry Rees in the hallowed number-nine shirt. After six games on the sidelines, the Golden Vision returned for a 4–2 win at home to Aston Villa on 28 February and an inspired win over league leaders Tottenham by the same scoreline at White Hart Lane a week later. All looked to be well with Everton, now in sight of the top of the table and finally hitting a rich vein of form. Not for Catterick, though.

The Monday after the Spurs game, Everton's manager shocked English football by smashing the British domestic transfer record when he bought Blackburn Rovers striker Fred Pickering for £85,000. Although neither as quick as Vernon nor as skilful as Young, Pickering, a converted left back who had found his niche leading the Blackburn attack, had a dangerously hard right-foot shot, which had earned him the nickname 'Boomer'. A tireless worker, he could unlock the tightest of defences by outrunning them and finding gaps, which he exploited mercilessly. Blackburn fans, who had also seen Vernon leave them for Goodison almost exactly four years earlier, were understandably frustrated and angry at the departure of the man whose goals had transformed them from mediocre nonentities into Championship dark horses. Many Evertonians – knowing that their signing would replace Young or, at the very least, break up the Scot's prolific partnership with Vernon – greeted his arrival with similar bemusement.

Yet Pickering marked his début in spectacular fashion, scoring a hat-trick in the seemingly annual 6–1 thrashing of Nottingham Forest, now managed by Johnny Carey. Despite the win, which lifted Everton to second, fans were unhappy about Young's absence. A last-minute goal by Temple on Pickering's return to Blackburn, a week later, which stole a 2–1 win, meant that Everton were top with 46 points. Beneath them, on 44, were Spurs and Liverpool, although, respectively, they had played one and two games fewer than Everton. West Bromwich Albion were Friday-night visitors to Goodison on 27 March, but Everton could not break them down and came out with a 1–1 draw. 'Everton looked ordinary; certainly not a championship team,' said the *Echo*. After the match a crowd demonstrated in front of the directors' box chanting, 'We want Young, we want Young.'

Twenty-four hours later the Golden Vision was back, heading home three minutes from the end to seal a 3–1 win over Blackpool, which kept Everton at the top. Liverpool, however, had closed the gap to just a point.

The next Tuesday – 31 March – Everton travelled to the Hawthorns for the return match with West Bromwich Albion. Here, an appalling defensive performance cost them dear, and they slunk away having been defeated 2–4. Catterick was defiant: 'We have been written off about six times already. I expect this will be the seventh, but we shall keep on pegging away, match by match, and see what happens then.'

The reality facing Catterick was that Liverpool's 3–1 win over Spurs a night earlier meant that not only had Liverpool replaced Everton at the First Division summit but their neighbours needed just seven points from their last six games to be crowned champions. The next Saturday Everton lost 2–3 at lowly Stoke, while Liverpool beat Manchester United 3–0 at Anfield. A scrambled draw on 11 April with Wolves virtually assured Liverpool of their title, which they confirmed a week later. However, the morning after Everton had played Wolves, worse news arrived.

On Sunday 12 April 1964 the *Sunday People* printed allegations that a number of players had received bribes to 'throw' games. To the astonishment of everyone involved with Everton, Tony Kay was named as one of them. The allegations, relating to his time at Sheffield Wednesday, were made by Jimmy Gauld, a one-time inside forward who had made a handful of appearances for Everton during the 1950s. Gauld had alleged that three Wednesday players – Kay, Peter Swann and David Layne – had accepted bribes to throw Wednesday's match with Ipswich Town in December 1962. Kay reportedly told the *People* that he had been convinced Ipswich would win anyway. 'It was money for old rope,' he allegedly said. Ipswich had indeed won 2–0, but Kay had won the man-of-the-match award and even the *People* – who were undoubtedly out to get him – acknowledged that he had 'put up a fine performance'.

Everton suspended him and he denied the comments attributed to him. 'It is a load of nonsense. I would never throw a match, no matter how much was offered me. I have too much to lose . . . I live for football and I would never do anything to stop me from playing.' Nevertheless the *People* passed their files to the Director of Public Prosecutions and the case was brought to court.

Nine months later, on 26 January 1965, Kay was sent to prison for four months for his part in the scandal and subsequently banned for life by the Football Association. The ban was lifted in 1974, by which time his best days were long past and he never again played beyond amateur level.

Harry Catterick was as bemused as anybody else by the case. Not only had he lost his captain for a crime committed at another club, but he had also lost the then huge £55,000 transfer fee. Although a notoriously strict disciplinarian, he said that the punishments meted out by the courts and the FA were 'far too severe for the offence'. He added, 'I read three newspaper reports for the match in which the offence was alleged to have been committed and Kay had rave notices.'

The sad irony was that the sum Kay received – less than £100 – would have been eclipsed within weeks by the signing-on fee, probably in the region of £3000, that he would have received on his arrival at Goodison.

Everyone associated with Everton was astounded by what had happened. That such an astute, tireless, committed performer, who had never been known to give less than 100 per cent for his team, could be charged and jailed for such a crime seemed, and still does seem, inconceivable to fans and fellow players alike.

One fan, Charles Mills's eldest son, Charles junior, was nearly twelve and had been a Goodison regular for seven years when Kay was jailed: 'It was one of the first occasions I felt real injustice. I was obviously biased, but I remember thinking, "How can you have thrown this game if you were man-of-the-match?" Even then – whether this is a chip on the Evertonian shoulder I'm not sure – I thought that they were after us. It may have had something to do with the aloofness of the club relative to Liverpool. Everton were never perceived as welcoming or warm-hearted, plus you had the 'Merseyside Millionaires' tag – they were there to be shot down. It was something that happened elsewhere and Everton suffered. It was one of a series of tragedies in the post-war history of Everton Football Club, which seriously hampered their progress at crucial times.'

Not only had Kay played his last game for the club, it seemed as the 1963/4 season drew to its close – with Everton finishing third and Liverpool champions – that Young's days there were numbered. After losing his place in the first team to Pickering, he had requested a transfer, which, after due consideration, the directors accepted at the season's end. The fans, who had come to idolize him, didn't want him to go and neither did Young. (He was the most modest of individuals yet quietly revelled in the adulation – he kept in his wallet a photograph, sent by a fan, of a wall bearing the legend 'Alex Young the Great'.) Joe Mercer's Aston Villa were rumoured to have a strong interest in the Golden Vision, but when the 1964/5 season opened

Young was still an Everton player and, moreover, making up a three-pronged forward line with Vernon and Pickering.

In fact, it was not Young whom 'Boomer' Pickering replaced, but his long-time forward partner, Vernon. The Welshman made just 16 appearances in the 1964/5 season, scoring only three times, and was sold on to Stoke City at the end of that campaign. He never scaled the heights he had once climbed with Everton and, after playing briefly with Halifax Town, retired from the game in 1969. His superb acceleration, rocket shot and lively personality made him Alex Young's favourite strike partner and the Scotsman later said of him, 'We were up front together for about three years and hit it off together pretty quickly and were a good foil for each other.' Always a heavy smoker and a bad trainer, Vernon once – tongue perhaps in cheek – claimed he was among the three best strikers in the game, along with Greaves and Law. A little less indulgence in his vices might well have proved him right.

Although Young withdrew his transfer request, he endured a miserable 1964/5 season, making just a handful more appearances than Vernon and concluding the campaign with the same measly haul of goals. The problem was injury and, more specifically, his unnaturally soft feet – which earned him the tag Tenderfoot; they were exceedingly prone to blisters and kept Young out for large tracts of the season. Nothing could rid him of the problem. When his devoted followers became aware of his affliction, 'My home and the club offices were absolutely deluged with letters giving me advice on just what to do in order to get back into the soccer scene,' he later remembered.[9] One fan suggested he paddle on Crosby beach three times a day, to benefit from the salt water, and another that he wrap his feet in newspaper. Others suggested rubbing them with a lemon, or even a potato.

Pickering was the star of the season, scoring 37 times in 51 league and Cup games, which earned him three England caps, the first of which came against the USA when he scored a hat-trick. Everton finished fourth, too far off the pace to mount a serious title challenge. It was a campaign of consolidation, with Catterick adding a number of new players to the Everton set-up.

Brian Harris reclaimed the number-six shirt from the disgraced Kay and played with the consummate pride and dedication that had characterized his play before he had been forced into the periphery

in December 1962. Those Evertonians who had been unable to travel
to the San Siro in September 1963 had had to wait a further six
months before they caught a glimpse of Harvey in a first-team shirt,
but during the 1964/5 season he established himself in the Everton
midfield, bringing poise and elegance to the side. Harvey's progress
edged out Dennis Stevens, who was eventually sold to Oldham in
December 1965 for £20,000. Later he played for Tranmere Rovers
and made his last professional appearance against Everton in an FA
Cup fifth-round tie at Goodison in March 1968.

Another senior professional whose chances had been limited by
the progress of a promising youngster was Alex Parker. He started
the 1964/5 season as club captain, but lost his place to Tommy
Wright and moved to Southport, where he was reunited with his
former team-mate Bingham, who had recently been installed as Haig
Avenue manager. Wright, a converted inside forward, was to provide
nine years of distinguished, dependable and fiercely brave service,
earning 11 England caps, and league and FA Cup winners' medals.

On the other flank of defence, Huddersfield Town's England
international left back Ray Wilson had been bought in the summer
of 1964. In an era when 'freedom of contract' was still an unknown
phrase, lowly Huddersfield Town had managed to hold on to him
until he was 29 before cashing in on their prized asset, who was by
then recognized as one of the most complete full backs in the world.
Even in the Second Division his calm, collected and fluent style of
play had attracted the attention of international selectors, who gave
him the first of his 63 England caps against Scotland in 1960. Wilson
possessed a change of pace more commonly found in attacking
players, which enabled him to stick like glue to opponents, and he
was blessed with the ability to either jockey them out of possession or
dispossess them with the crispest tackles. He had a strong tactical
awareness and was blessed with precise and imaginative distribution,
never playing a team-mate into trouble or making an ungainly hoof
into the back of the stands. Nevertheless, his Goodison career got off
to a shaky start and a hip injury sustained in only his second game at
the club limited him to just 21 first-team outings in his first season.
Despite the injury problems the class that had attracted Harry
Catterick to him was immediately evident.

The steady progress of the 1964/5 season carried over into the
following campaign, and Catterick continued to chop and change his

side in search of the winning formula. While youngsters like Harvey and Wright were getting the chance to cement their places in the starting line-up and other stars of the future – such as John Hurst and Jimmy Husband – were making names for themselves, his decisions were not always popular or, for that matter, winning ones.

On Saturday 15 January 1966 Everton met Blackpool at Bloomfield Road. With it came an incident that epitomized Catterick's managerial style and spoke volumes for the way in which many Everton fans regarded both him and their hero Young. Despite flashes of early-season brilliance, such as a hat-trick in the 5–1 demolition of Sheffield Wednesday on 31 August, there were creeping signs of complacency in Young's play. With an FA Cup third-round tie with Sunderland the following week being Everton's only remaining avenue to silverware, Catterick deemed it provident to give the Scot a short, sharp shock to kick-start his season back into action. He dropped him.

A gangly 16-year-old, who later replaced Young as the fans' hero and even further down the line managed the club to FA Cup glory, filled the Golden Vision's hallowed place in the Everton line-up. His name was Joe Royle. It was an inauspicious start to his career, with Everton falling to a 0–2 defeat against a poor side. After the game, visiting Evertonians were in uproar, and some decided to stay by the team coach to protest at Young's omission. Eventually the players came out to be greeted with rancour, which increased in volume when the manager appeared. As Catterick was about to get on board, there was a surge forward and he was jostled to the ground. The following day's newspapers were full of stories about the incident. 'I feel a bit sore this morning in more ways than one,' he told reporters at Bellefield, Everton's training ground, on Monday. 'But I'm all right. I am more concerned at the distress it caused my wife, who heard it on the radio before I arrived home.' Nevertheless, Catterick's reminder to Young of his fallibility worked wonders and he was back to his best the following weekend when Everton met Sunderland. Young scored in a 3–0 win, and Everton were set on the path towards Wembley.

Yet the matter was – and remains – extraordinary. On the one hand there was the manhandling of the individual who had led Everton to an almost unprecedented spell in the upper echelons of the First Division; who had promised winning football to Evertonians and provided it; and was shaping a side for still more success. On the other there was the sheer level of anguish felt at Alex Young's omission. Incredible talent though he was – his genius had repeatedly bedevilled opponents in his five years at Goodison – he had not been firing on all cylinders for some weeks. As such, Catterick had every right to drop him, perhaps more than when he had bought Pickering two years earlier. However, Young was no ordinary player, no standard hero even.

Everton's FA Cup third-round victory saw them pitted at non-league Bedford Town in the Fourth Round. A 3–0 win there and a victory by the same scoreline in the fifth round against Coventry City led them to a tough quarter-final meeting away at Manchester City. A goalless draw at Maine Road was followed by a second at Goodison before another replay was staged at neutral Molineux on 5 April. On a muddy pitch, Everton struggled to find their composure in the first 20 minutes, but the return of Gabriel from illness aided the drive of the team and tightened the back line. When Everton took the lead in the thirty-seventh minute it was against the run of play, but finished City's hopes of victory. From Scott's floating free kick Temple timed his run expertly to beat the offside trap and hit a superb volley shot past Dowd. A second goal followed just prior to half-time. Harris's chip over the City defence found Pickering, who struck a fierce shot past Dowd to continue the remarkable record for both him and Temple of having scored in every round.

With Everton's hopes of the Championship long since extinguished and aspirations of European qualification all but over, all attention was focused on the FA Cup. So much so that they were later fined £2000 for fielding a weakened team against Leeds United the week before the semi-final. Everton had been drawn to meet Manchester United at Bolton, a fixture that was viewed with even more fortitude after Pickering had limped off injured against Sheffield United two weeks earlier and was still to recover. Replacing him was Mike Trebilcock, a 21-year-old Cornishman for whom Catterick had paid Plymouth Argyle £20,000 earlier in the season.

Interest in the semi-final was enormous. Fans had slept overnight in their cars to gain admittance to Burnden Park, with considerable crowds forming outside the ground from 7 a.m.; British Rail laid on extra trains from Liverpool Exchange station to cope with the extra numbers. Ominously it was Bolton's biggest crowd since the 1947 disaster, when 33 people had died. Indeed, Burnden Park was ill-equipped to deal with the huge attendance and at half-time the fencing gave way in one corner of the ground and hundreds watched the second half sitting on the cinder track that circled the pitch.

Until then they had seen only a sloppy Everton performance characterized by poor defending and stray passes. In the second half they built up momentum but chances were still sparse. With 12 minutes remaining Everton took the lead. From Wilson's clearance, Young back-headed to Temple. He darted down the left before switching the ball to the unmarked Harvey, who let fly with a low shot into the corner of Harry Gregg's net. It was the goal that sent Everton back to Wembley after an interval of 33 years.

In the final, Everton were to meet Catterick's old club, Sheffield Wednesday, on 14 May. For Evertonians, the big worry was getting hold of tickets. With only 15,000 available, the club allocated them to fans whose season tickets ended in certain digits. On the day they announced the lucky numbers, Evertonians held their breath. 'I remember being at school and listening to a radio at lunchtime with my mates,' recalled Charles Mills junior. 'Three of us in the group got them . . . others weren't so lucky.' Those who weren't were left to barter, blag and beg. Others relied on contacts within the club. 'My father was the ticket man,' said Charles junior. 'He used to work at the market in town, which was a bit like Liverpool's Covent Garden. There were all sorts of characters there, and some of the footballers used to drink in the pubs nearby. We were going in a coach from our church, and I still don't know how he did it, but he got tickets for everyone in our party.'

Everton still had three league games to play before the final and Pickering played in each of them; Tommy Wright – who had also missed the semi – two. It was naturally assumed that both would take their places in the starting eleven when the big day came. Yet a week before the final, Catterick hinted that Pickering should presume nothing, telling journalists: 'I feel he is not playing with the confidence he was showing in his play before he was injured.'[10]

Given Catterick's reputation for pulling surprises, nobody knew what to expect. Yet when he announced the 11 men to face Wednesday there was shock and some consternation when Pickering (England international, 107 Everton appearances, 68 goals) was dropped and Trebilcock (Cornish rookie, eight Everton appearances, two goals) picked ahead of him. Pickering was understandably 'angry and upset' at his omission. Sandy Brown was more accepting: he had deputized for Wright – against United playing to 'the limit of his ability', according to Young, and clearing off the line from Law with three minutes remaining. True to character, he shrugged that it was merely 'part of the game'.

London was awash with the blue and white of both clubs on the day of the final. Peter Mills, Charles's other son, was then aged 10. The event left a lasting impression on him. 'It was a big day,' he recollected, 'thirty-three years since we'd last been in the final. It was a twenty-four-hour day – we left at six in the morning and got back around the same time the next day. One of the blokes, a guy called Jack Fleming, was the only man to walk to and from Wembley. We had this coach, and from the minute we left to the minute we got back, he never sat down once. Up and down he'd walk, chatting and joking, up and down.'

Many fans had travelled to London on overnight buses that arrived not long after dawn and some, killing time in Hyde Park, bumped into Muhammad Ali out on an early-morning run. Hundreds more turned up at Downing Street to meet the Prime Minister, Harold Wilson, whose constituency was Huyton in Liverpool. True to form, Wilson came down to meet them.

Come three o'clock, Catterick's gamble appeared to have failed. Just four minutes after kick-off, Jim McCalliog put Wednesday in front. Everton struggled to break down the Yorkshiremen and went in at half-time still a goal down. 'I have never known a dressing room so quiet,' Catterick revealed later. 'The players were slumped on the benches – they couldn't believe what had had happened to them. Some of them were getting on a bit and I can remember saying, "I'm looking round this dressing room and I can't see many people who are coming back here. This must be your last chance of winning a Cup winners' medal at Wembley. What are you going to do about it? Go out there and roll your sleeves up. I'm not asking for more ability, you've got that. I'm just asking for a bit more determination."'[11]

Things failed to improve after the restart. Everton's chances remained few and the midfield was struggling to provide ammunition for the attack. Then, on 59 minutes, disaster struck. David Ford scored Sheffield Wednesday's second: 0–2. With only half an hour left, Everton's task seemed hopeless.

Nobody, however, had banked on Mike Trebilcock.

Within two minutes he had pulled a goal back, driving the ball past Springett from Temple's knock-down. Three minutes later he had pulled the scores level, knocking home Scott's free kick from close range.

Evertonians on the brink of despair just minutes earlier were suddenly in Dreamland. 'Once they'd scored,' remembered Peter Mills, 'it was never in doubt. It was like flicking on a switch.' For one fan – Eddie Kavanagh – it was too much and he famously made his way on to the Wembley turf, with a mazy run that would have done Alex Scott proud, evading the attentions of chasing policemen who groped forlornly at his empty coat, in order to congratulate his heroes. The image of the ecstatic Kavanagh trying to hug Labone, with the grinning Brian Harris trying on one of the fallen policemen's hats, was to be one of the afternoon's most enduring.

With 10 minutes to go the ball slipped away from the control of Wednesday centre half, Gerry Young, on the half-way line and into the path of Derek Temple. 'As soon as he got that ball,' recalled Dick White, who had travelled down with the Mills family, 'I knew he'd score. Temple was lethal from that position.'

'As Gerry was the centre half, I knew there was nobody behind him except the goalkeeper, Ron Springett,' remembered Temple. 'I also knew that I would be expected to score. I was helped by the fact that Springett did not come far off his line. As I got to the edge of the penalty area, I aimed for the far post, and although the keeper got his fingers to the ball, he could not keep it out of the net.' It was the concluding goal in one of the most dramatic turnarounds in FA Cup Final history.

Shortly after, Trebilcock could have completed his hat-trick. A mistake by Megson let in Young and with only Springett in front of him, he unselfishly squared to Trebilcock, who, instead of shooting first time, tried unsuccessfully to take the ball round the Wednesday keeper. It didn't matter, the game had already been won. Moments later the referee Jack Taylor blew the final whistle, which ensured Everton's first FA Cup win in 33 years, sparking wild celebrations in Wembley and on Merseyside.

Catterick, who had risked his entire reputation by including Trebilcock, was ecstatic, claiming it to be 'the thrill of my footballing life'. Years later, in semi-retirement, he reflected: 'That was my greatest moment. The Cup hadn't been to Everton for many years and it was wonderful to bring it back to Merseyside and receive the acclaim of the crowds as we returned to the city.'[12]

At the post-match banquet the club presented its players with gold watches, and they were joined by members of the 1933 FA Cup-winning side – minus Warney Cresswell who was ill, and Jimmy Dunn, who had died. 'I think Alex Young had a great match,' said an elated Dixie Dean. 'He did everything right for me.' Albert Geldard was equally generous in his praise, saying of his successor on the Everton flank: 'Derek Temple's goal was one of the greatest I've seen. Those sort of openings can be missed so easily.' Joe Mercer, who had been on the first-team fringes in 1933, was still struggling to come to terms with what he had witnessed. 'I still can't believe how they got off the floor to win,' he said. 'For an hour, an Everton victory was not on, but it was the greatest Wembley recovery ever. They didn't play well, but what a final it turned out in the end.'

Two months later Ray Wilson was back at Wembley, this time in the white of England in the World Cup Final against Germany. It might well have turned out to be his finest hour, the day his name was immortalized in national legend, but he had definitely played better games. With only 13 minutes played, Held floated in a strong centre. Wilson was so well placed that his nearest opponent Haller never even attempted to close him down. Yet his uncharacteristically poor header fell at Haller's feet and he made no mistake in putting the Germans a goal ahead. It was later revealed that a furious Nobby Stiles shouted across to him: 'In the fourteen years I have been playing with and against you, the first time you make a fucking mistake is in a World Cup Final!' History has fortunately forgotten Wilson's mistake, and Hurst's hat-trick was to bring England their most famous victory and Everton their first World Cup winner.

Little over a month later, Wilson and Liverpool's Roger Hunt paraded the Jules Rimet trophy in front of the 63,329-strong crowd who had assembled at Goodison to watch the Charity Shield meeting between the FA Cup winners and the previous season's champions. Liverpool won by a single Hunt goal, but his solitary effort did not do justice to the extent of Liverpool's dominance. 'Liverpool almost walked the ball through,' wrote Leslie Edwards in the *Liverpool Echo*. 'Everton were always struggling; always making the inaccurate passes which let in their opponents for another spell of command of the ball and their opponents.'[13]

Again, Catterick had not made a significant pre-season signing, but two days after watching his Everton team outclassed by their neighbours he entered the transfer market again. The man he brought to Goodison was Blackpool's 21-year-old World Cup winner, Alan Ball. Once more Catterick broke the British transfer record, shelling out £112,000 for the feisty midfielder.

Ball had long been the hottest property in British football and the World Cup win had only added to his fame. Ball's father, Alan Ball senior, who had himself been a professional footballer with Southport, Birmingham City and Oldham Athletic, and was now manager of Stoke City, had long ago decided that his son would be the player he had always endeavoured to be. Throughout his son's upbringing, everything had centred on football and Alan junior grew up a driven, fiercely ambitious individual. He was signed by Blackpool at 15, and promised his father he would make his international début by his twentieth birthday. It was a pledge he met with three days to spare, against Yugoslavia in May 1965. A year later he was providing the cross for one of Hurst's three goals in the World Cup Final.

By then the ambitious youngster had decided that a crumbling Bloomfield Road and meagre crowds were no stage for one of the world's finest players. His pursuit of glory would come to nothing in the tangerine shirt of Blackpool and a higher level was needed. As he later put it: 'It was fame not fortune, which concerned me most . . . If you like, I was big-headed enough to think that I could come to be acknowledged as one of the world's finest footballers – if not the world's best – and this was a reputation I couldn't win, so long as I stayed at Blackpool.'[14]

Leeds United's Don Revie was Ball's biggest admirer and made no secret of his desire to bring him to Elland Road. All along he was favourite to land the midfielder, and during the summer of 1966 column inches were filled with speculation as to when Leeds would sign Ball and how much they would need to pay to take him away from Lancashire.

Catterick was an admirer too. The difference was that nobody – least of all Ball – had any inkling of it.

On the Monday after the Charity Shield (14 August) Catterick and his chairman E. Holland-Hughes turned up at Blackpool, apparently unexpectedly. An impromptu meeting ensued between Ball, his manager Ronnie Suart and the two Everton men. They agreed to Blackpool's price, then Catterick was allowed to hold further talks with Ball. He laid out his offer of a contract, its duration, the amount Everton were willing to pay and the role he envisaged for Ball in his Everton team. He impressed upon him the 6 p.m. deadline for eligibility in the European Cup Winners' Cup campaign. In short, the Everton manager had cornered both Blackpool and Ball. The Seasiders had not envisaged their price tag being met, and although Revie had caught wind of the deal, they were wary of opening negotiations with another club, lest the whole sale fall through. Catterick got his man as Revie was speeding towards Blackpool for an unsolicited appointment with Suart.

Catterick later revealed that he had allowed the football world to think Everton could not be considered contenders for Ball's signature, and let the press make out that it was a one-horse race. When previously questioned on the matter, he had merely told journalists with characteristic aloofness: 'Ball is a fair player.' At the same time, he made Suart assure him that Everton would have first option on Ball. It was a carbon copy of the Alex Scott transfer, when it had been assumed that he was to sign for Spurs. Before the new season was out, he was to pull off another transfer coup of equal magnitude.

Everton began the 1966/7 season in winning form, with Ball grabbing the only goal of the game on his début away at Fulham on the first Saturday. The next Tuesday they lost 1–2 at home to Manchester United, but that was quickly forgotten as minds focused on the following Saturday's meeting with Liverpool at Goodison.

Ball was one of just three changes in the line-up of two weeks earlier, coming in in place of Gerry Glover, while Morrissey came in for Scott and Pickering for Trebilcock. Nevertheless it was Ball who made the telling difference to the previous lethargic display. According to Catterick, his arrival had already lifted the standard of the other players' contributions by 10 per cent and the turn-around in events from just two weeks earlier was indicative of the newcomer's influence.

After only 10 minutes he had put Everton ahead, finishing off a Johnny Morrissey shot, which had deflected into his path; seven minutes later, he took advantage of a mix-up between Ron Yeats and

Gordon Milne and crashed the ball into the roof of the net to put Everton 2–0 up. 'When the second one went in,' Ball said, 'I'd never heard so many people singing my name or encouraging me like that in my life – even by comparison with the World Cup – and I've never experienced it again.' Despite a Tommy Smith goal, Liverpool could not force a comeback and Sandy Brown sealed a 3–1 victory seven minutes from time.

Everton made steady progress in improving on Catterick's worst finish to a season since he had taken charge. It was clear to all Evertonians that in Ball they had a new hero. His effect on some other players was arguably more than the 10 per cent Catterick had spoken of. For instance, some Evertonians had been slow in taking to Colin Harvey in his early first-team days, in particular criticizing his rashness in front of goal and sometimes his work rate. A combination of relentless dedication on the training pitch and Ball's work rate in the centre of the park elevated Harvey's game to the extent that when 1967 came round it was considered only a matter of time before he, too, would link up with Ball in the England midfield.

When Everton were drawn to face Liverpool in the fifth round of the FA Cup on 11 March 1967, Ball had the opportunity to reaffirm his status as the scourge of Anfield. Interest in the match was greater than ever, with Liverpool beaming the match live on to cinema screens at Anfield. Mile-long queues formed for both sets of tickets as soon as they went on sale. To add spice to the occasion, Catterick signed Preston North End's young midfielder, Howard Kendall, from under Bill Shankly's nose on the eve of the match.

Ball took his opportunity with relish. His angled volley was the only goal of the match and brought a roar of elation from Everton supporters. 'I think it was Gordon Milne who mis-hit the back pass,' Ball later said. 'The wind held it up and it looked like it was going out. I thought, "You lucky devil, you've got away with that." But the wind had taken it away from the goal and I just gambled and went after it. I smacked the volley from an acute angle right in the other corner. I've never hit a volley as sweetly in all my life. I finished up right in the corner by the flag, and I don't think I got away from there for about three minutes. These days, I'd have been charged with bringing the game into disrepute!'

Alex Young – whose unparalleled popularity the firebrand Ball had begun to dent – had been having a good season. Injury to

Pickering had allowed him to reclaim his number-nine shirt, after two years with the numbers eight or 10 emblazoned on his back, and he had been ever present in each of Everton's first 33 games. At 30 he had lost some of his pace, but his technical brilliance and flickers of genius more than compensated.

Injury struck him down following Everton's disappointing FA Cup quarter-final exit at the hands of Nottingham Forest a month after the Liverpool match, but when Everton met Sunderland for their final fixture of the season, Young was back. He was brilliant too, his mark clear on each of Everton's four goals, and only the team's over-confidence in trying to finish moves from close range, and a great display by Montgomery in the Sunderland goal, prevented more being scored. In the end they took the match 4–1 with Morrissey grabbing a hat-trick. 'Young spread destruction through their ranks with his wonderful ball distribution, artistry and sheer cheek,' wrote Michael Charters in the *Liverpool Echo*. 'In this he was matched by Ball and their superiority was so pronounced that they almost put on a music-hall double act at times.' According to Labone, it was the best individual performance he had ever seen from Young, and Alan Ball wanted him – not Morrissey – to have the match ball at the end. 'Young beat Sunderland almost on his own that night,' claimed Labone. 'He played on the wing and I never felt so sorry for a man as I did for the Sunderland left back. For him, it was a nightmare. For Young, it was a great personal triumph.'[15] It was the zenith of Alex Young's genius: a virtuoso display of grace and trickery.

Yet the game as a whole had changed considerably. Don Revie's Leeds United, since their promotion in 1963, had been exponents of a new style of play characterized by cynicism and defensiveness. It had introduced a new mindset into English football, not previously considered outside the context of meetings with Continental rivals in European competition. There had been defensive hatchet men from the 'reckless' Alec Dick to Herbie Roberts and Ron Yeats, but while their purpose had been to curtail individuals – men like Young – it was still a new phenomenon to try to stifle an entire team. Midfield destroyers were now in vogue: Ball himself could be – and was – used as one. More and more the likes of Young were deemed a luxury, an anachronism in the modern game. As Brian Labone put it in 1968: 'An examination of Young today is, at the same time, a joy and a sadness. A joy because he is just about the most perfect ball-playing footballer around ... but sad because for all that skill and sheer natural talent, Alex is becoming a misfit in modern soccer. He belongs to a breed that is almost extinct ... that can no longer survive and flourish in the hard-driving, hustling and ruthless business we are in now.'[16]

Young himself recognized the emerging status quo. In the 1967/8 campaign, his strike rate, which had at one time been a goal every other game, had now fallen to less than one in every four games. He was a declining force.

His last game in an Everton shirt came on 11 May 1968, a month after the screening of *The Golden Vision*, Neville Smith's BBC1 play about him. Although he lined up alongside virtually a reserve team, as Catterick rested players for the following Saturday's FA Cup Final with West Bromwich Albion, he ran the show with an imperious performance that drew loud applause even from West Ham fans.

A few weeks later Young left Everton to manage Glentoran in Northern Ireland, an unhappy experience cut short after two months. He returned to the North West and played 23 times for Stockport County, scoring five times. Edgeley Park, however, was no fit stage for a legend like Young, and when he was struck down by a knee injury at 32, he called time on his playing days.

On finishing his career he returned to Scotland. He ran a pub in West Linton for a while, then took over another in the village of Pebble Shore. After a period of unemployment, he started a soft-furnishings firm in Edinburgh. His son Jason played for a short time in the Third Division of Germany's Bundesliga, continuing the tradition boldly set by his father. In recent years a lounge was named in his honour at Goodison, and he was also named on the Football League's '100 List', two fitting tributes to an all-time great.

Back in 1968, as his time at Goodison drew to a close Young recognized the changing times in football. 'Everton, like the other top sides, have had to surrender much of the free-flowing style that was their hallmark, and adapt themselves to a tighter system in order to compete,' he wrote in his 1968 memoirs.[17] The Harvey-Kendall-Ball triumvirate had begun to blossom, thrilling Goodison with a new brand of football, but the statistics didn't lie. In both Young's first and last seasons at the club Everton had finished in fifth place with a similar amount of points. However, the goals-for-and-against columns revealed how much their pattern of play had fundamentally altered in the seven years under Catterick. In 1960/61 they had scored 87 and conceded 69, finishing with 50 points; in 1967/8, they had gained 52 points, scored 67 and conceded 40 goals. Young was appreciative of Everton's new stars, but unsure of the new path football was taking. 'I hate method,' he complained. 'It isn't my game. Football should mean the same as entertainment. Nowadays,' he lamented, 'that concept is missing.'[18]

8

The Three Graces

DESPITE HIS DOUR, often emotionless persona, Harry Catterick was a man of frequent surprises. From the inclusion of the untried Colin Harvey in Milan's San Siro, to the replacement of the seemingly untouchable Young with the gangly boy-wonder Royle, or Trebil-cock's inclusion ahead of the England international Pickering in the FA Cup Final, Catterick's first six years at Goodison had been littered with the unexpected. Yet it was in the transfer market that his machinations were the most unforeseen. One story – perhaps involv-ing the signing of Alex Scott from Rangers in 1963 – had Catterick and Harry Cooke, then a scout, at a black-tie function. Catterick told Cooke that they had to go to Scotland to sign a player. 'When? Tomorrow?' asked Cooke. 'No – now,' replied Catterick. With that the two left, still in evening dress, got snowed in on the way, spent the night sleeping in the car and signed the player the next day. The transfers involving Scott and Fred Pickering had each been a con-siderable coup, but the signing of Alan Ball from under Don Revie's nose had made Catterick's secretive buys the stuff of legend. But Catterick's *coup de grâce* was still to come.

The 1964 FA Cup Final had seen West Ham's highly attractive team, which included the core of the England side who had won the Jules Rimet trophy two years earlier, pitted against Second Division Preston North End. Many eyes, however, were turned not on West Ham's posse of emerging internationals but on Preston's brilliant young midfielder, Howard Kendall, who, at 17 years and 345 days, was the youngest player ever to appear in an FA Cup Final. West Ham won the day 3–2, but over the next couple of years Preston's youngster built on his early prominence to establish himself as one of the best players outside the top flight. For the ambitious Kendall, though, Deepdale offered little real hope of progression, although in

1964 Preston narrowly missed out on promotion. In 1965 they finished mid-table, flirted with relegation in 1966, and looked no better than a mid-table side the following season. Disillusioned, Kendall soon became the subject of transfer speculation, which, according to newspapers, linked him to Bill Shankly's Anfield. Indeed, the gossip seemed to have substance when Liverpool made an official bid in October 1966. Preston rejected it, but promised to keep Shankly abreast of developments.

Rumours, however, continued to abound. Fed up with the prospect of losing their star to Liverpool, the Deepdale crowd took to singing 'Stay away, Shankly!' Despite the potentially unsettling rumours, Kendall still shone. Then, on Friday 10 March 1967, as Merseyside braced itself for its FA Cup fifth-round derby, the inevitable seemed to have happened. 'Kendall Signs!' screamed the *Liverpool Echo* billboards. Expectant Liverpudlians rushing to seek confirmation of Shankly's purchase were in for a surprise. He had joined Everton.

Catterick had again hijacked a deal, this time stealing in before his Liverpool counterpart knew that Kendall was available. On the Wednesday Catterick had caught wind of an £80,000 offer from Stoke City and immediately travelled to Preston before Kendall could meet with them, or Shankly heard of the bid, and intervened. Aware of Catterick's imminent – and unsolicited – arrival, the Preston manager, Jimmy Milne, went to fetch Kendall, who was at home with his parents.

'I've got a club for you,' said Milne.

'Is it Liverpool?' asked Kendall's father.

'No, next door,' replied Milne. Kendall junior and senior were completely surprised. At no point had Everton expressed any interest. 'Hurry up, get ready,' said Milne. 'Mr Catterick is at Deepdale and we're meeting him in half an hour.'

It was vintage Catterick. The Everton manager told Kendall he wanted to play him in midfield (he had been playing in defence) and offered terms. Yet Kendall did not sign immediately. The Stoke City manager, Tony Waddington, and Alan Ball senior, who was now on the Stoke coaching staff, had also travelled to Preston, and Kendall, with his father, met them soon after. Waddington and Ball laid out their case for Kendall to move to the Victoria ground and offered personal terms similar to Everton's. Then Kendall senior – like Ball's father, the key influence on his footballing son – posed the killer question to Ball: 'If Stoke is the right move for my lad, why didn't your boy come here?' From that moment Kendall knew he would become an Everton player.

The following day he travelled to Merseyside and completed the transfer. The speed of the deal had caught Shankly unaware and the first he heard of it was in the local press.

Everton's new signing watched the FA Cup victory cup-tied and sat in the stands. The following Monday he began training and drove in to Bellefield in his bright red MGB GT. Catterick took one look at the car and warned, 'Either get it resprayed or be prepared for the worst. You've no idea what they're like down here.' Within days he had bought a blue one.

He made his Everton début in a 0–1 home defeat to Southampton the following Saturday, but made just three further appearances during the remainder of the season, cut short by injury. It was clear, however, that Catterick had a new vision for his Everton team and Kendall was to play a big part in it.

Harry Catterick seldom used pre-seasons to buy or sell players, but the summer of 1967 was notable for a number of high-profile departures, not all popular. Fred Pickering, plagued with injury and disappointment since the FA Cup Final, was sold to Birmingham City for £50,000; Alex Scott, with his thirty-first birthday approaching, left to join Hibernian for £15,000. Kendall's arrival spelt the end for Jimmy Gabriel, still only 26, who joined Southampton, having played exactly 300 matches for Everton. As both player and 'minder' of the junior members of the squad, the mark he left on the club was as indelible as it was on the memories of those prodigious youngsters. One, Colin Harvey, when he became manager, brought about his return to Goodison as a coach in 1990. In September, Derek Temple departed for Preston in a £35,000 deal, which helped fund Ernie Hunt's £80,000 arrival from Wolves a fortnight earlier. Hunt was a highly experienced, not to mention prolific, inside forward, but he failed to settle at Goodison or gel with his new teammates, and was sold to Coventry City within the season at a £10,000 loss.

Catterick's side indisputably had a new and youthful look to it. When Everton opened the 1967/8 season at home to Manchester United, newly crowned as European champions, his selection showed the basis of the team that was to be established over the following three seasons. In goal was Gordon West, and lining up in front of him were Wright, Wilson (later replaced by Sandy Brown and Keith Newton), Labone and John Hurst. The soon-to-be-famous Kendall, Harvey, Ball axis made up the midfield with Johnny Morrissey, who had reclaimed the number-eleven shirt the previous season. In attack, Alex Young (who would be edged out at the season's end by Jimmy Husband) partnered the man who had once displaced him, Joe Royle. Everton were to win 3–1, but Catterick's selection was a statement of intent. Moreover, in Royle and Hurst he had staked his faith in youth.

The unassuming figure of John Hurst had first arrived at Goodison as a 15-year-old England schoolboy international centre forward in May 1962. Quickly burdened with comparisons to Tommy Lawton, it was not as a striker but wing half and then centre half that he made his name. After plying his trade in the Central League and winning an FA Youth Cup winners' medal in 1965, Hurst made the step up to the senior side in August 1965 when he was named as twelfth man for the opening-day clash with Northampton Town. He had to wait another week to make his début when he came on as substitute for Fred Pickering in the game against Stoke City. During his début season in the first team, Hurst made 19 appearances, plus two as a substitute, and got on the score-sheet twice, yet did not feature once in the victorious FA Cup run. After providing competent cover for Jimmy Gabriel, Brian Harris and even Fred Pickering he eventually settled in the centre-back position alongside Labone, establishing himself in the latter half of the 1966/7 campaign. Come Everton's FA Cup meeting with Liverpool, he had the chance to show the footballing world his credentials. Entering the game as a largely unknown 20-year-old, he was up against Roger Hunt, a World Cup winner just nine months earlier and striving to add to his tally of medals. Hurst proved unflustered and marked the Liverpool man out of the game, leaving him to hunt around for scraps and himself winning the man-of-the-match award.

Royle's entry to the first team had been altogether less auspicious, with the hullabaloo surrounding his début leading to one of the more notorious chapters in Everton history. He had made just one more appearance in 1965/6 season before a gap from first-team duties that lasted nearly a year. Catterick, however, was convinced that he had something special on his hands. At the tail end of the 1966/7 season he threw Royle, who had been scoring prolifically for the reserves, back in at the deep end. By now the former Lancashire Schoolboys skipper was the complete article, and he duly repaid Catterick's faith by scoring three times in four games. At the start of the 1967/8 season, Catterick handed the 18-year-old the hallowed number-nine shirt. His reward over the next four years? Ninety-five goals in 190 games, spanning an FA Cup Final in 1968 and two semi-finals in 1969 and 1971, a League Championship triumph in 1970 and the first of six England caps in 1971.

The six-foot-one, 13-stone Scouser was very much the archetypal targetman. His large, flat forehead undoubtedly added to the power of his heading, but Royle used it intelligently, regularly bringing into play his team-mates from midfield as Dean had done decades earlier. Before long many Evertonians idolized Royle – the local lad made good. 'They're peculiar about their number nines here, the way Liverpool are about their number sevens,' he said, nearly thirty years later when, as manager, he had broken the Everton transfer record to bring Duncan Ferguson to Goodison. 'Whether it was Bob Latchford or Alex Young or Dixie Dean or Tommy Lawton, they've always loved them.'

Victory over Manchester United aside, Everton's start to the 1967/8 season was shaky. They lost five of their opening 10 league games and were knocked out in the third round of the League Cup.

Then, on 21 September 1967, came another blow. To the shock of everyone involved with the club, Brian Labone announced his retirement from football. The 27-year-old revealed that he wasn't enjoying playing and would be quitting the game at the end of his contract in May 1969, or sooner if Everton could find a suitable replacement. He said that it was too much of a responsibility to continue playing such a key part in the Everton defence when he was not enjoying the game and that he would sooner go into his father's central-heating business. Catterick, not normally one to applaud an individual, took the opportunity to give the defender a glowing reference. 'It's typical of Brian's top-class character,' he said, 'that he has told me eighteen months before the end of his contract that he is going to leave the game. Many a player would not have told his club until the last possible minute. Brian is one of the greatest club men I have ever known . . . and we shall be sorry to see him go.'

That setback aside, Catterick soon found the right blend in his team and by Christmas Everton had risen to fifth.

It was in the midfield where the renaissance started. A unique understanding had developed between Howard Kendall, Colin Harvey and Alan Ball in five-a-side matches in Bellefield's gym. 'Sometimes I wished we could have got the games televised,' Catterick said later of the training sessions. 'It was absolute magic.' It did not take long for such prowess to be transferred to the Goodison pitch. Each man complemented the others perfectly: Ball the firebrand was offset by the cool panache of Harvey; what Harvey lacked in aggression Kendall made up; if Kendall was occasionally lacking in goals, Ball's incredible strike rate compensated – 51 league goals in his first three seasons at Goodison, including 20 from 34 games in the 1967/8 campaign. 'As three players we hardly ever needed any coaching,' recalled Ball. 'We could find each other in the dark.' Everton supporters soon adopted their favourites. Ball had come to replace Alex Young as many Evertonians' hero, but Harvey was also hugely popular (Catterick later said, 'In terms of pure skill and ball control, Colin was probably the best of the three'). Others discerningly plumped for the more unsung virtues of Howard Kendall. 'It was a revolutionary kind of football, a stepping stone to the modern game,' recalled Dick White. 'It was a revelation the way these three played, ran into open space, turned up in odd positions – but they were always back when they were wanted.'

The rise to prominence of this Holy Trinity coincided with the start of the 1968 FA Cup, which Everton marked with a 1–0 victory over Southport on 27 January. A week later Kendall's solitary goal beat Liverpool at Goodison. Catterick, noting that Everton had also won the reserve derby 3–1 at Anfield, recycled the old Shankly gibe: 'I see the best two teams in Liverpool won today.'

Alex Young was now being edged out by another footballing wizard. A 20-year-old Geordie, with lightning pace, teasing skill and a low centre of gravity (which contributed to his mesmerizing body swerve), had come to stake a claim for the number-seven shirt, latterly occupied by the Golden Vision. His name was Jimmy Husband. Signed from school by Everton, he had made his full Everton début in April 1965 against Fulham, when he was marked by a veteran Bobby Robson, and made 19 appearances the following season. Yet it was only with Royle's establishment in the first team that this roving novice fully blossomed and became a mainstay of the Everton attack. He was both hero and villain of the 1968 FA Cup run, and in the fourth round added to his growing reputation with a goal in the 2–0 win at Carlisle.

That victory set up a fifth-round derby with Tranmere Rovers at Goodison Park on 9 March. Nearly 62,000 turned out to see Royle and Morrissey goals knock out their neighbours, with only the Tranmere goalkeeper, Jim Cumbes, preventing a rout. Evertonians had to wait a further week for a deluge of goals. They came at the Hawthorns where débutant Alan Whittle inspired Everton to a 6–2 victory with Alan Ball claiming four goals. The League Championship contest had by then turned into a four-horse race between Liverpool, Leeds and the two Manchester clubs, with Everton leading the chasing pack, some half-dozen points off the pace. In the FA Cup quarter-final against Leicester City on 30 March, Husband scored twice and Kendall added an exquisite volley to give Everton a 3–1 win.

Everton, however, were facing an injury crisis, which had given the likes of Whittle, Terry Darracott and Roger Kenyon a chance to prove themselves. Things were not helped by a gruelling run of eight league games in April or by Ball's dismissal against Newcastle a week before the Leicester match, after disputing a disallowed Husband goal. It was to cost him a place in the league matches with Sheffield Wednesday, Chelsea and Nottingham Forest.

It also meant that he missed the FA Cup semi-final with Leeds United on 27 April at Old Trafford. Also away was John Hurst, who had been struck down by jaundice, which opened the way for 21-year-old Tommy Jackson, a recent signing from Glentoran, and Kenyon. The game was won by a single goal from the penalty spot. Johnny Morrissey, taking over the responsibilities from the absent Ball, held his nerve to score the goal that sent Everton to Wembley. After the match, hundreds of Evertonians ran on to the pitch to mob their heroes. 'I am delighted that we have got through,' said Catterick. 'I feel that we did very well when one considers the blow of being robbed of Alan Ball, Sandy Brown and John Hurst. I regard Hurst as the king pin of the defence.'

It set up an FA Cup Final with West Bromwich Albion on 18 May 1968, with Everton overwhelming favourites to win. Not only had they beaten Albion 6–2 as recently as mid-March, but their

late-season league form was highly impressive, taking in 11 wins in
the final 16 matches. It was a sharp contrast to the disappointing
run-in two seasons earlier – when they had won the trophy – and
their sense of self-belief was enormous. 'The Everton boys are chock
full of confidence that we will win,' said Labone, a few days before
the final. 'It is not being over-cocky to say that. Having beaten Albion
twice in the league this season will give us a big psychological
advantage. I'm certain the boys will bring the Cup back to Liverpool
on Sunday night.'

Come the day of the final, Wembley was soaked after a deluge
of heavy rain in the morning. Disappointment abounded before the
match had even begun, when more than three thousand distraught
Evertonians were turned away from the turnstiles having been sold
forged tickets that had been introduced to Merseyside by a London
gang. The demand for tickets – always insatiable for a Cup Final –
was even greater after the Football Association's disgraceful allocation
of tickets: only 16,000 to a club whose average attendance was just a
shade under 47,000. The let-down continued after kick-off. Everton,
playing in amber and blue, found a dirty and defensive Albion side
difficult to break down. Before long, the crowd began pleading with
chants of 'We want football!' Then, just four minutes from time, and
with the score still deadlocked at 0–0, a cross was whipped into the
Albion penalty area where the unmarked Husband lurked. 'I could
almost have swallowed it,' he later admitted, 'but just as I was about
to stick it in, Alan Ball shouted. He did the right thing because he
was probably in a good position but the call put me in two minds.
It was my mistake. It was the biggest mistake I ever made. And I had
to do it at Wembley.'

Goalless, the game went into extra time and looked to be heading
for a replay. Then, three minutes from the end, after a rare foray
into the Everton half, came Jeff Astle's 20-yard volley. Everton,
rightly, felt robbed. As Ray Wilson put it: 'You don't mind when you
play badly and lose. You can congratulate the others. But when
you are the better side and lose, that's when it really hurts.'

The following Tuesday, Everton concluded their league campaign
against relegated Fulham at Goodison. A crowd of 40,000 turned out
– despite the essential meaninglessness of the fixture and an 11-week-
long bus strike, which had crippled local transport – to see Everton
turn in the sort of performance that had been sadly lacking the

previous Saturday, romping to a 5–1 victory. Hurst (2), Ball, Morrissey and Royle were the Everton scorers, yet it was Jimmy Husband – the previous Saturday's 'villain' – who got the loudest applause of the night. After the match the crowd, revelling in the feast of football they had just witnessed, refused to leave Goodison and stood singing the names of their heroes long after they had left the pitch. Catterick ordered his players out of the bath and told them to parade before addressing the crowd himself, promising that the brand of football they had witnessed that night would be 'the pattern of things to come'.

Indeed it was. The Everton team of the 1968/9 season has often been described by those who witnessed it as the club's best footballing side of the post-war era, better even than the side who won the title a season later. Yet again Catterick let the summer pass without making any signings, despite Alex Young's departure to Glentoran and the serious knee injury suffered during the pre-season by Ray Wilson, which would restrict him to just four league appearances, diminish his pace and ultimately precipitate his departure to Oldham at the season's end.

Although Everton lost the opening fixture at Manchester United (0–2) and won just two of their next five matches, by the end of September they had risen to fifth. On 28 September 1968 came the chance to avenge May's FA Cup Final defeat when West Bromwich Albion were the visitors to Goodison. Twenty of the 22 players who had turned out at Wembley were present in a game Ball dominated from start to finish. He opened the scoring from close range on two minutes, ran the midfield, adding to his tally on 59 minutes with a volley into the roof of the Albion net, and on 73 minutes from the penalty spot. Harvey completed the scoring with a spectacular solo effort. The Albion victory launched a run that took in victories over Manchester City (2–0), Southampton (5–2), Stoke City (2–1) and Wolves (2–1) during October, and left Everton in the top spot, for a week anyway.

If this Everton team had a problem it was that domination on the pitch was not always translated into results. They drew with Ipswich on 9 November and lost against Leeds on the twenty-third, despite opportunities to take each game. Unquestionably Everton had players capable of winning the Championship, but the squad perhaps lacked the mental strength or experience (the average age was only 22) that would carry them to the crown. 'There were other guys too,' recalled Charles Mills junior. 'They just couldn't get in. Gerry Humphreys was one, Terry Owen [father of Michael Owen] another – I'm sure if Owen was playing for any other side he'd have broken through.' Although they conceded the top spot in the first week of November, at home to Leicester City on the last day of the month they grabbed their biggest victory in six years, winning 7–1. Royle (3), Ball, Gerry Humphreys, Hurst and Husband were Everton's goalscorers. 'The sustained play, the intelligent build-up, the remorseless pressure came from an Everton side operating smoothly on all cylinders with the super-charged drive coming from those marvellous men in the middle, Ball, Kendall and Harvey,' raved Mike Charters in the *Liverpool Echo*.[1] Everton went off to standing ovations at both half- and full-time.

'I take the view,' claims Charles Mills junior, three decades later, 'as do many Everton supporters of the time, that that side, even though it had the same players, was better than the one that won the Championship the following year. That side was outstanding. The type of football they played was brilliant. It was still a side of promise, but some of the football they played was just superlative. That was the time that we thought – these three . . .'

Off the pitch, meanwhile, speculation persisted about Brian Labone's future. His shocking announcement 15 months earlier had coincided with an upturn in form and a recall to the national side. A national press campaign to persuade him to stay in view of the forthcoming World Cup in Mexico had been mounted, while on Merseyside the situation had been the cause of much rumour, including front-page headlines in the local papers. Tellingly Catterick had not bought a replacement and had scarcely blooded Roger Kenyon. Finally, on 7 January 1969, came the decision everyone had been waiting for. 'Mr Catterick asked me if I would be prepared to reconsider my decision,' Labone told the footballing world, in a written statement. 'He feels my experience is necessary to the present youthful side. It would also appear that I may be required for international duty at a later date. In the circumstances I have agreed to stay on for the period I am needed. I am glad all the conjecture is over – I am pleased to be playing on.'

Buoyed by that news, Everton continued to impress in the league and embarked on another FA Cup run. Victories in the early rounds

over Ipswich Town (2–1), Coventry City (2–0) and Bristol City
(1–0) led them to a quarter-final meeting with Manchester United
on St David's Day. In a well-matched battle, with little to choose
between the two teams, Everton scored the only goal of the game on
78 minutes from a close-range Joe Royle header, following Ball's
corner. It set up Everton's third semi-final in four seasons and Royle
had scored in every round.

Three weeks later Everton travelled to Villa Park to play United's
Mancunian neighbours. With both Harvey and Kendall having
suffered recent injuries, Everton's now famous midfield triumvirate
had played together just once in the first three months of 1969. Now
recovered, they came up against Manchester City's own exciting
threesome – of Summerbee, Bell and Lee – and it promised to be
among the great FA Cup semi-finals. Such hopes were unfounded
and the game proved a defensive stalemate, unlocked only in the last
minute when Tommy Booth hit the winner from close range.

The defeat left Everton to concentrate on the league. Standing in
third, but 10 points behind Leeds, albeit with two games in hand it
looked like a tall order and so it proved. Even if Everton had won
their remaining 11 fixtures, they would have finished one point short
of Leeds's record haul of 67 points. In the event they beat Arsenal in
their last home game to secure third place with 57 points, behind
Liverpool (on 61) and Leeds. Yet Everton had been the great stylists
of the First Division, providing the most attractive and exciting
brand of football in the league. They had also finished top scorers
with the total of 77 coming from all areas of the pitch. Royle had
finished the campaign with 22 goals, Husband 19, Ball 16. Things
looked good for the following season.

With the Mexico World Cup looming, the 1969/70 campaign
was to be compacted into eight months, instead of the more usual
nine. The schedule involved a gruelling run of seven games in the
first three weeks of the new season, and for Everton that meant a
particularly tough baptism: it included home and away ties at
Manchester United, visits to Arsenal and Manchester City and a
home match with champions Leeds. Again, Catterick had made
no new pre-season signings, despite Wilson's departure, although
speculation repeatedly linked him to Blackburn Rovers' England
left back, Keith Newton.

The new campaign opened on 9 August 1969 at Highbury.

Everton were missing Ball through suspension, but had Kendall – seeking to complete his first competitive match since 23 January. He lasted just 36 minutes before limping off injured again. Everton took the game 1–0, controlling affairs, without ever fully dominating, and it was won by man-of-the-match Hurst's goal eight minutes from the end. Four days later Everton travelled to Old Trafford, and, lining up against a team that boasted the famous Charlton-Law-Best forward line, won 2–0. Ball was back in the starting line-up and overshadowed the magical Best, while Law was wholly subdued and Charlton reduced to making long-range pot-shots. Again, Hurst was on the score-sheet, opening with a thirty-eighth-minute cross-shot after being played through by Ball. 'Here one of the greatest destroyers in modern football showed that he had not forgotten the schoolboy days when he was England's centre-forward,' thundered Horrace Yates, in the following morning's *Daily Post*. 'A scorer also at Arsenal on Saturday, he firmly underlined his claims to all-round status. His achievements made a mockery of the fact that Sir Alf Ramsey had named eight Everton players in his World Cup squad and still found it possible to omit Hurst.' Ball finished off United with a seventieth-minute downward header from Royle's perfect centre into the United box. 'With a start as blisteringly successful as this,' concluded Yates, 'the season could easily be the most fantastically successful in the history of the two Liverpool clubs.'[2]

The next Saturday Crystal Palace were seen off by two goals to one in Goodison's opening fixture and the following Tuesday Manchester United travelled to Liverpool for the return fixture with Everton. Hopes of revenge were soon out of the window as Everton stormed to a 3–0 lead after just 26 minutes following goals by Ball, Morrissey and Royle, an advantage they maintained to the delight of the 53,000-strong Everton crowd, who taunted United with chants of 'Easy, easy, easy.'

United's neighbours, City, proved a sterner test when Everton travelled to Maine Road the following Saturday. Despite racing into a Johnny Morrissey lead after just two minutes, City proved tough opponents with Kendall's understudy Tommy Jackson, Ball and Harvey having to do their utmost to stem the flow of play away from City's forward line. On 53 minutes they finally relented and gave up their lead, holding on to a draw and, with it, the top spot. A 2–1 win over Sheffield Wednesday midweek maintained that position and served as the perfect prelude to Everton's meeting with Leeds United on 30 August 1969 – the seventh fixture in a frantic opening three weeks of the season.

Although only seven games into the new season, the outcome of the match was decisive in terms of a psychological boost so early on in the title race. Leeds were unbeaten since the previous October, an incredible run that spanned 28 league matches. Kendall was still missing with the injury that had seen him withdrawn from the opening day's fixture, but Everton were otherwise at full strength. Few fans, however, could have either anticipated or hoped for what was to follow. As they had done against Manchester United 11 days earlier, Everton streamed into a three-goal lead. Jimmy Husband put them one up after only four minutes, but it was Royle who stole the show with a virtuoso display. On 20 minutes he crashed a header against the bar but recovered quickly enough to head into the empty net. Four minutes after the interval he spun and shot into the top right corner to make the score 3–0. Leeds pulled the scoreline back to 3–2 with goals from Johnny Giles and Billy Bremner, but the day was Everton's, thanks to the imperious Royle – who the *Football Echo* claimed had had 'the game of his life' – and they retained their place at the top of the league.

Kendall returned to action the following Wednesday – 3 September – for Everton's League Cup opener with Darlington, a 1–0 win. With the famous midfield triumvirate again reunited, Everton maintained their dominance in both play and results and by the end of October had played 17 league games, winning 14, drawing twice and losing just once, taking 30 points. Their form was as sparkling as their results. The entertainment factor was still as visible as ever, but with it there was an additional resolve that would see off opponents who might in the past have held out even under intense Everton pressure for a draw or even a win. 'They had hardened up,' recalled Charles Mills junior. 'Any team with Harvey, Kendall, Husband in it was going to be an attractive entertaining side, but they sacrificed an element of the daredevil stuff.' At the same stage in the previous season, Everton's points haul had been 25, but then vital points were not being won against their rivals at the top, be they Manchester United, Liverpool or Tottenham Hotspur.

November and early December saw a slight slump in fortunes by previous standards. Tommy Wright's second goal for the club in nearly 250 appearances was enough to see off Nottingham Forest on 1 November, but a defeat at West Bromwich Albion the following Saturday and a draw at Chelsea on 15 November saw them far from their best. The next week a 2–1 home win over Burnley was gained only after a few shakes.

Victory over Burnley had been achieved at a cost: Jimmy Husband, excellent all season, had left the field injured. His absence opened the way for Alan Whittle to deputize. Whittle had first broken into the Everton first team aged 18 in March 1968, when he had also come in as deputy for an injured Husband, and he made a handful of appearances that season, adding a further five the next. Nicknamed the 'blond bomber', his return to first-team action could not have been more timely, although he could do nothing to prevent Liverpool beating Everton 3–0 at Goodison when he played his first match of the 1969/70 season. Nevertheless, he had done enough to keep his place for the following week's encounter against West Ham at Upton Park. Playing on a quagmire of a pitch, Everton had been drawing blanks until a poor back pass by Bobby Moore was intercepted by Whittle, who sped 50 yards down the pitch, evading challenges by the West Ham full back Stephenson and Moore, before hitting the ball into the back of the Hammers' net. Ten days later and two days before Christmas, Whittle was on hand again to score the only goal of the game in a 1–0 win over Manchester City, and he grabbed the consolation when Everton fell to their third defeat of the season, losing 1–2 at Leeds, two days after Christmas.

Whittle was not the only man adding fresh inspiration to Catterick's table-topping team. Keith Newton, Blackburn Rovers' left back and long-standing England understudy to the recently departed Wilson, was finally signed for a fee of £80,000. A fine tackler, strong in the air and magnificent in his distribution, he had long been unsettled at Ewood Park. With Wilson's retirement from international football he realized that the step up from the Second Division was a necessary move to stake his case as heir to the England number-three shirt. For both Everton and England he proved a worthy successor.

During much of November and all of December, Colin Harvey had been missing from the Everton team. Indeed, his entire career had been put in real jeopardy when it was reported that he had lost the sight of his right eye after an infection. Specialist treatment and a complete two-month break from football followed and by mid-January, to the relief of the fans, he had returned to the first team. By then Alan Ball was missing from the line-up.

Ball was the engine running the Everton midfield, a veritable bundle of energy who would cover every inch of the pitch and drive the team forward with his rousing style of play. His work rate was an inspiration, and his verbosity also stirred his team-mates. Sometimes it got the better of him, particularly when it involved referees. He had already been sent off twice since he joined the club. Dismissed again, the Football Association cracked down and imposed a five-week ban.

Fortunately it encompassed only four games, but with Harvey's injury it meant that Everton's Three Graces had been separated for three months. In the 11 league games they had been apart, Everton had won six, drawn two and lost three – hardly Championship form. They also conceded the top spot to Leeds, and Sheffield United put paid to FA Cup dreams. Finally, on 21 February 1970, the three-some was reunited for Coventry City's visit to Goodison. But Everton could only muster a 0–0 draw that day, then the following week a 1–1 draw with Nottingham Forest. Winning ways were restored on 7 March with a 2–1 victory over Burnley, but Everton's title hopes were dealt a further blow when it was announced that Brian Labone would miss the remainder of the season with a back injury. Not only would his absence leave a gaping void in the Everton rearguard at a crucial stage in their pursuit of the Championship, but the team would be all the poorer without their captain's leadership, particularly given the youth of many of its members.

Catterick, however, pulled a master stroke. He appointed Ball captain. 'It is a psychological move to give Alan more responsibility and make him more aware of referees' and players' problems,' he explained. In reality, it was an attempt to channel Ball's aggression positively and it paid immediate dividends. He played his first game as Everton captain against Tottenham Hotspur on 11 March and was in truly inspired form. 'Success at the finish was a combination of so many things,' reported the *Daily Express*, 'none more telling than the presence of Alan Ball, courageous and penetrating. A warrior in white boots.' Whittle grabbed the winning and only goal of the game on 19 minutes. Newton's free kick had found him in the Spurs penalty area and, avoiding the temptation of a first-time shot, he veered intelligently to the right and let fly with a screaming shot past Pat Jennings. It was enough to restore Everton to the top.

Three days later the two clubs met again at Goodison. In a more open, if not scrappy encounter, Everton beat Spurs 3–2, although the Londoners twice came back to equalize goals from first Whittle and then Ball. Royle scored the winner 15 minutes from the end with his twentieth goal of the season.

It put Everton three points clear at the top, ahead of the following week's derby encounter with Liverpool at Anfield. When the two great rivals had met in December, Everton had rounded off a calamitous 0–3 defeat with a spectacular own goal from the head of Sandy Brown. The return match was a different story. Everton beat Liverpool 2–0, with goals from Royle and Whittle, in front of 54,496. Even the *Football Echo*, passionately (and sensibly on such occasions) non-partisan, reported, 'A brilliant display by Everton, in which they outclassed and outplayed Liverpool in the derby at Anfield today, put them well in front with goals by Royle and Whittle ... Everton dominated the game in midfield where Ball was brilliant, and in attack Royle frequently beat the tall Liverpool defence in the air, something that brought the first goal and helped make the second.'[3]

Everton were now back on top form. A blistering performance saw a 5–2 win over Chelsea, the next visitors to Goodison, including two goals in the opening three minutes. Two days later a superlative performance in goal by Gordon West held Stoke, who were seen off by a solitary Alan Whittle goal.

A win at Goodison over West Bromwich Albion on 1 April 1970 would secure Everton's seventh League Championship. Prior to the game, Catterick had taken his squad for two days' training in Knutsford to get them away from the tense atmosphere that hung over Liverpool.

It paid off. With play under way, Alan Whittle – all season superb – on 19 minutes sent Everton on the way with his eleventh goal in 14 games. When Colin Harvey's shot had been blocked, the ball had come out to the blond teenager and he brought it down, killed it and shot into the back of the Albion net with the help of a slight deflection. Harvey – whose career had been threatened just months earlier – completed his comeback with the goal that secured the Championship on 65 minutes. Indeed, few titles have ever been won with such spectacular efforts and Harvey's goal has gone down in the annals of club history as one of the greatest Goodison has been fortunate to witness. 'First he moved towards goal, changed his mind and veered out, as though to bring Morrissey into play,' wrote Horrace Yates in the following morning's *Daily Post*. 'Seeing Morrissey was covered he doubled back to the edge of the penalty area and while on the run sent a crashing drive soaring into the net with Osborne leaping spectacularly, but vainly across goal ... Everton sparkled in their play to the sparkle of their fans' applause.'[4] They clinched the title to a non-stop roar of chants, including 'Ever-ton', 'We are the champions', 'We're on our way to Europe', 'Send our team to Mexico' and even a couple of choruses of 'When You're Smiling'.

The sound of the final whistle was the prompt for thousands of victorious Evertonians to run on to the pitch, chanting, 'We shall not be moved.' The players later returned to receive the Championship trophy, cheered on by nearly sixty thousand fans, an attendance that hoisted Everton's aggregate for the season past the million mark. 'They have won it by playing football, by applying their individual skills to the team as a whole,' gushed Catterick. 'And I would like to believe they have also managed to entertain spectators all over the country in the process ... Our success has been a team effort and the credit must be shared all round.'

Success was down to many factors. Royle had a haul of 23 goals, Whittle 11 from 15 games, many of which had been scored at critical junctures. Johnny Morrissey was often overshadowed by the Kendall-Harvey-Ball partnership, but played a crucial role on the left of the Everton midfield. 'It was one of the scandals – if you like – that that team has been remembered for the Kendall-Harvey-Ball midfield,' claimed Peter Mills. 'It was a four-man midfield! Johnny Morrissey has often been forgotten.' As Catterick put it, 'When we are talking about those three, we mustn't forget the great part played by Johnny Morrissey – he was always available to receive the ball whenever one of the three was in trouble, and he played a great part in our style.'[5] In defence, Labone (and latterly Roger Kenyon), Hurst, Wright and Brown had all given sterling performances, while Keith Newton and Tommy Jackson played with distinction. Behind them, the unorthodox genius of Gordon West was a consistently excellent last line of defence.

Yet it was the stunning midfield trio for which the champions were rightly famous. They controlled and dominated games, provided the impetus and direction of the play, acted as a blanket in front of the defence, set up attacks and weighed in with their own haul of strikes. Catterick later said, 'I've seen some great midfield trios, but in terms of spectator value, pure skill and entertainment Ball, Harvey and Kendall formed the best I've seen.'[6] The decision to hand Ball the captaincy had been inspired. Having previously shown signs that they might flag at the crunch, Everton won seven of their last eight games of the season. 'Everyone in football knows his ability as a player but I think he has shown in his last eight games of the season that he has the temperament to act as captain as well,' said Catterick. 'He can inspire the others; he is respected by them.' Ball himself added, 'I don't think anything will change my temperament, but being captain helped me keep out of trouble. I could ask questions of referees instead of screaming at them as I used to do.'

Gibes about the 'Merseyside Millionaires' no longer held true. The team had cost just £275,000 to build, with £112,000 of that spent on Ball. Harvey, Hurst, Husband, Labone, Royle, Whittle and Wright had all been home-grown players, with Brown, Morrissey and West acquired for comparatively small amounts (by 1970 standards, anyway). Moreover, it was a young side, whose average age was just 24. Ball predicted confidently, 'I can see five great seasons ahead. This team is certain to go better. We have lots of skill and every player works hard for each other. With that behind us, how can we fail?'

◊

EUROPE WAS EVERTON'S next target, but the club's England internationals first had to set about conquering the world. Ball, Labone (recovered from his back injury), Newton and Wright all made the trip to Mexico as England sought to retain the World Cup. It was a gruelling and protracted affair, with the team spending 10 weeks overseas preparing, acclimatizing and playing. At almost every stage the touring England team were unsettled by controversy, discomfort or misfortune – from Bobby Moore's framed 'arrest' in a Colombian hotel gift shop, via the lung-busting problems caused by playing at altitude, to the food poisoning suffered on the eve of their quarter-final. On the playing side, it was a World Cup full of enduring memories, and when England bowed out to West Germany, each of the Everton men had made an impact.

However, at the start of the 1970/71 season, Everton's quartet of England stars were jaded, which impinged on their club's efforts to retain the title. It took Everton until the seventh match of the season to record their first league win, and by the midway point in the campaign they were as low as twelfth place. Injuries took their toll – Husband, Labone and Newton were all victims – but there was a more worrying decline in form. The Holy Trinity in particular were conspicuous for failing to reach previous heights. Ball, who had been made captain on a permanent basis in the summer, struggled with form, yet the desire was still there. Vexed with himself and frustrated with his team-mates, he often furiously urged them on, sometimes almost coming to blows with them. The captaincy that had proved so inspirational in the closing stages of the previous campaign was clearly causing problems. Howard Kendall said later that the players came to accept his captaincy, but acknowledged the confrontations that sometimes arose: 'The men who play under him accept him as the natural leader. We've all found him a bit difficult at times, but we've learned to understand him. This is the way he's made. If he sees something wrong, he speaks his mind. We may not always agree with what he has to say, but we think it's right that he says what he thinks.'[7]

Either way, it was a stark contrast to the affable manner of his predecessor Labone.

While Everton's Championship defence was all but over by Christmas, they took strides towards European success in the Champions' Cup. Keflavik, of Iceland, were seen off 9–2 on aggregate in the opening round, which set up a clash with the German champions, Borussia Moenchengladbach – who could boast the likes of Gunter Netzer, Bertie Vogts and the veteran Luggi Muller – in the second round. After a highly creditable 1–1 draw in Germany on 21 October, including a vital 'away' goal, the two teams met at Goodison on 4 November 1970.

It was an epic encounter. Mike Charters of the *Liverpool Echo* compared it to the famous Everton v. Sunderland FA Cup match 36 years earlier, and described it as a personal 'thrill of a football lifetime'.

On a sodden pitch Everton took a shock early lead when

Wolfgang Kleff in the Moenchengladbach goal misjudged a straight-forward Morrissey cross, which skidded off the wet pitch and went past him. Just 24 seconds showed on the clock. It was a solitary aberration and Kleff more than atoned for his misjudgement, making a succession of superb saves to deny Everton time and again. Yet the wet pitch was a curse to both goalkeepers, and Borussia Moenchen-gladbach got their equalizer on 34 minutes, when Rankin was unable to hold on to Laumann's header and the German followed up to score. As the game progressed into the second half Everton laid siege to the German goal, but Kleff redeemed himself with a succession of superlative saves. The match went into extra time and Everton had a let-off when Koppel hit a post, but even after a further 30 minutes it was still deadlock.

For the first time in Everton's history, that meant penalties. The game turned into a duel between Andy Rankin and Wolfgang Kleff. Everton were first up and Royle saw his penalty saved by Kleff. Sieloff and Ball both scored; then Laumann hit his penalty well wide to keep the scores at 1–1. Morrissey, Heynkes, Kendall and Koppel each converted their shots to keep the scores level at 3–3. Up stepped Sandy Brown for Everton's final kick, and he made it 4–3. Rankin's moment had come. Luggi Muller stepped up, hit his shot hard and to the right but the Everton goalkeeper dived superbly to parry the ball away. Game over.

Four months later, in the quarter-finals, Everton met Panathin-aikos of Greece at Goodison on 9 March 1971. A slight upturn in league form had lifted Everton to ninth place in the First Division, and they had strung together an FA Cup run, reaching the semi-finals three days earlier after a 5–0 win over giant-killing Colchester United. Panathanaikos were considered the easiest of all the quarter-finalists. Managed by Ferenc Puskas they mixed a well-organized defence with a touch of gamesmanship, and were aided against Everton by luck in no small degree. Royle had a header cleared off the line, Wright's header hit the bar, Ball missed a gaping chance. And so it went on. Rankin was not called into use until the sixty-sixth minute. A quarter of an hour later, with only their second shot of the night, the Greeks went in front through Antoniadis. Everton laid siege to the Greek goal and the breakthrough came in the final minute from Everton's seventeenth corner of the night, when David Johnson slammed the ball past the goalkeeper. Catterick, who had earlier spoken of the necessity of taking a three-goal lead to Greece, said, 'We played all the football. We created sufficient chances to have won easily – but we didn't stick them in the net.'

Two weeks later, Everton travelled to Greece. Like the England team in the previous summer's World Cup, they were plagued by bad fortune and intimidation: the plane could not land until the early hours of the morning; the hotel was circled by cars beeping their horns well into the following night; and the Everton secretary, Bill Dickinson, received a death threat before the game. Once play began, things got little better. On a rock-hard, bumpy pitch the Greeks closed Everton out by fair means and foul – 'They were spitting in our faces and gouging at our eyes by sticking their fingers into them,' complained Catterick – holding on for a 0–0 draw and progression to the next round via away goals. Everton's European dream was over.

They returned tired and dejected, and not ready for the task of playing Liverpool in the FA Cup semi-final less than 72 hours later. Ball, Royle, Harvey and Morrissey had all picked up injuries against the Greeks, but battled on gamely. The form book was against Everton, but surprisingly Ball put Everton in front on 10 minutes. After a blistering start from Everton, Liverpool came back into it, although the Everton defence seemed to be holding out under the imperious stewardship of Labone. The turning-point came when he went off injured with a thigh strain in the fiftieth minute. On 58 minutes Alun Evans grabbed the equalizer and from then on Everton were under the cosh. Liverpool's winner came from Brian Hall 18 minutes from the end. It sank Everton and effectively ended their season.

Indeed, Everton won only one more of their remaining eight league games, finishing the 1970/71 campaign a disastrous four-teenth. Hopes that their disappointing showing was a hangover from the Mexico World Cup, or the high tempo sustained in previous seasons, were not realized when the 1971/2 season kicked off in similarly disappointing fashion. By the end of November 1971, only six league matches had been won and an 8–0 trouncing of South-ampton proved a false dawn. Unhappy at the performance of his team, Catterick took the decision to alter it fundamentally.

o

THREE DAYS BEFORE Christmas it was announced that Keith Newton had been transfer-listed. There was little surprise: after he had returned from Mexico, Newton had been in and out of the team because of injury and loss of form. Then, in October 1971, Catterick had publicly criticized him for his tendency to dwell on the ball and again dropped him. Unable to regain his place in the side he had requested a transfer, which, after due consideration, was accepted. Yet the news of Newton's (possibly) imminent departure was quickly overshadowed when it emerged later on that day that Alan Ball was to be sold to Arsenal for £220,000.

It was an incredible development. Only the previous spring Catterick had been asked for a valuation of Ball, and replied, 'I would not dream of selling him, but of course every player has his price. Alan's is one million pounds.' When asked if he would sell, should such a sum be offered, Catterick replied, 'No, but I would consider it first.'

Now, within a year, he was to be sold (with Catterick's previous – albeit only half-serious – valuation apparently forgotten). The news was as much of a shock to Ball as it was to his adoring Evertonians. He told reporters, 'I don't think I would ever have asked to leave Everton but when you are faced with a situation like this you have no alternative. I shall play my heart out for Arsenal just as I did for Everton. I am not bitter about it at all – just a trifle sad.'

That morning Catterick had summoned Ball to his office and told him, quite simply, that he was being sold. Ball told him that he didn't want to leave Goodison and that he loved Everton. Catterick simply responded: 'There is a man in the next room from a top London club. It will be a good move for you and you'll make some money out of the transfer fee. I want you to sign for him.'

Later, Ball revealed: 'It was then that I realized what this game of football really is. It's a business in which players are moved around like slaves. I must admit, I became really cynical about life that day, but in my heart I had to admire Catterick and I certainly had no animosity towards him. Catterick had bought me for £110,000 and now he was selling me five years later for £220,000. That's got to be good business and he was quite right to do the deal.'[8]

Other people, of course, held their different opinions. There was a sense that Ball had not been at his best since the Mexico World Cup. Michael Charters wrote in the *Liverpool Echo*: 'My own view is that Ball has played his slight frame beyond the limits of his physical capacity. He has given 100 per cent so often that now he cannot give 100 per cent although his heart wants him to. In a phrase, I think Ball could have burned himself out.' Catterick announced that Ball's departure marked the start of the construction of a new team. 'I have been extremely patient, giving them every chance to regain their form and attitude to the game. Now my patience has ended.' Most Evertonians were understandably up in arms over the deal, but one fan, George Orr, later wrote in his book *Everton in the Seventies: Singing the Blues*:

> There were rumours about gambling debts and unrest in the dressing room. I was at his last match at Derby and remember Howard Kendall playing a blinder and only making one bad pass, Ball turned round and screamed at him. Kendall walked towards Ball and gave him a look that could kill. This to me was the fault: Ball was a great player but his mouth was never shut; arguing with referees or linesmen cost him many bookings and forced Everton into team changes for avoidable suspensions. If you look back, players from that team, Lyons, Darracott, Kendall, Harvey and Royle, have all gone to serve the club in some form of management but there has never been a place for Ball. Isn't there a pointer there?

Ball served Arsenal for five years, also captaining England for a short time while at Highbury. The Gunners sold him to Southampton midway through the 1976–7 season and he remained there until 1980, when he left for a short, unsuccessful spell as Blackpool player-manager before returning to the Dell less than a year later. He played briefly in Hong Kong before ending his career with Bristol Rovers. Several managerial appointments followed but he failed to transfer his hugely successful career on the football field to one off it.

For Catterick, who had made his managerial reputation by taking gambles and pulling surprises, selling his best player was the biggest yet. This time, however, it did not come off.

9

Decline and Fall

FROM THE OPENING BEAT of 'Love Me Do' in October 1962 to the last strain of 'The Long and Winding Road' eight years later, the city of Liverpool had stood at the height of its cultural powers. The Beatles were the most famous and enduring product of the Merseybeat scene, but when they weren't topping the charts with one of their 29 number-one singles, they were often replaced by any one of a number of Liverpool-based groups who emerged in their wake. This renaissance extended into literature, poetry and drama, bringing vitality and confidence to a city that had been on the wane since the turn of the century. Liverpool's inner city began to be cleared and new towns, such as Kirkby, Skelmersdale and Widnes, were created. With the latest architectural designs, wide boulevards and masses of open green space, they promised a quality of living that was an age away from the confines of the Dickensian two-up two-downs they had replaced. The zest and appetite for change saw a so-called 'City in the Sky' of tower blocks rise up in Everton Valley; a new Catholic cathedral was built, to the boldest and most daring architectural design in the world for a place of worship; and St John's Tower, a 450-foot revolving restaurant and observation point that afforded spectacular views across this new cityscape, was nearing completion when Catterick's men were winning the 1970 Championship.

Charles Mills junior remembered, 'We thought we were the centre of the world. You were made to feel – if you came from Liverpool – that there was something about you. In the sixties, you really did feel as if Liverpool was the centre of the world. It was a very vibrant place, but there was no sense that it would move on.'

Much of the hype about Liverpool in the sixties hid the socioeconomic problems it continued to face. It was still indisputably a poor city, whose port, its main source of revenue, continued to decline. Expensive and ambitious government-backed schemes – such as Ford's heavily subsidized Halewood plant – met with only limited success, and struggled to keep pace with the loss of jobs in other parts of Merseyside. The grandiose municipal planning and building schemes quickly became a byword for folly: they desecrated the inner city and created concrete jungles on Liverpool's fringes, which were cut off from the city's heart, marginalizing their populations. The cathedral – 'Paddy's Wigwam' – leaked, and the tower stood dormant for nearly three decades.

Much of this was still to come, though, and in December 1971, Liverpool still lived on the crest of the 1960s-induced wave of optimism. During the sixties, Evertonians had seen their fortunes rise with those of the city. The decade had rightly been recognized as a golden era, a time of unparalleled prosperity in Everton's league fortunes, when they had won the Championship twice and only once dropped out of the top five at a season's conclusion. Even then that had been the year the FA Cup had returned to Goodison Park. Many tipped the 1970 Championship team to dominate English football for years and it seemed inconceivable that Everton could again experience the troughs of the 1950s. But just as others had tipped Liverpool to emerge once more as the capital of England's North, they were wrong. Indeed, as Everton's rise had been in synch with the city's renaissance in the 1960s, so too was its decline in the 1970s and early 1980s.

The problems Harry Catterick faced following Ball's departure were immense. Injuries accounted for Harvey, Husband, Kendall, Labone, Royle and Wright for large chunks of the 1971/2 season, and took their toll on team performance, contributing to another disappointing end-of-season finish at fifteenth. Yet the malaise cut deeper than injuries. It seemed that the Catterick regime had stagnated, while the careers of many stalwarts of the previous five years were fading. The impression given by later interviews and memoirs is of a squad struggling to come to terms with not being as good as they once were, and a manager who had lost control of his player and his appetite for the game. A party culture had resulted in some players developing drink and gambling problems, which reflected on their domestic lives (divorce was rife), performances on the training pitch and, crucially, on Saturday afternoons. Catterick was an introvert and the daily pressures soon caught up with him. The 51-year-old had previously suffered ill-health and had been absent for several weeks after the game against Panathinaikos. Stress might or might not have been a contributory factor, but it undoubtedly resulted in the more serious illness that probably ended his career as Everton manager.

On 5 January 1972, while driving back from a League Cup semi-final between Stoke City and West Ham United in Sheffield, Catterick suffered a heart-attack. Perhaps only because he had the good fortune to stop near the home of a Pennines district nurse did he survive, though he spent several subsequent days in intensive care. He was back at the centre of things within 10 weeks, but he estimated later that it took him 18 months to recuperate fully.

Neither the rest nor his rushed return did much to revive Everton's fortunes. They won just three times in the last 24 league games of the 1971/2 season, finishing fifteenth. Catterick's purchases with the proceeds of the Ball transfer had been at best undistinguished, at worst inept. First, he laid out £140,000 for the chunkily built midfield scrapper Mike Bernard. Wholehearted and committed though Bernard was in his 170-match Everton career, he was no Alan Ball. From St Johnstone came the spindly flanker, John Connolly, whose considerable talents were often wasted during his time at Goodison, first through a lack of expertise up front, then two broken legs within a year.

What these men lacked in finesse or luck was as nothing compared to the shortcomings of the striker, Bernie Wright. Everton bizarrely signed him after coming up against him in an FA Cup match in February 1972, although he had played only a handful of games for Walsall. Although a bewildered Everton crowd saw him play on fewer than a dozen occasions, Bernie 'the Bolt's' woeful lack of top-flight ability and frightening appearance saw him go down in Goodison notoriety. One of his appearances is often quoted by bemused fans and former players. Everton were playing Sheffield United at Bramall Lane and Wright was up against their Scotland centre back, Eddie Colquhoun. As Wright bravely went for a diving header, Colquhoun kicked his head. Wright got up and brushed himself down, but the Scot had to be substituted: he had broken a toe.

As well as these recruits, a new school of players had graduated from the youth and reserve teams to establish themselves in the senior side.

The catalogue of injuries suffered by Brian Labone had given Roger Kenyon the opportunity to impress, though few had cause to doubt his credentials. When injury had ruled out Labone during the 1970 Championship run-in, Kenyon, a virtually untried 21-year-old, was charged with the task of filling his captain's place. He rose to the challenge, and in the last eight games of the season Everton remained undefeated, winning seven and drawing only once. Although he did not win a medal for his services (he had not played the required number of games) his performances led the *Liverpool Echo* to marvel, 'Kenyon will be difficult to move from this side, he improves with every match and is already a model of composure with a bite in every tackle.'

Gary Jones, an often brilliant winger, had also made his first Everton appearances, having pulled himself up through the club's youth ranks. At his best he was sublime, completely untouchable in the way he could wriggle past opposing defenders with an aura of effortless skill. He seemed to have it all: acceleration, change of pace, and an abundance of ingenious flair, which could ignite the Goodison crowd into raptures of appreciation.

Others who were as committed, but without perhaps sharing such ability, also emerged. Terry Darracott, Peter Scott and Archie Styles all put in stints at full back without ever staking a case for long-term inclusion. Mick Buckley, a sometimes elegant midfielder who made more than 150 Everton appearances, was perhaps best summed up by one writer as a 'less inspired version of Colin Harvey'. Like his colleague Bernard, he had much to live up to.

One man who was painfully aware of the legacy of the School of Science and the expectations that went with it was Mick Lyons. A later manager quipped that if you cut Lyons in two he would bleed blue, such was his love for Everton. He had made his début against Nottingham Forest in March 1971, scoring in the 2–3 defeat at the City ground, but it was another year before he established himself in the first team, playing in a variety of roles with the vigour of a 10-year-old. He was, of course, achieving a childhood ambition, and had watched Everton from an early age in the Gwladys Street end with his older brother. He witnessed the 1962/3 Championship triumph and the 1966 FA Cup win. In 1968, without a ticket for the FA Cup Final, he used his initiative and vaulted the turnstile, only to find himself among the West Bromwich Albion supporters. When

Everton next won a trophy, the 1970 League Championship, he was on the fringes of the first-team squad, but this was the closest he came to a medal.

Set against these additions to the playing staff were a number of sales and retirements. Keith Newton was sold to Burnley, and Johnny Morrissey, who had long been troubled by Achilles tendon problems, went to Oldham Athletic, where he made just six appearances before his retirement; the £10,000 outlay Catterick had made for him a decade earlier had been well spent.

Brian Labone also announced his retirement. On his return from the Mexico World Cup he had made only 26 more appearances for Everton, playing his last game in a League Cup tie against Southampton in September 1971, before hanging up his boots due to an Achilles tendon injury. Harry Catterick had christened Labone 'the last of the great Corinthians', a fitting testament to the unstinting respect Labone commanded be it from team-mates, fans or opposing players. He was a great servant to the club, a great gentleman and player.

Finally, Catterick's purchase of the England under-23 goalkeeper, David Lawson, in the summer of 1972 all but spelt the end of Gordon West's days at Goodison. He retired, some say prematurely, a year later, aged 30. He returned to football in 1975 with Tranmere Rovers as cover for their first-team goalkeeper and remained at Prenton Park for four years, picking up 17 appearances to add to the 399 he had made for Everton. It wasn't until a barren decade had passed that a replacement was found of his calibre.

Given this state of flux, it was perhaps a little surprising that Everton's start to the 1972/3 season was so promising. Unbeaten in the first eight games, they topped the table in mid-September, silencing the growing band of Catterick's snipers. Yet success belied many of the problems behind the scenes.

At the heart of these problems was Catterick's poor health, which was not only impeding his enjoyment of the game but making him even more withdrawn from day-to-day affairs. Although it was accepted that he was not a tracksuit manager, his appearances on the training ground had become even less frequent. Tommy Egglestone took virtual control of the running of the first team, but even on important matters such as contract negotiations or disciplinary matters – where Catterick had taken a central role – the manager was less and less involved. He had trouble dealing with his players and would avoid them rather than face confrontation. On one occasion, when Bernie Wright had attacked the coach Stewart Imlach with his fists, Catterick had escaped in his car rather than deal with the problem.

The spell of early-season success was brief and just one win in October (a month that started with yet another derby defeat) was followed by a miserable run of six straight defeats, stretching through November and into December. Catterick responded irrationally, claiming that his players preferred to play away from home because of the barracking they were getting from the Goodison crowd – 'This is an indictment of our supporters,' he said. The players 'are frightened to try something different; they have lost the confidence to express themselves, to use their skills, because they feel the crowd will be on their backs as soon as they make a mistake.'[1]

His remarks did little to endear him to the Everton support. 'When is he going to take some of the blame for his pathetic team?' asked J. Meade of Aigburth Vale, in the following week's *Football Echo* letters page. 'For the past two and a half seasons we have been watching the worst bunch of players (Kendall and Lawson excepted) that I have watched in my 33 years as a supporter.' More than a couple of irate fans called for a boycott of matches: 'Perhaps then Everton will realize what we have to say,' grumbled R. Chambers of Liverpool 4.

The problem was goals. Everton still had the best defensive record in the division, despite their slump, but could not find the net. Central to this was the absence of Joe Royle, who missed the remainder of the season with the back injury that dogged the rest of his Everton career. While Catterick's remarks about the Goodison crowd might have hinted at a man out of touch with his job, he was aware of where the problem lay and missed the Coventry City game five games into the run of defeats to go to Scotland, apparently to watch a new striker. The man in question was Joe Harper, Aberdeen's prolific goalpoacher, whose 38 goals the previous season had put him in third place for the European Golden Boot award. Even before Christmas 1972 he had another 24 strikes to his name. A week later Catterick brought the Scot to Goodison for £180,000, on the same day selling Alan Whittle to Crystal Palace for £100,000. Since his exhilarating run of form in the 1970 Championship-winning campaign, Whittle had never been given a proper run in his side, and elsewhere failed to live up to his billing as the 'next Denis Law', eventually playing out his career as far afield as Australia and Iran. Nevertheless, he was still a popular figure at Goodison and when his departure was announced at half-time on the day Everton played Wolves – with no mention of the Harper deal – the news was greeted with slow handclapping. Just 24,170 had turned out to watch Everton lose 0–1.

When Evertonians caught wind of the Harper transfer, though, some enthusiasm returned. His début against Spurs on 16 December added an extra 7000 to the gate, which, along with his presence, inspired Everton to a 3–1 victory, finally ending their run of defeats. Not even a missed penalty by the débutant could dampen expectations, and Harper goals in subsequent games with Chelsea and Birmingham earned Everton 1–1 draws on both occasions, helping to stem the Blues' decline. But the season's nadir was still to come.

After beating Aston Villa 3–2 at home in the third round of the FA Cup, Everton were drawn to meet Third Division Millwall at Goodison on 3 February 1973. The game was catastrophic. Catterick watched as his team were outmuscled, outfought and outspirited. Cushions were hurled in disgust from the stands as Millwall's full back Cripps moved, unchallenged, to head home Eamonn Dunphy's free kick past Lawson; then, two minutes from the end, came Wood's header to secure a famous 2–0 win. Catterick admitted that the fans had been let down, adding, 'We have got to try and make it up to them . . . We have not given them much to cheer about at Goodison for three seasons. We have had some bad luck, but played some football as well.' John Moores and his vice-chairman, Alan Waterworth, visited Bellefield the following week to 'try and work out an incentive to get things right after last Saturday's Cup defeat'.[2]

Off the pitch, the Millwall match had been marred by violence on the terraces: 11 Millwall supporters were stabbed when they entered the Gwladys Street terrace before kick-off. The victims included a 17-year-old who was seriously injured with a punctured lung. A Millwall fan, A. J. Campbell, a solicitor's clerk, claimed: 'There was no provocation. It was just an out-and-out attack because we were at their end of the ground and they came down to get us. This is the first time I have ever been to Merseyside. I never thought that anything like this would happen to me.'[3]

More defeats followed the Millwall débâcle, including the third consecutive loss to Liverpool. Patience had long been wearing thin among Evertonians, but at boardroom level it was about to break. On 11 April 1973 it was announced that Catterick – aged 52 – would 'retire' and move to an as yet unspecified executive position. The search for a new manager was to begin immediately.

That he was not fired outright was testament to the high esteem in which he was rightly held for his 12 years of largely outstanding service. There was also a desire to utilize his experience. Rather than give him a lump-sum pay-off for the remainder of his contract, which would have amounted to £50,000, he continued to draw his salary – which was rumoured to be in excess of that of his successor – for what turned out to be a mere scouting role. Later he put in a two-year stint as Preston North End manager, but failed to restore former glories to Deepdale.

Typically Catterick gave away nothing about his feelings, but on this occasion his upset was plain: 'It is a heavy blow after being manager for more than ten years,' he said, 'but I believe this great club, with many splendid players, will continue to have success.' Catterick's association with Everton had spanned two-thirds of his life, and though his love for the club seldom surfaced in public – in contrast to his contemporaries Shankly and Busby – it was unquestionable. 'Many people have criticized my lack of rapport with the ordinary supporters and probably rightly so,' he admitted. 'I am not an extrovert. My nature is to be a quiet person. But no one is a bigger Evertonian than me, no matter how loudly he shouts. I came here at sixteen and there has never been anything else for me since.'[4]

Catterick's record as manager had been hugely impressive, yet the state of transition that followed the Championship win had become unacceptably protracted. Moreover, he did lack camaraderie with much of the support. As Peter Mills put it: 'There was never any great affection for Catterick. He was, sort of . . . tolerated. Possibly, as a contemporary of Shankly, he was unfairly compared.'

The need to bring a quick fix of success to Goodison was important, but even more so a methodical, scientific approach to the running of the club, which would elevate Everton not just to more domestic success but to triumphs on the European stage. Bill McGarry of Wolves and Brian Clough emerged as the leading contenders for the job, yet as the 1973/4 season drew to another disappointing conclusion – seventeenth place and a brief flirtation with relegation – speculation put another, less obvious, name in the running.

Billy Bingham's Everton career had effectively ended with the arrival of Alex Scott from Glasgow Rangers in February 1963. At the season's end, Port Vale made a move to secure his services, and with his thirty-second birthday approaching he found the chance to play regular first-team football again irresistible. At Vale Park he saw out the remainder of his career, and retired after breaking his leg in spring 1964. From the Potteries, Bingham returned to Merseyside where he enjoyed a three-year tenure as manager of Southport, which ended with a move to Plymouth Argyle. Devon brought varied fortunes for the Ulsterman and he was sacked for breach of contract after travelling to Wrexham for a training session with the Northern Ireland under-23 team. A brief spell in charge of Linfield followed, but this ended, after they had been crowned Northern Irish Champions, when the Greek FA asked him to become manager of their national team. After his failure to take Greece to the 1974 World Cup Finals in West Germany, his contract was not renewed. His successes as a manager had therefore been mixed, but his reputation as a progressive, modern coach stood high. He had experience of English, Irish, international and European football, and was a disciplinarian and an advocate of new and advanced training techniques.

On 26 May 1973 Bingham was formally appointed manager of Everton. A wave of optimism spread through the club. 'There was great hope when Bingham arrived,' recalled Charles Mills. 'He'd been a very popular player – a seasoned Evertonian.' John Moores described him in similar terms – a 'true Evertonian' – and Bingham admitted that he was 'dying to have a go at the job'. Others were more cautious. The *Daily Post*'s Horrace Yates wrote, 'He is a stickler for discipline and it is only his Irish charm that takes the sting out . . . I have no doubt at all that Bingham will prove an amiable boss – so long as his aims are achieved.'[5] Others asked questions about his lack of top-flight experience and even his pedigree at lower levels. Yet he promised success in Europe and, given his brief though exotic experience, there was cause for hope.

Which was just as well. The 1973/4 football season in Britain was overshadowed by a cloud of unremitting gloom. Industrial unrest in the coalfields led to dwindling stocks and restrictions on day-to-day life. Street-lighting was reduced by 50 per cent and heating in offices and commercial premises fixed at 63°F. Petrol rationing was considered, and the speed limit reduced to 50 m.p.h. Later, Prime Minister Edward Heath imposed a three-day working week. All of this added to the rising sense of despondency on Merseyside, where 55,000 people were now unemployed and more than a hundred factories stood vacant.

In football, the autumn of strikes and power-cuts meant the banning of floodlights. The Football League were obstinate in their refusal to extend the season, which meant that fixtures were played during most people's working days. The drop in attendances for many clubs was considerable, although Bingham's new charges began to turn a tide of steadily decreasing attendances.

Bingham was quick to change the coaching staff: he replaced Tommy Eggleston with Ray Henderson and used Catterick in a scouting role. At the AGM two months after Bingham's appointment, Moores had told the gathering, 'The King is dead, long live the King. And I think I have a good king in Billy Bingham.' However, despite the promise of £300,000 for the purchase of new players Bingham began the new season without having made any forays into the transfer market, but he soon started to put together the side he wanted. After five straight wins, he picked up the October manager-of-the-month award. His first signing was Dave Clements, a muscular left-sided midfielder with an array of Northern Ireland caps, bought from Sheffield Wednesday for £60,000.

Little by little, Everton took on Bingham's imprint. The squad was unquestionably fitter, with players set weight targets and made to run 3000 metres a day. They were also more organized and became a difficult side to break down. Not everyone liked them, though. The Derby County assistant manager, Des Anderson, later branded Bingham's side 'robots' and the London press, making reference to Everton's orange away strip, called them the 'Clockwork Orange'. As one of Bingham's later stars, Martin Dobson, put it: 'His tactics were always geared towards the team and had more to do with organization than with individual creativeness.'

While a level of consistency lacking in previous seasons returned to Everton's results, goals were still in short supply. Joe Royle continued to be plagued by back trouble, and although he made 22 league and Cup appearances, he scored just twice during the 1973/4 campaign.

The sale of Joe Harper in February 1974, along with the departures of Rod Belfitt, Henry Newton and Jimmy Husband, brought in a combined total of £400,000, and with only £60,000 laid out for Clements, speculation mounted that Bingham was going to buy Everton a desperately needed big-name striker. He insisted that he would not be rushed, but the newspapers linked him with moves for Peter Osgood of Chelsea, Stuart Barrowclough and John Tudor of Newcastle, and Duncan McKenzie of Nottingham Forest.

Just as tabloid tittle-tattle had been wrong in its guesses for Catterick's successor eight months earlier, so too were they in predicting Bingham's choice of star striker. The man Bingham viewed as being the centre forward who would help propel Everton back to former glories was Birmingham City's bustling home-grown number nine, Bob Latchford.

With a team that could boast players like Gordon Taylor, Bob Hatton and a young Trevor Francis, not to mention Latchford, Birmingham City had been an attractive free-scoring Second Division side, gaining promotion to the top flight in 1972. Although they had struggled in making the transition to First Division football, Latchford – who had made his début alongside an ageing Fred Pickering in March 1969 – continued to stand out as their star player.

Bingham was a keen admirer of Latchford and had an abundance of cash at his disposal, but Birmingham – who were struggling to avoid relegation – were adamant that no amount of money could take him away. Eventually, Bingham talked their manager, Freddie Goodwin, into a compromise: Birmingham would allow Latchford to leave if they could get in return a top-class midfielder and a defender that they said must be of 'near international class'. This meant Howard Kendall and Archie Styles, plus a cash sum.

Goodwin's demands left Bingham with an impossibly tough choice. On the one hand the need for a new forward to spearhead the Everton attack was as obvious as it was sometimes desperate: in the previous two seasons, Everton had scored, on average, less than a goal a game, and by February 1974 had managed only a fraction above that, despite their upturn in league form. On the other, while Styles was only a fringe player, if a promising one, Kendall had been

Everton's best player by a long stretch over recent troubled seasons. Although injury had kept him out through much of Bingham's spell in charge, his ability then and in the future – he was still only 28 – was seemingly crucial to Everton's renaissance.

It was a tough call, but in the end Bingham went for goals. The deal was concluded on Valentine's Day 1974: Kendall was valued at £180,000, Archie Styles at £90,000, and £80,000 cash followed them to St Andrews.

The sale of Kendall prompted outrage. He had played 267 senior games for Everton – 227 in the league – scoring 29 goals. However, as the *Liverpool Echo* noted: 'The statistics cannot describe the polished contributions to Everton's cause as captain, sportsman and quality player.' Its postbag over the following weeks was jammed with letters bemoaning his departure. 'Kendall's transfer ranks as the biggest blunder at Goodison since Harry Catterick sold David Johnson,' wrote J. A. Norris of Whiston. 'Everton badly need fresh goal power and Latchford is a great player, but this is not the way.' 'Everton's Kendall-Styles-Latchford deal is ludicrous,' complained D. A. Lynch of Billinge. 'Of course Everton need a striker, but no striker can succeed without assistance. If Latchford is that good, why are Birmingham not much higher in the table?' Kendall himself said, 'You don't leave a club like Everton without a lot of thought, without a lot of worry that you are doing the right thing. But I believe that I am going to another good club in Birmingham.'

Despite the many misgivings about the transfer, Evertonians – although they didn't appreciate it at the time – benefited twice over from the deal. Most obviously, they got a desperately needed goal-scorer in Latchford, who was Everton's most important player for the remainder of the decade. Second, Kendall's move to St Andrews marked the start of his apprenticeship in management. Like many of his contemporaries, Kendall had found Catterick sometimes difficult, often aloof, while his relationship with Bingham was not always smooth-running. Goodwin, his new manager at Birmingham, was different: not only did he spark Kendall's ambition to be a manager, he nurtured and encouraged it. The midfielder's time in Birmingham lasted three years, before a move to Stoke City. Here he became a player-coach and began his formal journey into management, which later brought both him and Everton extraordinary success.

Everton's new boy made an immediate impact. Averaging more

than a goal every other game – a ratio he kept up pretty much throughout his seven-and-a-half-year Everton career – he took little time to win over fans. The fact that Latchford came within two goals of becoming top scorer for the season after just 13 games speaks volumes for his ability and epitomizes the extent of the Goodison goal drought that had brought about his move.

Everton finished the 1973/4 season a more creditable seventh. Stability, if not progress, had been achieved. Evertonians had a renewed sense of optimism, strengthened by the news that Bill Shankly was retiring as Liverpool manager: it was hoped that, without him, the red and white edifice would crumble.

Although it might have come through gritted teeth, Shankly subsequently enjoyed a respect unmatched among Evertonians for anyone exclusively associated with Liverpool Football Club. The transformation he had overseen at Anfield, where Liverpool were still the city's second team but had nevertheless made impressive gains, was cause for grudging admiration. If resentment of Shankly or his achievements has since emerged it is not generally directed at Shankly the man, more at those who have fabled and mythologized his record and created a mini-industry whose sole purpose has been to exploit his good name. It is an outcome that this most venerable and often modest of Scots would surely have hated.

Those associated with Liverpool Football Club, who do so well out of Shankly's name today, might have done better to afford him more respect when he was still alive. From the first day of his retirement, he saw himself as a shunned figure, never called on to advise, seldom invited on away trips, left to feel awkward as an Anfield spectator. Stuck for a way to fill his days he began to visit Bellefield, which was near his West Derby home. During the last seven years of his life he was a regular, using the impressive facilities to train, or relax in the sauna. 'I might add that I count Everton among the clubs who have welcomed me over the last few seasons. I have been received more warmly by Everton than I have by Liverpool,' he wrote in his 1976 autobiography. 'It is scandalous and outrageous that I should have to write these things about the club I helped build into what it is today.'[6] Later Howard Kendall encouraged his visits: 'He'd pop in for a cup of tea. I think he felt awkward at Melwood, but we loved seeing him. He'd say, "First thing you do each morning is put your tracksuit on." He knew how much you

could get bogged down in the office and that the important thing was
to get among the players. It was wonderful to just sit there and listen
to him talk about the game.'[7]

During the summer of 1974 Bingham added the blond-haired
Jim Pearson to the ranks, bought for £100,000 from St Johnstone.
A few games into the 1974/5 season he bolstered his team further,
taking on Burnley's Martin Dobson for a record cash fee of
£300,000. Dobson's career had nearly ended before it began. The
six-footer had played his youth football with Bolton Wanderers as
a centre forward but at 18 was not offered professional terms. 'I
thought the world was going to end,' he lamented later. Bolton's loss
was the gain of their neighbours Burnley. Here he moved into central
midfield, an inspired switch that saw his promotion to captain by the
time he was 21. When he made his England début the year Bingham
bought him, the pundits were describing him as a player 'of immense
skill', his calm, fluent distribution 'a delight to the eye'. His doubters,
however, wondered whether such a player could be accommodated
within the hustle and bustle of the modern game. Such questioning
became even more vociferous when – after his Goodison switch – he
struggled to blend into the team pattern, which a later team-mate
attributed to his 'playing better with the ball than without it'.
Nevertheless his bedding-in period was not overly protracted and
Dobson, like Latchford, became one of Everton's star performers for
the remainder of the decade.

He took the place of the last of the Three Graces, Colin Harvey,
who was sold to Sheffield Wednesday the same week. 'We called him
the White Pele,' said Charles Mills junior. 'To think that he got just
one England cap, against Malta, and Emlyn Hughes got sixty . . . It
just beggars belief.' His time at Hillsborough was brief, and after
quitting playing due to injury in 1976, he returned to Goodison on
Bingham's coaching staff. A few weeks later, Joe Royle's back
problems, plus competition from new faces, prompted Bingham to
sell him to Manchester City for £200,000. Royle had achieved much
and, but for injuries, would probably have done more, but the fee
received was generous for a man who had found the treatment table
more often than the net over recent seasons. He helped Manchester
City win the 1976 League Cup, and later played for Bristol City
– where he earned an England recall – and Norwich City, before
a knee injury ended his career. Charles Mills remembers him as 'a

wonderful character, a great player, in my opinion Everton's best post-war centre forward and probably worthy of a mention in the same breath as Dean and Lawton'. On retirement, Royle moved into management with Oldham Athletic in 1982, forging a successful career that led to his eventual return to Everton.

Fifteen games into the 1974/5 season, Everton had lost just once, but won only four times. The inordinate amount of matches they drew cost them dearly at the season's end. Still, they were a difficult side to beat, which meant that once more they occupied the upper echelons of the First Division. On 14 December 1974 Everton travelled to the Baseball Ground to play Derby County. 'Derby are, in my view, the most effective and attractive team in the division – on their day,' opined Norman Fox in *The Times*.[8] Yet it was Everton who emerged 1–0 winners – the goal coming from Latchford – to go to the top. A week later Carlisle United, who were enjoying their solitary campaign in football's top flight, visited Goodison. It was a game that Everton should have won easily, and although they missed the direction of Dobson in their midfield, two well-taken goals from Latchford – the first hit home cleanly after Connolly's header had hit a post, the second on the half-volley from Connolly's right-wing corner – propelled them into a 2–0 half-time lead. In the second half Carlisle immediately struck back, scoring two goals in three minutes and a third soon after. Despite laying siege to the Cumbrians' goal for the final 25 minutes Everton found their defence impossible to break down and fell to an inglorious 2–3 defeat. 'Better to put your money on Carlisle than Everton,' concluded the following Monday's *Times*.

The calculated percentage game practised by Bingham's men was seldom reminiscent of Catterick's great stylists of five seasons earlier, but it was effective – there was no doubting that – and Everton were back at the First Division's summit, with an excellent chance of winning the Championship.

A 2–1 win over Queens Park Rangers at Goodison on 8 March 1975 consolidated Everton's position at the top with just 10 games to go. A fifth-round FA Cup exit to eventual finalists Fulham focused minds, and Bingham promised, 'The chase is almost over and the prize is almost won. We are not cracking in the crunch.' A goalless draw with Leeds, a 0–2 defeat at Middlesbrough and a 1–1 draw with Ipswich showed some signs of slippage, but Everton travelled

Everton's 1906 FA Cup Winners. Thomas Keates wrote 'they were the observed of all observers, the cheered idols of everybody wherever they walked, rode or sat.' Back (left to right), J. Elliott (trainer,) Harold Makepeace, Walter Balmer, Jack Taylor, Bill Scott, Jack Crelley, Walter Abbott. Front: Jack Sharp, H. Bolton, Sandy Young, Jimmy Settle, Harold Hardman.

William Ralph 'Dixie' Dean and his teammates parading the FA Cup after victory over Manchester City. Dean later said, 'That made me feel so proud. I was walking ten feet tall because it meant I had won every honour in the game. That cup medal completed my collection.'

Above. Everton's 1938/39 team. Lawton, Jones, Sagar and Mercer stand from left to right on the back row, with Harry Cooke inbetween the goalkeeper and Mercer. 'They were a bloody good side,' Lawton later said, 'and the next year we should have won the League again, the FA Cup and the bloody Boat Race if they'd put us in it.'

Below, left. Hickson's extraordinarily courageous play would often see him put his head in places lesser (and saner) men would baulk at putting their feet.

Below, right. Harry Catterick described Brian Labone as 'the last of the great Corinthians'.

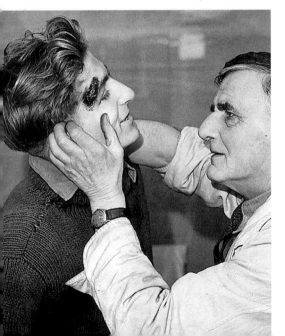

'The Golden
Vision'

Harry Catterick:
'That was my
greatest moment.
The Cup hadn't
been to Everton
for many years and
it was wonderful
to bring it back to
Merseyside and
receive the acclaim
of the crowds as
we returned to
the city.'

Above. 'The Three Graces'

Left. A modest, articulate man
Bob Latchford helped restore some
pride to Goodison at a time when living
in Liverpool's shadow was a way of life.

Opposite, top. 'When goals like Sharp's
at Anfield started to go in you knew
something was happening.'

Opposite, bottom. Howard Kendall
later said of Andy Gray, 'He was
blessed with the rare ability to lift and
amuse his teammates at the same time.
When things weren't going well I knew
that I could rely on him to instil a sense
of confidence into those around him.
He was invaluable to me and Everton.'

Above, left. 'We used to sing:
"He's fat, he's round, he's worth a
million pounds,"' wrote Carl Parker
in the iconic *When Skies Are Grey* fanzine
'To my mind Peter Reid was worth
much, much more than that
to Everton.'

Above, right. Neville Southall:
'The finest goalkeeper in the world'.

Left. In eighteen months during the
mid-eighties Howard Kendall dragged
a team from the depths to being the
best in the world. Later attempts to
replicate those glories eluded him.

Above, left. Tony Cottee on his spectacular debut against Newcastle United: 'Four goals in two league games, it was going like a dream,' he later wrote. 'But, as I realized in the weeks ahead, the flying start brought enormous expectations that would prove difficult to handle.'

Above, right. 'Johnson may have had perennial aspirations, some might say pretensions, to move up a level, but lacking the nous to put those into practice, he was always merely going to be just "Hamperman" – no more than the Birkenhead boy made good, perpetually swimming out of his depth.'

Right. Paul Rideout was just one of many men to have his career transformed in Joe Royle's 'Dogs of War team'. In six months he went from being an exiled reserve to the scorer of the winner in the FA Cup Final.

Left. 'I am joining the people's football club,' said David Moyes on his appointment. 'I want to win and I am sure the supporters want to win . . . I want the players to know what it is is like to win again and I want the supporters to know what it is like to win. We will try and play a brand of football that the people will enjoy, but when it comes down to it winning is the thing I want to do.'

Below. 'Remember the name . . . WAYNE ROONEY!'

to Carlisle United on Easter Saturday, 29 March, confident that the Cumbrians would not be a banana skin second time round. Bingham had seen them lose 0–2 at Birmingham the previous Tuesday, which had virtually assured their relegation. 'All season Carlisle have played good football without being able to put the ball in the net,' he said. 'That has been their great weakness . . .'[9]

Those words soon came back to haunt him. Carlisle strolled to an unlikely, though utterly deserved, 3–0 win. The same day Liverpool went to the top via a Keegan penalty, controversially awarded by Clive Thomas.

On Easter Monday Everton beat Coventry City 1–0 to return to the top with a game in hand, Dobson scoring the winner with a glorious knee-height volley from 25 yards. When they met Burnley the next Friday they were unable to add to Latchford's solitary goal and a late Noble header brought a draw. The next day Liverpool went ahead on goal difference, beating Leeds United 2–0 at Elland Road. But it was wickedly tight at the top. Stoke and Derby had pulled level with Liverpool and Everton. At the top were Liverpool who had played 39 games, Everton 38, Stoke City 39, Derby 38, all on 47 points. Next were Ipswich on 46 points from 38 games.

April 9 saw Everton travel to Kenilworth Road to face bottom-placed and already relegated Luton Town for their game in hand. In a match contested on a quagmire of a pitch, Everton outplayed the Hatters – Hurst hit a post, Latchford missed when put through by Smallman, Jones went close, all in the first half alone – yet could not add to Latchford's eighteenth-minute strike. Then they conceded two goals in a whirlwind four-minute period prior to the break. After half-time, Everton came out and continued the onslaught. Pearson went close within seconds of the restart, Jones had a chance cleared off the line, Latchford missed from close range and Barber saved a Pearson header. None of it was enough to break down the Luton defence. Bingham was vexed in defeat: 'We lost because we failed to take advantage of clear chances created by superior football. We outplayed Luton but lost.' But as the *Liverpool Echo* concluded, 'If you don't beat the team at the bottom, you don't deserve to win the title.'

The Championship was now slipping away from Everton, although a 1–0 win over Newcastle gave them a chance of pulling it off.

Not that Bingham's men did much to help themselves. In Everton's penultimate game of the season, Sheffield United were the visitors to Goodison. Despite streaking into a 2–0 half-time lead, through Smallman and Jones goals, they allowed the Blades back into the game. Eddy pulled one back on 48 minutes, and from there onwards it was Sheffield United who made the running. On 72 minutes Bingham sought to tighten up the midfield by bringing on Telfer for Pearson. A minute later Deardon equalized. Five minutes from time Tony Curry scored the winner. With Liverpool losing 0–1 to Middlesbrough and Derby being held 0–0 at Leicester, Everton could have closed the gap at the top to a point. Instead they had thrown away their best chance of winning the Championship for nother decade.

Everton's feeble Championship challenge had seen just two wins in the last 10 games and numerous openings at the top passed over. The *Observer* surmised that Everton had made an 'unscheduled stop at the top on their way to becoming a good team'. Maybe so. But in this frustrating decade of Everton's history, they could not win the most open Championship race of the era, which might have been taken by the lowest number of points in a generation, essentially because they could not beat, or even draw, Carlisle United.

○

WHILE THERE WAS undoubtedly room for improvement, Everton began the 1975/6 season – without major additions to the squad – reasonably well. Arsenal were knocked out of the League Cup, while champions Derby and Newcastle United were both comprehensively beaten in the league. Moreover, Everton were back in Europe for the first time in five years. Drawn against AC Milan they faced a stiff task, yet when the Italians arrived in Liverpool mid-September, they were a club torn by internal wrangling and takeover bids. *The Times* even suggested that factions within their ranks hoped to see them lose to speed up the takeover process. Everton performed creditably, keeping the Milan attack at bay, but were unable to crack the defence, and with two minutes remaining Mike Bernard was sent off for a foul on Benetti, the captain. Bingham was not happy. 'If you ask me what I learnt from this match, all I would say was how to organize a massed defence, foul cleverly and waste time, but this is what you must expect against teams like these.' AC Milan manager

Gustavo Giagnoni was more upbeat: 'This is just what we came for,' he said. 'Now we can have them on our ground.'

Prior to the second leg two weeks later, Bingham said, 'It will be a tight match. I cannot see it being anything else. But the players are optimistic.' The game was dominated by bad refereeing decisions from the East German official Rudi Glockner. Everton fell to a sixty-seventh-minute penalty awarded against Lyons for a handball. 'If he had not given a penalty then he would have invented some other offence by us,' said a furious Lyons, after the game. Everton had had two clear penalty efforts turned down: first, when Gary Jones was fouled – according to one report, '10 yards inside the penalty box' – only for a free kick to be awarded outside the area; later, when Jim Pearson was knocked down. A brilliant save from Albertosi to deny Martin Dobson a headed equalizer three minutes from time secured the Italians a narrow victory.

The turning-point in Everton's season and, for that matter, Bingham's managerial career, came 10 days after the defeat at the San Siro, with a 0–5 defeat at Queens Park Rangers. It marked the end of Bingham's 'London Luck' (since the start of the 1974/5 season Everton were undefeated in the capital, winning four and drawing four) as well as the onset of a miserable run of just four wins over the next four months. Crowds dropped considerably, with 13,000 off the previous season's average of 40,000, and searching questions were asked about Bingham's ability.

Things came to a head after a 0–3 defeat away at Manchester City on 21 February 1976, which left Everton in fifteenth place. After the game a number of fans protested outside the players' entrance. Inside the dressing room, a furious argument had broken out, which ended with Gary Jones and Mike Buckley demanding transfers. It was, according to Michael Charters, 'as poor a performance as I can recall from an Everton team', the dressing-room revolt 'unprecedented in my knowledge of Goodison affairs'. Buckley declined to comment, but speculation linked him with a move to Leeds. Jones was more open: 'Like any player I am ambitious for success and I do fancy a move to another club.' David Lawson's transfer request had already been turned down. Bingham held talks a few days later, aimed at clearing the air, but emerged despondent. 'To be honest I do not know if they will be happier but I hope they will.'

Jones was sold to Birmingham the following summer, and Buckley became, through a combination of injuries and loss of form, a peripheral figure at Goodison before his departure to Sunderland in August 1978. Neither man, despite their all too obvious disenchantment with Bingham, had done much to redress Everton's decline on the field and there followed a five-game losing streak through March and into April, which saw Everton fall to sixteenth. Only a late rally at the end of the season lifted them to the relative respectability of eleventh.

One bright spot in the final month of the season had been the emergence of Andy King, an extrovert footballer in an era of extroverts. Extravagantly talented on the field and gregarious off it, he was a crowd-pleaser and favourite in two spells that spanned eight years. Signed by Billy Bingham from Luton Town in April 1976, aged just 19, he responded to the challenge that if the team gained four points from the final three games of the season they would be rewarded with a holiday in Spain by scoring a memorable double against Derby County, which secured a 3–1 victory and the Spanish trip. The Derby win set a precedent for the midfielder, who scored 68 goals in an Everton career that encompassed 247 games. In Andy King Evertonians found someone not only with sublime footballing ability, but a chirpy personality and constant smile. He further endeared himself to fans when he said, 'I don't think of myself as a southerner, I'm a northerner with a funny accent!'

Pressure was still mounting on Bingham even before the 1976/7 season kicked off. Fans would tolerate football without style if there was substance in results, but drab football and disastrous results were anathema to Evertonians. Patience with the 'robots' was thin. Yet the team who had been so lacklustre all year long confounded their critics with an excellent opening-day display, thrashing the previous season's nearly-men Queens Park Rangers 4–0 at Loftus Road. Although still lacking consistency, Everton went into October in second place. But as was so often the case during this era, the foundations for success were shaky. Yet another defeat to Liverpool in mid-October, with more losses that month and in November, left Everton languishing in mid-table. Their growing tribulations held a hint of farce: when West Bromwich Albion beat them 3–0 at the Hawthorns on 27 November, one of their goals had resulted from a dog running on to the pitch and panicking Everton's incredulous defenders.

With a last throw of the dice, Bingham signed Bruce Rioch and Duncan McKenzie. Immediately both players captured the fans' imagination, but it was McKenzie whom they took to their hearts. He had been with Nottingham Forest between 1969 and 1974, and later claimed it was a club he never wanted to leave. Brian Clough had prised him away during his infamous 44-day stint as manager of Leeds United. At Elland Road McKenzie built up and made famous his repertoire of party tricks – which would probably have been better suited to a circus – and became as well known for leaping over his Mini and throwing golfballs phenomenal distances as he was for playing football. A spell with Belgian champions Anderlecht followed, before Bingham came in for him.

'Sign McKenzie and you're sacked,' was the popular wisdom of the day, which was unfair given the rapport that the maverick had soon built up with the Goodison crowd. Evertonians' love for McKenzie stemmed from his home début, a 2–2 draw with Birmingham City. Dobson told him to 'go out and do one or two tricks and the crowd will absolutely love you'. McKenzie duly obliged with two goals, one from the penalty spot and the other from a Terry Darracott cross-field pass. 'I was appreciative of them and their support,' he said later. The crowd were delighted by his skills and appreciative of his credo – 'Entertainment is what it's all about,' he once declared. 'Sure, it's important to win, but there's room for some fun and games along the way' – and he was soon a hero. 'In our street it was "McKenzie passes to McKenzie, who goes past one, past two, crosses for McKenzie, one–nil,"' Steve McManaman remembered. 'There were eleven Duncan McKenzies in our team!'

It was not enough to save Bingham, though. With more defeats over Christmas and no end in sight to his insipid brand of football, he was sacked on 10 January 1977. 'I've had pressures from every quarter, and I have tried to do the job as well as I could,' he said. 'Some people may debate whether that was the right way, but it was the best I could do.'[10] Maybe so, and perhaps he wasn't given enough time to find the right blend, but at a time when Everton's Anfield neighbours – whom they had not beaten for more than five years – were enjoying successes on both domestic and European fronts, the pressures of being overshadowed were too great. Bingham and the fans were left to rue the fact that his team of 'robots' could not bring the title back to Goodison.

In his place came Newcastle United's manager, Gordon Lee. For 11 years his towering figure had been a mainstay of the Aston Villa defence before he set out on a managerial path that took him from Port Vale to St James's Park via Blackburn Rovers, whom he had led to promotion in the 1974/5 season. He was a passionate, committed and decent man who had garnered an unfair reputation – perhaps because he had sold Malcolm MacDonald to Arsenal when he was Newcastle manager – for dour, workmanlike teams rather than, in his words, 'coffee-house ball-jugglers' or 'Flash Harrys'. Yet he was a lot better than his reputation implied and even those for whom he was said, erroneously, to have little time spoke highly of him. Duncan McKenzie, who was meant to be an early victim of the new status quo, said of Lee: 'I've found him fair, sympathetic on occasion, understanding often, and generally ready to do his best for me – as he is ready to do his best for everybody else on the playing staff.'[11]

Lee steadied Everton's slide down the table. Mike Pejic, a £150,000 purchase from Stoke City and one-time England international, added some gritty panache to the left side of the defence. By the end of the 1976/7 season, after a slow start, Lee's men had been steered up to the relative respectability of ninth place. By then, though, greater dramas had taken place in both domestic cup competitions.

In Bingham's final days as Goodison supremo, the League Cup had represented some compensation for a poor league campaign. On succeeding the Irishman, one of Lee's first tasks had been to guide Everton past a tricky two-legged semi-final with Bolton Wanderers – won 2–1 on aggregate – and on to Wembley. Here they met Aston Villa on 12 March 1977. Everton went into the match confident after five successive wins. Much was expected of McKenzie, and likewise of Villa's dashing Scottish striker Andy Gray – fresh from a dual victory as PFA Player of the Year and Young Player of the Year. In the event both proved disappointing in a 0–0 draw, the first stalemate since the game was first staged at Wembley in 1967.

Both teams converged on Hillsborough the following Wednesday for the replay. Dobson was missing with a hip injury and the game looked as if it was heading for another stalemate when, 10 minutes from the end, Roger Kenyon put the ball into his own net. Rather than demoralizing his team-mates, Kenyon's error focused the minds of an Everton attack that had been struggling to get into its stride, and they channelled men forward in an effort to gain an equalizer. Their efforts were rewarded in the dying seconds. McKenzie played in Pearson who found Latchford in the congested penalty area and he gleefully rammed the ball home.

It was nearly another month before the second replay was scheduled. This time the venue was Old Trafford, and for much of the game the prize looked to be Everton's. They opened the scoring late in the first half: Nicholl fouled Latchford and from the resulting free kick Goodlass hoisted the ball in, McNaught rose to head downwards and Latchford guided it home.

It remained so until 10 minutes from the end of normal time, despite an incessant Villa assault. Just as it seemed that the Everton defence would take everything the Midlanders could throw at them, they were breached twice: first, from Nicholl's left-footed shot, then two minutes later when Little squeezed the ball past Lawson from an oblique angle. Villa had barely finished celebrating when Lyons scrambled home an equalizer from a Goodlass corner. With the onset of extra time, both teams carried on doggedly, but the game looked as if it was going to be decided by penalties – then a novelty in domestic football. But with two minutes left, disaster struck. Brian Little kicked the winner when a deflection off the unfortunate Goodlass wrongfooted everyone and the Villa forward reacted quickest to steer the ball past Lawson. So, with five hours of play spread over three matches and more than a calendar month, yielding more than £500,000 in gate receipts, the game was lost in the most unfortunate circumstances. As was so frequently the case in the 1970s, luck had not been on Everton's side. The players were as forlorn as the fans. 'When the cross came over, the ball clipped my left foot and it spun away past me and past Terry Darracott,' said Goodlass. 'If it hadn't hit me he would have cleared it easily.'

'After it had been deflected, I just could not reach the ball,' said Darracott. 'It spun away from me and went through to Little just a few yards away and that was that.'

Ten days later, Everton had the opportunity to return to Wembley in the FA Cup semi-final. First, though, they needed to overcome their mighty Anfield neighbours. Martin Dobson's 30-yard effort in the previous October's derby defeat had been Everton's first goal against their neighbours since David Johnson's strike had beaten them five years earlier. Since then, Everton's record had been: played 11, won 0, lost 6, drawn 5, goals for 1, goals against 6. The semi-final offered the double whammy of avenging that miserable run and restoring some pride to Merseyside's success-starved Blues.

Interest was as feverish as ever, and Everton's revival of fortunes under Lee had given the fans cause for cautious optimism, despite the absence of Bob Latchford through injury. Yet Liverpool scored first when Terry McDermott sent a beautiful chip over the head of Lawson. McKenzie equalized when Jim Pearson disposed of Emlyn Hughes and crossed for the fans' favourite to score. Jimmy Case's looping header put Liverpool back in the lead, but McKenzie glided in from the right and crossed for Rioch, who cancelled Liverpool's advantage.

As the match seemed to be heading for a stalemate, Lee sent on Bryan Hamilton for Dobson as the attacking onus passed to Everton. Hamilton, a £40,000 signing from Ipswich Town in November 1975, had earned something of a reputation as a goalscoring midfielder at Portman Road, but struggled to be more than a fringe player in his second season at Everton; when given the chance, though, he worked tirelessly down the right side of midfield, with a blend of skill and tenacity.

With the scores balanced at 2–2 and just minutes remaining, Goodlass cut in from the by-line and played a centre for Hamilton. Running into the six-yard area Hamilton deflected the ball past Clemence and into the Liverpool net. He had scored better goals in his time, but none was more important. Everton were 3–2 in front. The blue half of Maine Road rose in wild celebration to what would surely be the winning goal, and the Liverpool players looked forlorn as they faced the inevitability of a rare defeat. Their despondency, however, was short-lived.

Clive Thomas – the referee – disallowed the goal and instead gave Liverpool a free kick. His decision was inexplicable and met with incredulity from both sets of players. During the match he told Ken McNaught that Hamilton had 'obviously handled the ball'. Then afterwards all he would say was that there had been 'an infringement of the rules of the Football Association'. On the following Monday he said that Hamilton was offside, although his linesman had not flagged. He later said in *A Celebration of the Merseyside Derby*,

'From the angle of the cross there was no way Bryan Hamilton could have controlled the ball without the use of his arm. In no way could I say that from behind I could have seen the ball make contact with his hand or his arm. But I was 100 per cent certain that he couldn't have controlled it any other way. So I disallowed it. For handball.'

In other words Thomas had denied Everton a place in the FA Cup Final for imagining an infringement. While bad luck had seen off Everton's chances in the League Cup, their best chance for years of, simultaneously, getting one over Liverpool and reaching Wembley had been wrecked. The following Wednesday Liverpool swept to a 3-0 victory in the replay and Everton were left to rue missed opportunities.

The day after the semi-final, the luxury cruise liner *Monte Granada* sailed out of the Mersey. It was expected to be the last cruise out of the port. Another proud part of the city's heritage had seemingly been lost.

◊

GORDON LEE SPENT the summer of 1977 setting his mark on his new club. He signed George Wood from Blackpool for £150,000, in an effort to rectify Everton's inconsistency between the posts, and sold Dai Davies – who never shook off the tag 'Dai the Drop' – to Wrexham in September. A year later David Lawson departed for Luton Town.

The brilliant and often unerring accuracy of England international Dave Thomas's crosses prompted Lee to pay Queens Park Rangers £200,000 for the winger's services. The dashing flanker had originally made his name with Burnley where he won a host of England under-23 honours. Soon a number of big clubs were coveting his signature including Leeds, Manchester United and Everton. Surprisingly, he rejected their advances and opted for Second Division QPR in October 1972 at a cost of £165,000. After gaining promotion at the end of his first season with the club, he came agonizingly close to winning the Championship with them in 1976. This was after picking up the first of his eight England caps, against Czechoslovakia in October 1975. Famous for his rubber-soled boots and socks rolled down round his ankles without shinpads – a dangerous habit, given the reputations of one or two defenders of his era – Lee bought him for the purpose of increasing service to Bob

Latchford. It was an inspired move. Although he rarely contributed with goals of his own – he scored just six times during his two-year spell at Goodison – his direct style wrought havoc among opposing defences. While most wingers can either cut inside or run to the by-line before crossing, Thomas could do both to equally devastating effect. 'He was a fine player, Dave Thomas,' remembered Charles Mills. 'As good a crosser of the ball as I'd seen since the thirties.'

Ken McNaught was sold to Aston Villa and in his place the promising young centre back Mark Higgins established himself in the first team. Football ran in the Higgins family's veins and his father John had been a member of the Bolton Wanderers team of the 1950s that twice reached the FA Cup Final and won it in 1958. Lee admired him for his youthful authority, fleet foot, dominance in the air and excellence in tackling. His place in the first team was secured by injury to Roger Kenyon in only the second match of the campaign, which saw him figure in the next 21 games.

The 1977/8 season undoubtedly belonged to Bob Latchford, though. Aided by the arrival of Thomas, who liked to get in early accurate crosses for Latchford to bundle into the back of the net, the big striker prospered and the net bulged. After taking five games to get on to the score-sheet he opened his account in the 5–1 mauling of Leicester and then, after a goal against Manchester City, he hit four past QPR. Of Latchford's second goal, a diving header from a Thomas cross, Lee commented, 'That was the kind of goal I was dreaming about when I bought Thomas. Latchford is deadly when he gets the ball in the area at the right time and with the right pace behind it. Thomas can do this for him.' A brace in the thrilling 4–4 draw with Newcastle on 29 October took his total to nine by the start of November.

Early in the season the *Daily Express* had offered a £10,000 prize for the first player to score 30 league goals that season, and local bookmakers had originally offered 100–1 for Latchford to reach the magical total. A brace against Birmingham on 12 November, then a hat-trick against an improving Coventry side at the end of the month, had those odds tumbling and the fans salivating. Coventry had started their day in third place, level on points with Everton, but Latchford's treble, along with goals from Dobson, King and Pearson, had seen them off 6–0. *The Times* commented that Thomas 'tills the flanks skilfully, flights his centres perfectly for the big men, particularly

Latchford, who needs the ball where he can reach for it or run on to it to be most effective'. Higgins also attracted praise and they added that he 'has given the defence a central firmness'.

Everton were riding high in the league and ended 1977 – the year they had started, under Bingham, in fifteenth place – second to runaway leaders Nottingham Forest. By then Lee had added the bite of Arsenal's Trevor Ross to his midfield at a cost of £180,000, and while he did his best to talk down Everton's Championship challenge, many were tipping them for the title. A shock 2–6 defeat at home to Manchester United on Boxing Day had, however, exposed some of the side's frailties, and in the event the Championship was beyond Everton. They finished the season in third place on 55 points, nine behind champions Nottingham Forest.

Latchford had, however, given success-starved Evertonians something to cheer about. A long-awaited England call-up against Italy came shortly before Christmas – his first appearance of a 12-cap career in which he bagged five goals. Domestically he was excelling himself and by New Year was two-thirds of the way to winning the £10,000 prize. After something of a lean patch, in which he scored just twice in the first nine league games of 1978, five goals in four games over the Easter period saw him well on course. After reaching 28 goals with three games remaining, one local restaurateur said that if Latchford did not score in the next game he would shave his head. When Everton played Middlesbrough, their next opponents, no one from either side managed to score and only George Telfer got on the score-sheet in the following match against West Bromwich Albion. So Latchford had to wait until the final day of the season – when Everton met Chelsea at Goodison on 29 April – to see if he could score the necessary couple of goals. It seems strange now to consider the hype whipped up by the *Express*'s prize in an age when even journeymen players can command such amounts for their weekly pay packet, but in 1978 £10,000 was a small fortune. For Evertonians it provided a focal point, to which hopes and expectations could be channelled in the absence of a Cup Final or credible title assault.

Nearly forty thousand people packed into Goodison to see the game but when Everton swept into a commanding 3–0 lead without Latchford getting on to the score-sheet, many expected his luck to have run out. But Latchford was indomitable. He scored the fourth, and with 10 minutes left Everton were awarded a penalty. Latchford made no mistake in finishing off the 6–0 drubbing to set Goodison wild with cheering and collect the money. It was the week of the fiftieth anniversary of Dixie Dean's 60-goal haul, and in a gesture that his generous predecessor would have smiled on, half of the prize money went to the PFA Benevolent Fund while the rest was split among the other players and ground staff. Latchford himself took home just £192, and four years later was still trying to convince the taxman that he did not owe anything!

At the season's end, Lee again wheeled and dealed to try to bring a winning mix to Goodison. Jim Pearson was sold to Newcastle United and Mick Buckley to their north-eastern rivals Sunderland. More controversially, Duncan McKenzie was sold to Chelsea.

If any one player has come to symbolize the Lee era it is McKenzie. Despite the upturn in results and McKenzie's protestations that their relationship was the picture of cordiality, the antipathy between the gaunt-faced manager and his showboater forward was sometimes barely suppressed. Much has been made of McKenzie's absences from the side – perhaps too much. When asked about McKenzie and his supposed preference for rugged triers, Lee would throw back a question in response: 'If a team of Duncan McKenzies played a team of Terry Darracotts who would win the game?' Before reporters could begin to speculate, he would answer the question for them: 'The Terry Darracotts would win 5–0 every time because no one on the Duncan McKenzies' team would be willing to go and win the ball.' (McKenzie often had the same conversation with his boss, but would turn the argument on its head and rubbish Lee's claims – on the basis that Darracott was no good in goal!) Even so, Lee selected McKenzie more often than Darracott.

McKenzie's relationship with the Goodison crowd remained remarkable. When he returned the following November with his new Chelsea team-mates, neither they nor he could believe what happened. In a game from which Everton emerged 3–2 winners, McKenzie scored for Chelsea to be greeted with an ovation from the home crowd.

The man bought to replace the mercurial McKenzie was Blackpool's Micky Walsh. A brave, quick striker, who had made his reputation as the winner of the BBC's Goal of the Season award and as a prolific lower-league scorer, earning the first of his 22 Ireland caps while at Bloomfield Road, he never quite lived up to his

£325,000 fee. Out of sorts for much of his solitary season at Everton, he departed for Queens Park Rangers in a straight swap that carried Peter Eastoe in the opposite direction. Geoff Nulty arrived from Lee's old club, Newcastle, but – honest and committed trier though he was – ultimately lacked the calibre to be more than a fringe player.

The purchase that captured fans' imaginations came in September when Colin Todd arrived from Derby County for £300,000, equalling the record fees paid for Bob Latchford and Martin Dobson. Few doubted that Lee would get value for money from signing him, even though he was nearing his thirtieth birthday. A winner of Championship medals with Derby in 1972 and 1975 – the same year he was decorated with the PFA Player of the Year award – and 27 England caps, the blond north-easterner was one of the best defenders of his generation. Yet Goodison Park saw only rare glimpses of the form that once earned him comparisons with Bobby Moore. One of the reasons behind this was Lee's insistence on playing one of the finest centre backs of the era in the unfamiliar right-back position, as a result of which Todd's form suffered and his Everton career lasted just 35 games.

By the time Todd had arrived, Everton were off to a flying start to the 1978/9 season. They won four of their first six games, including the opening three against Chelsea, Derby County and Arsenal, as well as an 8–0 trouncing of Wimbledon in the opening round of the League Cup, which featured five goals from Latchford and a Dobson hat-trick. Everton were regarded among the Championship favourites.

However, the opening day's fixture at Stamford Bridge has come to be remembered not for Andy King's solitary goal but for one of the worst days of football hooliganism involving Everton supporters. On the day when Latchford had completed his haul the previous April, all manner of trouble had broken out (as it frequently did, wherever Chelsea visited) at the end of the game, and Chelsea's mob had departed for London bruised and battered. Revenge was sworn. Mindful of this, when August came the Metropolitan Police had been extra-vigilant when escorting Everton's 500-strong visiting contingent back to Fulham Broadway tube station after King's goal had defeated Chelsea. Once on the train, it seemed that the intermittent fighting that had broken out around Stamford Bridge was over. Two stops down the line, at Earls Court, a gang of Chelsea fans piled into the last carriage and, as the train pulled away, began to attack anyone who looked even remotely like an Evertonian before making their way to the next carriage where they repeated the process. Further down the train Everton fans quickly caught wind of the commotion and went to help.

When the train stopped again at Kensington High Street, the platform was full of Chelsea hooligans, local skinheads and punks. Some were there for the thrill of a fight, others for some 'Scouse-bashing'. As the doors opened, they bombarded the train with bricks. The chaos inside turned to panic, as the mob on board ran through the carriages and attacked those who had escaped so far. The gang on the platform barred the doors with fire extinguishers so that the train could not move off and fought to get inside. Those who did tried to drag out Evertonians to be lynched on the platform by those who could not fight their way in. By then the few remaining British Transport police officers had run for reinforcements.

When they arrived several Everton supporters had been stabbed and many needed hospital treatment. It had been a vicious and expertly planned ambush, and for the victims, a terrible reminder of the hazards that came from following Everton in the seventies.

Living and watching football in more sanitized times, it is perhaps difficult to put into context or explain the violence that blighted football in the seventies and early eighties. Hooliganism was by no means confined to this era, and as far back as the nineteenth century there is evidence of riotous crowds at Everton and elsewhere. Today 'firms' of football hooligans arrange fights with rival gangs for 'pleasure', while in bookshops an entire subgenre of hooligan memoirs – mostly loaded with exaggeration, idle boasts and posturing – sit alongside more traditional works. Football hooliganism has tended to be perpetrated by a minority of fans, some fuelled by love of violence, others by alcohol or other stimulants. Sometimes it has been planned, at others it has been spontaneous; victims have usually been predesignated, though occasionally selection has been random.

In the seventies and early eighties the wrong-coloured scarf in the wrong street or pub at the wrong time would make almost any fan a target, sometimes with horrifying consequences. Both now and until the late sixties, the minority of perpetrators was tiny, but in the seventies and early eighties it was sizeable enough to taint the name of football and put off some followers for life. In his diary of the era,

George Orr wrote that at away games, 'If you ran you got caught and were given a good hiding and if you stayed and fought, the local police would try and arrest you.' Attendances dropped, grounds fell into dilapidation and what happened off the pitch was often more talked about than what happened on it.

Football violence was a cancer that ate away at the game during the seventies, and not just at Everton. Nevertheless, the Blues had their own exclusive problem perpetually glaring at them from the other side of Stanley Park. Without a trophy themselves since 1970, and lacking a win in a derby since November 1971, or even a goal between then and October 1976, Everton had had to watch as the Anfield machine collected trophy after trophy.

On 28 October 1978 Everton met Liverpool at Goodison. Having failed to beat Liverpool in 362 weeks, they faced the indignity of watching the run top seven years if they didn't manage it this time. Lyons, who had endured almost all of Everton's inglorious run, was missing with a knee injury, and Roger Kenyon stepped up to make a rare appearance in his place. Goodison was a 53,000 all-ticket sell-out, with a banner in Gwladys Street proclaiming, 'Andy is our King.' And so he was. When Pejic looped a long, high ball forward, Dobson got his head to it and the ball fell to King, who hit it from the edge of the Liverpool area and into the back of the Liverpool net. It was the afternoon's solitary goal, the run was over and no one was happier than Lyons, the man who hadn't played. 'People were smiling as they walked along on Sunday morning,' he wrote on his captain's page in the programme, a week later. 'Some came up to me with congratulations, even though I hadn't played. They would say: "You were happy yesterday." But I think they really meant it as much for themselves.'

In a pique of ungraciousness, Graeme Souness, who had tried to block the shot, claimed that King mis-hit it and Phil Thompson claimed that it took a deflection. The occasion was made even more memorable when the BBC's Richard Dukenfield was interviewing King at the end of the game for *Match of the Day*: he and King were unceremoniously removed from the touchline by a policeman before they had completed the interview. The inspector in charge of that area of the pitch told the BBC reporter, 'My instructions are that at the end of the game there will be nobody on the pitch . . . and that means NOBODY!'

King ended the season as top league scorer with 12 goals, and further endeared himself to Liverpool supporters by scoring the equalizer in the return derby at Anfield the following March. 'King's Drive', as his goal has subsequently come to be known, was the midfielder's greatest moment. Reflecting on it, he said, 'If I die tomorrow, I've done something that millions would give their right arm to have done.'

Everton remained unbeaten throughout November 1978, and continued to shadow their neighbours at the top of the league. The top slot continued to elude them, though. On 2 December 1978, their visit to West Bromwich Albion was called off because of bad weather, and the following week only Liverpool ending Nottingham Forest's record-busting 42-game unbeaten streak prevented Everton drawing level at the top. A week later, against Leeds, a late direct free kick four minutes from time by Trevor Ross secured Everton's record as the First Division's only unbeaten team, grabbing a 1–1 draw. Finally, two days before Christmas, Everton lost it against Coventry, but a single Billy Wright goal on Boxing Day was enough to beat Manchester City and maintain momentum at the top.

Gordon Lee had become the hottest managerial property around. He revealed that two clubs had made tentative bids to steal him from Everton, but he had rejected both out of hand. 'I don't think I will ever want to leave Everton. I cannot think of another English club I would rather work for. My only concern is to make Everton the most successful side in the country and by that I mean winning the First Division Championship.'[12] Despite his show of loyalty, Lee was often struggling to win over sections of the Everton support, even when his team were riding high. Perhaps it was his adherence to hardworking triers ahead of mavericks and entertainers, or even his long, stern face, which belied his passion for the game and love for Everton. It might have been his lack of firm roots at the club, or elements of all three, but he seemed to be trying perpetually to prove himself. Over time, the Lee era has come to be perceived as one of dour teams and dour football, but for more than half of his reign Everton were an attacking, winning team, challenging for honours.

As James Callaghan's Britain entered its winter of discontent, with strikes, power-cuts, mounting piles of rubbish and bitterly cold weather, games fell victim to the ice and cold. At the end of January

1979, after a gap of a month, the league programme resumed, although by then Everton had been knocked out of the FA Cup by Sunderland. They topped the table for a week after beating Bristol City on 10 February, but from then on their title challenge slipped away. As under Billy Bingham four years earlier, there had been too many draws. Everton won just five games after Christmas, losing six and drawing the remainder, and Latchford's goals dried up – he managed just three of his total of 19 (only 11 of which came in the league) – after Boxing Day. Not even the late-season additions of Brian Kidd or Peter Eastoe could bolster Everton's Championship challenge and they finished fourth on 51 points, well behind champions Liverpool.

With the season ending on a downbeat note, unrest spread in the dressing room and among the supporters. Dobson was one of the first departures, refusing the offer of a two-year contract extension. When Lee would not give the 31-year-old the three years he was demanding, he moved back to Burnley for £100,000. Always an elegant and stylish player, he had appeared in 230 league and Cup games for Everton, scoring an impressive total of 40 goals. Darracott and Kenyon left for America; Pejic for Aston Villa. Thomas and Latchford were thought to be unhappy that Lee reportedly wanted to use them as bargaining chips in a £1 million move for Wolves' Steve Daley, a deal that collapsed on the season's eve. Two months into the 1979/80 season, Thomas was on his way to Molineux anyway, without having played a further game for Everton. By then, Colin Todd had left Goodison, sold to Birmingham City for £275,000 just three days into the new season – a clear case of a considerably talented player being under-utilized.

Supporters lacked optimism as the 1979/80 season opened. Only John Bailey had been added to Everton's ranks and season-ticket sales were down 24 per cent. Supporters did not like the defensive nature of Lee's teams, despite the previous season's brief flirtation with glory. 'Goodison will never warm to the sight of players passing the ball around their own area,' wrote Wilf Heslop of Crosby, in the *Football Echo*'s letters page. 'They should go forward.' Other fans were less generous. 'Gordon Lee is too small for Everton,' said C. Smith of Liverpool 15. 'I blame everything on him.'[13] Chairman Philip Carter nevertheless spelt out his intentions for the season: he stated in his annual report that his ambition was to win the league. Lee admitted, 'I am under pressure. I realize this. But I will do things my way and sink or swim on that basis.'

Pre-season concerns about a lack of new players were allayed with the early-season additions of John Gidman, Garry Stanley and Asa Hartford as Lee tried vainly to find the right mix. Latchford was alternately injured or out of form, and Everton's previous over-reliance on his goals was brutally exposed. They floundered around the nether regions of the First Division in a woeful campaign in which they eventually finished nineteenth, having scored just 43 times.

On 1 March 1980, while watching Everton fall to a 1–2 derby defeat, Dixie Dean collapsed and died of a heart-attack. He was 72 and in a frail condition, having undergone the amputation of his left leg a few years earlier. He was revered by fans and fellow players alike. Joe Mercer described him as 'bigger and better than life', and Matt Busby said, 'He'd cost a ransom today.'

A week after Dean's death on 8 March, Everton had an opportunity to gain some solace from their wretched campaign. They met Ipswich Town in the quarter-final of the FA Cup following early-round wins over Aldershot, Wigan and Wrexham. In a storming performance full of the conviction that had been lacking all season long, Everton ran out 2–1 winners through a twenty-ninth-minute Latchford header and Kidd's scorching seventy-seventh-minute left-footed shot, after King's tapped free kick.

Five weeks later, they travelled to Villa Park to meet West Ham in the semi-final. The tie ended in a 1–1 draw, but that match and the replay in Leeds were dominated by the poor refereeing of Mr Seel from Carlisle. In the Villa Park game Everton went ahead, having been awarded a contentious penalty when Devonshire was judged to have held back King as they both rose for a cross. Kidd dispatched the penalty with aplomb, but was later sent off for tangling with Ray Stewart. Stuart Pearson eventually set up a replay at Elland Road.

Latchford – who had scored in every round until the first match of the semi-final when he appeared as a substitute – was back in place of the suspended Kidd, but again it was the controversial Seel who took centre stage. In the first 10 minutes of the second half he disallowed shots that found the net from both Latchford and Eastoe, each for handball, and one from Billy Bonds on the pretext of a foul. In extra time Devonshire's goal was cancelled by Latchford's diving header. The game was heading for a second replay when, two minutes from the end, Lampard broke Everton's hearts with the goal that sent his club to Wembley and sealed another trophyless season for the Blues.

'There was a feeling that they'd let us down again,' recalled Charles Mills junior. 'We'd gone through the '77 débâcle with Clive Thomas and the disallowed goal; and we'd lost in the League Cup Final second replay and that was bad luck. But by the time we got to the West Ham loss, we were definitely feeling let down. And Liverpool were winning everything at the time. There was a real feeling that we were owed some consolation.'

○

Lee was fast running out of ideas. He spent a frustrating summer of 1980 fruitlessly trying to bring inspirational new faces to Goodison, most notably Peter Reid, and had more fallings-out with his players. One, Andy King – Lee's most consistent performer during his three and a half years in charge – was sold to Queens Park Rangers for £425,000, while another, the previous season's Player of the Year, John Bailey, also looked set to leave.

Undaunted by his critics' readiness to write off Everton before the season had even begun, Lee announced his faith in youth. He opened the 1980/81 season with the untried novices Gary Megson, Steve McMahon, Kevin Ratcliffe and Graeme Sharp in his line-up to face Sunderland. Sharp, aged only 19, had been signed for £120,000 the previous April from Dumbarton. It took him a further – often frustrating – 18 months to make any real impact at Goodison while Aston Villa and Aberdeen, who had both tried to prise away the youngster from Dumbarton, rode high in Europe.

Ratcliffe – whom Lee played on the left of defence but who was in reality a centre half – had been taken on as an apprentice professional straight from school in June 1977. He won Wales under-15 and under-18 honours before making his Everton début in a goalless draw at Old Trafford in March 1980. The *Liverpool Echo* concluded that he had had an 'impressive début' giving Joe Jordan 'little scope'. Megson, son of the Sheffield Wednesday stalwart Don, had been a £250,000 purchase from Plymouth Argyle the previous

February. The 21-year-old red-haired midfielder played 25 games for Everton, without much distinction, later turning out competently and loyally for a number of other top-flight clubs, despite lacking the all-round finesse of the other members of Lee's young foursome. The final member of the quartet, Steve McMahon, made the most initial impact, although he was eventually to shine elsewhere. Showing authority and skill beyond his 18 years he remained in the side for nearly all of the rest of the season. Lee admired his tough tackling and quick distribution style, which was not dissimilar to that of Peter Reid, whom he had tried unsuccessfully to prise away from Bolton that summer. Despite playing in such a deep-lying position – just in front of the back four – his name appeared with some regularity on the score-sheet, and during his first season he notched five goals.

Alongside this young composite were the marginally more experienced Billy Wright, aged 22, and Joe McBride, 20. It was a daring move, and the subsequent trophy- and international-laden careers of Ratcliffe, Sharp and McMahon testify to Lee's ability in spotting potential. Yet what they had in promise they lacked in experience and fell to a 1–3 defeat to Sunderland. Lee changed his line-up and seemed to have struck the right formula when Everton embarked on a six-match winning streak in September and October, but it was not enough. Indeed, they won only six more times in the league all season. Some pride was restored with a win over Liverpool in the FA Cup fourth round, the first and only time Mick Lyons played for the victorious side in 20 derby appearances.

As the 1980/81 season drew to a close, speculation was rife about Lee's future. His contract as manager was drawing to its conclusion, and the board of directors remained tight-lipped. They seemed ambiguous in their dealings with Lee who, when pressed by journalists on the issue, did not appear to know if he was staying or going.

Everton closed the season on 4 May 1981 with a 0–0 draw against Wolves at Molineux, which lifted them to fifteenth place following a run of form that had seen just one win in their final dozen league matches. Within hours of the season's end Lee had been sacked. 'Gordon Lee has since been unfairly criticized,' said Charles Mills junior, 'if you look at the sides we had, and some of the players we had, flair players, Goodlass, McKenzie, Thomas, Latchford. Forest and Villa were winning the European Cup at the time, but we weren't far behind and it wouldn't have taken much to step up a gear. The last two years were poor, but I think, in hindsight, Gordon Lee deserves a degree of sympathy. Much underrated.'

Days later, Howard Kendall was installed as his replacement.

◊

SEVEN YEARS had passed since the final addition to Everton's Holy Trinity had departed Goodison, but even in that relatively short time the place had changed almost beyond recognition. Crowds were at their lowest level in living memory; the standard of the playing staff – though blessed with a plethora of promising youngsters – was the worst it had been since the austere fifties. And the days when John Moores's bountiful financial resources could be utilized in the transfer market were seemingly over.

The city of Liverpool had changed markedly too. The seventies had been a particularly harsh decade, with the port continuing to decline, further factory closures and mounting unemployment. Kendall's bedding-in period as manager was against a backdrop of violent inner-city riots, which dominated the national news.

At Goodison, a monumental task lay ahead of him. 'Nothing has happened here since 1970,' said Kendall, 'and it will take a bit of time to put it right. But we are geared to win trophies and that is what we aim to do.' Expectations were high, despite the scant resources available to him. As one newspaper put it, 'They're not asking much from Howard Kendall – only a three-minute mile, a century before lunch and a successful assault on Everest.' Yet his credentials were certainly promising and the fans were on his side. As Peter Mills said, 'There was great affection for Kendall. I think everyone had monitored his progress.'

After serving his managerial apprenticeship under Freddie Goodwin at Birmingham, then as player-coach at Stoke, Kendall had been appointed manager of Blackburn Rovers in the summer of 1979 after their relegation to the Third Division. He kicked off his career by winning promotion back to the Second Division and the following season Rovers finished fourth, missing promotion only on goal difference. With him he brought his assistant manager from Blackburn, Mick Heaton, and made seven close-season signings: Jim Arnold, Mike Walsh, Micky Thomas, Mick Ferguson, Alan Biley, Alan Ainscow and Neville Southall. The first six members of this 'magnificent seven' – a goalkeeper, a centre back, a winger, a striker (who stood at six foot three but wore size 6½ boots), another striker and a midfielder – were like many of Lee's later signings: doughty triers without the necessary skills to elevate them to the top level. The final member of the ensemble, then a virtually unknown 23-year-old goalkeeper, today needs little introduction.

Always one to spurn convention, Neville Southall came into football via a succession of non-league sides. As a schoolboy he played for Caernarfon District, both as goalkeeper and centre half. His manager was a fortunate man indeed because he had two men in his side who would go on to keep goal for Wales: Southall's rival at that time was a youngster by the name of Eddie Niedzwiecki, later to play for Wrexham and Chelsea before injury prematurely ended his career. Southall also played for Llandudno Swifts, and on leaving school played for a succession of semi-professional teams to supplement his income. His full-time jobs were as unglamorous as the teams he played for – Bangor City, Conway United and Winsford Town: he was a labourer, a hod carrier, a bin man and ended up at the Ritz, a café in Llandudno, where he worked seven days a week for the princely sum of £18. By then he had attracted the attention of several scouts, and Bury gave him his first taste of league football. Under the guidance of Bury's coach, Wilf McGuinness, the former Manchester United boss, Southall blossomed, but was still incredulous when he read in his newspaper one morning that Everton were going to sign him. He sought to clarify what he thought had been a mistake, but his manager, Jim Illey, told him that the deal was finalized, provided they could come to an agreement with Winsford, Southall's last non-league club, over their cut of the fee.

Southall initially thought he would be rivalling Jim McDonough and Martin Hodge for the goalkeeping slot, but Kendall surprised everyone by going back to his former club, Blackburn Rovers, and signing Jim Arnold, who went straight into the first team. 'I started the first season,' Arnold later recalled, 'but Neville's ability later came through and I ended up being more of a spectator than a goalkeeper.' Nevertheless, the two friends had to battle it out for more than two years before Southall secured the number-one shirt.

It was also a time of departures. John Gidman left for Manchester United and Asa Hartford followed him down the M62 in the early stages of the new season, when he joined the sky blue of City. Garry Stanley was another early-season departure, to Swansea City. At the

Vetch Field he linked up again with Bob Latchford, who had been the biggest name to move on during the pre-season. Just as his arrival had served as the prelude to Kendall's departure in 1974, so Kendall's return seven years later precipitated his own exit, at a price of £125,000. Latchford spent two years at the Vetch Field before spells at NAC Breda, Coventry City, Lincoln City and Newport County; on retiring he took a job with Ladbrokes but later returned to football as Birmingham City's youth coach.

A modest, articulate man, he helped restore some pride to Goodison at a time when living in Liverpool's shadow had become a way of life. Latchford's name is still synonymous with his 30-goal haul: 'The money side of the award is secondary to me. The prestige and sense of achievement in reaching the record is the part that has thrilled me,' he had said, on reaching his target. 'Proud is too strong a word – pleased with myself would be nearer the mark. And very tired.'[14]

The 1981/2 season was one of consolidation and experimentation. Little of note happened on the playing side, with Everton finishing a more healthy eighth; average attendances dropped by a further 2000 to just over 24,000; and early cup exits occurred in both domestic competitions. Yet it was also a time when potential young stars were establishing solid reputations in the first team. Southall, Ratcliffe, Sharp, Gary Stevens and Kevin Richardson all enjoyed extended spells in the side.

Kendall also smashed the club-transfer record, paying £750,000 to bring a young attacking midfielder, just short of his twenty-first birthday, to Goodison. His name was Adrian Heath. He had made his début for Stoke City in a League Cup tie at Northampton Town aged 18. However, it had not been he who grabbed all the headlines the following day but his future employer Howard Kendall, who scored twice in a 3–1 victory. Kendall paid close attention to him and throughout his career, as player and coach, acted as his mentor and, in many ways, benefactor. Heath made his début in a royal blue shirt in January 1982 against Southampton, and spent much of the remainder of the season flitting between a midfield and an attacking role, scoring six times in 22 appearances, but failing to impress highly expectant sections of the Goodison faithful. On occasion, he found himself on the receiving end of barracking from the terraces. Much of this could be attributed to his inability to hold down a regular position in the side. 'I've never considered myself to be an out-and-out striker,' said Heath, 'because I think there is more to my game than being a goalscorer.' Eventually, of course, he found his niche.

○

AT THE SEASON'S END Kendall continued his rebuilding programme. Again there was a significant departure: Mick Lyons – the man who would bleed blue – was allowed to join Sheffield Wednesday. On the day of the transfer, so the oft-told anecdote goes, a supporter found him in a pub crying his eyes out. 'It was as if his wife had left him,' recalled the fan. 'Of course she hadn't, he'd been sold by the club he loved, but I wonder whether he would have been as upset if she had ditched him.' In all he had appeared 460 times for his beloved Everton over 12 seasons, earning England under-23 and England B caps as well as the club captaincy. Success had eluded him, though, as did derby victories, almost until the end. His critics derided his play as crude and his presence as a jinx, but such sniping does a disservice to his spirited, resolute and brave service. Indeed, he had been inspirational in various Everton sides throughout the seventies.

As one favourite left Goodison, another returned. Andy King had spent an unremarkable 18 months in West London before being sold to West Bromwich Albion, where he failed to live up to the unfairly high expectations of being Bryan Robson's successor. Over the summer of 1982, after begging Howard Kendall to give him a second chance at Goodison, he proved his commitment to Everton by turning up at Bellefield to train even though he was still a West Brom player. His attitude impressed Kendall and he decided to exchange Peter Eastoe for him. Although he started in impressive fashion with a 25-yard curler against Aston Villa, a persistent knee injury hampered his chances, and he was edged out.

Kendall went to Anfield to buy Kevin Sheedy for £100,000, making him the first player to cross Stanley Park since Johnny Morrissey in 1962. Sheedy couldn't run particularly fast or tackle particularly hard; he had a tendency to drift out of games and was prone to injury. In fact, in an era in which modern midfielders raced around the football field as if their lives depended on it and tackled everything that resembled an opponent, it could have been argued that there was little room for a player like Sheedy. Yet he possessed something that set him apart from his contemporaries: the finest left foot in football. The son of a publican in Builth Wells on the Welsh borders, he had begun his career with Hereford United where his delicate and precise passing earned him a transfer to Liverpool. Faced with competition for a place in the side from the likes of Jimmy Case, Sammy Lee, Graeme Souness, Terry McDermott and Ray Kennedy, many of whom were seasoned internationals, his appearances were restricted to just three games in nearly five years at Anfield.

It was surprising for fans of both clubs when Sheedy made the £100,000 switch, which was settled by tribunal. Bob Paisley had been unhappy to lose such a potentially good player, but was equally loath to break up his midfield to include an untried 21-year-old. Sheedy was an instant success at Goodison and weighed in with 11 league goals in his first season, playing in more games than any other Everton team member, with hindsight an impressive feat given the injury problems that later blighted his Everton career.

A man who tasted more success at Anfield was David Johnson, who followed Sheedy to Goodison for an indentical fee. After his misguided sale to Ipswich nine years earlier he had returned to Merseyside in 1976, having won the first of his eight England caps. However, he didn't thrive in his second spell at Goodison and was sold 20 months later to Manchester City.

Everton began the 1982/3 season erratically. A 0–2 opening-day defeat at newly promoted Watford was followed by a 5–0 demolition of newly crowned European champions, Aston Villa, then an impressive win over Spurs. Five games without a win were followed by a three-match victory streak that was ended by Southampton. It represented progress of a sort, and Kendall's precocious young team was beginning to settle. Or so it seemed.

November 6, 1982, marked the first meeting of the season with Liverpool. Midweek before the game, Kendall had gone back to Blackburn to bring in their experienced centre back, Glenn Keeley, on loan as cover for the injured Higgins. 'Keeley replaces Higgins for what is likely to be a memorable day one way or the other,' said *The Times* – ominously – on the morning of the match. 'Everton have played some sparkling football at Goodison this season and the speed of their attack in pursuit of the sweeping passes of Sheedy could expose Liverpool's Achilles heel.'

History tells us otherwise. Keeley was sent off on the half-hour mark for blatantly hauling back Dalglish with a despairing snatch at his shirt, which left Everton – already a goal behind – with a hopeless task: Liverpool had the space now to cut through them with ease. Rush scored four times, Lawrenson grabbed the middle goal. Everton were humiliated. 'People have gone overboard about the game,' said Kendall, attempting to rationalize after the débâcle. 'We were beaten by a very good side and we only had ten men for most of the time. Any side is going to have to do it all against Liverpool.'

The letters page of the *Football Echo* was, inevitably, devoted to soul-searching. Criticism centred on a lack of bite and imagination in midfield and pace in defence. Billy Wright was alternately too small, too fat or too slow. Readers suggested that Ratcliffe and Higgins should be given a chance in central defence, perhaps Derek Mountfield too; while David Johnson was not the answer to the lack of goals up front. Kendall seemed to escape the anger of most fans and the mood was more contemplative than vitriolic. 'What has happened to Everton?' pondered Vic Ferns of Ormskirk. 'Where are the great games, the School of Science . . . ? Recently Goodison Park is a depressing place. I would like to think things will be like old times again, but for me, I am sure this is only a dream.' C. D. West of Formby directed his ire at the Everton directors. 'Maybe last week's débâcle might wake the Everton board to the fact that they have been conducting the affairs in a downmarket manner. We are now in the sad position of being happy with just surviving in the First Division.'

The match was a turning-point of sorts. After it Gary Stevens, who had spent the previous 18 months vying for the right-back position with Brian Borrows, was brought back to the first team. Borrows never returned and his career passed creditably though almost unnoticed with Bolton Wanderers, then Coventry City. Kevin Ratcliffe, who had mostly been played on the left of defence, moved to his favourite central position.

A month later Kendall signed Peter Reid from Bolton Wanderers for £60,000, a tenth of the price Gordon Lee had been prepared to pay for him two years earlier when the deal had collapsed over personal terms. Yet the man whom Kendall later regarded as Everton's most important signing since the war was utterly out of sorts in his opening days at Goodison, off pace and untidy in his play. When he succumbed to injury just 10 games after signing and missed the final three months of the season, Kendall regarded the buy as a mistake and his youth-team coach, Colin Harvey, who had scouted Reid, recommended him and even set up the deal, went as far as apologizing for his part in it.

Everton ended the 1982/3 season in seventh place, helped in great amount by a run of six wins in the final eight games. What looks like progress today – the burgeoning Heath-Sharp forward partnership, the establishment of Stevens and Ratcliffe in defence and Sheedy in midfield – was not viewed as such then. Again eyes were cast over to Anfield where Liverpool were picking up their fourteenth league title and the European Cup. Everton had finished far off the pace and domestic – not to mention Continental – success seemed as distant a prospect as ever. Only 12,872, a post-war low, turned out to see the penultimate home game of the season, against Coventry City, while the average attendance barely teetered over 20,000.

The slump in spectators could be explained in part by the nationwide economic recession, which was biting Liverpool with a vengeance. The recently published 1981 census results revealed the true extent of the city's malaise with 17.8 per cent unemployment and one in five households classified as 'economically inactive'. The population was shrinking too, as people left their homes to find work elsewhere. Between 1971 and 1981 Merseyside experienced a decrease in population of 8.7 per cent to 1,511,915. Over the following decade it fell by a further 9 per cent. A heroin epidemic was sweeping the city with five thousand registered users and children as young as 12 or 13 caught up in it. 'We are on the verge of catastrophe,' warned Bill Skellinn, chair of Merseyside Drugs Council. The city's once proud cultural heritage was being ripped apart by the puerile television satire *Bread*. More serious dramas such as Alan Bleasdale's *Boys from the Blackstuff* were misinterpreted: outsiders saw his social realism as almost jocular – the affable, laughable Scouser, perpetually on the take, encapsulated by Yozzer Hughes's plea, 'Gissa job.'

Kendall had no money, either. Everton had had to change banks from the Midland to TSB to get overdraft facilities that would allow them to buy Peter Reid. He could not or would not accede to the highly promising Steve MacMahon's contractual demands and sold the midfielder to Aston Villa, using the £300,000 to pay Burnley for their virtually unknown 19-year-old wideman, Trevor Steven. Along with a move for Liverpool's recently released utility man, Alan Harper, this represented his only transfer business during the summer of 1983. Many Evertonians thought him mad: not only had he sold one of the club's most promising players and blown the proceeds on a rookie, he had also picked up a Liverpool reject after an Anfield backroom purge. Moreover, when the 1983/4 season opened, Harper replaced the highly promising Stevens, while Steven struggled to make an impression.

Goals were the problem as the 1983/4 season opened amid waves of pessimism. Everton managed just seven in their opening 10 fixtures and at the end of their tenth game, a 1–0 win over Watford, chairman Philip Carter delivered a vote of confidence: 'We are not complacent about our present problems – we are most concerned – but let us state unequivocally that our manager, Howard Kendall, has the absolute support of the board . . . This is not just a club chairman trotting out a hackneyed phrase, I am stating that categorically.'

November 1983 saw another derby defeat – Kendall's fourth in five as manager – and another crocked veteran, by the name of Andy Gray, was signed, this time from Wolves. Fans saw him as another Peter Reid, simply looking for one last big pay-day before the inevitable surrender to the injuries that had plagued his recent years. Reid, who had missed the start of the season, was now back in the side and playing surprisingly well. Few expected it to last.

Kendall was under intense pressure in December 1983 when Gray had done nothing to stem the goal drought. Letters rained into the *Football Echo* calling for him to go. 'Howard Kendall's appointment was welcomed by supporters as a link with the club's great days, but unfortunately he has now obviously failed as a result of his buys (Sheedy and King excepted), his tactics and the team's inconsistency,' wrote M. J. Molloy of Hightown. 'Isn't it time Howard Kendall resigned before Everton becomes a sick joke? The catalogue of disasters is becoming ludicrous,' opined B. G. Fareley of the Wirral.[15] Some fans took more drastic action: on returning home from training one afternoon, Kendall found his garage daubed with the words 'Kendall Out'; the same slogan had been sprayed on a wall further down his road. Earlier, leaflets had demanded, 'Kendall and Carter Out. Bring Back Attractive Winning Football to Everton.'

The goal famine continued over Christmas, taking in an abysmal

0–0 draw at home to Sunderland on Boxing Day. On 27 December Everton travelled to Gray's old club Wolves, who were bottom of the table and without a home win since the previous April or even a goal at Molineux since October. Everton were trounced 3–0 with Gray, who was captain for the day, catcalled throughout: 'Andy, Andy, what's the score?'

'The Blues have hit rock bottom and it's heartbreaking to witness their demise. Howard Kendall should prove his love for the club by resigning,' wrote Disgruntled Blue of Liverpool 13 in the following Saturday's *Football Echo*. Little did the writer know that that was exactly what Kendall had done. Carter rejected his resignation, saying that he had faith in Kendall's ability to succeed.

Few shared his confidence in either Kendall or even the club's ability to keep top-flight status. Charles Mills junior, now married with a child and teaching in London, had seen the Wolves débâcle during the Christmas holiday. On the long journey back to Merseyside with his family they stopped in Sandbach for a drink and postmortem on the afternoon's proceedings: 'I do remember actually considering that this was the end for the club. That was the low point. We did genuinely think it. Gates were poor, we'd been beaten by the bottom team, and where was the money going to come from? I remember my father – and he's the eternal optimist – saying, "I can't see the club surviving – they'll slide down the divisions and literally go out of business." It looked like it could be the end of Everton. It was that bleak . . .'

10

Gray Skies Turn to Blue

Two WEEKS AFTER the distribution of the 'Kendall Out' leaflets and with the passing of yet another derby defeat, Howard Kendall entered the transfer market. It was the second week of November 1983 and his team had managed just seven league goals between them. Graeme Sharp was struggling with injuries, confidence and form. His name, joked some newspapers, seldom bore any relation to the standard of his finishing. His colleagues in the Everton attack were doing little to share the burden: David Johnson had but one league goal to his name, Adrian Heath none. Nevertheless, the injury-battered striker that Kendall brought in was, for many fans, the last addition the beleaguered manager would be able to make to attempt to resurrect his ailing side. For others, mindful of Kendall's track record in the transfer market, which included Peter Reid who had suffered a similar catalogue of injuries prior to his joining the club a year earlier and had only played in a dozen games since joining, the buy was a waste of money. Few could possibly have envisaged the effect that this crocked but talismanic Scot would have on Everton Football Club.

Just four years earlier Andy Gray had been the subject of a British record £1.5 million transfer between Aston Villa and Wolves, but a combination of serious injury, a poor team and inconsistency had meant that he had failed to recapture the form that had led to the Midlands club paying so much for him. He had initially captured Aston Villa's eye while playing for Dundee United and signed for the Birmingham club midway through the 1975/6 season. Here, he cultivated a reputation as a cavalier centre forward who would win at all costs, and earned the move to Molineux. Later financial difficulties at Wolves meant that when Kendall offered £250,000 for the striker they were not in a position to turn down his bid.

Gray's signing was initially made on loan so that he could make his début two days later against Nottingham Forest. An under-pressure Kendall told reporters, 'I was grateful to have the money available to buy such a quality forward. In this price bracket Gray is top of the list and I see an exciting partnership ahead with Graeme Sharp.' The press asked Gray why he had come to Everton. 'To win things,' he answered. When they wearily told him that others had said the same, he replied, 'You've never heard it from me.'

It was the first demonstration to Evertonians of Gray's self-assurance, which sometimes bordered on arrogance. For his team-mates, amongst whom confidence was rock bottom, it was to eventually have a galvanizing effect. Although Everton marked Gray's début with a rare victory over Forest, it took a further month for him to find his feet, by which time the club had dropped to eighteenth place.

On a more positive note, the highly rated youth-team coach, Colin Harvey, had been promoted to first-team duties. Peter Reid, after an injury-ravaged first year, had played in a run of games and – fitness permitting – was at times looking to be the midfield dynamo lacking at the heart of the Everton team since Kendall's transfer to Birmingham a decade earlier. Neville Southall, recently returned from a spell on loan at Port Vale, had begun to shine, and Sharp, who had partnered Gray only once, was coming back to fitness. Nevertheless, confidence among the team was low and results continued to go from bad to worse. A turning-point was needed, and the FA Cup provided it.

○

ON 6 JANUARY 1984 Everton travelled to Stoke for the third round of the FA Cup. Eight thousand fans had made the journey to the Potteries, despite the abysmal showing against Wolves just 10 days earlier. It was a day of surprises. Holders Manchester United were knocked out by Third Division Bournemouth (0–2), West Ham by Wigan (0–1) and Arsenal by Second Division Middlesbrough (2–3). At Stoke, something was in the air.

'There was just this . . . feeling beforehand,' recalled Charles Mills junior, who had met up there with his family. 'I remember getting out of the car – a good walk away from the Victoria Ground – and hearing this noise. We got into the ground, and it was a freezing day, and it was just mayhem. It was bedlam. It was like one last final throw, as if everyone was saying, "Can we actually drag this team to do something?" It was really hairs-on-the-back-of-your-neck stuff. That was the pivotal point.'

Kendall's team talk that afternoon was the stuff of legend. With the Victoria Ground already half packed with Evertonians and the noise deafening, he got up and opened every window of the dressing room. 'Just listen to that,' he said. 'Are you going to let them down?' They didn't. With Sharp fit again and on a heavily sanded pitch, Gray put Everton in front with a spectacular diving header that soared into the Stoke City net on 67 minutes. Alan Irvine added a second with six minutes left, drilling an angled shot into the roof of the goal. From then on, Kendall's men never looked back.

Goodison mythology has often dictated that the turning-point in Everton's fortunes was Kevin Brock's back pass in the League Cup quarter-final with Oxford United 12 days later. Many who were at both Stoke and Oxford maintain that the earlier game was the most important. Others thought differently: Andy Gray said it came when Everton beat Birmingham on 2 January; Howard Kendall said it was the Oxford game; Southall, the fourth round of the FA Cup against Gillingham; Jim Greenwood, the club secretary, the League Cup semi-final with Aston Villa.

Nevertheless it is worth turning briefly to that dramatic night at the Manor Ground. Oxford, then in the Third Division, had already seen off Leeds, Newcastle and Manchester United in the League Cup. Everton's scalp was expected to be next and the gloomy predictions about their fate seemed to be coming true when they fell behind to Bobby McDonald's goal on a frosty night. Deprived of Gray, who was Cup-tied, Everton seemed bereft of ideas as to how to break down their opponents. Then, with just nine minutes left, a miracle. Kevin Brock passed the ball back to his goalkeeper, Steve Hardwick. Heath read it superbly, ran on to the loose ball, took it past Hardwick and, from an oblique angle, hit home the equalizer. Everton were saved.

When the two sides met the next week, Everton had no problems in dismissing the Third Division side. Goodison's highest attendance of the season – though still only 31,000 – watched the game kick off in a light snow shower, which soon became heavy, and marked the arrival of an orange ball. By then Everton were 1–0 in front. After nine minutes, Harper's chip was headed down by Sharp into the path of Kevin Richardson, who scored his first goal of the season. Despite the slippery conditions Everton began to control the play and their second goal on the half-hour mark was not unexpected. Peter Reid beat his man and ran to the by-line, and though his cross was too deep for Sharp, Sheedy met it with a shot too powerful for Hardwick, in the Oxford goal, to stop. Heath added another, and although Paul Hinshelwood scored a consolation goal in the last minute, Sharp's measured lob over the stranded Hardwick restored Everton's three-goal margin.

In the FA Cup fourth round, lower-league opposition again briefly caused Everton problems. On the Saturday after they had seen off Oxford (28 January), they met a Gillingham team who could name Tony Cascarino and Steve Bruce among their numbers. They held Everton to 0−0 draws in the first tie at Goodison and first replay at Priestfield the next Tuesday. For the second replay on 6 February, also staged in Kent, Andy Gray was recalled to the side, having been on the substitutes' bench for the previous meeting. In a game that was dominated by gale-force winds, Gray was an inspirational force playing a crucial role in each of Everton's three goals. For the first − on 27 minutes − he flicked on Reid's measured pass to find Sheedy, who scored. Five minutes later, Heath accepted a pass from Gray to give Everton their second. Then, seven minutes after half-time, Gray robbed possession to tee up Sheedy, who scored his second and Everton's third. After the game, Kendall, delighted at the prospect of a fifth-round tie against Second Division Shrewsbury Town at Goodison, said 'Our confidence is back. Now we have started scoring a lot of goals my lads have started to believe in themselves.'[1]

Everton's glory days were to be dominated by Cup ties, and 1984 was only the start of them. Before they had the chance to play again in the FA Cup, Everton had the first leg of the League Cup semi-final against Aston Villa to play. They met on 15 February, seven years to the day since Everton had last got to Wembley, by beating Bolton Wanderers to reach the League Cup Final. Facing their eventual conquerors from 1977, Everton again set themselves towards Wembley with a 2−0 victory. In a poor, scrappy game, they took a twenty-eighth-minute lead through Sheedy, thanks to a mix of fortune and farce in the Villa penalty area. His dipping left-footed cross should not have caused the Villa defence too many problems, but a three-way mix-up in the Villa penalty area, between Paul Mortimer, Gary Williams and Nigel Spink, saw it dribble past the befuddled group of claret shirts and into the net. Sheedy's goal did little to raise the standard of play, although there was little doubting the quality of Everton's second, eight minutes from time. Des Bremner headed out Alan Irvine's cross and Richardson's crisp drive sent the 40,000-strong crowd wild. A week later at Villa Park, Everton held on to their aggregate lead, despite losing 0–1, to reach the final against Liverpool.

After the two-legged match with Aston Villa, confidence continued to grow. Shrewsbury Town were easily overcome, beaten 3–0 thanks to efforts from Reid and Irvine plus an own goal from Griffin, while in the league their new-found form saw Everton rise up the table. A draw away at Watford on 25 February showed just how far Kendall's team had come, with Everton three times overcoming two goal deficits to end 4–4, after Heath finally pulled the scores level in injury time.

At the start of March, Everton had a dress rehearsal for the League Cup Final with their second derby match of the season. Having been outplayed for most of the match and fallen behind to Rush's inevitable goal, it looked like Everton were going to fall to yet another defeat against their neighbours after Sharp's tamely hit penalty was saved by Grobelaar 13 minutes from the end. Yet eight minutes later they got their equalizer. Headers by Gray, Sharp and Heath found the feet of substitute Alan Harper who tucked a shot inside the post. It was his first goal since arriving from Anfield the previous summer.

A week later, ten thousand Evertonians travelled to a sodden Nottingham for the FA Cup quarter-final with Notts County. In the wind and the rain, Kevin Richardson – wrist set in plaster after fracturing it in the League Cup semi-final – put Everton in front after just six minutes, heading home a Stevens throw-in from close range. Notts County fought back gamely and only a series of impressive saves from Southall held them at bay until John Chiedozie equalled the scores on 20 minutes. On a muddy pitch and with the scores tightly balanced, the game needed a *coup de grâce* to take the tie.

In the most unlikely fashion, it came from the head of Andy Gray. On 47 minutes Everton gained a free kick. Kevin Sheedy took it and lifted the ball over the heads of Graeme Sharp and his marker David Hunt to the back post where Gray dived – virtually touching the ground – to head the ball into the back of the County net. It was enough to win the game and Kendall, unable to conceal his delight after the match, admitted that he didn't think that Gray's nose could have been more than an inch off the ground when he scored. Looking ahead to both the League Cup Final and the mid-April semi-final with Southampton he added, 'Once the players have smelt the Wembley atmosphere, it will give them a tremendous incentive.'

In nearly ninety years of Merseyside derbies, in which success was rarely far away from one or both of the two clubs, it seemed remarkable that Everton and Liverpool had never played each other at Wembley. The 1984 League Cup Final was to be just the first of five such occasions over the next half-decade, in a series of clashes that Liverpool were to come out of as 2–1 winners, with two games drawn.

Liverpool's League Cup record in previous seasons had been extraordinary, with wins in the previous three competitions. Indeed, one had to look back some 38 matches and 1525 days to see Liverpool's last defeat in the competition, when Nottingham Forest had beaten them in the 1980 semi-final. Despite the formidableness of their opponents Everton's need to win was desperate. Since the club's last title, the Championship win of 1970, Liverpool had won a remarkable 17 trophies.

Everton began the final the more assured of the two teams. Indeed, they were robbed of a clear chance to go in front as early as the seventh minute. Heath stole the ball off the wayward Grobelaar on the edge of the penalty area and hooked it towards the Liverpool goal. It sailed towards the gaping net until it was heroically blocked by Alan Hansen. Well, Alan Hansen's hand, anyway. It was a clear penalty and Hansen should have been sent off for illegally obstructing a goal, but play carried on. Everybody in the ground except the referee, Alan Robinson, seemed to have seen him handle the ball. Even *The Times* reported that Hansen 'handled so blatantly that the offence was clearly visible from 100 yards'.[2] Nor was that Liverpool's only escape of the first half. Richardson and Sheedy both went close with volleys that hit the side-netting and Lawrenson's outstretched boot respectively, and went in at half-time having restricted Liverpool to just two shots.

Experience began to show in the second half: out of Everton's team, only Southall and Ratcliffe had ever previously played at Wembley, and Everton's early dominance diminished. Whelan and Alan Kennedy both had goals disallowed for offside, while Southall saved spectacularly from Rush's volley. Honours were even at the final whistle, and Everton returned north to face Liverpool in a replay at Maine Road – a venue still haunted by the spectre of another bizarre refereeing decision against Liverpool seven years earlier. Kendall was delighted with the efforts of his young team, saying that he 'could not have asked any more' of his players. Even Joe Fagan was generous in his praise of Everton, saying that Liverpool were lucky not to have gone in at half-time 3–0 down.

Everton lived to regret those early missed chances when the two teams met in Manchester four days later. In the rematch Fagan's team were not nearly so munificent in their defending, and although Heath caused problems in the early stages, Liverpool's dominance took hold after their captain, Souness, broke a deadlock that had lasted 141 minutes with his left-footed volley. Desperately missing the Cup-tied Gray up front, Everton's attacks broke down all too easily and they seldom threatened. Souness's solitary goal proved enough to win Liverpool their fourth consecutive League Cup and keep Everton lurking sadly in their shadow.

The FA Cup, however, still provided an opportunity for Everton to step back into the light. The semi-final, against favourites Southampton on 14 April, saw another trip to London, and this time Highbury was the venue. Kendall restored Terry Curran to the side after a lengthy absence from injury, and Graeme Sharp was confined to the bench. In a tight and intriguing game, Heath went closest for Everton with three excellent early opportunities. Although Everton were dominant in possession for long stretches, Southampton enjoyed the best chances and only Southall kept them at bay with a string of saves that 'were brilliant [enough] to earn him a place in any national team, let alone that of Wales', opined *The Times*.[3] Indeed Southall, who had just begun to claim the number-one jersey as his own and reduce his friend and rival Jim Arnold to the permanent status of a spectator, kept Everton in a match that looked as though it was heading for a draw. Then, deep into extra time, Adrian Heath overcame his early profligacy. Peter Reid's free kick was nodded on by Sharp – only playing as a substitute for Trevor Steven – and

Heath stole in to score the winner and the most important goal of his life. Everton were going back to Wembley.

'That game isn't given the credit in Everton's history that it should,' recalled Charles Mills junior. 'Nor is that goal given the credit in Everton's history it should.' His brother Peter, who was with him that afternoon, described it as 'the best afternoon of being an Evertonian. Inchy scored with just minutes to go and it went wild. A minute or so later the referee blew the whistle, and everyone thought it was the final whistle and ran on the pitch. It was chaos, and we were convinced that the match might have been abandoned. It wasn't until we got to near Charlie's flat in Goldhawk Road [West London] that we were able to stop off at a pub and confirm that the result had actually been confirmed!'

Success against Southampton galvanized Everton's league form still further. A late-season flurry of good form saw them rise from fourteenth to their final placing of seventh, taking in a 1–1 draw that virtually ended any title aspirations of second-placed Manchester United, and a 3–1 win over third-placed Queens Park Rangers. Until New Year they had scored 11 goals, yet in the latter half of the campaign managed 33.

○

WHEN HOWARD KENDALL had turned out in the lily-white of Preston North End in the 1964 FA Cup Final, he was the youngest ever player – at 17 – to do so. Twenty years later, he was the youngest manager to take his team to Wembley in the same competition. For Everton's opponents, Watford, owned by pop star Elton John, it was their first ever FA Cup Final, and although they had finished second in the league a year earlier, Everton went into the match overwhelming favourites. Perhaps crucially, Watford's captain, Wilf Rostron, was missing through suspension, but they still had some of the best early chances. John Barnes (twice), Maurice Johnston and Les Taylor each went close for the Hornets, while Graeme Sharp headed Trevor Steven's cross marginally wide and Kevin Richardson hit the side-netting.

On 38 minutes Everton went in front. Richardson's cross from the left looked aimless enough until Gary Stevens met it with a shot. Sharp, marginally onside, stopped the ball, turned, and shot into the Watford goal via the inside of the post. His goal transformed the game, and Everton's dominance was never seriously questioned. Without the experience and influence of Rostron, Steven and Stevens were allowed to maraud down the right flank, while their roles and that of Richardson on the left also suppressed all threats from Watford's widemen Barnes and Nigel Callaghan. It was from an attack down the right that Gray scored Everton's second, with a controversial header. Steven's deep cross was reached for by Sherwood – who was groping backwards – and Gray seemed to make contact with the back of the goalkeeper's hands as he rose to head the ball home. Video footage later showed that the collision was legal, but the goal killed off any remaining hopes that the Hertfordshire team might have harboured and, finally, Everton had their hands on a trophy – for the first time in 14 years.

Delighted by the Wembley triumph, not to mention the turnaround in fortunes, Kendall added a new face to his midfield. His name was Paul Bracewell, and Kendall paid Sunderland £250,000 for the highly promising 22-year-old midfielder, who supplanted the slightly unlucky Kevin Richardson from the heart of the Everton midfield. A strong tackler and exemplary passer of the ball, he was the bargain of the summer and evoked memories of the playing days of the man who had bought him.

Everton returned to Wembley for the 1984/5 season's opening fixture with Liverpool in the Charity Shield. For the first time in years they went into the match no longer feeling that they would be challenging Liverpool merely for the afternoon. There was an indisputable sense of optimism among Evertonians that the balance of footballing supremacy on Merseyside was shifting back to the Goodison side of Stanley Park. Liverpool were without Graeme Souness after their captain's summer transfer to Sampdoria, while Everton's midfield was boosted by the addition of Bracewell. Their 1–0 victory was richly deserved, even if the only goal of the game came after Sharp's close-range shot pinballed around the Liverpool area and bounced off Grobelaar into his own net.

However, on the opening day of the league programme – 25 August – Everton were humbled 1–4 by Spurs at Goodison. Perhaps the parading of the FA Cup and Charity Shield prior to the game had lulled the team into a sense of overconfidence. As *The Times* pointed out, what happened that afternoon 'confirmed the feeling that talk of Everton as potential Championship challengers is unduly optimistic'. Hindsight tells us how wrong their correspondent was, but a lame 1–2 defeat at the Hawthorns two days later must have strengthened his conviction. Glory, though, was not far away.

September and October were more prosperous. A win away at Chelsea on the last day of August set in motion a run of just one defeat in the next 13 games, spanning the opening rounds of the league and the European Cup Winners' Cup, in which Sheffield United and University College Dublin were disposed of respectively, and taking in an incredible 5–4 win over Watford.

Kendall further strengthened his team by signing Birmingham City's steely left back Pat Van Den Hauwe, who had a reputation as a hardman during his days at St Andrews. Many Evertonian purists deemed the tough-tackling left back to be 'the wrong sort of player' for the Goodison School of Science. Moreover, he replaced the popular John Bailey, who had done little to deserve being dumped in the reserves other than perhaps lacking the aggression of his successor. Born in Belgium in December 1960, Van Den Hauwe had come to Britain in the late seventies to play for Birmingham City. By opting out of national service in his native country he scuppered his chances of playing for the Belgian side (and perhaps the opportunity to show off his talents in the World Cups of 1986 and 1990). Instead he adopted Wales and made his international début for them against Spain in February 1985. At Everton he shored up what was an occasionally leaky defence. Prior to his signing, Everton had already conceded four goals on two occasions and when he was ruled out of the game against Chelsea in December they lost 3–4. Although his methods were often unconventional, sometimes blatantly illegal, there was no denying that Van Den Hauwe *was* effective. Where Gary Stevens on the other flank had Trevor Steven to cover for him, Van Den Hauwe enjoyed no such luxury with the defensively shy Kevin Sheedy.

When Everton met Liverpool at Anfield on 20 October 1984 it was their first real test of their credentials. The win in the Charity Shield had been their first in the previous nine meetings with their great rivals and they were without a league win over them since the 'Andy King Derby' of October 1978. Liverpool had had a poor start to the season and were six points and 10 places behind Everton, who were sixth, yet could not be discounted, especially since they had Rush back from injury and in their side for the first time that season. Yet Everton's nemesis was unfit and his team-mates out of sorts, while the Blues were at the peak of their form. Reid dominated the midfield, while Stevens and Van Den Hauwe marshalled the flanks with distinction.

The only goal came from Graeme Sharp. It was the worthy winner of *Match of the Day*'s Goal of the Season competition. Gary Stevens had hit a long ball up the field – 'He got a lovely touch over Alan Hansen,' Peter Reid later recalled, 'and volleyed it past Grobelaar and the ground exploded. It was a great moment for Evertonians after all those years of coming away from Anfield with nothing.' Even the Liverpool manager, Joe Fagan, so often defiant in defeat, was moved to say, 'It was a bloody good goal, worth winning any game. It would almost have been a shame for us to score after a goal like that.' As Peter Mills put it: 'When goals like Sharp's at Anfield started to go in you knew something was happening.'

Midweek after the derby, Everton flew out to Czechoslovakia to meet Inter Bratislava. They held on to a lead gained by Paul Bracewell's first goal for the club – a sixth-minute header from a Trevor Steven cross – to give them an excellent chance of victory when the two teams met at Goodison two weeks later.

The next Saturday Manchester United arrived at Goodison. In spite of the victory over Liverpool, Ron Atkinson's multi-million-pound team, which had cost six times that of Kendall's side, were still favourites to rival Liverpool to the Championship. October 27, 1984, marked the full extent of the change in Everton's fortunes: exactly 10 months earlier they had been humbled by an abysmal Wolves team and looked like relegation candidates; against Manchester United, Everton won 5–0 in a performance that was less a victory and more a piece-by-piece dissection of their rivals.

In terms of the range of passing, level of skill and 90-minute-long dominance, this was one of Goodison's great performances. The rout began on five minutes with a rare headed goal from Kevin Sheedy. Showing the sort of bravery more commonly associated with his team-mate Gray, he out-jumped Kevin Moran to angle home Everton's first, his efforts leaving a gash on his forehead that took six minutes and three stitches to patch up. Eventually the cut became so bad that he had to be substituted, leaving the field with his shirt soaked in blood. Before, then, there had been time to add a second: on 23 minutes Heath played Sheedy through and he drilled home with stunning precision. Heath himself added a third 12 minutes later, firing home with a close-range shot.

By then the Goodison crowd's appetite was whetted for a massacre and the Everton waves of attack were greeted with triumphant shouts of '*Olé!*'. Heath could have added his second after the interval, but watched as his header was cleared off the line by Arthur Albiston. The fourth goal came in the final 10 minutes, when Stevens lashed home from 20 yards via the post. Finally, four minutes from time, came Everton's fifth. Sharp, imperious all afternoon, was rewarded for his exemplary forward play when he stole in at the near post to head home a Heath corner.

Peter Mills, who had seen Sharp's goal a week earlier, remembered, 'There's no doubt it was the Manchester United game which made everyone sit up and notice. United were a good team but we blasted them out of sight. I remember taking my brother-in-law, who doesn't follow the game that much but is a Red, and he was just bowled over by the performance.' Joe Mercer, present on so many great days for the club as a player, fan and manager, was in the crowd and said it was the best Everton performance that he had ever seen. A little overstated, perhaps, but as *The Times* – which had mocked Everton's title aspirations on the opening day of the season – noted, 'It brought the realization that after winning at Liverpool and Inter Bratislava during the previous week, they had completed the transformation from an ordinary team to a formidable one.'[4]

Three days later Everton did it again, knocking Manchester United out of the League Cup in front of nearly fifty-one thousand at Old Trafford. A Sharp penalty cancelled out Alan Brazil's fortuitous opener, before John Gidman headed into his own net four minutes from the end to give Everton a 2–1 victory. The next Saturday Everton beat Leicester City 3–0 at Goodison to go top. With the exception of a short spell over the Christmas holiday they remained there until the season's end.

Midweek after going top, the attention turned back to Europe with the Cup Winners' Cup second-round, second-leg tie with Inter Bratislava. Twenty-five thousand fans turned out to watch Everton walk to a 3–0 victory through goals by Sharp, Sheedy and, in the second half, Heath.

Adrian Heath's form had been inspired all season. He followed up his goal against the Czechoslovakians the next Saturday with a late effort that took all three points against West Ham. The Saturday after – 17 November – he scored a brace against his former club, bottom-placed Stoke City, in a 4–0 win. It brought his total up to 11 goals in the first 15 league games and sealed his position at the top of the First Division scoring charts.

While Heath's form had been impressive in the latter half of the previous campaign, he had shown only glimpses of the ability that had moved Kendall to pay a hefty £750,000 for an untried 21-year-old. Three years after his arrival, that fee was still more than twice the amount Everton had ever paid for any other player, and was still occasionally burdensome prior to the 1984/5 season. Only now was he fully justifying Kendall's faith in him and his form had attracted the notice of the England manager Bobby Robson.

By the start of December he was on the verge of an England call-up when disaster struck. Turning out in a 1–1 home draw with Sheffield Wednesday he came out worst in a tackle with Brian Marwood and left the field injured. It turned out that he had wrenched a knee, which kept him out of the rest of the campaign and saw off his England chances for ever.

Heath's terrible injury opened the way back to the first team for Andy Gray, who had barely featured all season long. Although it was in the most unfortunate of circumstances, it was perhaps a timely return for the inspirational Scot as Everton's form had begun to stutter. In the game prior to the Sheffield Wednesday draw they had lost 2–4 away at lowly Norwich City and had also been knocked out of the League Cup by Grimsby Town four days before that. Gray's return to a starting place in the first team saw a typically gutsy performance on Queens Park Rangers' awkward Astroturf pitch and a week later, on 15 December, he featured prominently in a 5–0 mauling of Nottingham Forest. Although Everton lost 3–4 at home to Chelsea three days before Christmas and were temporarily knocked off the top spot, a 2–1 win over Sunderland on Boxing Day, subsequent wins over Ipswich, Luton and Newcastle, set them back on course, so that by 12 January – when they knocked four past the Geordies without reply – they were back at the top of the league.

While Gray's buccaneering performances were inspirational to his team-mates he seemed to be having some difficulty in finding the net himself. One of his team-mates who was facing no such problems was Derek Mountfield. He scored both goals in the Sunderland game, the first with a header, the second with his foot, which contributed to his remarkable tally of 14 league and Cup goals that season. Mountfield, a boyhood Evertonian who had begun his career on the other side of the Mersey with Tranmere Rovers, had been snapped up just 26 appearances into his Prenton Park career for the bargain sum of £30,000 in June 1982. It took him another 16 months, and the untimely retirement of Mark Higgins, to establish himself in the Everton side (he made his league début in April 1983 against Birmingham City). Shortly after the FA Cup Final victory over Watford he made his one and only appearance in an England shirt, for the under-21 side against Spain.

By the time Everton were back on top of the First Division, they had begun their defence of the FA Cup beating Leeds United 2–0 in the third round. In the fourth, they defeated Leeds's Yorkshire neighbours, Doncaster Rovers, 2–0. That win set up an intriguing fifth-round tie with non-league Telford United, who were only the fourth non-league side ever to reach that stage of the competition. Kendall was sufficiently impressed by Everton's opponents to note: 'They are one of the best non-league sides I've watched. They don't play and rush, and it's easy to see why they've beaten so many league teams.' With most of the day's other matches a victim of the icy weather that had frozen Britain, Everton won 3–0 with goals from Reid, Sheedy and Steven in a physically bruising encounter in front of 47,402 – Goodison's largest crowd so far that season.

A week later, on 23 February, Everton returned to league action away at Leicester City. With Graeme Sharp injured, Trevor Steven partnered Gray in attack. With just a single goal to his name all season, the Scot did not let any of his team-mates down, scoring both goals in a 2–1 victory. It was a well-timed return to goal-scoring form.

The FA Cup run continued with a quarter-final match against Ipswich Town at Goodison. In a game that was later described as 'the perfect Cup tie', Everton opened the strongest, their dominance in the early stages suggesting that they might win with embarrassing ease. Yet such were the twists and turns in this enthralling encounter that, with five minutes remaining, it looked as though Everton were facing FA Cup defeat. The drama began on five minutes when Kevin Sheedy scored twice from the same free kick. With the first kick he bent the ball over the wall into the right-hand side of Ipswich keeper

Paul Cooper's net, but unfortunately the referee hadn't blown for the kick to be taken. While the crowd buzzed with disappointment Sheedy kept his cool and bent another shot over the wall to Cooper's left. Ipswich battled back strongly and Neville Southall, all season long a seemingly impenetrable presence in the Everton goal, made an uncharacteristic error and allowed Kevin Wilson's opportunistic 25-yard shot slip under his body. It was only the second goal he had conceded in 17 hours of FA Cup football over the previous 14 months. On 32 minutes he conceded a second: Romeo Zondervan volleyed home after a three-man move. Ipswich, who had been knocked out of the League Cup just days earlier, defended their lead doughtily and Everton found it difficult to break them down. After Steve McCall was sent off by Alan Robinson for a late high tackle on Trevor Steven, just past the hour mark, Everton bombarded the Ipswich half with wave upon wave of attack. Finally, five minutes from the end, it paid off when Mountfield touched home his ninth goal of the season to secure a replay.

The joy of winning was soon subdued by the sad news that Harry Catterick, at that time Everton's most successful manager and the last man to lead them to Championship glory, had died of a heart-attack after the game. After winning the Championship in 1970 Catterick had shared his football philosophy with the world. 'When I go to a match,' he had said, 'wherever it may be and whoever might be playing, I go to watch a contest. I go to be entertained . . . Quality of performance is so important.' Only fifteen years after his last Championship win an Everton side was again fulfilling his lofty credo. He was 65 years old and, like Dixie Dean five years before him, had spent his final moments at the place to which he had brought so much joy and success.

After a three-month break, Everton returned to European action at the start of March against Fortuna Sittard, a Dutch club of modest traditions who were playing only their first European campaign. Everton were expected to win comfortably, although Kendall was still mindful of his experience as a player in 1971 when the club had been knocked out in the same stage of the European Cup by Panathanaikos on away goals. He need not have worried. His defence were flawless against a side who were but an intermittent threat on the break. Gray led the charge in attack, scoring all three of Everton's goals to capture his first hat-trick for the club. It was a deserved reward in a match that both he and Everton dominated. A fortnight later, on 20 March, Reid and Sharp goals in the Netherlands secured Everton a semi-final against the competition's favourites, Bayern Munich.

Days after returning from the Continent Everton ended fourth-placed Arsenal's Championship ambitions with a 2–0 win at Goodison, and rounded off March – on the thirtieth – with a 2–0 win over Southampton, their first victory at the Dell in 13 years. Until that day, when they had lost at home to Aston Villa, Tottenham had been neck and neck on points with Everton virtually all season. Nevertheless, when the two teams met four days later at White Hart Lane, a win would have seen the London club pull back to level pegging, albeit having played a game more. More crucially, perhaps, it might have upset the momentum that had carried Everton undefeated since December.

Spurs were no pushovers and deserved their lofty position. They had, after all, thrashed Everton 4–1 at Goodison on the opening day of the season and, like Everton, had enjoyed a commendable European run, in the UEFA Cup – a title they were defending, having beaten Anderlecht a year earlier in the final. It was a scrappy game with Mountfield an early addition to the referee's notebook, and Gray might have joined him when he got involved in an off-the-ball fracas with Graham Roberts. Yet capitalizing on two mistakes from the Tottenham defence, Everton punished Spurs. First, Paul Miller had trouble dealing with Southall's long clearance and he headed the ball into the path of Gray, whose drive into the Spurs net was instant and spectacular. Then, in the second half, with Gray injured, Steven pushed up front. He robbed Mark Bowen, danced around Roberts and Ray Clemence in the Tottenham goal, then rolled the ball into the empty net.

With the midfield controlled by Everton, the attacking forays of the infinitely gifted Spurs midfield partnership of Glenn Hoddle and Ossie Ardiles were limited and it was not until the second half that Southall had been threatened. Yet the complexion of the game changed on 73 minutes when Roberts pulled back an unlikely goal, scoring from 30 yards. Suddenly Everton were put under immense pressure by the Londoners. With just three minutes left the moment came for which the match has rightly been remembered. Mark Falco bulleted a header towards the roof of the Everton net. It looked like a goal all the way until Southall somehow turned mid-air and managed to tip the ball over the bar. After the game, Spurs manager Peter Shreeves said, 'The talk in our dressing room was all about the save near the end that stopped us getting the draw. It was world-class.' Southall's description was altogether more modest. 'Everyone went on about it,' he shrugged, 'but it was straight at me.'

○

'THAT NIGHT,' Gray wrote later, 'we felt the title was ours and suddenly the chance of taking a treble was still alive.' Everton now had the upper hand in the Championship race, but were still a stage away from reaching the finals of both the FA and European Cup Winners' Cup. On top of a gruelling league programme that would take in a further four league games in April alone, Everton were scheduled to meet Bayern Munich on the tenth and twenty-fourth in the European Cup Winners' Cup, and Luton Town at Villa Park on the thirteenth in the FA Cup.

First up was the trip to Bavaria. The away match against Bayern Munich promised to be the hardest, with the Germans – marshalled by Lothar Matthaus – chasing a treble of their own. Bayern were a side of infinite quality, replete with internationals throughout their ranks. Belgian goalkeeper Jean-Marie Pfaff was a formidable last line of defence; in front of him he could rely on the presence of Klaus Augenthaler and Wolfgang Dremmler, a World Cup full back with West Germany in 1982. Alongside Matthaus in midfield was Soren Lerby; up front Dieter Hoeness was a fearsome and aggressive striker, superbly complemented by the pacy Ludwig Kogl.

The task facing the Everton team was made all the more difficult when Sheedy and Gray failed fitness tests on the morning of the match, and Kevin Richardson and Alan Harper were brought in in their places. The two reserves did not let their team-mates down in a performance of iron resolve in which the Everton team stuck to their task of keeping the Bayern attack at bay. Only once did they break through in a packed Olympic stadium: Michael Rummenigge, younger brother of the legendary Karl-Heinz, beat Southall with a shot only to see Richardson clear it off the line. It was enough to keep the scores pegged at 0–0 and give Everton an excellent chance of victory in the second leg.

Next they travelled to Villa Park to play Luton Town for the FA

Cup semi-final. By now Everton looked invincible, and even Luton's best efforts could not sink them. The Bedfordshire team battled and scraped and prevented Everton gaining the sort of rhythm that had proved so effective all season in gaining them success, edging in front on 36 minutes after Ricky Hill's thunderous shot went in off the post. Although Bracewell hit the post early in the second half, it was Everton's opponents who looked the more dangerous through their attacks on the break, while Steve Foster stood solidly in defence. As time began to run out, Mountfield was pushed into attack and his gangly presence soon took effect resulting in an eighty-sixth-minute free kick just outside the Luton area. Sheedy stepped up, and with his deadly left foot curled a shot wickedly around the Luton wall and beyond the grasp of Les Sealey. Luton were shattered.

As the game moved into extra time Everton finally found their feet and when Brian Stein fouled Reid, Sheedy again took the free kick. This time he crossed it and Mountfield was on hand to head home the winner. 'If you saw my celebration after scoring you'd understand how I felt,' Mountfield recalled later. 'Really we had no right to be in the game at that stage. We didn't play well in the first half and went in one–nil down, but we came out in the second half with a lot more steel. We equalized very, very late on to get extra time, and to score that winner was a great feeling.' Everton were going to Wembley again.

League wins over West Bromwich Albion and Stoke City reaffirmed the belief that the Championship was a closed case, and Everton went into the second leg of their European Cup Winners' Cup semifinal with Bayern Munich almost convinced of their own infallibility.

On a balmy April night that has gone down in Everton folklore Bayern Munich were outfought on the pitch by the players and sung off the park by the fifty thousand Evertonians who thronged Goodison. The return to fitness of Gray and Reid meant that Everton had a full-strength side to face the Germans, yet it was Bayern who took the lead on 38 minutes, when Southall conceded his first goal in the competition to Dieter Hoeness. Kogl had been played in behind the Everton defence by Matthaus, and one on one with Southall had seen the Welshman save, only for Hoeness to put in the rebound past two defenders on the line. Everton were perhaps unfortunate to go in at half-time a goal down. In the early moments of the game, Trevor Steven had flashed a shot wide, and Kevin Sheedy had twice gone close, first being denied only by the onrushing Pfaff, and again with a trademark free kick that left the Bayern goalkeeper scrambling to his far post. In the middle of the park, Reid and Bracewell were dominating their more experienced opponents as Everton took the game to the Germans.

At half-time Kendall told his players to maintain their tempo and continue to take the game to Bayern. They entered the second half to a wall of noise from the Goodison crowd. As Gray put it, 'I don't think I've ever been overcome by so much noise and you could see that Bayern was suffering.'[5] Both players and fans were abundantly aware of the size of the task: that Everton needed two goals to overcome the Germans who now had a crucial away goal. Within three minutes they had got one back. Gray back-headed Stevens's long throw-in and Sharp glanced home his twenty-ninth goal of the season. The Goodison crowd roared the team on, and on 73 minutes they got their reward in a reverse of the roles that had led to the first goal. Stevens launched another long throw into the Bayern area. This time Sharp flicked it on and, with Pfluger inadvertently impeding his own goalkeeper, Gray was allowed to steal in with a header and make the score 2–1. All night long the physical presence of Gray had unsettled the Bayern Munich defence and one of their centre backs had had his nose broken after a zealous challenge by the Scot. Now his strength and bravery had cost them again.

Everton's third and final goal came late on. Paul Bracewell played a ball to the buccaneering Gray, who found himself in space just inside the Bayern half. He played the ball first time, without looking up, into the path of Trevor Steven. Steven raced clear of the straggling Bayern defence, held his nerve and calmly drew Pfaff out of his goal as he advanced unchallenged, then dispatched the ball past the exposed goalkeeper and into the bottom corner of the Gwladys Street net. Everton's place in the final in Rotterdam was secure.

With the sound of the final whistle Goodison erupted. Gray was the last man to leave the field. Once inside the tunnel he caught sight of the Bayern coach, Uli Hoeness, brother of their striker Dieter, who was complaining bitterly, 'That was not football, you are crazy men.' Gray's response was short and to the point: he told Hoeness to 'fuck off'. Given the chance to cool down, Hoeness was more generous, saying that Everton were 'the best team in Europe'. Still shaken by their swashbuckling Scottish forward, he added, 'Gray should be playing rugby not football!'

Sitting in the Bullens Road Stand, Dick White, then in his sixty-third year as a supporter, was struggling to come to terms with the brilliance of the performance he had just witnessed. 'I didn't have the strength to stand up,' he recalled. 'Eventually we got up and walked along, and as we walked to the end of the gangway, there was a knot of people all around this one person at the end of the row. And as we got nearer, it was a dear old lady who was dressed from head to foot in blue and white. She was just sitting there, dazed, and people were saying things like "You all right, love?", "Are you able to get up and get out?" We passed her by and I put my hand on her shoulder and said, "You all right? Are you going to be okay?" She looked at me and said, "Yes, son, I'm all right . . . weren't they bloody marvellous?"'

○

IN THE FINAL OF two competitions, Everton returned to the league programme, where they still had to tie up the Championship. A 3–0 win over Norwich City on 27 April, the Saturday after the Bayern win, put them 11 points clear of second-placed Manchester United with three games in hand. They were in an untouchable position, and after the Norwich win, *The Times* paid tribute to the Champions elect: 'The beauty of Everton is that everybody can rely on everybody else. They avoid doing what they cannot do, and what they can do, they are constantly improving on. In their celebration of mutual faith they have made pragmatism exciting. They will be worthy Champions.'[6]

The First Division Championship was sealed with five games to spare, on 6 May 1985 – the May Day Bank Holiday – against Queens Park Rangers. That day Neville Southall had been awarded the Football Writers' Player of the Year Award, an accolade that no Everton player had previously been accorded. In the poll Everton players had amassed 60 per cent of the total vote, and the newly crowned PFA Player of the Year, Peter Reid, was placed second. The announcement of Southall's award marked the start of a huge party for Everton with Mountfield and Sharp goals enough to see off the West London team and secure Everton's eighth League Championship. Sir John Moores was watching from the stands: now aged 89, he had lived through all but one of Everton's previous titles. He was as ecstatic as any of the other watching Evertonians: 'I never thought I'd live to see another Championship come to Everton,' he said. 'It's great to feel free of the domination of Liverpool.'

Victory hangovers over, attention soon turned to the European Cup Winners' Cup Final with Rapid Vienna the following week. From the outset the day was a carnival affair: Everton fans mingled freely and without confrontation among their new Austrian rivals in central Rotterdam in the hours leading up to the match.

Rapid Vienna began the match nervously. Kienast and Garger made early mistakes while Lainer had to fling himself to head clear in front of Konsel, their hesitant goalkeeper. Stevens's throw-ins were proving troublesome for the Austrians and Sheedy saw a right-footed shot parried awkwardly by Konsel. Perhaps surprisingly it took Everton 57 minutes to break the deadlock. Gray, who had already had one goal disallowed, scored after Sharp had intercepted Wein-hofer's back pass and pulled the ball back for his fellow Scot to volley home. Fifteen minutes later Everton doubled their lead through Steven's tap-in at the far post, after Mountfield had caused chaos in the Vienna penalty area with a dummy run following Sheedy's corner. With six minutes remaining Hans Krankl scored an unexpected goal, but any concerns that he might have caused were short-lived. A minute later Sheedy shimmied through the Rapid Vienna defence to score Everton's third goal and seal the club's first and, to date, only European trophy.

The win was richly deserved, a point generously acknowledged by the Rapid Vienna manager, Otto Baric. 'Everton were the better team and we could not cope with their speed and aggression,' he said. 'We were without three important midfield players, but even on our best form we could not have lived with Everton tonight.'

Kendall was thrilled by what he had seen. 'It was something special tonight, a truly tremendous performance,' he told reporters. 'We showed everybody what a good side we are. In terms of possession football you will see nothing better. Everyone in the side was magnificent. We deserved every bit of our win. I think the treble is definitely on.'[7]

Everton had a mere 64 hours to prepare for their second consecutive FA Cup Final. On a high after their seemingly never-ending run of victories, they arrived at Wembley almost giddy with success. As Gray later commented, 'The triumph in Europe hadn't given us any time to worry or grow nervous about the FA Cup Final and most of us thought we could float through Manchester United on a high.'[8] Since Christmas they had played 30 league and Cup matches, losing just one, drawing four and winning an incredible 25. No team in living memory had ever embarked on such a run. A win over Manchester United would place Everton in the history books: neither Arsenal nor Tottenham, the two other sides to win domestic doubles, had matched it with a European win.

But an FA Cup Final victory was beyond Everton. The luck that had assisted in their triumphant run abandoned them, and the gods smiled on Manchester United. Twice, fortune worked against Everton: on 10 minutes Peter Reid's volley deflected off Gidman and on to the post; then, with the game goalless and into extra time, Bryan Robson inadvertently headed against his own bar. Not even the second-half sending-off of Kevin Moran – the first player to be dismissed in an FA Cup Final – could help Everton overcome United. The game was lost as it seemed to be heading for a replay. Norman Whiteside turned Van Den Hauwe on the right flank and unleashed a shot from outside the area that curled inside Neville Southall's post.

◊

THE CRUSHING BLOW of losing to Manchester United could not detract from the greatness of this Everton side. The Wednesday after returning from Wembley, a single Paul Wilkinson goal defeated Liverpool to lift Everton's total of points to 90. Although teams packed with youngsters and reserves lost the final two matches, the haul of points was a new record.

Howard Kendall's achievement was immense and he was soon rightly declared the Manager of the Year. In 18 months he had dragged a team from the depths of that awful defeat at Wolves to being the best in the world – a fact acknowledged at the end of the year by *World Soccer* magazine, who named Everton their 'World Team of the Year'. With the exception of Adrian Heath, Kendall had made no big-money signings, but optimum use of his youth players, astute bargains and grizzled veterans. They played in a manner and spirit befitting the finest traditions of the School of Science, and after sitting for so long in the shadow cast by Liverpool's endless catalogue of success over the previous 15 years they had come marching out of it.

As the national newspapers endlessly reminded their readers, this was 'the team with no stars'. The tag was more reflective of the fact that many of Kendall's team had risen – literally – from nowhere than any slur on their abilities. Indeed, most of that great side were dominant figures in their respective national sides throughout the remainder of the decade.

Starting from the back, Neville Southall had been an indomitable presence between the Everton posts. The one-time hod carrier, who, to the amusement of his team-mates, cycled to training each day, had risen meteorically from the lower leagues to become the finest goalkeeper in the world. At a number of crucial moments, an outstretched arm or trailing leg had proven a match winner, none more so than his stunning point-blank save from Mark Falco, which virtually assured Everton of their Championship crown. Southall's contribution to Everton's successes then, and to the team as a whole during the following 13 years, is incalculable. Records of matches tend to focus on goalscorers rather than stoppers, and goalkeepers are usually forgotten, except for their mistakes. Southall's failures were few, and any Evertonian who ever witnessed the eccentric genius who dominated the Everton goal during this era will remember the immensity of his presence.

The partnership of Ratcliffe and Mountfield had stood at the heart of the Everton defence. Rightly, much emphasis has been put on Mountfield's impressive goalscoring – to the neglect of his defensive attributes. Tall and commanding, with a knack of being able to make a timely interception or block, the future for the gangly defender looked immensely promising. What Mountfield might have lacked in pace was made up for by Kevin Ratcliffe who, at only 24, had a Bobby Moore-like maturity and authority. His turn of pace meant that he was a formidable opponent for even the paciest attacker. Alongside the centre backs stood the snarling Welsh Belgian, Pat Van Den Hauwe. He added an edge of steely resolve and aggression to the back line.

On the right stood Gary Stevens and Trevor Steven. The two should be viewed as a partnership in defence and attack, each complementing and covering the other, dominant along the wing, providing both an exciting attacking force and, when needed, a defensive blanket. It is no coincidence that when each player struggled during the early part of his Everton career – Stevens vying for the number-two shirt with Brian Borrows then Alan Harper, Steven finding it hard to justify Kendall's decision to sell Steve MacMahon to fund his transfer to Goodison – it was without the presence of the other man in the team. As Tommy Wright, one of Stevens's predecessors in his position, said at the time, 'I think Trevor has helped him a lot and they worked well together and complemented each other perfectly.' Stevens was already regarded as Everton's finest full back since Wright and the former defender spoke highly of the young star: 'He has great attacking qualities with a good eye for goal and did play more as a right-winger. But gradually he changed and I think he was told to restrict himself by the coaches. He adjusted and stopped belting helter-skelter down the wing and realized he was meant to be a defender and that was when his skills in that department improved.' His skills improved sufficiently to earn him an England call-up for the friendly international against Italy at the end of the triumphant 1984/5 season and he soon – like Steven – became a fixture for the national side. He played a part in the World Cups of 1986 and 1990 as well as in the unsuccessful European Championship campaigns of 1988 and 1992. In all he won 46 England caps in an international career that spanned seven years.

Trevor Steven finished the title-winning season as second top scorer with 12 league goals, including winners in the games against Coventry, Newcastle, Watford and Luton. He also provided much of the ammunition for Gray, Heath and Sharp, who all finished the season in double figures. In the European Cup Winners' Cup it was Steven's solo goal against Bayern Munich that ensured Everton would take part in the final, and in the final itself he scored the second goal, which put the Blues in an almost unassailable position. His contribution to the Everton cause that season won him two England under-21 caps before he was finally called up to the full squad, making his début against Northern Ireland in November 1985.

On the left was that most graceful of left-footed maestros, Kevin Sheedy. When the midfielder had not been taking teams apart with his pinpoint passing from open play, he did it with the dead ball. Of Derek Mountfield's tally of goals that season, many came from corners or free kicks taken by Sheedy. When he was not providing goals Sheedy scored them: his total of 17 in all competitions is a remarkable figure for a midfielder, and many of them sealed or secured important games such as the 5–0 victory over Manchester United that lifted Everton to second position, or his goal in the European Cup Winners' Cup Final, which vanquished any threat of a Rapid Vienna comeback. It seemed that whenever Sheedy got a free kick within 40 yards of goal he was going to score. 'In terms of a provider of goals and scorer of goals Kevin will always be up there with the best,' reflected Kendall. 'He is one of the best left-footed players I have ever seen.'

In the heart of the team, Peter Reid had been the dominant presence. The uninitiated should remember that Reid could not run particularly fast, he did not score many goals, and he could not head the ball. In fact if you listened to the gibes of Liverpool fans, envious after losing Souness, they would have you believe he was fat as well. The key to Reid's success was the simplicity of his technique. He rarely needed more than two touches – he would get it, give it, move into space and demand it back. This was, of course, only part of his contribution to the Everton cause. His will to succeed not only saw him return from a horrific catalogue of injuries, but also acted as a huge inspiration to others. Peter Reid was a leader among a team of leaders.

Besides winning Championship and European Cup Winners' Cup medals, he also picked up the PFA Player of the Year Award. In recording the fact *Rothmans Football Annual* said,

> A few years ago injury and disputes seemed to have ruined the first-class career of this midfield player. During one spell of almost five years at Bolton Wanderers he failed to make a score of appearances in any one season. Transfer to Everton proved the breakthrough he needed and last year he was the mainspring in the Goodison Park midfield machinery which churned out Championship and European success in impressive fashion. Then winning his first full international cap for England at last put his career in pole position.

Reid said of the award, 'When you talk about awards, you can't be given a greater honour than one voted for by your own profession. Winning that is something I'll never forget.'

Paul Bracewell, his junior partner, had been equally instrumental from his very first outing in the Charity Shield. 'We controlled the game,' Kendall had said after it, 'especially in midfield,' pointing at the contribution of Bracewell and Reid. For his part Reid had initially been sceptical about the partnership: 'I remember thinking when we bought him that we might be too similar to be effective. We were both tacklers, getting the ball and giving it, engine-room players. But it worked. We stayed solid in the middle and left Trevor Steven and Kevin Sheedy to get on with it wide.' Reid also spoke of a 'telepathic' understanding. 'If he went forward I was always in behind him, we had it worked out to a tee. As a midfield partnership we played against all the top teams and I don't remember us coming off second best to anyone.'

Graeme Sharp was now regarded as one of the most complete centre forwards in the league. Domestically he scored 21 goals in 36 league appearances, and was a key figure in the two Cup runs, scoring from the penalty spot in the FA Cup quarter-final against Ipswich Town and netting the equalizer against Bayern Munich in the European Cup Winners' Cup semi-final. His form, that triumphant season, earned him the first of his 12 Scotland caps, against Iceland. Adrian Heath's early-season excellence should not be discounted either, and only the cruellest of injuries prevented wider recognition for his contribution.

And then there was Andy Gray. His goals and extrovert person-ality had been the inspiration for a glut of Everton success. What he lacked in pace or even ability, he made up for with his aggression on the pitch and personality in the dressing room. As Howard Kendall later commented, 'He was blessed with the rare ability to lift and amuse his team-mates at the same time. When things weren't going well I knew that I could rely on him to instil a sense of confidence into those around him. He was invaluable to me and Everton.'[9] The injury to Heath had given him the chance to fill his unfortunate team-mate's boots after a spell on the sidelines. He seized it with gusto, and Everton subsequently embarked on a run that saw them drop just four points in four and a half months, with Gray averaging a goal every other game in the league. Deprived of the chance to play a part in the League Cup campaign, after his team's early and unceremonious exit at the hands of Grimsby Town, he came into the side for the European Cup Win-ners' Cup quarter-final against Fortuna Sittard and won the match with a hat-trick. He missed the first leg of the semi-final against Bayern Munich but returned in the second leg to bombard the opposition defence in a famous 3–1 victory. When Howard Kendall was asked about the difference between his side's performance in the first and second legs he quipped, 'They hadn't seen Andy Gray in the first leg!'

In the final, Gray volleyed home Everton's first in their 3–1 win over Rapid Vienna, which made him Everton's top European scorer with a total of five goals. Although Manchester United thwarted Everton's ambitions for a treble in the FA Cup final, Gray's tally of medals was still impressive. When he had first come to the club, reporters had scoffed at his suggestion that he had come to win things. An FA Cup, European Cup Winners' Cup and League Championship later it was Gray who had the last laugh.

As a player Kendall had seen complacency after success undo Catterick's 1970 Championship side. Now he had no intention of resting on his laurels and was set to strengthen even further his extraordinary team. What he sought was more pace in the Everton attack, and the man he knew could provide it was Leicester City's exciting young England striker, Gary Lineker. In a new club record transfer, Kendall paid £800,000 to bring the 24-year-old to Goodison in July. With Adrian Heath coming back to fitness, this gave him four top-grade strikers to choose from, plus the England under-21 forward Paul Wilkinson, whom he had bought from Grimsby earlier in the year. Spoilt for choice, he began to ponder the permutations. Although he had few doubts about either Heath or Sharp lining up with the new striker, he had misgivings as to whether a Gray-Lineker partnership would work. What swung it was the prospect of leaving Gray to play reserve football. 'If I had done that it would have destroyed him. He was a big-name player who needed a big stage and if I couldn't offer him that stage then I wanted him to move on and find somewhere else.'[10]

When a £150,000 bid came in from one of Gray's former clubs, Aston Villa, Kendall thought the unthinkable, then acted on it. He accepted their offer.

Everton supporters were in uproar. Petitions were drawn up in protest, and hundreds of fans wrote to the club begging for Gray to stay. It was all to no avail. In an emotional farewell address sent through the pages of the local press Gray wrote:

My Dear Friends, and I trust we shall remain so. I received so
many cards from you regarding my departure that I felt I must
write to thank you all. I have never felt so moved or humble as
I did when your letters started to arrive. I knew we were close
but I didn't realize how close. I have so much to thank you for
over the last two seasons and I am proud to have been part of
the Everton revival. The club will always be a special place for
me as it gave me two of the happiest years of my life. All I
basically want to say to you, to Colin Harvey, Mick Heaton,
Terry Darracott and the best bunch of lads I have ever worked
with is 'Thank you for the memories'. God Bless You All and
may your amazing success continue. Your mate forever . . . Andy
Gray.

A series of knee injuries meant that during his second period at
Villa Park and in subsequent spells with Notts County, West Bromwich Albion and Glasgow Rangers Gray never again reached the
heights he hit at Everton. Following his retirement in the summer of
1989, after winning a Scottish Championship medal with Rangers,
he embarked on a career in the media, also briefly holding down a
role as Ron Atkinson's assistant at Aston Villa. When Sky TV won
the rights to screen Premier League football, Gray took up his media
role full time, and has since become one of television's leading
pundits.

It had been a rich and varied playing career, with plenty of lows
and many highs, most of which came in twenty thrilling months on
Merseyside. Leaving Goodison Park, Gray was in a reflective mood:

As I took one last look at Everton I thought of two things. I'd
proved I could walk in the footsteps of the Goodison greats.
Dean . . . Lawton . . . Young . . . and now Gray. I felt I'd won
my personal battle. Secondly, I was just proud to be part of a
team that will go down in history. Just like England fans reel off
the 1966 World Cup-winning side, you'll not find an Evertonian
who can't recite the team that brought Goodison Park its first
European trophy: Southall, Stevens, Van Den Hauwe, Ratcliffe,
Mountfield, Reid, Steven, Sharp, Gray, Bracewell, Sheedy; and
the rest, such as Adrian Heath, who were with us in spirit.
Everton was, and still is, a great club and wherever I go I'll
always be proud to say I was once part of it.[11]

11

The Devastating Impact of Heysel

TWO WEEKS AFTER Everton had won their first European trophy, Liverpool travelled to Brussels to play Juventus in the European Cup Final. It was the reigning European champions' fourth final and they had never been defeated at the last stage, while Juventus – who could boast the likes of Platini, Tardelli and Boniek – were strong contenders looking to overcome a disappointing domestic season. The game promised to be the best in years, a veritable feast of football to rival Liverpool's famous victory over AS Roma in the final a year earlier. The only mismatch of the day was the choice of venue: the 60,000-capacity Heysel Stadium was a decaying wreck of a ground, with crumbling terraces and flaking walls. It was not the type of venue that befitted a meeting of Europe's two supposedly best teams.

The pre-match build-up in Brussels was characterized by heavy drinking among Liverpool supporters, which by the end of the afternoon had turned into an orgy of obscene drunkenness. The *Times* reporter wrote of Liverpool fans urinating openly in bars where they had stood drinking for seven or eight hours, and of a looted jewellery shop. As kick-off approached and fans left La Grande Place – Brussels' main square – a trail of broken glass, scattered chairs and debris littered the city's streets.

At the ground Liverpool and Juventus fans had not been properly segregated, and at one end all that separated them was an empty area marked out by flimsy temporary fencing. As kick-off approached a hail of bottles and missiles showered on the Italian supporters from across this no man's land. Inevitably they responded in kind, which served only to provoke the hordes of drunken Liverpool fans. Quickly, the fencing, which consisted of four-foot-high poles joined with wire, was broken down and a mob of Liverpudlians charged across the open terrace towards the Juventus section.

The Italians panicked, turned and ran towards an exit. In the chaos that ensued, many were trampled underfoot in the rush to escape. Worse was to come. A wall collapsed under the pressure of thousands of fleeing supporters, causing them to fall on their comrades. Dozens were crushed to death. With the suddenness of events the emergency services were overwhelmed, struggling to help save the injured and contain the rioting mob of Liverpool hooligans. Even the Liverpool manager, Joe Fagan – who had that morning shocked the world of football by announcing his retirement – could not quell the fighting when he appeared on the pitch to appeal to the out-of-control fans. By then they had turned on the riot police who had arrived in the stadium.

Amazingly the match went ahead some eighty-three minutes late. The result – a 1–0 victory to Juventus – was immaterial. The deaths of thirty-nine Italians and the shame that Liverpool supporters had brought to the English game, not to mention their home city, were what figured most prominently in people's minds.

Disgust with the drunken mob was universal. 'After years of punishment which never fitted the crimes of English soccer thugs abroad, Brussels was the ultimate shame,' wrote the *Daily Mirror*. 'We gave football to the world. Now we give it our national disgrace.'[1] *The Times* wrote, 'England's involvement in European competition can surely not continue.'[2] The rest of the world united in its condemnation of the rioting supporters and the poor policing. *Corriere dello Sport* spoke of 'Assassins on Parole and Absent Police'. *La dernière Heure des Sports* condemned the 'Liverpool animals' and added that the tragedy could have been avoided if police had reacted more quickly and there had been better segregation between rival fans. Signor Agnelli, the Juventus chairman, said, 'The first thing to do to prevent such dreadful incidents happening again is unfortunately ban English fans from European soccer.'

Politicians in London moved quickly. Margaret Thatcher emerged from a two-hour emergency cabinet meeting and said that her blood had boiled to see the scenes shown on television. 'It isn't that we're numb, we're worse than numb. Everything, but everything, must be done.' She summoned Bert Millichip, the chairman of the FA, who was on tour with the England team in North America, to London. He returned immediately and gave reporters who greeted him at Heathrow Airport a hint of what was to follow: 'I believe the behaviour of hooligans over the past year culminating in the terrible events in Brussels may well mean that we may not see our football in Europe. Enough is enough and we cannot put up with these problems any longer.'

On Friday, two days after the tragedy, Liverpool's chairman John Smith who had earlier tried to blame the fighting on National Front infiltrators, announced that Liverpool would not be participating in the following season's UEFA Cup. It didn't matter. Hours later, the FA, acting under intense pressure from Margaret Thatcher, banned all English clubs from European competition for one year. An Everton spokesman stated that it was unfortunate the FA had come to their decision so quickly: it would have been better to wait for UEFA's.

If Everton expected a more sympathetic hearing from the European governing body they were wrong. UEFA sought to make an example of English football by taking an impossibly hard line. Two days later, they announced that they were banning all English clubs from European competition indefinitely. Jacques Georges, the UEFA president, said, 'The decision to ban English clubs from UEFA club competitions for an undetermined period of time was made deliberately to give flexibility. We suspect the ban will be for two or three years, but it could be moderated because obviously some clubs may prove that they have civilized supporters and could be allowed to participate in European events.'[3]

The reaction of both the English FA and UEFA had been in the wake of the disaster, when contempt and disgust were so great that rational discourse had not been possible. In the heat of the moment, fury was directed at English football in general, rather than the Liverpool fans who had behaved so appallingly. The unimpeachable behaviour of Everton supporters visiting Rotterdam two weeks earlier had been forgotten. The same newspaper that had reported Liverpool fans urinating as they stood drinking in Brussels, had said of Evertonians in Rotterdam two weeks earlier: 'From the moment the Dutch police, with good humour and astute diplomacy, zealously took part in impromptu football matches organized in the market square here by Everton and Rapid supporters, we knew the day was bound to end happily. The behaviour of Everton's followers was impeccable from sunrise to sunset and a credit to Britain.'[4]

It would be wrong to suggest that Liverpool were the only English team with a hooligan element. Despite the claims of all manner of self-appointed sociologists who said in the days and weeks that followed that the riot was a symptom of nationaal degradation, football hooliganism was not an exclusively English disease. It was a problem that transcended national boundaries. Heaping punishment on the English game – even in the naïve expectation that it would allow English clubs 'to get their house in order' – did nothing to rectify the problem and merely inflicted far-reaching sporting and financial consequences on all the innocent parties involved. Indeed, it took a further tragedy, at Hillsborough four years later, and the advent of all-seater stadia in the top two divisions, before the plague of football-related violence began to fade from the English game.

It is of crucial importance not to lose sight of the fact that Heysel was, above all else, a human tragedy. Thirty-nine Juventus fans died because they were trying to watch a game of football. Their deaths will for ever be on the conscience of the supporters of Liverpool Football Club.

It was a disaster for football too. What should have been the 'Old Lady' of Italian football's finest hour – its first European Cup win – was its most traumatic. In England, the ban had enormous consequences for the game too, not least for Everton.

Along with the four other European qualifiers from the 1984/5 season, Everton went to the High Court in an effort to have the ban overturned. Their case was thrown out, leaving them to face the prospect of missing out on the opportunity to prove themselves on Europe's élite stage. Howard Kendall later said that, in light of what had happened, the ban was right; he did not want to discuss whether it was fair because so many had died. But he admitted, 'The ban came as a massive body blow to Everton Football Club. We had won the League and with it the right to contest what is arguably the most sought-after piece of silverware in world football. I had been so looking forward to seeing the cream of Europe play at Goodison Park in front of one of British football's most knowledgeable crowds.'[5]

In the five years that the ban stood, Everton missed out on qualification to the European Cup in 1985 and 1987; the European Cup Winners' Cup in 1986; and the UEFA Cup in 1988, and probably 1990, when reduced entry meant that sixth place was no longer high enough for qualification. The financial costs were considerable, with lost gate receipts amounting to some £300,000 per tie, not to mention sponsorship, TV rights and prize money. It meant that English clubs were forced to concentrate on domestic honours, although the European ban, initially anyway, did little to quell Everton's appetite for further glory.

Yet the consequences were even more far reaching. The loss of the distraction of competing with Europe's best and the inevitable end-of-season race to gain qualification for the following year's competition via a high league position saw the domestic programme stagnate. Crowds dropped, sapping revenues further. Players, without the additional challenge of European football and with clubs unable to meet their salaries when rivalled by their Continental contemporaries, moved overseas or even to Scotland. The decline of English football was a self-perpetuating circle until UEFA lifted the ban in 1990.

By then it was too late for Everton. The cost of the ban had been far greater than exclusion from the 1985/6 European Cup. It had seen the loss of three of its best players, plus their greatest ever manager. Because of the appalling actions of Liverpool fans one night in Belgium, a club at the height of its powers had been cast into a decade-long decline from which it has never properly recovered.

○

THIS EROSION OF fortunes did not, however, manifest itself in the short term. Everton began the 1985/6 season at Wembley, and did what they had been unable to manage at the end of the previous season: they beat Manchester United 2–0 to win the Charity Shield. Their new-record signing, Gary Lineker, took little time to settle, following up a winner against Spurs with a hat-trick against Birmingham City at the end of August. 'I thought it was a fantastic signing,' recalled Peter Mills. 'Gray was knackered and Lineker was super. It wasn't his fault that they never subsequently won anything with him in the side . . .' In spite of his early promise, though, Lineker found it difficult to win over sections of the Everton support, who were unhappy that his arrival had led to the departure of their old hero.

Charity Shield and early promise from Lineker aside, the form of the team was patchy. They had lost the opening fixture 1–3 at Lineker's old club Leicester, and when they were defeated in their September meeting with Liverpool, fell to sixth.

It would be an injustice to skirt over that day in September 1985 simply because it ended in a 2–3 defeat for Everton: 51,509 fans, who had packed into Goodison to see what was to be one of the all-time great derby matches, barely had time to take their seats or vantage-points on the terraces before Liverpool's new player-manager, Kenny Dalglish, had opened the scoring after only twenty seconds. Two minutes later, Lineker went close but failed to control a through ball. Liverpool, who were playing with a sweeper – Molby – with Hansen and Lawrenson in front of him, soaked up the Everton pressure and hit them on the break. They went in at half-time 3−0 up. During the interval Kendall brought off Ian Marshall and replaced him with Adrian Heath. Sharp scored early on in the second half and Lineker, who had clipped the bar moments earlier, added a second with eight minutes left, which had Goodison shaking with a crescendo of noise. As Everton sent everybody forward Dalglish could have twice added a further goal for Liverpool while Lineker again went close for Everton. And then it was over.

The England manager, Bobby Robson, watching his first Mersey-side derby, barely had time to draw breath. 'I don't recall seeing a better game in my life,' he said. 'It was glorious – a match no other country in the world could produce.' *The Times* was equally spell-bound: 'It was a game enriched by imaginative tactics, extravagant skill, controlled power and astonishing finishing as well as a deafen-ingly vociferous crowd.'[6] Even Peter Reid, who was watching from the stands, and by his own admission not a good loser, wrote in his diary of the season: 'It was just unbelievable, an amazing game. Great skills, great passes, shots, saves, misses, goals, an electric atmosphere. It was a disappointment to lose, but even so I loved every minute of it.'[7]

Result aside, the only other cause for regret was a dispute between the Football League and TV companies that kept football off the screens until Christmas and meant that the game was not captured for posterity.

Despite losing, the epic match with Liverpool marked the begin-ning of a turnaround for Everton. A 6−1 win over an improving Arsenal team at Goodison at the start of November underlined their credentials, and by Christmas they sat second to Manchester United, who had won their opening 10 fixtures, while Lineker was atop the First Division scoring charts.

At the start of February Peter Reid, who had missed almost all of the season through injury, was ready to make his comeback. The game against Spurs was Reid's first in five months. He was returning to the side after consecutive operations on his right and left Achilles tendon, and the injuries – along with those suffered by Mountfield – had undoubtedly contributed to Everton's burdensome goals-against column. 'We've been giving plenty of entertainment,' said Reid – tongue firmly in cheek – prior to the game.[8] In a match that Everton needed to win to go top they tried everything in their power to break down Spurs in a lopsided game in which they dominated possession and the Spurs half of the pitch but struggled to create chances. It took the eighty-second-minute intervention of returnee Reid – moments before Kendall was set to take him off – for them to break down the stubborn Tottenham defence. Meeting a cross on the edge of the Spurs area that had evaded the heads of an array of blue shirts, which had massed in the box, Reid hit home the winner off the underside of the crossbar.

Three weeks later Everton confirmed their status as Championship contenders with a 2–0 victory over Liverpool that sent them three points clear. It took 73 minutes and a touch of luck for their first goal when Kevin Ratcliffe, with only one strike to his name in 250 previous appearances, hit a long-range shot, which skidded under Grobelaar's body. Minutes later Lineker beat the Liverpool offside trap to chip Grobelaar and seal the points for Everton. It was Liverpool's first defeat at Anfield in 11 months and only their third at home to Everton in 16 years. After the other two in 1970 and the previous season Everton went on to win the Championship: the omens were good.

In the FA Cup, things were looking equally prosperous. After beating Exeter, Blackburn and Spurs in the early rounds, they came up against Luton Town in the quarter-finals. Overturning a two-goal deficit when the two teams met first time round, a solitary Lineker goal was enough to win the replay and set up their third consecutive semi-final.

Ten days later they met Luton Town again, this time in the league. This was the point at which, Kendall later came to believe, Everton's season unravelled. At the start of the season Luton had taken the controversial step of laying an Astroturf pitch, a move that was paying dividends as a plethora of teams unfamiliar with the awkward artificial surface were defeated. With revenge for the FA Cup still fresh in the players' minds, Luton sought to claim the scalp of the champions. Yet Everton seemed set to continue an unbeaten run that stretched back more than three months when Richardson's shot shortly after the break took a wicked deflection off Steve Foster to put Everton in front. Foster atoned for his error in the eighty-second minute, heading home Ricky Hill's free kick. Four minutes later he headed down David Preece's corner, which Mike Newell diverted past Southall to secure a 2–1 victory for the Hatters.

After the disappointment at Kenilworth Road, Everton's host of internationals flew off to join their international squads to play their respective midweek fixtures. Wales – complete with Neville Southall and Pat Van Den Hauwe – were scheduled to play the Republic of Ireland in Dublin. Ireland's footballers share Lansdowne Road with their country's rugby players and the notorious bog of a pitch had been made even worse by a recent international. Indeed, the country's failure to provide a pitch worthy of international football had appalling consequences for Neville Southall. Going to collect a relatively easy high ball under a challenge from John Aldridge, one of Southall's feet landed in a pothole causing him to fall in a heap. He was stretchered off amid fears of a broken leg. The injury: a severe dislocation and ankle ligament damage kept him out of contention for the remainder of the season and for the start of the next. The injury was a devastating blow to Everton. Bobby Mimms – an England under-21 international whom Kendall had signed for £100,000 from Rotherham United a year earlier – performed creditably. 'He was a good player,' recalled Peter Mills, 'and he played well in Nev's place.' Nevertheless, the absence of the world's greatest goalkeeper and one of the dressing room's most charismatic members was a crushing one.

Everton had to persevere without their Welsh colossus. Days later they met Sheffield Wednesday in the FA Cup semi-final. As well as Southall, Lineker was missing through injury, as was Kevin Sheedy. To make Everton's task harder, Trevor Steven limped off with a groin injury early on in a physically draining encounter against Howard Wilkinson's typically demanding Wednesday side. The frenetic pace of the first half was to their advantage as Everton struggled to break Wilkinson's team down. The breakthrough came at the start of the second half as the pace of the game finally slowed. Alan Harper, on for the injured Steven, latched on to Mountfield's header into the Wednesday penalty area, beating the onrushing defenders who were trying to play the offside trap. Martin Hodge in the Wednesday goal committed himself, giving Harper the chance to lob him and put Everton in front.

Wednesday fought back and Carl Shutt equalized to bring the game into extra time. Again, they began strongly with a succession of corners early on in the additional period, but the Yorkshire side were clearly tiring. The winner came when Everton again beat the Wednesday defenders trying to play the offside trap: Bracewell chipped the ball in for Sharp, then held off Mel Sterland to volley spectacularly home. Late on Mimms came of age, saving Peter Shirtliff's stunning drive, which ensured Everton's victory and third successive FA Cup Final place. The day's other tie, hosted at White Hart Lane, between Liverpool and Southampton, ended with Liverpool victorious. The scene was set for a thrilling climax to the season: the FA Cup's first all-Merseyside final.

On the same day that Liverpool and Everton were securing their places at Wembley, Manchester United beat Coventry to remain in contention for the Championship. They sat in third place on 68 points, Liverpool top with 70, Everton sandwiched between the two clubs, level on points with Liverpool and just a single goal behind. It was the closest and most exciting Championship race in a decade. Two weeks later, Manchester United were out of the running. Everton and Liverpool had each picked up maximum points from their next three games, and Everton still had a game in hand. If they won their final four league games, they would again be champions going into the FA Cup Final.

Everton's league form had been extraordinary. In their 100 previous matches they had won 64, drawn 18 and lost 18, scoring nearly 200 goals. Lineker, their star striker, had just collected both the PFA and Football Writers' Player of the Year Awards and had bagged 35 goals in an Everton shirt already. It had been an incredible run that spanned two and a half seasons. Something, somewhere, sometime had to give, and at a critical juncture in the 1985/6 season, it did.

It began with four games left. Everton visited the City Ground and recorded a goalless daw with Nottingham Forest. No matter, Everton still had a game in hand away at lowly Oxford, who were fighting for First Division survival. It was not without irony that Everton's fate was being decided at the Manor Ground, the same venue where their revival had been sparked two years earlier. If Everton won, and followed it up with victories in their remaining fixtures against Southampton and West Ham, they would be champions by at least a point. Peter Reid had failed a morning fitness test and Kevin Richardson took his place. Ominously, Lineker had left his 'lucky' boots in Liverpool and had had to borrow a pair. The significance of this should not be overlooked. When he got them back he scored five times in the last two league games of the season and again in the FA Cup Final a week later. He even had them patched up prior to the Mexico World Cup and returned to England as Golden Boot winner.

The game – a midweek fixture – was characterized by scrappiness and the inevitable tension of two teams with so much to play for. There were few chances either. Everton's best came on 66 minutes, falling to Lineker. Put through by Sheedy he was one on one with Alan Judge, the Oxford goalkeeper, in a situation that had borne him so many goals already that season. His shot was blocked in what Lineker later described as the miss of his life. Minutes later Billy Hamilton touched the top of the Everton bar. Then, on 88 minutes, disaster struck when Les Phillips scored from a free header to win the game for Oxford. Worse still, at Filbert Street where Liverpool were playing Leicester, Rush and Whelan goals had given them a 2–0 victory. The following Saturday, Liverpool got the win they needed against Chelsea to become champions. Not even a Lineker hat-trick in a 6–1 thrashing of Southampton could prevent the title returning to Anfield.

In an ordinary season, Everton's tally of 86 points would have been enough for them to retain the Championship. They were convinced that they had lost the title only by default. Most watchers saw Everton as the best team in the division. David Pleat – then Luton manager – said: 'Today Everton comprise all the features of the traditional English game. They can play it short or long. They're very well balanced and tactically it is very difficult for footballing sides to get their game going against them. They push out so quickly from defence, they don't let you breathe.'⁹ The following Saturday, at least, they had the opportunity to redress the balance in the FA Cup Final.

The interest was enormous. The demand for the 50,000 available tickets had been so immense that a number estimated to be equal to that of those actually possessing them was said to have also converged on Wembley. Some 200 million people were to watch the match in more than twenty countries. It was Merseyside's day, though, and it emphasized to the watching world the city's command of English football. As *The Times* was to write after the match, 'Only a wild optimist would foresee the end of Merseyside's crushing domination next season. It could stretch far into the future.'[10]

After such hype and anticipation, the game – as Cup Finals and derbies often are – might have been anticlimactic. While not a classic, it was a gripping encounter with shifting balances of play and, inevitably, of fortunes too. Everton enjoyed the early dominance. On 18 minutes they should have had a penalty when Steve Nicol wrestled with Graeme Sharp in the Liverpool area. Their claims were forceful, if not legitimate, and the fact that the man who turned down the Everton appeals was Alan Robinson of Hampshire – the same referee who had 'missed' Hansen's blatant handball in the 1984 League Cup Final – was lost on few Evertonians.

That injustice was soon forgotten. Ten minutes later Dalglish lost possession and Reid struck a superb through ball. Lineker evaded the attention of Hansen and raced on to it. Grobelaar surged out of his goal and blocked Lineker's shot, but the striker reacted most quickly and struck the rebound past the flapping keeper.

Everton were unequivocally on top, while Liverpool stood in disarray. An argument between Grobelaar and Jim Beglin highlighted their lack of cohesion and it was the blue half of Merseyside who went in at half-time as deserved leaders. Shortly after the interval both Sheedy and Steven went close to doubling Everton's lead.

It was against the run of play that Jan Molby – Liverpool's best player – latched on to Gary Stevens's aimless cross-field ball on the hour mark. The Dane played through Rush, who sidestepped Mimms and pulled Liverpool level. Rush had scored in 121 previous Liverpool fixtures. They had lost none and drawn just 19. Suddenly, the portents for victory were looking less positive.

Yet, moments later, a header from Sharp was tipped over brilliantly by the backpedalling Grobelaar. That was to be the closest Everton came to a winner. Six minutes after he had scored, Rush played in Molby, who turned the ball across the Everton goal. Dalglish missed the chance, but the ball fell into the path of Craig Johnston at the far post, who touched home Liverpool's second. Kendall responded by bringing off Stevens – at fault for the first goal and tainted with a hint of culpability for the second – and sent on Heath. It was a move that yielded no reward. In the eighty-fourth minute, Whelan crossed for Rush to head home Liverpool's second and kill off hopes of an Everton revival. They joined just Preston, Tottenham and Arsenal as the only winners of a League and FA Cup double.

The teams travelled back to Liverpool together, Everton so near to more glory but sitting firmly in their rival's shadow. The next week Barcelona lost to Steaua Bucharest in the European Cup Final, a competition Liverpool had robbed Everton of the chance to enter. It reminded the watching Peter Reid of what Everton were missing out on. 'It really brought home to me how much we had lost because of the Heysel disaster,' he wrote, 'because I'd have backed us to beat either of the two teams.'[11] His observations more than likely mirrored those of his colleagues, not least Gary Lineker.

○

BY THEN BOTH Lineker and Reid, along with Gary Stevens and Trevor Steven, had joined their England team-mates, and Graeme Sharp his Scottish compatriots, in Mexico to prepare for that summer's World Cup Finals. Scotland, under the temporary management of Alex Ferguson, fell at the first stage, but England's performance – after a slow start – was more impressive. With the Everton contingent featuring prominently, they reached the quarter-finals and were unlucky to be knocked out by an Argentina side aided by equal measures of impudence and brilliance from their star player, Diego Maradona.

The other indisputable star of that tournament was Lineker. He had finished top scorer with six, a tally that included a hat-trick against Poland, a brace against Paraguay and England's solitary goal against Argentina. For Barcelona, who had been following his progress during the latter stages of the previous season, it was the final confirmation they needed of his pedigree. They made a £2.2 million bid for his services and, to their delight, Howard Kendall refused to stand in Lineker's way of a move to Spain.[12]

With Lineker in the side Everton had become more direct. Kendall spoke of the two-pass goal: Southall to Sheedy to Lineker, who would use his pace to run on to the through ball. While this new directness had brought Everton to the verge of more success, Kendall was firm in his belief that Everton could go out and add to their trophy cabinet without Lineker. Indeed, Peter Mills thought that Everton had become too 'one dimensional ... despite Lineker's feats – that had been their downfall'. At the same time Kendall did not believe it fair to stand in the way of either the financial rewards – Lineker was to receive an almost unheard-of yearly salary of £250,000 for eight years – or the chance to participate in European competition. For a variety of factors Everton could not match such a salary, while European football – for obvious reasons – was also off the agenda. As Kendall asked later, 'How can you stop someone leaving when Barcelona are involved? Liverpool couldn't stop Ian Rush going abroad, and most other top-class English players have gone, haven't they?' He added, 'At the same time, I did honestly feel we could still go on and win the title by reverting to our previous way of playing.'[13] For his part Lineker admitted that it had been a 'difficult' decision to make, adding that he was 'extremely happy' at Everton. 'But,' he said, 'I have a desire to play in European football. It is a shame English clubs are banned from Europe – I believe they need each other.'[14]

Sanctioning the sale of Lineker was a considerable gamble for Kendall. However, his generosity in allowing the England forward to pursue his career elsewhere did not come back to haunt him, and the 1986/7 season saw further additions to the Everton trophy cabinet.

Everton began the 1986/7 season, as they had for the previous two years, at Wembley for the Charity Shield match, in a rerun of the last game they had played there, against Liverpool. They were not only missing Lineker: Southall was still absent, Reid was injured, so too was Mountfield, and Bracewell – who had been operated on during the summer – was just beginning a two-and-a-half-year exile from the first team. On a scorching August afternoon in a venue that was quickly becoming a second home for Everton, honours were shared in a 1–1 draw, Adrian Heath opening the scoring for Everton on 80 minutes, with Rush equalizing a couple of minutes later.

The next week Kendall went out and spent some of the proceeds of Lineker's transfer, breaking Everton's record by buying Dave Watson for £950,000. Watson's transfer, the biggest domestic deal of the summer, was likened by Ken Brown, the Norwich City manager, to losing an arm. Looking back now, on more than a decade and 500 appearances of imperious service, most Evertonians could understand where his former boss was coming from: finally Everton had found a commanding centre back truly worthy of filling the boots long since left empty by Brian Labone.

Like his new team-mates, Alan Harper and Kevin Sheedy, Watson had begun his career on the other side of Stanley Park, at Anfield. He left without playing a game and was rescued from obscurity by Norwich City. At Carrow Road his career finally picked up and by the age of 22 he had made his England début, playing against Brazil at the Maracana on the day that John Barnes scored his famous solo goal. He captained Norwich to success in the 1985 Milk Cup Final and to the Second Division Championship a year later.

Yet Watson's early days at Goodison were plagued with occasional inconsistencies, and at times he seemed to lack the qualities that had transformed him from a Liverpool reject into an England international. The settling-down process was made even harder by a small but vociferous contingent of supporters baying for the return of their hero Derek Mountfield, the man whom Watson had come in to replace. 'He'd been a very, very good player,' recalled Charles Mills, 'but after Watson came, he just seemed to disappear.' Kendall kept faith in his record signing, and eventually began to justify his hefty fee. 'The fans gave me some stick because I wasn't playing well,' Watson reflected later, on the most turbulent time of his Goodison career, 'but I don't just think it was me. If anyone is playing badly, they are likely to get on his back, but I must say that Evertonians are as quick to praise you.'

As well as Watson, Kendall brought the precocious talent of Neil Adams, a winger, from Stoke City, and the midfielder Kevin Langley from Wigan Athletic. Both young signings were to make enough appearances to earn Championship medals, though neither showed the sort of pedigree that would suggest they could impact on the highest stage. Langley was sold to Manchester City mid-season and played out his career in the lower leagues, while Adams later featured on the fringes of both the Oldham and Norwich City teams – a competent player, who performed largely without distinction. The signing that seemed most unusual was that of Paul Power, the 33-year-old captain of Manchester City, whom Kendall had bought for £65,000. An articulate man who had studied for a law degree before embarking on a decade-long career at Maine Road, Power's experience and versatility – he played at left back, left and centre midfield – were crucial factors in a season in which Everton's squad was ravaged by injury.

They began their league campaign with a 2–0 home victory over Nottingham Forest, Sheedy claiming both goals. On the following Monday, a bank holiday, they came back twice from behind to draw 2–2 away at Sheffield Wednesday, Langley setting up Sharp for the first, then scoring himself with a deflected shot to equalize again on 69 minutes. The next Saturday they drew 1–1 with Coventry, thanks to an Ian Marshall equalizer. It seemed – initially at least – that the absence of Lineker was impacting on the team.

Indeed, it took Everton until the seventh game of the season, against Manchester United, to get into their stride. Just 25,843 at Goodison joined millions watching on TV to see Everton crush Manchester United 3–1 and leave them just a place off the bottom of the table. It was only five minutes before Sharp headed home Power's cross via the underside of the crossbar, and although Robson equalized 10 minutes later, Everton continued to dominate. Sheedy's volley just before half-time sent Everton in with a deserved 2–1 lead at the break. In the second half Everton's play heightened the discomfiture of United's under-pressure manager, Ron Atkinson, and their supremacy was rewarded shortly before the end when Moran's error allowed Langley to chip the ball on to the head of Adrian Heath, who nodded home with aplomb to give Everton a 3–1 victory and second place in the table.

Lineker's absence, though, plus an extensive injury list, meant that inconsistency plagued Everton until late November. A 3–1 win over Manchester City at Maine Road on the twenty-ninth saw two Heath goals interspersed with one from Paul Power, who was returning to the club he had previously served all of his professional career. 'I really didn't know how to react,' he said of his goal. 'If it had not been a more vital situation I would probably have regretted scoring.'

The Manchester City win saw Everton move into their stride. A 4–0 hammering of Norwich City the following week was less a contest than an exhibition match, with Pointon and Power getting unlikely goals and Steven scoring from a penalty after Steve Bruce had handled Sheedy's shot on the line. Heath later added a fourth, the best of the match. Spotted by Southall on the half-way line, he exchanged passes with Sheedy, who scooped the ball to the running Heath, who hit it on the volley past Bryan Gunn in the Norwich City goal. 'When we have everybody available,' said Kendall, in the post-match press conference, 'I will have an embarrassment of riches. It is nice to be embarrassed.'[15]

Kendall was still without Peter Reid, however, and it was becoming apparent that Paul Bracewell's injury was worse than had originally been envisaged. With that in mind, he added Ian Snodin to his squad, paying Leeds United £840,000 for the 23-year-old midfielder. A superb athlete with an excellent range of passing and a biting tackle, this proud Yorkshireman (he insisted that his son was born within the county boundaries so that he would be eligible to play for the county-cricket team!) seemed a natural heir to Peter Reid. Although he was at Everton for the best part of eight years, the comparatively low number of appearances he made – less than 200 – would suggest that he was little more than a bit-part player. Sadly, like the man he had been bought eventually to replace, Snodin's career was plagued by injury, the most serious of which came midway through the 1989/90 season, when he stood on the verge of an England cap. Thereafter, he never seemed the same.

Nineteen eighty-seven bore happier times for Snodin, though, and he marked his Everton début with a goal in the FA Cup fourth-round tie against Bradford City. By February his new team was also boosted by the return of Stevens, Van Den Hauwe and, crucially, Peter Reid. When they beat Coventry 3–1 at Goodison they topped the table for the first time that season. Coventry had actually out-played Everton in the first half and were unlucky to go in level at half-time after Stevens's shot moments before the break had taken a fortuitous deflection off Nick Pickering to cancel out Cyril Regis's opener. Luck was again on their side when Lloyd McGrath was harshly judged to have handled inside his own area, and Steven scored the resulting penalty. Heath added a third late on. Unlike a year earlier, the breaks were falling Everton's way. Nevertheless, for the first time since March 1983, when Manchester United had beaten them in a sixth-round tie, Everton were defeated in an FA Cup match not played at Wembley. Their televised visit to Plough Lane yielded a 1–3 defeat by Wimbledon.

That same month the English FA met with UEFA representatives to try to gain readmittance to European competition in time for the

Football League's forthcoming centenary season. Their efforts came to nothing. 'There is no question of English clubs playing in Europe next season,' said a UEFA spokesman. 'The executive decided last autumn to continue the indefinite ban.'

FA Cup defeat aside, Everton maintained their table-topping league form, but injuries were still taking a considerable toll. With the continued absence of Graeme Sharp, Kendall again entered the transfer market. This time he bought striker Wayne Clarke from Birmingham City for £300,000. The youngest member of the five-brother footballing dynasty, the most famous of whom was Allan, a star of Don Revie's 1970s Leeds team, Clarke proved a timely addition to the side. His first goal for the club – a delectable 25-yard lob that took all the points at Arsenal – was his first major contribution in an Everton shirt, but more was to come.

Clarke's signing, coupled with the return to form of Reid, was instrumental in Everton wresting the Championship trophy from Liverpool. Despite his return to action in February, Reid had been less than happy with the level of his performances, and Kendall admitted after the meeting with Chelsea at the start of April that he had been close to dropping him. 'He'd had seven games and not been at his best. It was a question of persisting with him or taking him out,' he said. 'I had good players, like Harper, in reserve.' Even Reid admitted that he was 'running out of excuses'. In the days leading up to the match with Chelsea, Reid had overdosed on Just For Men hair dye and entered Stamford Bridge – to much sniggering – with his grey hair suddenly jet black. However, with his newly regained youthful looks, he provided a display with a similar level of vigour, dominating the midfield. Neville Southall was back to his best too, producing a stunning one-handed reflex save from a close-range header with the scores level at 1–1. Two minutes later Harper scored with an audacious 25-yard swerving shot to win the game. It kept Everton top on goal difference, but with a game in hand.

The next week Everton tore West Ham apart, beating them 4–0 with all the goals coming in the first half through Clarke, Reid, Steven and Watson. A single Kevin Sheedy goal beat Aston Villa a week later on Easter Saturday. Two days later a superb Wayne Clarke hat-trick against Newcastle, coupled with the news that Peter Davenport's goal for Manchester United, 90 seconds from the final whistle, had been enough for United to beat Liverpool at Old

Trafford, meant Everton went into the following Saturday's meeting with Liverpool knowing that a win would almost certainly clinch the title.

Liverpool did enough to prevent the ignominy of seeing their neighbours take the League Championship off them in their own home. Rush, playing what many assumed would be his last derby before signing for Juventus, scored twice and beat Dixie Dean's record of 19 derby goals in a 3–1 victory for Liverpool. It was a result that still meant Everton needed to win only two of their remaining three home games to win the title, and, at the end of the match, Everton fans sang, victorious in defeat, 'Champions! Champions!'

That eluded them. It was their solitary away fixture at Norwich City on the May Day bank holiday where they finally clinched the title. After drawing 0–0 with a Manchester City team doomed to relegation two days before, Everton brought 7000 fans with them to Norfolk. Pat Van Den Hauwe – not long back from injury – scored the only goal of the game after just 90 seconds to bring Everton their ninth League Championship.

It was a stupendous achievement for a club that had been so rocked by injuries. Reid, Southall, Van Den Hauwe, Sheedy, Mountfield, Sharp and Stevens had all suffered lengthy spells on the sidelines. Considering the complete loss of Bracewell, plus the sale of Lineker, Everton's success was all the more impressive. With the timely return of both Reid and Sheedy, the versatile experience and adaptability provided by Power, as well as the signings of Snodin and Clarke, Everton had risen to the occasion. In total Kendall used 23 players, a figure unheard-of in the days of only one substitute. Aston Villa, for instance, had won the Championship with only 14 players just six years earlier.

The manager was understandably delighted. 'Losing out to Liverpool last season in the league was very hard to take. Today we have produced an emphatic answer. But we still have a long way to go to match Liverpool's achievement of 16 titles and that must be our target.' The desire to match Liverpool's astonishing run of success of the 1970s and to become Everton's answer to Bill Shankly or Bob Paisley did not appear to be burning deeply for Kendall, though. His ambitions, as it emerged, lay elsewhere.

○

ALL THROUGH THAT eventually triumphant season speculation had linked Howard Kendall to the Barcelona manager's job whose current incumbent, Terry Venables, had been coming to the end of his contract and was said to be considering a variety of options. The rumours were not unfounded. Barcelona had approached Kendall earlier that season when it was revealed that Venables might leave the Spanish giants. He met Jose Lluís Nuñez, the club president, and Joan Gaspart, its chief executive, in the Connaught Hotel in London. He even signed a provisional contract, which would have seen him reunited with Lineker and manager of arguably the biggest club team in the world. In the event Venables signed for a further year against, as he later admitted, his better judgement, and Kendall's deal fell through. Despite his obvious disappointment at missing out on the Nou Camp, the idea of managing abroad had been firmly implanted in his mind. It was 'a longing which burned deep inside of me and one which I knew I had to get out of my system'.[16]

In April 1987, as Everton teetered on the brink of the Championship, Kendall met with a representative from a second Spanish club. Athletic Bilbao, the representatives of Spain's Basque capital, were the unlikely team that had captured his imagination. Like Yorkshire Cricket Club, they had a strictly adhered-to policy of using only indigenous players, a factor that contributed to their status as perennial underachievers in La Liga.

Yet their representative, Fernando Ochoa, sold the idea of managing the Basque club to Kendall. Even the efforts of the Everton board – he was offered and turned down a contract that would have made him the highest-paid manager in England – could not keep him at Everton. On 19 June 1987, after feverish speculation, he revealed his departure to a press conference held at Goodison Park. 'After six years something inside you says go out and start again,' he said. 'There are many aspects to management in England and I felt that I just could not devote enough of my time to the aspects of my job I find important. I am at the stage where I do not want to spend my life sitting behind a desk.' Philip Carter, also making reference to Lineker's transfer a year earlier, rued his departure: 'Spain has had its fair share as far as Everton are concerned.' He added, 'It is a problem for English football.'

Like Lineker, Kendall's ambition to try his luck overseas had ultimately taken him there. Money, the cultural experience and the need for a change all played a part in each man's departure, as they did – to a lesser extent, perhaps – in later seasons for Gary Stevens and Trevor Steven. The attraction of European football and the need for a man at the peak of his profession to test his talents at the highest possible level contributed to the departure of all four. As such the European ban, imposed after Heysel, could not have failed to wield an influence. As Kendall himself later said: 'One of the major reasons why I felt so drawn to the continent was the UEFA ban on the participation of English clubs in European competition . . . I missed those nights of European glory very much indeed.'[17]

For Everton, after three years of unprecedented success, their decline had begun.

12

The Unbearable Weight of Expectation

GOODISON'S PRESS ROOM was packed. Journalists primed their pens and dictaphones, while photographers clambered to gain a vantage-point from which to snap away at their diminutive target. Then, to a flurry of excitement, the club secretary Jim Greenwood, manager Colin Harvey, and finally Everton's new record signing, Tony Cottee, appeared at the front of the room. It filled with the blinding light of a hundred flashgun bulbs and echoed with the clatter of camera shutters.

'I don't feel under any pressure because of the fee,' Cottee told reporters. 'I am just glad the talking has finished and I can get on with the job I do best – playing football.' Harvey, clearly delighted at signing Cottee under the noses of Arsenal, told the assembled press corps, 'You have to go after players even if their market value is high.' He added, 'I know Everton would rather have a quality player than two million in the bank.'

Cottee's arrival at the price of £2,050,000 was not just a new Everton transfer record but a British domestic one too. Moreover, it signalled that after a disappointing year following their 1987 Championship win, the Merseyside Millionaires were back. Liverpool, who had looked invincible when strolling to the 1987/8 Championship, would be facing their biggest challenge yet. Expectation was high, and Cottee was all too aware of it. 'I was no longer Tony Cottee,' he later remembered. 'From here on I would always be referred to as the Two Million Pound Man – and it was a burden that would weigh very heavily on my shoulders . . . The pressure was on.'[1]

When he made his début at Goodison Park nearly a month later that weight failed to show. Indeed, few could have doubted the new striker's pedigree or his team's credentials as Championship con-tenders as he scored a brilliant hat-trick against Newcastle United in a 4−0 opening-day victory. Cottee was irresistible, taking just 34 seconds to score his first goal for the club. Fellow débutant Neil McDonald hoisted the ball up to Graeme Sharp, who controlled and shot at Newcastle keeper Dave Beasant. He parried the ball and Cottee gleefully swept home a left-footed shot from the edge of the area. Just after the half-hour mark he added his second. A neat through ball was played by Peter Reid, which Cottee hit first time past Beasant and it went in off the post. His hat-trick came on 61 minutes. Pat Nevin played the ball into space, with Cottee reacting most quickly, flicking the ball over Beasant, before rolling it into the empty Newcastle net. A week later against Coventry he scored the winner, a header from a long cross by Neil McDonald, which put Everton top. 'Four goals in two league games, it was going like a dream,' Cottee later wrote, 'but, as I realized in the weeks ahead, the flying start brought enormous expectations that would prove difficult to handle.'[2]

The incredible weight of expectation was to plague Cottee during his six years at Goodison, and cloud most Evertonians' assessment of him. Likewise the performance of his manager, Colin Harvey.

When Howard Kendall had left for Spain at the end of the 1986/7 season, there was little doubt in the eyes of the board or the fans that Colin Harvey was the best man to take over and maintain the success Kendall had brought to Goodison. Then aged 42, Harvey had been at Goodison for all but two years of his professional career. His credentials first as a player, then youth coach and finally as Kendall's assistant were impeccable. As Charles Mills junior put it: 'He's quiet, loyal − if you wanted to put a marker down for the greatest Evertonian of all time, put it by his name.' Indeed, if any individual could continue Everton's unprecedented glory years, few looked further for him than Harvey.

Yet there were sceptics. Charles's brother Peter was one of them: 'I just think − and did at the time − that Harvey was the wrong appointment. Everton thought that they could just follow the Liverpool template and appoint from within. Harvey was the real coaching brain behind Kendall, but Kendall knew how to handle people. Harvey was too much one of the players, always there on the pitch warming players up before the match, but didn't seem to have the same command.'

In his first summer as boss he did not enter the transfer market, preferring to stay loyal to the team who had just been crowned champions. They began the 1987/8 season positively, initially anyway, by beating the previous season's surprise FA Cup winners, Coventry City, 1–0 in the Charity Shield. Wayne Clarke got the goal in a team that was without Southall, Snodin and Stevens, and still missing Paul Bracewell. A more telling challenge came a few weeks later when Everton flew to Spain to play the reigning Spanish champions, Real Madrid, in an exhibition match. During the ban on English teams from European competitions such prestige games took place relatively often, along with a plethora of other long-forgotten trophies such as the Screensport Super Cup, the Simod Cup and the Mercantile Credit Challenge. It made up in some way for the loss of European competition, although it was scant compensation for lost entry into the glittering Champions Cup. Perhaps it was as well that few placed any great importance on such matches: Real thrashed a weakened Everton side 6–1.

Fortunately Everton's league form was not so poor, although at very best it could only be described as indifferent. Their win over Manchester United on 19 September, thanks to two goals from Wayne Clarke, was just their third in the opening eight league games. When they slumped to a 1–2 defeat at Coventry a week later they fell to ninth place. October saw a rally. Sharp scored all four goals in the away romp at Southampton, and at the month's end Everton beat Liverpool 1–0 in the League Cup; Gary Stevens, just fit from a lengthy injury lay-off, grabbed the only goal of the game with a shot deflected by Gary Gillespie in the eighty-third minute. A 2–0 win over Manchester City in the same competition a month later set up a two-legged semi-final with Arsenal in the New Year.

It was only when 1988 came that some much-needed consistency returned: a five-match-long winning streak – completed without conceding a goal – that spanned from the start of January until March saw Everton move to fifth place. They put an FA Cup run together too, although they made hard work of it. It took three replays to overcome Sheffield Wednesday in the third round before a scintillating 5–0 away win at Hillsborough – with all five goals, including a Sharp hat-trick, being scored in the first half – put them into the fourth round. This time, Middlesbrough required three games before they were finally beaten, which set up an intriguing fifth-round tie with Liverpool on 21 February. The derby game, the season's third, was sandwiched between Everton's two-legged League Cup semi-final with Arsenal. The first match at Goodison resulted in a 0–1 defeat, with a missed penalty by Trevor Steven doing little to aid the Everton cause. Two weeks later they were unable to overcome Arsenal at Highbury where they lost 1–3. This effectively marked the end of Everton's season, as Liverpool had knocked the Blues out of the FA Cup with a 1–0 victory at Goodison the previous weekend.

By then there were already murmurs of discontent among Evertonians. Some questioned the team's will to succeed and suggested that complacency had begun to set in. Harvey had made just one signing, the Scottish international midfielder Ian Wilson, who was bought as cover for Sheedy. Fresh blood, said many, was needed for progress. Gary Lineker was just one of the names being linked to Everton, with a £2 million return from Barcelona attracting considerable press coverage, but other players were mentioned frequently too. Few fans were yet questioning Harvey's competence as manager, despite the continuing indifference of his team's performances. Most thought that, with an injection of fresh blood, Everton would win honours.

On 20 March 1988, Everton had their opportunity to wreak revenge on Liverpool for knocking them out of the FA Cup. Unbeaten in the league and now through to the semi-finals of the FA Cup, Everton had been the only side to inflict defeat on Liverpool with the win in the League Cup the previous autumn. A draw between Liverpool and Derby County, midweek before the two neighbours' fourth meeting of the season, had seen Liverpool equal Leeds United's 1973/4 record of 29 unbeaten games from the start of the season. In six months the bookmakers' odds that Liverpool would remain unbeaten throughout the league programme had fallen from 100–1 to 6–4 and between them their estimated liability stood at £1 million.

By dint of fate, Wayne Clarke, whose oldest brother, Allan, had been a member of that great Leeds team, was lining up for Everton that afternoon. Indeed, from the minute he stepped out on to the pitch there was a sense of inevitability about what was to follow. In the fourteenth minute Grobelaar came for a left-wing corner and failed to catch the ball. It dropped to Wayne Clarke, who struck it low into the corner of the Liverpool net. It was to be the only goal of a closely fought match. The following day the newspapers were full of photographs of Allan Clarke kissing his younger brother's cheek. Leeds's record stood equalled, but unbeaten.

Liverpool still walked to the Championship. They were untouchable, conceding a paltry 24 goals and matching Everton's 1985 record of 90 points, having played two games fewer. Everton finished the season in fourth place, though could have improved on that had they won more than half of their last eight matches. But without European qualification to play for, the remainder of the season was anticlimactic. When Everton played Arsenal on the last day of the season, a match they went into in third place, Arsenal in sixth, just 22,445 turned up to see a game Everton ended up losing 1–2.

○

ALTHOUGH HARVEY had inherited a side fresh from their second League Championship in three years, the squad was too small to allow for injuries and loss of form. A combination of the two had undone Everton in his first season in charge, with Stevens, Sheedy and Bracewell all suffering long-term injuries. Age was taking its toll on Peter Reid, likewise that other stalwart of the 1986/7 season, Paul Power. At the end of the 1987/8 season Power announced his retirement from playing and took up a coaching role at Goodison. Yet there were positive signs too. The defence had had its best season in the club's history, conceding just 27 goals, while fourth position was by no means a disgrace. Yet Harvey clearly wanted to put his own mark on the team and set about a reconstruction programme that he believed would make Everton great again.

In July 1988 Everton signed Pat Nevin from Chelsea. They had originally bid £400,000 for the out-of-contract winger, but when Chelsea asked for £1.7 million, it went to arbitration at the Football League, which a set a record fee for a tribunal of £925,000. Gary Stevens left for Glasgow Rangers in search of European football, and in his place came the England under-21 international right back, Neil McDonald, for £525,000. His three-year spell at Goodison was, for the most part, beset with uncertainty about his optimum position – he spent his first seasons flitting between left and right back – which inevitably took a toll on his consistency. Stuart McCall came from Bradford City for £925,000, an energetic midfielder who many hoped would match the success of his flame-haired predecessor Alan Ball. Out went Ian Wilson to the Turkish club, Kocaelispor, and

Derek Mountfield – who had found his chances limited because of a combination of injuries and the arrival of Dave Watson – to Aston Villa. Early on in the season Adrian Heath followed them, moving to Barcelona's second club, Espanyol. The man whose goal against Oxford United some said had been the most dramatic turning-point in the club's history had suffered a drop in form since the departure of Kendall, and with the arrival of Cottee, it was clear that his days at Everton were coming to an end. His spell in La Liga was as unhappy as it was short-lived and he returned to England after 12 months to sign for Aston Villa. He later joined Manchester City and it was perhaps fitting that when they met Everton in September 1990 it was Heath who scored the winner against his old club.

Arguably, a greater loss was Alan Harper, who left for Sheffield Wednesday. The man the fans dubbed 'Zico' had been an unspectacular and unsung hero of Everton's glory years, filling every outfield position in his quietly effective manner. While perhaps few supporters would have necessarily chosen him in their dream line-up, his presence as a versatile squad member, particularly in the days before more than one substitute was allowed, was invaluable.

The transfer activity Evertonians were most excited about was undoubtedly that involving Cottee. But the hype and sense of expectation were soon confounded. Cottee himself admitted later that he couldn't understand the size of the fee, given that West Ham had valued him at just £1 million a year earlier; he added that while he knew he was a good player, he was all too aware that there were better. His performance against Newcastle was probably his best in an Everton shirt, a view with which he concurred: 'I would have thought it was my best performance,' he said, 'and it was probably the best and worst thing that I ever did. Obviously it was the best thing because of the performance which I put in, but from an expectation point of view, everyone thought that I could get a hat-trick every game and I felt that I put a lot of pressure on myself by scoring the hat-trick on my début.'[3]

After winning the first two matches of the 1988/9 season, Everton slumped. They won just one match in the following two months and were knocked out of the League Cup by lowly Bradford City. Things were not looking positive. Yet they struck together a 10-match unbeaten run, which lasted until the New Year, hauling them up to fourth place. Had Everton turned the corner? No. Their league form over the next three months was wretched and they won just once, falling down as far as eleventh place.

○

DECEMBER 1988 marked the publication of the first issue of the fanzine *When Skies Are Grey* (*WSAG*). Football fanzines had been sold around the country since the early eighties and Everton were one of the few big names without one. It was founded by Chris Collins, who was soon joined on the editorial staff by Graham Ennis. He took full charge some three years later with the publication of issue 15. 'It was a strange time for Everton,' they later quipped, 'where the only similarity with the team that had won the Championship eighteen months earlier was the kit they wore.' Typewritten, smeared with globules of Tipp-ex and filled with spelling mistakes, Collins's first editorial boasted, 'At last you the fan's have you're own platform to air you're views on Everton FC . . . I will not make any apologies for ruffling any feathers though. What's got to be said will be said, unlike the programme which would have us believe that all is rosy in the Goodison Garden. The football I've seen over the last eighteen months or so tells me otherwise.' Len Capeling of the *Daily Post* welcomed its arrival. 'Hardened Everton fans who've suffered the slings and the arrows (plus the occasional bouquets) of the last 20 years will instantly warm to the tone of torment in the Goodison fanzine *WSAG*. Of course the title gives the game away. Depressingly downbeat, it forcibly reminds us that every silver lining has a cloud.'[4]

When Skies Are Grey was by no means the only Everton fanzine, but it was the first, the longest-running and most widely read. *Blue Wail* came out soon after, and lasted for a few issues before fading away later in the season. The magazine had to be pulled after the Hillsborough disaster as it contained an article – written before the tragedy – judged by the editors to be in bad taste. That decision left the fanzine facing ruin and it disappeared soon after. *Speke From the Harbour* was launched at the start of the 1989/90 season by John McAllister of the Northern Ireland Everton Supporters Club (NIESC). It was originally sold only twice a season, on the NIESC's biseasonal visits to Goodison. At the start of the 1993/4 season its present editor Mark Staniford took up the reins and it still goes from strength to strength. My own effort appeared at the start of the 1994/5 season, entitled *Gwladys Sings the Blues*, and ran for three years.

Blue Blood, edited by George Orr, a prolific Everton chronicler, came soon after. Finally, *Satis?* first appeared at the start of the 1998/9 season, boasting the credo: 'We don't hate Liverpool, we don't hate Manchester United. We don't hate anyone – it's only a game.'

Fanzines were, and indeed still are, a crucial forum for fans, who were increasingly dispossessed, alienated and priced out by their clubs. Amateurishly produced, often libellous and sometimes bitingly funny, they made for essential half-time reading and, as Chris Collins said in his first editorial, they were almost always more pertinent than the match-day programme. Indeed, Colin Harvey might have done well to read some of the criticism levelled at him and his expensive team.

In February 1989 Peter Reid left for Queens Park Rangers on a free transfer. It was evident that his best playing days were past him, although he was not, and never really has been, adequately replaced. *When Skies Are Grey* paid tribute to him on his departure. 'We used to sing: "He's fat, he's round, he's worth a million pounds",' wrote Carl Parker. 'To my mind Peter Reid has been worth much, much more than that to Everton.'[5]

In a season that was quickly falling apart, the only positive note came in the FA Cup where Everton began to put a good run together. In the third round they beat West Bromwich Albion in a Goodison replay after drawing the first match 1–1 in a game marred by crowd trouble. In the fourth they drew again with lower league opposition, 1–1 away at Second Division Plymouth Argyle, overcoming them in emphatic fashion three days later at Goodison in a 4–0 win, with Sharp scoring twice, and Nevin and Sheedy getting the other goals. In the fifth round they beat Barnsley 1–0 at Oakwell with a single, Sharp goal. That set up a televised quarter-final with Wimbledon, which was won 1–0 with a scrappy Stuart McCall goal.

Cup run aside, Harvey's new signings were struggling. Cottee was out of sorts, while McDonald and McCall were both dropped early on in the new season. Nevin was one bright spark, although his Goodison career might also have got off to a better start. Just three games into it he was substituted after having suffered the worst injury of his career. A torn anterior cruciate ligament kept him out of the reckoning until Christmas, and when he did get back into the team his consistency was questionable. Slowly he hit a vein of form, and by April was firmly established in the side, scoring a winner against Charlton Athletic that had fans positively drooling. Dancing past two defenders, Nevin played a wall pass to Graeme Sharp, then scooped the ball over goalkeeper Bob Bolder. Scotland's manager Andy Roxborough was in the crowd watching, and such a fine goal led him to marvel, 'That was just about the best goal I've seen all season. It was quite brilliant.' The following week Nevin scored the goal that put Everton into the FA Cup Final.

April 15, 1989, is not, however, a date that has come to be remembered for Pat Nevin's goal in a sterile 1–0 FA Cup semi-final victory over Norwich City at Villa Park. In Sheffield, events at the day's other tie between Liverpool and Nottingham Forest had taken on an altogether more epic complexion. Overcrowding in the streets outside Hillsborough prior to kick-off had led a senior police officer to order that a gate be opened. This allowed hundreds of Liverpool fans, crowded outside the ground, to move inside. They surged forward into a central pen in the Leppings Lane end where thousands of supporters were already crammed. As hundreds of expectant fans entered the ground there was a surge forward, crushing those at the front into the metal fences at the bottom of the terrace. Unaware that their fellow fans were dying, latecomers pushed forward, trampling more people underfoot and causing those at the front to suffocate. This included several children, standing there for a better view. Eventually, at 3.06 p.m., aware that something was not right, the referee took the two teams off and the gates were opened letting the crush of fans move out of the pen and on to the pitch. It was too late. Nearly a hundred Liverpool supporters had already died and countless more were injured. Advertisement hoardings were ripped down and used as stretchers. Ambulances were soon on the scene, but the Sheffield emergency services were overwhelmed by the enormity of the tragedy.

In the cruellest and most appalling of ironies, perimeter fences, implemented to control hooligan mobs, such as those who had wreaked catastrophe at Heysel four years earlier, killed scores of innocent supporters. Even if the Hillsborough tragedy had occurred only as the most indirect result of it, the deaths of those 96 fans were the worst legacy of football hooliganism, and an indelible stain on the consciences of the Heysel perpetrators.

At Villa Park, few, if any, fans were aware of the unfolding tragedy. The players were equally oblivious to it. The day's hero, Pat Nevin, later remembered, 'As soon as the game was finished we just jumped up and down celebrating, having a great time. I'd scored the winning goal and that was one of the biggest moments of my career and the boys were on an incredible high. We went into the dressing room expecting champagne. I just looked around and there was a quietness, a kind of hush.'[6] Even then the scale of the tragedy was not fully known. 'Bulletins started to appear on the radio on the way home,' recalled Harvey. 'The mood went from being ecstatic to sombre. We couldn't put over how badly we felt. By the time we got back to Liverpool everyone's devastated because then you start to realize you've got friends at that game . . . Then you see how important the news was, and how little your own joy was from that day. Basically you'd won a game of football, which was nothing then.'[7]

The city of Liverpool was united by its biggest tragedy in living memory. Ninety-four fans had died on the day, and 150 were seriously injured. Of those a further two died later of their injuries. The next morning the 14-ton bell of the Anglican Cathedral – only used previously to signal the death of a monarch – rang out, and the gates of Anfield were opened as Liverpool's ground became a shrine to the dead. More than a quarter of a million people came to pay their respects, turning the Liverpool pitch into a carpet of floral tributes. The Prince and Princess of Wales visited the survivors in hospital, as did Margaret Thatcher, while the sixties pop legend Gerry Marsden recorded a tribute record to benefit the disaster victims.

The football programme was suspended and Liverpool, Everton and Tranmere Rovers were given indefinite leave to postpone their fixtures. One match that would go ahead was the FA Cup Final, although many felt it should have been abandoned. Even Tony Cottee, who had never experienced an FA Cup Final and was desperate to end his disappointing season on a high, felt it should have been abandoned: 'Although it would have been very disappointing to miss out on the Cup Final, I felt the heart and soul had been ripped out of the competition. The magic and romance of the FA Cup had died along with those 96 fans.'[8]

Everton restarted their faltering season a week after the tragedy, but it was nearly three weeks before their great rivals and neighbours were ready for a return to action. Fittingly the scene of that match was Goodison, for the second league derby of the season. Despite Colin Harvey's appeals for a typical 'ding dong' affair, the occasion was marked not by the standard of football on offer but for the show of unity between rival sets of supporters. At half-time the pitch, previously ringed by the metal fences, was circled by a chain of 96 red, blue and white scarves to commemorate the dead. A 40-foot banner, draped among the ranks of Liverpool fans massed at the Stanley Park end, gave a message to the watching nation: 'The Kop thanks you. We never walked alone.'

Days later, Liverpool beat Nottingham Forest to set up the second all-Merseyside FA Cup Final in four years.

It was a frantic, incident-packed match, where sentiment was soon forgotten and Liverpool emerged winners. John Aldridge had put Liverpool ahead on just four minutes, and although Everton pressurized in the second half, it looked as though the Anfield team were cruising to victory. Even when Dave Watson was pushed up front late on and Everton increasingly laid siege to the Liverpool penalty area, it looked as if their neighbours would hold firm. Then, with just seconds remaining, another searching ball into the Liverpool area found substitute Stuart McCall, who bundled the ball into the Liverpool net to bring the match into extra time.

Only four minutes of extra time had elapsed before Everton fell behind again. Typically it was their old adversary, Ian Rush, who scored, controlling a centre from Steve Nicol, turning Ratcliffe and driving the ball into the far corner of the goal. Everton's response was speedy and spectacular. Eight minutes later Alan Hansen headed out a Ratcliffe free kick, which fell to McCall, who controlled and volleyed the ball thunderously into the Liverpool net from 25 yards.

This time Everton's elation lasted just two minutes. John Barnes floated the ball into the Everton penalty area and, with a flick-header, Rush, yet again, scored. It was one blow too many, and only Neville Southall prevented the scoreline being increased, spectacularly stopping Rush completing his hat-trick and denying Ray Houghton, Peter Beardsley and Barnes late on.

Cottee was distraught by the 2–3 defeat. Marked out of the game by Alan Hansen he had failed even to have a shot on target. 'When I got to within fifty yards of the tunnel,' he wrote later, 'tears began streaming down my face. The game had passed me by . . . I just thought I'd let myself down, I'd let the club down and I'd let the other players down.'⁹

In the wake of the FA Cup Final defeat, Harvey again set out to make his mark on the Everton squad. His first task was to resolve Trevor Steven's future at the club, which had long been in doubt. After a relatively disappointing 1987/8 campaign he had refused to sign a new contract: his was up for renewal at the end of the following season. With the arrival of Pat Nevin in the summer of 1988 he then found himself playing in a much deeper role, which only added to his unhappiness at the club. 'I've hardly played in my traditional wide position,' he complained, in an interview during Christmas 1988. 'While I've been happy to help Colin Harvey out when we've had injuries, I still prefer to play out on the right.' The fact that rumours linked him with moves to Manchester United and Liverpool did little to endear him to the home support. 'The fact that things haven't gone so well has had a bearing on my thinking,' he admitted, 'and is something I will have to address at the end of the season.' The speculation even led to one supporter invading the pitch during the FA Cup Final to remonstrate with him.

That was to be his last game in the royal blue of Everton, and throughout the summer speculation continued to link him to Liverpool (Kenny Dalglish was later to recommend Steven to Marseille). Eventually he moved to Rangers after a bitter cash wrangle between Everton and his new club. Everton had wanted a British record fee of £2.5 million but a tribunal set it at £1 million lower. It proved a woeful undervaluation of his abundant ability, later shown when Steven signed for Marseille just two years later for three times that amount. At Marseille his presence undoubtedly helped Jean-Pierre Papin win the European Footballer of the Year award for his free-scoring exploits during Steven's one full season with the French club. Tellingly, at both Marseille and Rangers (where he returned just over a year after leaving), he was able to show his ability in the European Cup for seven seasons, an opportunity that had been taken away from him at Everton. He later cited the Heysel ban as a major factor in his leaving the club. 'We were all set to challenge for the European Cup the following season and that was a crashing blow. It threw a hell of a cloud over the English league. It's one of the reasons I came away from English football. At the time it didn't look as though we'd get back into Europe.'

Steven's was not the only departure that summer. Mike Newell arrived from Leicester City in a part-exchange that took Wayne Clarke in the opposite direction, while Pat Van Den Hauwe left for Spurs shortly after the start of the new season. Paul Bracewell, who had made his Everton début in a Wembley match against Liverpool, in the 1984 Charity Shield, turned out also to have played his last for the club at the same venue and against the same opposition. He departed for Sunderland after the FA Cup Final. Long-term injury had clearly taken its toll on Bracewell and many compared him unfavourably with the player who had once run the Everton midfield so successfully with Peter Reid. Perhaps such comparisons were unfair, and maybe Harvey's decision to sell him to Sunderland was a touch hasty. At Roker Park he helped lead Sunderland's charge for promotion and within a year of his signing they had restored their top-flight status, although their spell in the First Division lasted just a year. He moved across the North East in 1992 to join Kevin Keegan's Newcastle where he enjoyed three productive seasons. In 1995 he was bought by his old team-mate Peter Reid, then Sunderland manager, for a nominal fee. It was the third time he had been bought by the Wearsiders – they had originally taken him as a 20-year-old from Stoke City in 1983. He was also to win promotion to the Premiership for the third time in 1996 as a player-coach. It was a return to the level of football that his qualities merited.

In addition to Mike Newell, Harvey made three further signings. Norman Whiteside, scorer of Manchester United's winner against Everton in the 1985 FA Cup Final, was signed for £600,000. Of all the young United players to be burdened with the tag of 'the new George Best', Whiteside had, at that time, probably come closest to emulating the great man. Like his compatriot Best, Whiteside had been elevated to fame as a 17-year-old, when he was the youngest player ever to participate in the World Cup Finals just 42 days past his seventeenth birthday. Later, just as his compatriot was turned away from Old Trafford for disciplinary problems, so too was Whiteside. On the pitch Whiteside had built up something of a reputation as a hardman, and at times his temper got the better of him. Off the field, his reputation was as dubious. He had been a member of Old Trafford's infamous 'drinking club', which United's recently installed manager, Alex Ferguson, sought to break up. First he sold Paul McGrath to Aston Villa, then Whiteside to Everton, which left Bryan Robson as the sole remaining 'ringleader'. By this time a series of knee injuries had curtailed much of the Ulsterman's early promise, although at 24 his best days should still have lain ahead of him in the royal blue shirt of Everton.

Intriguingly, Harvey bought Everton their first foreign signing. Midfielder Stefan Rehn was signed from the Swedish side, Djurgaarden, in a move that was tainted with farce from start to finish. Even before Rehn had made his début, he was fined by FIFA for having turned his back on a previously agreed deal with the Swiss club, Neuchâtel Xamax. At Everton the Swede was given just two starts and four games as substitute (during one of these games he was substituted 15 minutes after coming on) before being sold only months later. After leaving Goodison, Rehn went on to win 45 international caps, the Swedish Footballer of the Year award, and figured in several European Cup campaigns with IFK Gothenburg.

Arguably, Martin Keown – bought from Aston Villa for £750,000 – was the best of Harvey's signings in his time as Goodison boss. For a time at Everton, Keown held the distinction of being one of the best man-marking defenders in Europe and he began a successful decade-long England career while there. Yet he only really excelled himself in less than half of his three-and-a-half-year stint.

◊

A YEAR AFTER STARTING the 1988/9 season as Britain's most expensive player, Tony Cottee began the new campaign at Coventry City on the substitutes' bench, supplanted by Mike Newell who partnered Sharp in attack. Days later he was fined two weeks' wages, having refused to return to Coventry to play for the reserves. After an angry meeting with Harvey, Cottee asked to be made available for transfer and he followed that up four months later with a formal written request to leave. Harvey listed him for £1.5 million, but nobody came in for the striker.

The £2 million man's unhappiness was not just down to the lack of certainty about his place in the Everton team: 'I felt I was being bypassed and the team wasn't playing to my strengths. Crosses were generally hit long towards the big man at the far post, few were delivered hard and low for my benefit.'[10] Fans were as aware as Cottee that the team was not playing to his strengths. 'Let's change the style to suit our £2 million striker. We did for Lineker,' wrote Chris Collins in his *When Skies Are Grey* editorial. 'The only people who want Cottee to go are the press in desperation for a good story.'[11]

Harvey's decision to leave Cottee out of the new season's opening fixtures was vindicated. Newell made a positive start to his Everton career, and his early-season form saw him called up to the England squad. His team-mates began the season every bit as impressively. A brilliant 3–0 win over champions Arsenal at the end of October saw Everton rise to the top of the table. In a performance that brimmed with confidence as Everton took the game to Arsenal, Keown, playing only his second game in a blue shirt, won everything at the back while Pat Nevin wove majestically through the Arsenal defence, scoring twice, the second of which – Everton's third – was the pick of the bunch. Cottee, starting in place of the injured Sharp, laid the ball on into space, allowing Nevin to run on to it, and, controlling it with his studs, he danced wide of Lukic in the Arsenal goal and slammed the ball into the roof of the net to seal Everton's rise to the top.

A week later, in an effort to strengthen his table-topping side still further, Harvey brought in Peter Beagrie from Stoke City for £750,000. The tricky winger with a penchant for back-flips went straight into the team for Everton's Bonfire Night visit to Aston Villa. In front of live television cameras, Everton were humiliated. 'It was an horrific combination of shuddering surrender and sheer ineptitude,' wrote the *Daily Post*. 'And Graham Taylor's in-form Villa took full advantage.' In their heaviest league defeat in 12 years, Everton left the field outplayed and 3–0 down at half-time. Harvey was left with little option but to gamble and attack Villa. He brought on Beagrie for the injured Dave Watson and Sharp for Whiteside. It was a risk that could only work with an early second-half goal. That goal came, but it was Villa who scored it, through David Platt on 50 minutes. Indeed, the deficit had doubled to six within 22 minutes of the restart, and Everton looked like they could concede more. Villa laid off their quivering opponents, but not even a late Tony Cottee strike or a Paul McGrath own goal could bring about any semblance of respectability. Villa, concluded the *Daily Post*, had 'inflicted a clinical execution on an Everton side that had the backbone of a jellyfish'.[12]

The Villa defeat destroyed the confidence of Harvey's team, which, even while Everton sat atop the First Division, was shaky. The good run of early-season form had papered over many of the glaring inadequacies of Harvey's squad, not to mention the divisions that lay within it. Two rival camps were building up in the dressing room: the old guard who had enjoyed such success under Kendall; and the new school, who had been signed at such expense yet failed to replicate their team-mates' glory. Harvey's signings were accused of being overvalued and overrated; and the remnants of the mid-eighties side, of complacency. 'Sharp in particular is the picture of what is wrong with Everton,' wrote Dave Jones in *When Skies Are Grey*. 'The way he ambles across the pitch, doing practically nothing all game, and he still gets picked every week. He still somehow carries a name for himself, people cheering every time he touches the ball and at every attempt at goal (albeit a rarity in itself) and if we sold him now we could probably get a million for him.'[13] Graham Ennis concurred: 'There is no room for sentiment if a player doesn't come up to standard, despite what has gone in the past, he will have to go.'[14] Murmurs suggesting that Harvey wasn't up to the job of managing Everton were becoming widespread. Equally vociferous was the criticism of the backroom staff, particularly Terry Darracott and Mick Lyons, whose previous coaching experience at Grimsby Town – Lyons manager, Darracott his assistant – had seen them relegated to the Third Division.

Harvey's managerial team was not the only one under pressure. On 14 November 1989, Howard Kendall was sacked by Athletic Bilbao having lost three games in six days. He was out of a job for less than a month. After Manchester City had sacked Mel Machin and Joe Royle turned down the vacant managership, Kendall was installed as Maine Road boss at the start of December.

Everton ended 1989 in tenth place. Their slide down the league ended then, although it was March before a truly impressive run of results was put together. In the FA Cup, they made typical hard work of the third round, only beating Middlesbrough at the third time of asking, 1–0 in the second replay at Ayresome Park. In the fourth round two goals from Norman Whiteside and a faultless display from Neville Southall saw off Sheffield Wednesday 2–1. It sent them through to their eighth consecutive fifth-round appearance. Here they met Joe Royle's Oldham at Boundary Park, complete with its plastic pitch. After drawing the first match 2–2, having conceded a two-goal lead, they met at Goodison where a hard-fought replay yielded a 1–1 draw. It set up a second replay back at Oldham where, after finishing the initial 90 minutes still level at 1–1, the game went into extra time. The deadlock was finally broken by an Everton old boy, Ian Marshall, scoring the winner from the penalty spot.

After the Oldham defeat the letters rained in to *WSAG*. 'The present regime just have an inability to motivate and an inability to come up with a winning formula,' wrote Mike Saunders of Liverpool. 'In short THEY ARE LOSERS. They might be good "Evertonians", and indeed some might say being a good loser and a good Evertonian are synonymous, but they are obviously not up to the job. They never have been, they never will.' A. Beesley of Manchester asked, 'Most Evertonians want Harvey to succeed, but at what cost to our club? He has definitely fallen short of what true fans want.' 'I feel now is the time for Colin Harvey to be sacked,' wrote Gary Norman of Stoke-on-Trent. 'The man has a squad of excellent players but the poor negative tactics he uses and the diabolical coaching staff he has employed are the main reasons for his continuous failings.'

Also causing debate was the news that Everton and Liverpool were giving consideration to the building of a new stadium. The local newspapers were full of stories during February about a private venture by Stadium Mersey Ltd to build a 70,000-capacity all-seater stadium on the outskirts of the city, which would be leased to the two Mersey giants. With the recent publication of the Taylor Report, which recommended that all-seater stadia be universally adopted throughout the top divisions, and with development land in Liverpool 4 at a premium it was clear that Everton were going to have to look at options that would address the inevitable drop in Goodison's capacity. The possibility of a joint stadium, which was never the cause for much enthusiasm from either the blue or the red half of Merseyside, was just the first of many solutions put forward.

Back in the league, Harvey's side confounded their growing number of critics with an upsurge in form. A run of three wins during March lifted them to fourth. When they met League Cup finalists Nottingham Forest at the start of April, the TV cameras were there to capture the possibility of Everton going third. With the memory of their last television nightmare to exorcize, they didn't let any of their fans down, waltzing to a 3–0 half-time lead with two Whiteside goals and an effort from Cottee. After the interval they showed no sign of letting up, with Cottee completing the rout four minutes from the end with a crisply placed header. The result left Brian Clough raging and after the game he compared his players to 'pansies'. Harvey, though, was full of praise: 'It was a good all-round performance,' he said. 'People played out of position, but they adjusted well.'

Everton were unable to sustain their good form, winning just one of their last five games to finish the 1989/90 season in sixth place. An extra win might have seen them finish as high as third, although Liverpool were, again, far ahead of their 60 points with 79. Another season in Liverpool's shadow was an unacceptable prospect, and Harvey went into the 1990/91 campaign in the knowledge that another success-starved year might bring an end to his managerial reign.

Just two new faces were brought into his expensive squad pre-season. Mike Milligan, a 23-year-old midfielder from Royle's Oldham, was signed for £1 million, and left back Andy Hinchcliffe came from Kendall's Manchester City, in a part-exchange deal consisting of Neil Pointon plus £800,000. Milligan, an exciting, hard-tackling and energetic midfielder in the mould of Bryan Robson, had been one of the summer's most sought-after acquisitions, but from the outset looked out of his depth in an Everton shirt. He lasted just a season and 17 starts before he was sold back to Oldham at a £400,000 loss. Hinchcliffe was another young player bought with one eye on the future. Harvey never saw the best of him, and neither, for that matter, did his two successors. It was only with the arrival of Joe Royle in 1994 that the quiet Mancunian blossomed.

The dressing-room uncertainty boiled on. Neville Southall, who had ended the previous season by asking for a transfer, made a formal written request to leave the club on the eve of the new season. Harvey made it known that offers would be considered, although they would need to be in the region of £3 million, a sum in excess of the British transfer record. Southall's unhappiness bubbled over in the opening fixture of the new campaign, against newly promoted Leeds.

After an abysmal first-half performance, Everton left the pitch two goals down to a chorus of boos. Ten minutes later a solitary figure emerged from the tunnel and jogged over to the goal Everton were set to defend and sat down. It was Neville Southall.

'It wasn't a protest,' Southall's agent, Neil Ramsey, claimed at the end of the game. 'Neville just wanted to get on with things but as the seconds ticked away and the other players didn't come out, he decided to sit down.' The sit-in cost Southall a week's wages and drew boos from Everton supporters. At the next home game a banner bearing the legend 'Once a bin man, always a bin man' was unfurled – a harsh but necessary reminder that no player was bigger than the club, even if they were Neville Southall.

Everton ended up losing the Leeds match 2–3, and followed it up with defeats at Coventry and Manchester City. To make matters worse for Harvey, when he took his players out for a Chinese meal to clear the air, the evening descended into a boozy punch-up between Martin Keown and Kevin Sheedy, with the latter needing four stitches to a head wound. Indeed, it was the end of September before bottom-placed Everton recorded their first victory of the 1990/91 season, a 3–0 home win over Southampton. The *Guardian*'s headline, however, spoke louder about the standard of the performance than any result: 'Soccer Junkies Watch Junk'.

The win over Southampton did not prompt a revival in Everton's fortunes. On 30 October 1990 they visited Bramall Lane to play Sheffield United in a League Cup tie. United were at the bottom of the First Division without a league win, while Everton sat only two places above them. In a dreadful match, which was swung by Dave Watson's sending-off on the hour mark, the Sheffield side won 2–1, with Nevin getting the Everton goal. 'It could prove to be another nail in his [Harvey's] managerial coffin,' remarked the *Guardian*. They were prophetic words. The next day Harvey was sacked.

His dismissal and its timing surprised few people. 'The display in the Cup at Bramall Lane was the final straw,' wrote Chris Collins in his editorial. 'An abysmal display against poor opposition. The board had no alternative.' Evertonians had been desperate for Harvey – whom they rightly saw as one of their own – to succeed, but after three and a half years, millions spent, and success ever more distant, even the most sympathetic supporters' excuses for him had run out and his departure had an aura of inevitability about it. One newspaper likened it to the passing of a friend with a terminal illness: 'The sense of loss at the demise of a manager they idolized as a player and liked and respected as a person was tempered by acceptance that the departure was the only way to end the suffering.'[15]

Harvey was obviously upset. 'It was heartbreaking to wake up and realize I wasn't going to Everton,' he said, 'but when the time is right I will go back as a fan. I will always be a fan.'

By the standards of the club's later troughs, his record as manager, fourth, eighth and sixth positions plus an FA Cup Final appearance, was not bad. Neither was his transfer record as awful as some would suggest. Harvey had brought young players into the squad clearly with the future in mind, and although he spent heavily, the fault lay not so much with the quality of his signings but the large prices he was willing to pay coupled with his inability to get the best out of them. Tony Cottee was the prime example of underachievement under Harvey, but he was also all too frequently made a scapegoat for the failure of others.

Harvey was also let down by a crippling catalogue of injuries. Paul Bracewell missed his first 18 months in charge; Ian Snodin, on the verge of England honours, his last. Kevin Ratcliffe, his captain, was absent for a long period, while Norman Whiteside played only twice after the end of the 1989/90 season, in which he had been one of the star performers. Injuries and arguably complacent senior players aside, the team unmistakably bore Harvey's imprint. In his final match in charge, seven of the 12 players involved were Harvey's signings, while an eighth – John Ebbrell – had broken through to the first team under him. It was clear for all to see on that cold autumn night in Sheffield that between them all there was a lack of motivation and appetite for success. The time was right for a change.

◊

SIX DAYS AFTER Harvey's sacking, the club arranged a press conference to announce his replacement. It was widely expected that Joe Royle, whose Oldham side were top of the Second Division, would be named in his place. Others, including Ron Atkinson and Arthur Cox, had been linked with the post, but Royle was hot favourite. However, not a single pressman speculated the right name. At the press conference, Philip Carter unveiled not one surprise but two. Howard Kendall was named as manager and Harvey his assistant, in a rematch of Everton's most successful managerial pairing. 'If Manchester City was like a love affair, Everton Football Club is like a marriage to me,' gushed the new manager. The move took everybody, not least Kendall, utterly by surprise.

Kendall had been approached by a go-between 48 hours after the sacking of Harvey. He later claimed that at that point he had not given consideration to the prospect of a return but as he dwelt on various matters – the indifference of Manchester City support to his managership, the chance to return to his team and rekindle Everton's glory – the more it appealed. The deciding factor had been the opportunity to try to transform Everton's fortunes for a second time. 'Deep down inside,' he later wrote, 'I knew that I ... wanted to make the club great again.'[16] With a clause loaded into his Manchester City contract that he might negotiate with another club should he so choose, he met with Philip Carter and told him that he would be delighted to return to Goodison.

Such were his reputation and Everton's standing that Kendall's return made the front pages of several national newspapers. It was viewed as a genuinely bold move that would restore glory to Everton. Most Evertonians were as surprised as they were delighted. Despite the problems of Harvey's managership, few doubted his ability as a coach, while the return of Kendall and the recent memory of his triumphs evoked broad smiles. Some voices stood out among the hyperbole, and one was Chris Collins's. 'I just had a feeling that a clean broom was needed right throughout the club. The appointment of Kendall and reappointment of Harvey was hardly that,' he wrote. Peter Mills's was another: 'I know it's a cliché,' he remarked, 'but you should never go back. I think we all felt that Howard's return was a mistake. He didn't have the strong characters like Reid and Gray around either.'

Nevertheless, Kendall had soon redressed Everton's decline, lifting them away from the relegation zone and back towards the respectability of mid-table. He was quickly linked to a plethora of new signings, although none came immediately. Cottee, to his immense frustration, was faring little better under Kendall than he had under Harvey. His vexation was almost palpable when, after scoring all four goals in a Zenith Data Systems tie with Sunderland, he was dropped barely a week later as the two sides met again in the league.

Yet Cottee's moment came – and in the most dramatic fashion. For the fourth time in six years, Everton met Liverpool in the FA Cup. On this occasion it was a fifth-round tie that was played at Anfield in front of TV cameras. In a compelling match that lacked nothing except goals, Everton came closest to winning. First Pat

Nevin was clearly tripped by Gary Ablett inside the Liverpool area in front of everyone, it would seem, except the referee Neil Midgley. Then, with the game drawing to a frenetic conclusion, McCall seized on a piece of careless play by David Burrows and released Nevin. His pass rolled perfectly into Neil McDonald's path, but his shot was snatched. Shortly after, the final whistle blew, to set up a replay at Goodison the next Wednesday, 20 February 1991.

What followed on that heady February night, in a match of high drama, extraordinary passion and excitement, went down for Cottee, along with his début against Newcastle, as his best game in an Everton shirt. Liverpool had Peter Beardsley back in their starting line-up in place of David Speedie, while Mike Newell came on in place of Kevin Sheedy, who had tweaked his hamstring in the first match. Cottee was named on the substitutes' bench. The scoring began in the first half when Rush seized on a mistake by his Welsh team-mate Ratcliffe. He moved in, beating Southall with his shot, which Hinchcliffe cleared off the line. The ball went only as far as Beardsley, who knocked it gleefully home. By half-time Everton were almost overrun but the rich tapestry of the match was still to unravel.

Two minutes into the second half Sharp's header brought the game level and suddenly the momentum was Everton's. It was short-lived. Beardsley was worked through by neat interplay from Burrows and Molby, and put Liverpool back in front with a left-foot drive that went beyond Southall's reach. Everton rallied again, and when there was a mix-up between Grobelaar and Nicol on the edge of the Liverpool penalty area, Sharp ran through, virtually unchallenged, to bring the scores level at 2–2. With the game still moving at full pelt there was little telling where the next goal would come from, but when Everton's nemesis, Rush, headed home a Molby cross on 77 minutes it looked as if the match would be Liverpool's.

On 86 minutes, in a move that looked little more than a last-ditch gamble, Cottee came on for Nevin. With just seconds remaining, and just one prior touch to his name, it paid dividends. McCall flicked the ball on and Cottee ran in to tuck it past Grobelaar: 3–3. Extra time beckoned.

Further twists were not far away. Barnes put Liverpool in front with a curling 30-yard shot that nestled into the top corner, confounding Southall who had saved brilliantly from Rush and Barry Venison just moments earlier. Lesser sides might have capitulated here, but Everton and Cottee were indefatigable. Six minutes from time he equalized again to set up a replay a week later, again at Goodison.

Everton took that match 1–0, thanks to Dave Watson's first-half goal and some doughty defending in the second period. However, the game was a pale imitation of what had preceded it, and Cottee was again occupying the substitutes' bench. Indeed, the talk on Merseyside in the days leading up to the match had not been the stunning 4–4 draw or Cottee's removal from the transfer list, but the shock resignation of Kenny Dalglish just hours after it. Citing the unbearable pressure of management, the unending demands for success and hinting at deep traumas left by Hillsborough, Dalglish announced he was retiring from the professional game. It was short-lived and he soon returned to football, managing Blackburn to the Championship four years later, and Newcastle after that, also playing a role at both Celtic and Rangers. Yet the formidable success of his mighty Liverpool sides of the mid- to late-eighties – Everton's biggest rivals in the period – was never to return, either for him or his former club.

Everton maintained a fitful progress under Kendall, finishing the 1990/91 season ninth. After their epic fifth-round FA Cup tie with Liverpool, they lost the quarter-final, disappointingly, at West Ham. The Polish international winger Robert Warzycha was signed from Gornik Zagreb for £400,000 and immediately staked a claim for inclusion in place of the popular Nevin. April 1991 had seen a visit to Wembley, albeit in the Zenith Data Systems Cup Final, which ended in a 1–4 defeat to Crystal Palace. Just 12,000 Evertonians had made the trip to London and the irrepressibly downbeat Southall shared the indifference of those who had stayed at home, refusing to collect his medal. 'Who wants a ZDS runners-up medal?' he scoffed.[17]

A month later Gwladys Street took its last stand for the final game of the season against Luton Town. The Taylor Report that came in the wake of the Hillsborough disaster declared that top-flight stadia must be all-seater by the start of the 1994/5 season. Everton were one of the first to put this into action, installing seats in all areas of the ground save for a small section in the Park Stand, then allocated to visiting supporters. Just 19,909 came to pay homage to the famous terrace, watching Everton grind out a 1–0 victory, with

Cottee claiming his twenty-second goal of the campaign. It was a downbeat end to a traumatic season.

○

THE MYSTERIOUS DEATH of newspaper tycoon and Derby County owner Robert Maxwell, days prior to Kendall's return to Goodison, had placed the future of the Midlands club into crisis. Faced with financial turmoil as the scale of the collapse of Maxwell's business empire unfolded, it became clear that the Baseball Ground's two favourite sons, Mark Wright and Dean Saunders, would be sold to make ends meet. Speculation led them to Merseyside where Liverpool's new manager, Graeme Souness, was said to be preparing a £2 million bid for Wright, and Kendall was ready to break the British transfer record to bring Saunders to Everton for £3 million. In the event, Souness surprised everybody by buying both players for a total of £5.1 million. The deal left a gap in the Everton attack, not to mention the Anfield bank account, and Kendall sought to rectify both by bidding £1 million for Peter Beardsley. To the surprise of many, Souness accepted, and the Geordie became only the fifth player in 30 years to cross Stanley Park.

In apparently crisis-hit times for football, with scandal and the taint of money seeming to corrupt the game almost daily, it was refreshing to find a player like Beardsley: a quiet teetotaller whose love affair with football was unremitting. He had not been signed by his local heroes, Newcastle United, as a youngster, and had got his break with Carlisle United where he emerged as one of the lower league's most exciting young talents. A spell playing in Canada and an extended trial period with Manchester United saw the young Beardsley prosper, but it was with the North American Soccer League (NASL) on the verge of financial collapse and his return to Britain with Newcastle that he flourished. Here, he fitted well into an attack-minded team, which included the likes of Kevin Keegan and Chris Waddle. Together they stormed to the Second Division title in his first season, and by the time his contract had expired in the summer of 1987 he had agreed to sign for Liverpool for a British record fee of £1.9 million. He spent four years at Anfield, picking up two Championship medals, and also played a starring role in the 1990 World Cup during which England reached the semi-finals. However, his last season at Anfield saw him in and out of the side, and after Kenny Dalglish's resignation, Graeme Souness's appointment and the record signing of Saunders, Beardsley had realized that his time at Anfield was coming to an end.

The summer of 1991 also marked the conclusion of Graeme Sharp's 11-year association with Everton. Although he was widely regarded as one of the club's great centre forwards, his goal tally was drying up and most Evertonians saw the £500,000 deal that took the 30-year-old to join Joe Royle – a fellow member of the pantheon of legendary number nines – at Oldham as good business. He was followed to Boundary Park by the disappointing Mike Milligan and, shortly after the start of the new season, Neil McDonald, who had shown signs of developing into a quality player. Stuart McCall was sold to Rangers, a clear indication of how highly Howard Kendall rated the England under-21 captain, John Ebbrell, whose place in central midfield was cemented by the Scottish international's departure. The unassuming Wirral-born midfielder never lived up fully to his potential, lacking the finishing touches to his game that would have fulfilled his youthful promise. He flitted in and out of the side under later managers and never got over the disappointment of being left out of the 1995 FA Cup Final team. Kendall later spent £1 million to bring him to Sheffield United in 1997, where Ebbrell should have kick-started his career. The move ended disastrously for both Ebbrell and the Yorkshire club after he limped out of action on his début. It was his last match as a professional, aged just 27, a sad end for a player whose future, in 1991, seemed so rich.

Along with Beardsley, Kendall brought in Mark Ward from Manchester City as well as Alan Harper. Ward, a £1-million signing, slotted into the right-hand side of midfield. Quick-tempered and never really looking as though he might justify his heavy price tag, he was sold to Birmingham City three years later, having failed to make his mark at Goodison, beyond a well-taken goal in the 1993 Goodison derby.

One final addition that summer came in the boardroom. Dr David Marsh, a former Walker Cup golfer, took over as chairman from Sir Philip Carter who stood down after 13 years in charge. Marsh later attracted criticism for holding tight the Goodison purse-strings, a not entirely fair criticism, as Everton, with Sir John Moores no longer playing an active role at the club, lacked a benefactor. Yet

Marsh seemed to lack the guiding presence of Carter and this poverty of meaningful direction and leadership from the boardroom later had a telling influence on the future of both Kendall and the club.

Everton began the 1991/2 season brightly, although they often struggled to turn their vibrant performances into results. One exception was the first home game of the season, a 3–1 win over champions Arsenal. Four days later they ran Manchester United ragged at Goodison, only the imperious Peter Schmeichel, making one of his first appearances for the Old Trafford club, keeping the scores blank. Indeed, one win in the opening eight league games of the season belied the genuine quality of some of Everton's performances. Beardsley showed glimmers of his abundant talent, but it took him six starts to register his first goal in a blue shirt. In the four matches that followed he added a further six, including a hat-trick against Coventry City. Kendall was elated by the immediate impact he made: 'I was delighted with the way Peter immediately settled in at Goodison and got on with his job. It could not have been easy coming straight from Liverpool.' His prolific spell of form earned him many plaudits, some saying that he was worthy of an England recall, but as ever he remained typically modest. 'I feel as though I could still do it,' he told *Shoot!*. 'But it's not up to me to decide if I'll get the opportunity.' Beardsley was a provider of goals as well as a scorer, no more so than when Everton met Spurs at Goodison in October and he laid on the first of Tony Cottee's hat-trick. Running through the Tottenham defence he shaped to shoot, fooling everybody, including the Spurs goalkeeper Erik Thorstvedt and, to the surprise of everybody, and delight of Cottee, squared the ball to his strike partner for the simplest of side-footers.

The effervescence of Beardsley and some of the bright build-up work aside, Everton were in essence a mediocre side and their finish of thirteenth did justice to the team's overall quality. As Graham Ennis, by then *When Skies Are Grey* editor, wrote a year on from Kendall's return, 'The team is a long way from the mess Colin Harvey left, but still is not quite right.' Kendall had sought to strengthen his forward line again with the signing in November 1991 of Maurice Johnston, the controversial Scottish international striker, from Rangers. Johnston had been the first Catholic to turn out in the navy blue of the Ibrox club in modern times and, as a proven striker in the Scottish and French leagues, was expected by many to reproduce such form in England. He was not, however, the answer to Everton's striking problems or the target man so desperately needed to add physical presence to an attack that lacked the recently departed Sharp, and also Mike Newell, who had been offloaded to Blackburn. Everton's forward line became known as the 'Diddy Men', and as the 1991/2 season drew to its conclusion, the need for a commanding centre forward had become abundantly obvious.

By the end of the season there was one noticeable absence from the starting 11: Kevin Ratcliffe had played his last game for the club the previous December in the 1–4 League Cup defeat by Leeds United: he was substituted at half-time after a torrid first 45 minutes, an inauspicious conclusion to the career of the club's most successful captain.

It is perhaps little coincidence that as soon as Ratcliffe was struck down with injury problems Everton's successes of the mid-eighties ground to a halt. He had led by example throughout that period, and when he was kept out for most of 1988 with groin and hernia problems his presence was sorely missed. On his eventual return in October that year his once hallmark pace had deteriorated, and ordinary strikers who would once never have got a look in began to get the better of him. Evertonians hoped that his form would return but more niggling injuries in the 1989/90 season halted further progress. Things got no better the following season when Colin Harvey had played him in the much-hated left-back position to accommodate Martin Keown. Following Howard Kendall's return, Ratcliffe was often part of defensive experiments that rarely proved successful.

A month after the Leeds game, Kendall signed Gary Ablett from Liverpool, the captain's armband was handed to Dave Watson and Ratcliffe was put on the transfer list. It was assumed that Ratcliffe, who had only just turned 30 and had stood out just months earlier when Wales rose to their finest ever victory, beating world champions Germany 1–0, would be immediately snapped up. Sadly that was not the case: he spent a year languishing in the reserves before he was signed by Cardiff City. There, his career enjoyed a brief resurgence and he returned to the international fold, playing his last game in Wales's 1993 win over Belgium. He later became manager of Chester City, then Shrewsbury Town.

Ratcliffe remained passionate about the club throughout his 15-year Everton career, and maintained the love affair even after he had left Goodison. Yet for all his trophies and honours it was the fans who brought him the most pleasure. 'Casting my mind back over the past ten years,' Ratcliffe had said in his testimonial season, 'it is amazing how many of my best memories are of the fans rather than the matches or goals. Even during the lean years there was a massive hardcore at every away game who lifted us more than they could imagine. And by the time we had lifted ourselves to Wembley and Rotterdam, they brought tears to our eyes. To play before supporters like that, to share their joy, has been an honour.'[18]

○

THE BEGINNING OF the 1992/3 season marked the start of a new era for English football with the inception of the Premier League. After years of procrastination the élite clubs had broken away from the rest of the Football League, having submitted their resignation en masse 12 months earlier. This 'Super League' had been agreed in principle in the Everton boardroom in March 1991, in a meeting presided over by Philip Carter, and was confirmed the following summer. Originally envisaging an 18-team division, with minimum standards for pitches, floodlights, stadium facilities and so on, it emerged as little different from the old First Division, albeit with 20 teams instead of 22 from the start of the 1994/5 season. In fact as David Dein, the Arsenal vice-chairman, admitted shortly after its formation: 'I'm getting increasingly embarrassed when people say, what is the difference between the Premier League and the old First Division? I have to face them and say, "Nothing, except there's more money swishing about."'[19]

Not that any of this money made its way into Howard Kendall's hands. Three weeks before the start of the new season, Everton announced annual losses of £2 million and debts totalling £3.6 million. Kendall brought in Barry Horne, Paul Rideout and Predrag Radosavljevic from the American Indoor League, having seen Sheedy, Nevin and Ray Atteveld leave towards the end of the previous season. Although Horne and Rideout eventually proved their worth, none of Kendall's summer signings inspired much hope for the Goodison faithful.

Nevertheless, Everton again began the season brightly. They followed up an opening-day draw with Sheffield Wednesday with a 3–0 victory over Championship favourites Manchester United, the blistering pace of Warzycha and the artistry of Beardsley tearing the eventual champions apart. 'The Reds,' wrote the *Independent*'s Joe Lovejoy, 'were drowning in an Everton blue sea.'[20] When Everton met hotly fancied Blackburn Rovers in mid-September, still unbeaten and with £10 million of recent signings in their starting line-up, few gave them a chance, less so when Mark Ward broke his leg after just eight minutes and Alan Shearer put them behind shortly after. Yet Everton rallied and an equalizer by Cottee was followed by another goal from John Ebbrell, set up by Warzycha. When Shearer added a second late on in the second half it seemed he might have saved Blackburn, but Warzycha struck again, gliding down the right to set up Cottee's winner. 'In a season in which it is fashionable to be unfashionable,' marvelled one newspaper, 'this branch of the aristocracy, at least, cannot be written off.'[21] Even *When Skies Are Grey*, so often full of pessimism, were moved to carry a cover with a photograph from the mid-eighties of Howard Kendall holding the Championship trophy, begging the question 'Rebirth of the Blues?'

Such optimism was short-lived. An issue later, Phil Redmond, now a co-editor, asked in an article aptly titled 'Jekyll and Hyde', 'How can a team that played so brilliantly at Blackburn be so bad just a matter of days later at home to Crystal Palace? . . . sometimes Everton really piss me off.'[22] Redmond's article summarized Everton succinctly: they simply lacked the strength and quality to be anything other than a mediocre, inconsistent side. Too often they were reliant on Beardsley to muster some creativity or Southall to rescue them at the back. The absence of an outstanding goalscorer had been a recurrent problem since Lineker's departure, and although Cottee had finally established himself as Everton's number nine, the lack of a top-class target man to partner him meant that his potential still went unfulfilled. Maurice Johnston had proven a huge disappoint-ment, burdened by injuries, bad form and rumours of disciplinary problems, and at the end of 1993 he moved to Hearts on a free transfer.

Yet, in the December 1992 meeting with Liverpool, one of the few outings he got into an Everton shirt, he struck the equalizer. Trailing to Mark Wright's header, Johnston let fly with a speculative left-foot curler that flew in off the right-hand post. His goal galvanized Everton and he could have added a second before Beardsley scored

Everton's winner six minutes from the end, sending a skimming shot from the edge of the D into the back of the Liverpool net.

Beardsley's winner was one of the few pluses in a bleak winter. His presence, coupled with the knowledge that Liverpool were enduring a similarly awful season, maintained the sanity of the Goodison faithful. When Everton met Wimbledon at the end of January 1993, just 3039 turned up at Selhurst Park to see Everton beat them 3–1. It was the lowest ever recorded attendance for a top-flight match. That win stemmed Everton's decline, but the club's financial problems were highlighted just days later when Martin Keown – then an England regular – left for £2 million to return to his first club, Arsenal. The departure of Keown and the arrival of his 'replacement', 34-year-old Kenny Sansom, on a free transfer, were indicative of Everton's decline as a big club and served to highlight the lack of ambition that was eating away its core. Optimistic fans waited patiently for a Kevin Brock backpass; others spoke of relegation. Either way, supporters were increasingly fewer as the average attendance plunged towards the 20,000 mark.

Relegation was averted and, by the standards of later seasons, quite comfortably: Everton finished thirteenth. Yet hope was a sparse commodity among Evertonians, and even more so when Kendall accepted a £1.2 million bid from Derby County for Beardsley in the hope that he could use the funds to buy his much-needed target man. Beardsley never became a Derby County player: Kevin Keegan, on hearing that his former team-mate was available, snapped him up for his newly promoted Newcastle team, bringing the Goodison career of one of Everton's most brilliant individuals to an end. At Newcastle Beardsley was recalled to the England squad, also helping Newcastle into Europe and to a league position at the upper reaches of the Premiership. His most successful days were evidently not at Goodison, but in the short period he was at the club he often managed to thrill the crowds and was easily the team's best performer. Tony Cottee later said of him, 'He is a quiet person who just gets on with his job in a professional manner. That's how he won the Everton fans over so quickly. He is the most creative player I have ever played with. It was an honour to play with him.' Peter Beardsley's genius was probably best epitomized during a 3–0 victory over Nottingham Forest at Goodison. After intercepting the ball just past the half-way line and seeing the goalkeeper off his line he made an audacious lob. The end result, however, was indicative of his and Everton's fortunes at the time. It hit the bar.

○

KENDALL SPENT THE 1993/4 pre-season forlornly trying to buy a target man. Attempts to sign Duncan Ferguson, Niall Quinn, Mark Hateley, Mark Bright and Brian Deane all came to nothing. When Everton opened the season they had no new signings in the team that beat Southampton 2–0 on the opening day of the campaign, although the deal to bring in Graham Stuart (who stood at just five foot eight, but was a veritable giant beside Cottee, towering two inches over him) was in the offing.

Stuart made his début in the third game of the 1993/4 season, a 4–2 win over Sheffield United at Goodison, in which Cottee scored a hat-trick, that took Everton – to the surprise of everybody – to the top of the Premier League. After the match Kendall was fulsome in his praise for Cottee, who had just signed a new three-year contract with the club. 'Cottee's general play was superb,' he enthused. 'He's linking well with Rideout, who has had three superb games for us and showing what he can do – which he didn't last season.' That win was Everton's third on the run, but yet again they were plagued by the sort of form that characterized this era, losing their next three matches. A win, with a solitary Cottee goal, away at Oldham in mid-September, stopped their slide down the table and left the Everton dressing room on a high prior to the following week's meeting with Liverpool.

If any one factor – beyond the gallows humour that inevitably pervaded in a ghostly Goodison – kept Evertonians' spirits alive during these days of decline, it was the mounting traumas that Liverpool were facing since Dalglish's departure. Graeme Souness's time at Liverpool had been beset by public-relations gaffes, bad signings, indiscipline and unrest among supporters. It was expected that he would lose his job at the end of the 1992/3 season, but to the surprise of many – and the barely suppressed delight of Evertonians – had somehow kept it.

The September 1993 derby effectively ended any remaining credibility Souness had among Liverpool fans. Everton romped home to a 2–0 victory, with Horne and Ebbrell dominant in midfield,

Beagrie weaving havoc from the left flank and Southall, unusually, seldom challenged. Mark Ward struck the first goal, thrashing home a 20-yard shot. That moment was remembered best not as the instant that Everton went ahead but for the punch-up in the Liverpool penalty area between Bruce Grobelaar and Steve McManaman that followed it. If the Everton dressing room could be accused of poor morale, it was seemingly nothing compared to that of their visitors. With Liverpool in disarray it never looked as if more than a goal would be needed to take the tie, but Cottee added another to make certain five minutes from time. Robbing his former West Ham teammate Julian Dicks, he ran into the Liverpool area, rounded Grobelaar and tucked in his fifth goal in eight games. As the game drew to a close Gwladys Street reverberated to the chorus of 'Souness must stay! Souness must stay!'

Their joy was short-lived. A week later Everton met Norwich City – who had finished the previous season third, having led the Premier League for much of it – and were thrashed 1–5 at Goodison. It was their worst home defeat since Liverpool had humiliated them 11 years earlier in the infamous 'Glenn Keeley derby'.

Moreover, it was hardly a fitting tribute to Sir John Moores, who had died at his Formby home that morning, aged 97. The patriarchal millionaire, who had restored Everton to greatness in the 1960s and twice served as chairman, lived by the maxim 'You look after your own.' In Moores's case his 'own' extended beyond his large family, to include the Littlewoods workforce, the people of Merseyside and Everton Football Club. How they could have done with someone of his ilk then.

On the pitch, things went from bad to worse and the positive start to the season was soon forgotten. Everton slid down the league with worrying ease and were knocked out of the League Cup by Manchester United. The nadir came when they were humbled by a depressingly ordinary Queens Park Rangers, who beat them 3–0 at Goodison, without even breaking into a sweat. Attendances were down and the squad bereft of quality. The board – uncertain anyway in the wake of Moores's death – lacked firm leadership, and morale seemed to be at an all-time low. Goodison was moribund. Work had started on the demolition of the Park Stand and by the end of the season there would be just three sides to the ground. As the wind swept through the open end, it added to the sense of desolation.

Two weeks later on 4 December 1993, a crowd of just 13,667 –
Goodison's lowest in almost a decade – turned out to see Everton
beat Southampton with a solitary Cottee goal. Evertonians left the
ground thinking that perhaps yet another corner had been turned
as they saw their side rise to eleventh position. Yet within an hour of
the final whistle, they were struck with the shock news that Kendall
had resigned.

The timing, rather than the resignation itself, caused most surprise. Goodison had been full of hope when Kendall had returned in
1990. Three years on his only ambition seemed to be consolidation.
Few talked of Everton as a major player any more, and no one, not
even the most wildly optimistic of Evertonians, talked of championships. It was hardly surprising that hope had died for Kendall too.

In the days that followed his departure, it emerged that he had
resigned after the board had refused to sanction the £1.5 million
signing of Dion Dublin from Manchester United. Perhaps they were
mindful of the calamitous signing of Maurice Johnston two years
earlier, but it was fair to say that Kendall, having sold Keown and
Beardsley for a combined total of £3.5 million that year, could have
felt that in some way he was 'owed' Dublin in recompense. In any
event the board were wrong. Dublin proved an able, prolific, if
slightly ungainly, top-flight striker who went on to earn England
honours. Arguably, with a more able and patient chairman than
the grim-faced Marsh, Kendall might have fared better, even if the
money was genuinely not available at the time. In the midst of
uncertainty over future ownership, a more capable leader, like Philip
Carter, would have persuaded Kendall to bide his time.

Jimmy Gabriel took control as caretaker manager and suggested
that he would like to take over permanently. The board did well not
to give serious consideration to this as Everton embarked on a
miserable December, which dragged on into January and saw them
go some six games without scoring. Joe Royle and Peter Reid were
the prime candidates to succeed Kendall, but the board of directors
raised a few eyebrows by overlooking both and appointing the
Norwich City manager, Mike Walker, on 7 January 1994.

Walker's rise to prominence had been meteoric. His playing
career had been undistinguished and confined to the lower leagues.
Having briefly enjoyed a spell in charge of Colchester United in
the late 1980s, famous only for his being sacked having just won the

Manager of the Month award, he joined the Norwich City coaching staff and was appointed manager in 1992, still virtually unknown outside Carrow Road. Perhaps more surprising than his appointment was the immediate transformation his managership had on a Norwich team that had never looked anything more than a good bet for mid-table anonymity. With a reputation for free-flowing, attractive football, they ended 1992 10 points clear at the top of the Premier League. But for a lack of depth in squad numbers they might have won the Championship that season, but their finish of third was still the best in the Norfolk club's history. Perhaps ominously, though, they had the unusual distinction for a club who had finished so high of having conceded more goals, 65, than they had scored, 61.

Yet Walker had enhanced his reputation still further in the half-season prior to his arrival at Goodison. The 5–1 walloping his team gave Everton in September belied some of their inconsistency in the league, but they still managed to knock the mighty Bayern Munich out of the UEFA Cup, losing out narrowly to Inter Milan in the next round. With this in mind Everton sought him as the man to restore their ailing fortunes and, moreover, to provide a clean break with the inertia that had come to typify the latter Harvey and Kendall years.

Swindon Town were the opponents for Walker's first full match in charge. He had watched from the stands as a side picked by Gabriel had scraped to an undeserved draw away at Bolton in the third round of the FA Cup a week earlier, and spent the following few days bringing in Brett Angell from Southend United. Angell, a lumbering centre forward and prolific lower-league scorer, was hardly the top-class target man most Evertonians had had in mind, but at least he was big. Everton won 6–2, with Cottee getting his second hat-trick of the season, but the scoreline was flattering. Having thrown away a two-goal half-time lead, Ablett put Everton back in front, and three goals in the final six minutes gave Gwladys Street a long-awaited smile.

It was brief, though. Four days later Everton were dismissed from the FA Cup by Bolton, losing 2–3, having again conceded a two-goal lead. In the league, they fared slightly better, beating Chelsea impressively and drawing with Arsenal. But when they visited Walker's former club on 20 March a slick-looking Norwich side routed Everton 3–0. Relegation became more and more of a threat, and it was reinforced a fortnight later when Sheffield Wednesday thrashed Everton 5–1 at Hillsborough; 3–0 reversals at Blackburn and Leeds pushed Everton closer towards the trapdoor, with only a win over West Ham blocking a seemingly irreversible tide. They approached the final match of the season against Wimbledon occupying the third relegation spot, lying behind Sheffield United whose result against Chelsea Everton would need to better in order to survive.

May 7, 1994, is one of those days that has gone down in Goodison folklore: 31,000, some queuing from before midday, packed the three-sided ground, with hundreds more watching from the trees of Stanley Park. Wimbledon were coming to the end of their best season ever, hunting a fifth-placed finish, with a trip to Las Vegas, paid for by their Lebanese chairman Sam Hamman, dangling before them as a reward if they managed it. The night prior to the match, the Wimbledon coach had been burned in an arson attack. 'Intimidation,' the conspiracists had bleated. 'Gamesmanship,' smiled those in the know. Wimbledon – who boasted a player called Peter Fear, an apt name if ever there was one on such a day – arrived at Goodison singed but unperturbed.

From the earliest stages of the game Everton looked doomed. In the fourth minute Limpar mysteriously handled inside his own area. Dean Holdsworth gratefully stepped up to take the resulting penalty and score his twenty-fourth goal of the season, the ball trickling agonizingly into the net after Southall had got both hands to it. Worse was to follow. Sixteen minutes later Dave Watson and David Unsworth jumped for the same high ball. It dropped to Andy Clarke, whose mis-hit shot found the net via the shins of Gary Ablett. Goodison, which had been an inferno of noise, was hushed.

Four minutes later the crowd was stirred back into life. Limpar, desperate to atone for his bizarre misjudgement, ghosted into the left of the Wimbledon penalty area. As he sought to shuffle past Fear, he appeared to have been caught and crashed to the ground. Penalty! A dubious decision, perhaps, but Graham Stuart kept his nerve to slot home a crucial goal.

Wimbledon still looked most likely to score, though. Holdsworth went close twice, and missed from four yards on a third occasion. At the other end Stuart nearly scored shortly after half-time with a low near-post drive after a mazy run, but one was still left to ponder where an Everton goal might come from.

Then, on 67 minutes, a miracle. Barry Horne, for so much of his first two years at Goodison out of sorts and with a single goal to his name, seized the ball on the edge of the centre circle. He rushed forward, and when the ball sat up invitingly, he sent a volley from 30 yards into the top corner of Segers's net. It was one of the finest goals Goodison had ever seen.

Two minutes later he nearly added a second, sending a similar effort inches over the crossbar. Everton surged forward searching for a winner. Walker brought Stuart Barlow on for Ebbrell with 10 minutes remaining. With his first piece of action he ran down the right flank and played the ball to Cottee. His flick on found Stuart who, from the edge of the area, hit a tame shot that squeezed in under Segers to make it 3–2. It was a scoreline they held until the referee's final whistle nine minutes later signalled that Everton were safe.

It was widely expected that the Wimbledon game and the imminent threat of relegation for the first time in more than forty years would be the lowest Everton would fall. A new takeover, which would see millions injected into the club, was on the verge of completion, and it would enable Mike Walker to rebuild the squad he had inherited. It was acknowledged that the road back to glory would be long, but the gloom that had come to grip Goodison Park in the seven years since their last Championship victory was lifting. Premiership survival, which had come about in the most dramatic fashion, was naturally a prerequisite for future success. After the Wimbledon match, with a new manager, a new owner and money to buy new players, a renewed sense of expectation emerged. Everton were about to enter a different era.

The most significant departure in Mike Walker's brief spell as manager was Tony Cottee, early in the 1994/5 season. Here was a player whose career had declined in parallel to the fortunes of Everton. When he first joined the club in 1988 as the most expensive player in Britain, he was a 23-year-old on the fringes of the England team, a proven goalscorer at West Ham and acknowledged as one of the country's finest talents. At the time Everton were England's pre-eminent team, save for Liverpool. They boasted a side packed with internationals, and although the 1987/8 season had ended without a trophy, it was expected to be a mere interlude before Harvey carried on with the successes of his predecessor. The Everton that Cottee left in 1994, despite the renewed optimism, held quite a different standing, as did his reputation. They were embarking on their worst start to a season in their history and he was a mere makeweight in the deal that brought David Burrows – one of Goodison's least distinguished sons – to Everton.

Cottee's six-year association with Everton was rather less impressive than his goal ratio – just short of one in every two games – or his tally of 99 might suggest. Too often he would labour ineffectively for weeks without return, then boost his goal tally with a hat-trick or a brace against lesser opposition. A run of goals followed, which eventually dried up. Then the cycle was repeated. Nevertheless, there was little doubt that the swap for Burrows was a mistake. For all his faults, Cottee had still been top scorer in all but one of his six years at Goodison, including the previous troubled campaign where he had scored 16 league goals. He was a proven goalscorer, who had the experience and ability still to find the back of the net regularly. It is perhaps unfair that any assessment of him is invariably made with reference to his record-breaking fee. Given that view, his time at Goodison was a disappointment, but most Evertonians were agreed that he was a player worth keeping.

Cottee was aware of the affection most fans had for him, and that few singled him out for blame as an individual. If he had any cause to doubt this, such thoughts were erased in his last game as an Everton player in the reserve derby at the start of September 1994. At the end of the match, 6000 supporters gave him a standing ovation. 'It was a wonderful end to my Everton career,' he later wrote, 'and I was genuinely choked by the reception I got.'[23]

13

Johnson's Odyssey

ON 19 MAY 1993, the *Liverpool Echo* broke the news on its front page that Everton was to be sold by the Moores family. 'Everton For Sale' ran a sensationalist headline that belied any firm evidence behind the story. Ken Rogers, the *Echo*'s sports editor, had been tipped off that the Moores family had instructed their bankers, Hill Samuel, to seek ways of refinancing the club. For some time rumours had circulated throughout the city concerning the club's future. Sir John Moores was 97, in poor health and confined to his Formby home. Infirmity and old age had precluded him playing a meaningful role in the club for some years. Neither of his two sons, John Moores junior, a successful farmer and chancellor of Liverpool John Moores University, nor Peter, a well-known patron of the arts, was said to share their father's passion for the game. Nevertheless, at that stage the club was still in the Moores family's hands and a spokesman for Sir John strongly denied the *Echo*'s claims. Yet the story brought many rumours out into the open, and for much of a summer bereft of transfer activity for the cash-strapped club, Merseyside's Everton-supporting fraternity was abuzz with speculation and intrigue. Richard Branson and the Sultan of Brunei were just two of the names linked – without any basis – with takeover bids for the club.

When Sir John died in September, Rogers's journalistic instincts were proved correct. The board of directors moved quickly to ascertain the club's future and it soon became apparent that neither of the Moores brothers was interested in continuing their family's association with the club in the same manner that their father had for more than thirty years. It was made clear that an offer, if made, would receive due consideration.

Two leading contenders emerged for control of the club: the long-time director Bill Kenwright, and Peter Johnson, the ambitious chairman of Everton's Merseyside neighbours, Tranmere Rovers. Kenwright, a former star of *Coronation Street* but by then a successful theatre impresario, was a lifelong Evertonian who travelled unfailingly from his London home to every match. He was an unstinting follower of Everton, as dedicated a fan as any who turned out in Gwladys Street. Johnson, like Kenwright, was a businessman, who had made his fortune selling hampers. His Park Foods empire was valued at £175 million and his interests extended into distribution, logistics and, later, to a chorus of sniggers from his critics, flavoured chips bizarrely named 'DJ Spuddles'. He had made his name in football as owner and chairman of Tranmere Rovers, taking them from the brink of relegation out of the Football League, to the verge of promotion to the Premiership in just six years. Johnson was said to hold the financial muscle, Kenwright the love of the club.

It was the theatre impresario who emerged as the early frontrunner in the battle for financial control of Everton. He quickly captured the enthusiasm of the supporters and, it would seem, of the Moores family. It had been suggested that the late Sir John had declared that any new owner of Everton should be 'selflessly devoted to the club' and 'a safe pair of hands'. Given those criteria, there was only one man for the job, as Johnson had been a boyhood Liverpool supporter. Kenwright met with the previous owner's sons in December 1993, along with their sister, Lady Granchester, who agreed to back his takeover bid. He left the Moores home with a signed statement to that effect.

From here on, though, Kenwright's dream began to unravel. Two months later, in February 1994, John Moores junior refuted the suggestion that his father had made specific requests about the club's future. 'During his lifetime, my father discussed with me on several occasions his wishes for the future of the club and hence his shares,' he said. 'He urged me to use the shares to ensure that Everton was kept on a sound financial basis and, above all, achieve success. At no stage did he mention to me "a safe pair of hands" or a "True Blue".'[1] By this stage, his brother Peter had passed his Everton inheritance on to Lady Granchester and Janatha Stubbs. It left John junior the main shareholder and power-broker, with a 21.2 per cent stake in the club. The December pact with Kenwright seemed to have been forgotten.

At the same time the allegiance of the Everton directors, previously allied to their fellow board member Kenwright, switched to a more neutral focus. Sir Desmond Pitcher had told the board that it was not in their remit to favour one candidate over another and that they had no alternative but to accept the offer that would best benefit the shareholders. Johnson was now talking in terms of £4000 apiece for each of the 2500 shares. As chairman elect, he was also prepared to underwrite the issue of a further 2500 at the same price. Not only would this boost the club's transfer funds to the tune of £10 million, it would also give Johnson a clear boardroom majority.

All of this was beyond Kenwright's financial capabilities and he admitted defeat. He retained his position on the board, and could take some consolation from the fact that Johnson's wealth would benefit the club. 'Because of my stand,' he said, 'Peter Johnson vastly improved his original offer and that can only be good for the Blues.' At an extraordinary general meeting of the shareholders, held on 26 July 1994, a resolution to double the number of shares was approved by 1659 votes to 22. Johnson's election as director was unanimous, and he was immediately installed as chairman. Mike Walker suddenly found himself with £10 million in transfer funds to spend. After the meeting, Johnson said, 'This is an opportunity for me to help revive a great club. I love my football and I would not have gone outside my home city for anything.'

The summer of 1994 had seen the fifteenth World Cup, staged for the first time in the United States. Perhaps it was indicative of Everton's decline that just one of their players, Anders Limpar, made the squad of one of the 24 teams. Sweden reached the semi-finals of the competition, beaten by the eventual winners Brazil, but Limpar was to play for just 17 minutes in the entirety of the competition. Back home, though, Everton were never far from the headlines, and summer-transfer speculation constantly linked Walker – transfer booty almost at the ready – with the stars of the tournament. After proving unsuccessful in bids to sign Jürgen Klinsmann, Oliver Bierhoff and Limpar's Swedish international team-mate, Martin Dahlin, whose £2.5 million move from the German side Borussia Moenchengladbach broke down at the last moment, they opened the new season at home to Aston Villa with just one new face. That was the midfielder Vinny Samways, signed from Tottenham Hotspur, who played in the 2–2 opening-day draw. It was the first match to be played in front of the newly redeveloped Park Stand, which had risen from the ashes of its predecessor at a cost of more than £4 million.

Walker finally got his World Cup star, two weeks into the new season when, to much euphoria, he signed the Nigerian international Daniel Amokachi from FC Bruges for a club record £3 million. The Nigerian had made his name in the competition thanks to a spectacular 30-yard strike against Greece that was later voted among the best of the tournament. He claimed to be able to run 100 metres in 10.1 seconds, and as only the second black player to turn out for Everton, his was hailed as a landmark signing in a club sometimes tainted by criticisms of racism.

Everton had been without a black player since the days of Cliff Marshall in the mid-1970s and had at times attracted gibes that the club was institutionally racist. Despite the best efforts of anti-racism campaigns by the club, the local newspapers and fanzines, it was an image they had found hard to shift until Amokachi's signing. For many the arrival of the Nigerian star heralded the onset of Peter Johnson's Everton revolution.

Because of work-permit restrictions Amokachi's début was delayed by a fortnight. Walker used the time to try to bring in the Brazilian international striker Muller. The 28-year-old São Paolo player was set to sign for £2.5 million when the deal broke down after he revealed that he expected his salary to be paid net of tax. The breakdown of the transfer was symptomatic of the Johnson years. Transfer deals were often talked of and hyped, bids made and talks with players held, but all too often players failed to agree to sign. Muller was arguably the most spectacular failure in Johnson's time, although on this occasion the loss was not Everton's.

Walker also brought in the former Liverpool left back David Burrows from West Ham in a deal that took Tony Cottee in the opposite direction. The player who arrived was an often sloppy, cynical and undistinguished hardman, who had attracted the ire of many Evertonians during his time at Liverpool. When he appeared along with Amokachi away at Blackburn, it was perhaps the first time an Everton player was booed upon making his début. It was a sharp reminder of how unpopular his arrival was, and how the discerning travelling contingent viewed his ability as a player.

Everton lost that match 3–0 to the eventual champions, and

although Amokachi scored on his home début against QPR a week later, Everton could only muster a draw. A 1–1 draw with Leicester followed, then a three-match losing streak, without an Everton goal. Although hugely popular, the team's new African star was struggling and he seemed to lack the spontaneity in front of goal to turn round Everton's worst-ever start to a season. His goal against QPR was not followed by a further effort until the next spring, a spell that, in fairness, he spent mostly on the sidelines. But, sceptical of the hype, one cynical supporter spoke for a number of doubters when he wrote in the fanzine *Gwladys Sings the Blues*, 'I just feel the devotion to a man who has earned it is justified, but the ridiculous hero-worshipping of a player who is yet to impress significantly can only lead to him thinking that doing the bare minimum is good enough for Everton FC. It is not.'

By mid-October, Walker's men were still without a win, and the situation was reaching crisis point. 'One of Everton's finest acquisitions was Sir John Moores,' wrote Charles Mills in the second issue of *Gwladys Sings the Blues*. 'He knew who to appoint and who to discard . . . Mr Johnson, please take note.'

Midfielder Iain Durrant and centre forward Duncan Ferguson were signed on loan deals from Glasgow Rangers at a cost of £35,000 per week plus their wages. Durrant was a creative midfielder who, after lengthy injury problems, had fallen out of favour with the Scottish giants. It was the signing of Ferguson, though, that attracted most interest. He had become Britain's most expensive footballer in July 1993 when he signed for £4 million for Glasgow Rangers from Dundee United, in the process rejecting the opportunity to move to England, where a number of clubs – including Everton, ironically – sought his services. He was far from a success at Rangers, though, notching up just one goal in his first season, although he was kept out for much of it with a broken leg. To add to the pressure of being deemed a failure by the Old Firm-obsessed Scottish press, his off-the-field antics earned him more unwanted headlines. Ferguson had already been involved in three assault cases in two years when he was handed a 12-match ban by the SFA for head-butting Raith Rovers defender John McStay during a league match at Ibrox in May 1994. He had not been booked, and McStay had made no formal complaint, but the incident had been beamed to hundreds of thousands on TV. He appealed against the ban, but while awaiting the outcome was also charged with assault by Strathclyde police. Thus it was with a 12-match ban and yet another court case hanging over his head – this time with the threat of a custodial sentence – that he arrived on Merseyside.

The two loan signings could not, however, avert defeat on their débuts away at Crystal Palace. Days later a rare draw was secured against Arsenal and a first win, at home to West Ham, courtesy of a single Gary Ablett goal, followed. However, with a 16-day break approaching due to international matches, the idea to sack Mike Walker had crystallized in Johnson's mind. The final straw for Everton's new chairman came following a sterile goalless draw at Norwich on Bonfire Night. 'I think the confirmation was going down to Norwich City,' he later said, 'and seeing two teams which he'd [Walker] managed within a period of X number of months in a dreadful match. We were certainly not going anywhere. Joe Royle, I felt, was the right man. He's Everton through and through, and wanted to come for many years and missed the job on a number of occasions, so we returned back to Everton basics.'[2]

Three days after the Norwich match, on 8 November 1994, Walker was sacked.

Walker's sacking brought to an end a wretched 11-month reign for the silver-haired Welshman. Everton had picked up just eight points from the first 42 of that campaign and had escaped relegation on the last day of the previous season by the narrowest of margins. 'I think Mike Walker would have to go down as our worst manager,' recalled Peter Mills. 'He was completely out of his depth, coming to fame very rapidly with Norwich on the back of some good backroom people like John Deehan. Walker was probably the absolute antithesis of David Moyes!'

Although some argued that the tide had turned and that Walker had had no time to prove himself, most anticipated an even more arduous relegation battle this time round. Some of his signings showed foresight – he had bought Limpar, Ferguson and the then unknown Joe Parkinson – others, such as Samways and Amokachi, never had a fair chance. At the same time there was increasing disharmony on the training pitch. Tony Cottee later mocked his training methods; others, such as Paul Rideout, admitted feeling alienated by him. Tellingly, no one ran to his defence after he was sacked.

After Walker's departure there was the inevitable speculation as to who would succeed him in the Goodison hot-seat, but the favourite of the fans and the board was, without question, the Oldham Athletic manager, Joe Royle. He had retired from playing aged 33 to begin his managerial career back in the North West at Boundary Park. Here he performed small wonders, taking tiny Oldham to the top flight for the first time in 68 years, where they were among the Premier League's founder members, and also to within seconds of the 1994 FA Cup Final, as well as the League Cup Final and FA Cup semi-final in 1990. Many had expected Royle to be appointed as Colin Harvey's successor that same year, and when he'd been overlooked in favour of Walker just over three years later, it was thought that his chance would never come.

Royle admitted that he had almost given up hope, but said that his heart flickered when he heard that Mike Walker had been sacked. 'Even when it seemed my chance had gone,' he said, 'I still believed I was destined to be manager of Everton.'[3] Such was his belief in that destiny that he accepted the job without entering into salary negotiations, or even signing a contract.

Charles Mills was as optimistic as most Evertonians when he heard the news. As he pondered in *Gwladys Sings the Blues*,

> Do twelve relatively successful years at Oldham constitute reasonable grounds for hoping that this obviously nice man will lead us out of the wilderness? I think he will. He's proven to have the gift of fidelity whilst at Oldham, resisting the lure of better-paid offers from other clubs, until at last his old love came along – some might say inevitably. He's displayed good husbandry, cutting the cloth according to its measure. He's good at personal relationships – invaluable when dealing with highly activated footballers, some of whom act as prima-donnas at an opera. He knows that there's a time to keep a distance and a time to get involved. He'll need to spend big money wisely – but don't we all?

Royle had 11 days to prepare and prime the bottom-placed team for the arrival of Liverpool on 21 November 1994. It was to be a record-breaking thirty-fifth derby appearance for Neville Southall, but the prospects of victory against the high-flying Liverpool were not good. Into the line-up Royle brought Andy Hinchcliffe and John

Ebbrell, who had been playing peripheral roles under Walker, and dropped Graham Stuart along with the much-maligned Burrows. Yet on a freezing Monday night, Everton won their second match of the season showing a will and an urgency to win that were lacking in the Anfield side.

The first half was a typically cagey affair, with Everton doing their utmost to contain the free-scoring Robbie Fowler and their old adversary Rush, but offering little in attack. At half-time Matthew Jackson went off injured, Barry Horne moved to right back, Amokachi to midfield and Jackson's replacement Rideout partnered Duncan Ferguson up front. Everton's attack was transformed. Amokachi, who had been insistent since his arrival that his best position was as a deep-lying forward, began to create problems by running at defenders and taking long shots. Hinchcliffe swung in corners with a previously unknown venom, and Ferguson and Rideout – previously untried as a forward pairing – showed signs that they might link up well together as a partnership. It was from a Hinchcliffe corner that Everton scored their first goal in the fifty-sixth minute, Ferguson rising unchallenged to send a bullet-header into the back of the Liverpool net. Soon after, Rideout nearly added a second when he hit the inside of the post. His moment came two minutes from the end, when the Liverpool goalkeeper, David James, pushed another good cross on to Ferguson's head. The ball fell to him and he scrambled it into the goal. Goodison erupted as Everton moved off the foot of the table.

Hard-tackling and hard-running, Royle dubbed his tenacious side the 'Dogs of War'. They won the next two games against Chelsea and Leeds, and went four without conceding a goal, making a total of seven matches – a new club record. The Leeds win saw Everton move out of the bottom three, and when Ferguson scored he was afforded hero status. For the final half-hour Goodison shook as 25,000 Evertonians sang 'Duncan, Duncan Ferguson' to the tune of the Village People's 'Go West'. The following day, Royle made the loan deal permanent at a cost of £4.5 million – then the second-highest fee ever paid by an English club. 'I don't think he came here to play for Everton,' admitted Royle. 'I think he came to get out of Scotland. But then he found the place was growing on him, and suddenly there was this adulation which has to be seen to be believed. You walk round Goodison today, and they've all got Ferguson shirts on. The "Big Fella" has got a charisma about him. He is a bit of a gunslinger, sometimes an anti-hero in people's eyes, but they absolutely adore him.'

By February 1995 the Dogs of War had brought Everton back from the wilderness. But as his new team rose up the table, Royle had his critics. Purists argued that he was 'borstalizing' the School of Science with the no-nonsense way his sides approached matches. Roy Evans claimed that his Liverpool team had been 'hacked' out of the January derby, to which Royle responded mockingly that 'a lot of dummies were thrown out of [Evans's] pram'. Kevin Keegan was another critic, accusing Royle's side of 'indiscipline' after Everton had had two men sent off and another five booked when they met Newcastle at St James's Park. Irrespective of the rough image his team had attracted, one that Royle found hard to shrug off in subsequent years, he still managed to accommodate the silky skills of Anders Limpar in his side who, he said, was 'reminiscent of Johann Cruyff'.

Limpar had flitted in and out of action under Walker, doing little to curry favour among Evertonians. The days leading up to the Wimbledon game on the last day of the previous season had been full of speculation that there was a 'get-out clause' in his contract, which would take effect should Everton be relegated; his bizarre handball in that match had diminished his reputation further. Later, when Walker substituted him against QPR, he had sarcastically applauded the fans, earning himself a public rebuke from his manager. The odd lapse aside, he was a prodigiously talented player, the most naturally gifted, Royle said, that he had ever worked with. 'It's latent ability, yes, but it's there,' he told the *Independent*. 'It's all in his ball control, his ability on the ball, the way he can run at people and go past them, his ability to pass and cross, and it's there in his shooting. He is two-footed, although he's more naturally right-footed. He can use both to good effect. He's capable of almost anything, even reaching world superstar level.'[4]

However, the core of Royle's new team was the club's four senior professionals: Barry Horne, Dave Watson, Neville Southall and Paul Rideout. Both Watson and Southall, then in their mid-thirties, had come in for criticism earlier in the season and a mounting tide of opinion suggested that their careers could or should be drawing to a conclusion. Days before Royle's arrival, Southall had been part of Wales's 0–5 humiliation against Georgia, providing an individual performance that inspired little confidence. Likewise, Watson's ever-decreasing pace was being exploited all too often. The school of thought that criticized them, however, tended to neglect the defensive frailties of others, and Royle rightly saw through it. Indeed, the two veterans were peerless after the arrival of their new manager. More marked was the improvement in the form of Horne and Rideout, and their transformation from peripheral team members to key ones.

Perhaps Barry Horne had already turned the corner when he scored his thunderous equalizer against Wimbledon on the last day of the previous season. He had been a revelation during Everton's pre-season tour of Scandinavia during the summer of 1994 but had sustained a back injury that kept him out of the first 10 matches of the new campaign, the miserable run of seven defeats and three draws. He returned with a man-of-the-match winning performance in the draw against Arsenal, and was prominent in the first win of the campaign, over West Ham. For a player whose first two years at the club had been a non-event, dogged by inconsistency and lack of confidence, this marked an about-turn in form. On the other hand, as the Wales manager Mike Smith – who had installed Horne as national team captain – said, the style of football Royle brought to the club was to suit the midfielder, and sustain his upturn in form. 'There is a lot more to Barry Horne than bravery. He is a good passer of the ball and I think the way in which Everton are now playing has allowed him to express himself more.' Horne's heroic exploits that season were to earn him the Everton Independent Supporters Player of the Year award: he amassed a massive 75 per cent of the vote. The half-sarcastic chants of 'Who needs Cantona, when we've got Barry Horne?' that had rung out at the end of the previous season suddenly took on a more sincere note.

The circumstances in which Paul Rideout found himself on Joe Royle's return to Goodison were less certain. For a start he was on the transfer list, and also out of the side. After a slow start to his Everton career (it had taken him two months to score his first goals for the club) and a first 18 months punctuated by niggling injuries, Rideout had struck up a relatively prolific partnership with Tony Cottee during the run-in to the previous season, and Cottee later cited Rideout as his favourite forward partner in his six years at Goodison. Their goals had helped save Everton from the drop, but it had not been enough to prevent Mike Walker selling Cottee and dropping Rideout after he had brought in Amokachi and Ferguson. Upset at being left out in the cold, Rideout asked for a transfer and was linked with moves to West Ham, Bolton and Preston.

Yet his fortunes changed dramatically with Walker's sacking. Royle had brought Rideout on as a half-time substitute for the Liverpool match, and the difference he had made to an Everton side that had rarely threatened in the first half was perhaps more telling than the late goal he scored would suggest. Confidence boosted by that performance, he formed a formidable partnership with Ferguson and their goals helped lift Everton off the bottom of the Premiership. Royle dubbed the partnership the 'RAF' (Rideout and Ferguson) and between them they averaged a goal a game, with Rideout finishing the season as top league scorer with 15 goals, including the one against Ipswich that secured Everton's Premiership status in the last week of the season. His crowning moment, however, was still to come.

Another player revitalized by the arrival of the new manager was Andy Hinchcliffe. The victory over Liverpool represented the turning-point in the left back's career. After spending more than four years under three different managers as a virtually anonymous figure at Goodison, the one-time England under-21 international's career was failing to live up to its early promise. Under the tutelage of Royle and his new assistant Willie Donachie – himself a former international full back – Hinchcliffe was transformed into one of the Premiership's most complete defenders and an England international.

The quiet Mancunian had shone from an early age. He was a superb all-rounder, representing Lancashire at cricket and lacrosse while turning out for Manchester City's youth team on Sundays. His progression into the City first team was swift and, along with other young pretenders like Paul Lake, David White and Ian Brightwell, he looked to be continuing the early promise he had shown for the youth side. However, Hinchcliffe's Manchester City career was brought to an abrupt halt in the summer of 1990 when his new manager, Howard Kendall, sold him to Everton. With Pat Van Den Hauwe's departure to Spurs a year earlier, the England under-21 international looked to be an ideal long-term investment, but injury and the general inconsistency of the team dogged his early days at Goodison. Then, just months after joining, Harvey was sacked and Kendall, the man who'd sold him to Everton, returned to Goodison.

Nevertheless, Hinchcliffe persevered and although he rarely played badly, he usually played without distinction. When Kendall left in November 1993 and Mike Walker took over, Hinchcliffe found himself an early casualty of the new regime. But so short-lived was Walker's spell in charge that an oft-rumoured transfer never came about.

The turnaround in Hinchcliffe's career can be attributed to two factors. First, the potency of his left foot was, for the first time, properly utilized. Neville Southall told him that if he could deliver the ball with pace and without too much height so that it cleared the first defender, it was virtually impossible to defend. With target men such as Ferguson, Rideout and Dave Watson to aim for, it was left to Hinchcliffe to exploit their height, which he did with devastating effect. Liverpool and Leeds were only early victims of a rejuvenated Hinchcliffe. Manchester United (when he delivered a text book-perfect corner for Ferguson to head home), QPR (after coming back from 2–0 down he scored the winner from a free kick with 'One of the best strikes I have ever hit . . .'), and Spurs in the FA Cup semi-final (with an in-swinging corner he found the head of Matt Jackson for Everton's first goal) were among the other victims in what turned out to be a vintage season for the left back. The second factor behind his renaissance was the confidence instilled in him by his team-mates and the new management. Asked by *Goal!* magazine if he was a naturally confident person, he replied, 'Not really. It's something that's come from people close to me such as Joe [Royle] and Willie [Donachie], and some of the older players at Everton, like Barry Horne and Neville Southall.'

There was some youthful vigour about the new team too. David Unsworth had already exploded on to the scene the previous season after Mike Walker had seen the 21-year-old's potential and brought him into the first team. Then a left back in the reserves with just a handful of first-team appearances behind him, he stormed into the starting line-up showing the sort of pace, presence and composure on the ball that belied his lack of experience. To many Evertonians he was the long-awaited heir to Kevin Ratcliffe and one of the few pluses in a weak team. More underrated was Joe Parkinson, who had been signed from Bournemouth on the same day as Limpar. Already with 150 appearances for the south-coast side and Wigan before them, the 23-year-old Lancastrian made his way into the team at the start of the 1994/5 season, working as an anchorman, his short, sharp passing and dogged tackling holding together the heart of the Everton team. Discerning Evertonians saw a bite return to the side that had been lacking since the heyday of Peter Reid.

By the time that champions Manchester United arrived at Goodison on 25 February 1995, a win would, for the first time that season, put clear light between Everton and the chasing pack at the bottom. Despite their resurgence in form it was still a tall order, although United had been rocked by the suspension of their star player, Eric Cantona, after his sensational kung-fu kick on the Crystal Palace fan Matthew Simmonds a month earlier.

Unlike Cantona, Duncan Ferguson was conspicuous by his presence. Even without Paul Rideout to partner him his readiness to hustle, his pace, link-up play and aerial strength kept United's formidable defensive pairing of Steve Bruce and Gary Pallister occupied. Horne and Parkinson ran the centre of the park, while Limpar and Stuart Barlow, playing the flanks as part of a five-man midfield, kept United's wingers in check. The single goal of the match came in the fifty-eighth minute when Ferguson connected with a trademark Hinchcliffe corner to send the capacity crowd into a state of delirium. Ferguson celebrated by ripping off his shirt and swinging it around his head. It was his eighth goal in 21 matches since his arrival from Glasgow, and Everton's first at Goodison against United since 1989.

The victory over Manchester United moved Everton to the relatively lofty heights of sixteenth, two places above the relegation zone in a season that was to see four teams relegated as the Premier League restructured. It also enabled them to concentrate on an FA Cup run that was gaining momentum. A 5–0 win over Norwich City had given them a quarter-final tie at home to Newcastle on 12 March 1995, who were pushing Manchester United and Blackburn strongly for the league title. Again, Everton were without Rideout and also the potent left foot of Andy Hinchcliffe. It was another close match, high in tension but short of genuine quality. Everton had the best of chances, with Barlow – a devastating finisher at reserve level, a lamentable one for the first team – twice put clear, having one shot tipped over the bar and skewing the other wide. In the end it was Everton's two survivors from the 1989 Cup Final, Dave Watson and Neville Southall, who won the match. Watson scored the only goal when he scrambled home a Ferguson knockdown. Then, with 12 minutes remaining, Southall played his part by making an outstanding point-blank save from Lee Clark, with Ruel Fox thrashing the rebound into the side-netting. That save, as much as anything, brought Everton their seventh consecutive Goodison win and within a single match of Wembley.

There followed a semi-final against Tottenham Hotspur at Leeds on 9 April. Elland Road had proved an unhappy destination for Everton, where they were without a league win in nearly fifty years. Spurs, who boasted Jürgen Klinsmann, just about to be crowned PFA Player of the Year, were hot favourites for a place in the final. Royle, always one to build up an underdog mentality, spoke sneeringly of the press's 'dream Final' between Spurs and Manchester United in the days leading up to the match. He made a play on the criticism that Everton were a mere rough-and-tumble side, a pub team who had progressed one round too far. Yet the manager knew what he was doing, that he was merely priming his charges to explode in the faces of their critics, and giving himself the opportunity to stick up the proverbial two fingers up at the newspapers.

Even before kick-off, Everton had a crucial psychological advantage over their opponents. At the time Elland Road boasted Europe's largest cantilever stand, seating some 18,000 spectators. Spurs fans took that, while the remaining three sides of the ground were crammed with Evertonians. By the time the two sides came on to the pitch the ground was awash with blue, and the only fans that could be heard were those from Merseyside.

While Everton's other most notable victories under Royle – over Liverpool, Manchester United and Newcastle – had been won through grit and guile, victory this time was attained by a footballing performance in the finest traditions of the School of Science. Limpar, the game's outstanding influence, was imperious. He destroyed Stuart Nethercott, Spurs' makeshift left back, time and again. Up front Graham Stuart, standing in for the suspended Ferguson, was tireless, linking defence and attack faultlessly. At the back Southall, Watson and Unsworth proved indomitable barriers to the attacking forays of Klinsmann, Nick Barmby and Teddy Sheringham. From the outset there was only one team in it. Three times in the opening 12 minutes Limpar tested Ian Walker in the Tottenham goal, the best chance coming from a sixth-minute volley after Nethercott had misjudged a cross. Everton looked dangerous from Hinchcliffe set-pieces, and it was from a thirty-fifth-minute corner that they got their first goal when Matt Jackson got goal side of Nethercott and headed in. After the interval, Everton maintained their tempo and were rewarded on 55 minutes. Walker mis-hit a free kick from his own penalty area, Rideout won the ball, and though the Spurs keeper saved his shot, Stuart tapped in the rebound. Walker was in tears, but his team-mates rallied and, seven minutes later, won a dubious penalty when Sheringham tumbled over Watson, which Klinsmann converted.

Shortly after came the game's crucial moment. With the match still in the balance at 2–1, Rideout picked up a knock and Daniel Amokachi was told to warm up. Royle had surprised many Everton-ians by omitting their hero from the starting line-up between his first match in charge until the following March. Although Amokachi was representing his country in the African Nations' Tournament for some of that time, with lesser players often picked ahead of him, it looked as though the Nigerian's Everton career was going to be shorter than expected. As he was about to be brought on, Les Helm, the Everton physio, who had been treating Rideout on the sidelines, indicated to the bench that he would in fact be okay. There was, however, no stopping Amokachi's boundless enthusiasm and he entered the field of play before the Everton bench could stop him.

Twelve minutes later, with just eight left, Nethercott's volley was saved brilliantly by Southall. The ball ran to Limpar, who surged upfield before finding Barry Horne. He laid the ball off to Stuart whose cross met Amokachi at the far post: he scored, to make the game 3–1. Seven minutes later Limpar broke again. He played it to Gary Ablett whose cross the Nigerian met, to score his second and Everton's fourth. Elland Road reverberated to chants of 'Amo! Amo!'

An elated Joe Royle later described it as 'the best substitution I never made!' He added, 'He was desperate to play, but he should not have been on. What a good mistake it was.' Indeed it was Royle, not Amokachi, who stole all the headlines the next day after his angry comments in the post-match press conference. 'I shouldn't be here, should I?' he asked reporters, many of whom had criticized Everton's robust style in the run-up to the match. 'Sorry about the "dream Final", lads. It could have been more in the end. I was disappointed when they got a penalty, which TV will tell whether it was or wasn't. We played a lot of good football, which is perhaps surprising to one or two of you having read the previews. So bollocks to you. And that's double L!'

Premiership safety, which looked unlikely when Royle took over, was secured with a league game to spare. By then all eyes had turned to the forthcoming Cup Final. Controversy abounded in the week running up to it, when the distribution of tickets ended in farce and, for many, disappointment. For those lucky enough to make the trip to north-west London, the tension of the afternoon ended once more in elation. In the adage of those heady days of Britpop, Everton were 'mad for it'. Manchester United, minus their French maestro Cantona, record signing Andy Cole, plus Andrei Kanchelskis, and with Ryan Giggs on the bench, never looked serious contenders. Yet it would do Everton an injustice to say that they only won the match because of United's absentees. Not so. Manchester United were a side who were defending the remaining half of the previous year's double, having been just a goal away from retaining the Championship a week earlier. The absences weakened them, but they were still a formidable team.

The game's only goal came in the first half. Paul Ince lost the ball in midfield and Limpar hit United on the break. Everton suddenly found themselves with four attackers to United's two defenders. The Swede played the ball out to Jackson on the right, who cut inside Pallister and crossed low for Stuart. His shot hit the underside of the crossbar and out to Rideout. In a moment that seemed to last an age, the 30-year-old rose to nod the ball coolly into the Manchester United net, before the onrushing defenders could block it.

Limpar then seized control of the match, his darts and passes hurting United. Again he robbed Ince and played in Stuart, but Peter Schmeichel saved his low shot. United found an answer to the mercurial Scandinavian only when they brought on Giggs for the injured Bruce at half-time. Yet Southall and Watson, as they had been since Royle's return, seemed invincible. Watson's perfect marshalling of his defence and victory in the physical contest provided by Mark Hughes won him the man-of-the-match award. Southall proved a similar colossus, making a superb double save from Scholes, and later gathering Pallister's header with the sort of veteran nonchalance that told Evertonians it was to be their day.

After Watson had lifted Everton's fifth FA Cup aloft, Royle gushed with praise: 'We only had eight points from fourteen games when I arrived, so escaping relegation has been the real battle, but winning this is the icing.' From Alex Ferguson, the homily was understandably more muted. Dignified and generous in defeat, he said of the goalkeeper who had done most to thwart their second-half comeback, 'When Neville Southall's in that form you need something special to beat him.' The scorer of the winning goal, Paul Rideout, experienced the disappointment of having to come off in the second half through injury, but that did not deflect from his sense of achievement. 'I have to give a lot of credit to Joe Royle for showing that he's got a lot of belief in me.' A week after the FA Cup Final, David Unsworth was called up to the England squad, the first time an Everton player had received a call-up since Martin Keown had left the club in February 1993. It rounded off a dramatic season on a high note.

◊

Joe Royle set about strengthening a squad that had barely escaped relegation to the First Division in consecutive seasons. The team that had won the FA Cup had performed wonders in bringing Goodison its first trophy in eight years, but the credit was all Royle's. He had turned a team of journeymen into Cup winners, but the Wembley victory belied the lack of genuine quality that was apparent throughout the squad. Some hopeful supporters tried to draw comparisons between the turnaround in fortunes under Royle and that under Kendall in the mid-eighties, but Neville Southall was quick to pour scorn on their optimism. 'We're still a fair way from matching the quality of the squad Howard pulled together,' he said. 'People should remember that it took Howard three or four years to get it right – Joe Royle hasn't even had twelve months yet.'

The manager set about bringing some much-needed pace and spontaneity to a forward line that had been criticized by some as immobile and pandering to long balls. His principal target was Nottingham Forest's temperamental but occasionally brilliant striker Stan Collymore. Forest slapped a price tag of £10 million on the head of their star turn, but even though that fee was unlikely to be met, it was clear to all observers that a similar offer would have to be made for them to part with him. Liverpool soon emerged as the main contender in the race for Collymore's signature, a battle they won, just as they had beaten Everton to the signing of Dean Saunders four years earlier. It was perhaps a sign of Everton's true standing that they were unable to bring Collymore to Goodison, despite apparently offering him more money than their neighbours.

After failing in an attempt to sign the Crystal Palace forward, Chris Armstrong, Royle then turned his attentions to Manchester United's Ukrainian winger, Andrei Kanchelskis. Late the previous season, Kanchelskis had announced that he was unable to work with Alex Ferguson and demanded a transfer. With Collymore going to Liverpool for a British record £8.5 million, the money was clearly there to spend and Everton were willing to meet United's £5 million valuation of the player. Such was the eagerness to bring him to Goodison that Everton were even prepared to meet an additional £1.2 million 'loyalty payment' that Kanchelskis was owed by the Old Trafford club as part of any future transfer. With the deal seemingly cut and dried Everton paraded their new signing to the press on 21 July 1995. Unknown to them, the registration of the Ukrainian had not been completed and no money exchanged by the clubs. Everton had agreed to hold off until 1 August to complete the formalities of the transfer – as an act of courtesy – to fit in with United's financial year.

Unfortunately this had damaging consequences. Kanchelskis' previous club, the Ukrainian team Shakhytor Donetsk, caught wind of the deal and on 27 July informed United that they were owed £1 million on the 'sell-on clause' that had formed part of the original deal that had brought the wideman to Old Trafford in 1991. United then told Everton that the deal was off unless they met the Ukrainian club's demands. Everton refused, claiming the deal had already been agreed. There ensued a public argument between Everton's commercial director, Clifford Finch, United's solicitor, Maurice Watkins, and Shakhytor Donetsk. It lasted nearly a month and looked to be reaching a state of deadlock. United would not release the registration, Everton refused to be held to ransom and pay Shakhytor Donetsk, and Kanchelskis was adamant that he would not return to Old Trafford. It meant that the Ukrainian missed the first three games of the season and the deadline for registration for European competition.

An extraordinary turn of events – later revealed in Alex Ferguson's memoirs – led to the argument's settlement and Kanchelskis becoming available to make his Everton début on 26 August against Southampton. Ferguson had arranged a meeting between himself, Watkins, the United chairman Martin Edwards and Kanchelskis, his agent Grigory Essaoulenko and adviser George Scanlon in an effort to bring the matter to a conclusion. Their discussions soon became heated with Essaoulenko demanding the player's transfer. The meeting came to a climax when the agent screamed at Edwards, 'If you don't transfer him now, *you will not be around much longer.*' Neither Ferguson nor Edwards doubted the seriousness of the threat. 'What are we going to do, Maurice?' asked a clearly intimidated Edwards, after the meeting had come to an abrupt end. Watkins's reply was terse but unequivocal: 'Sell him.'[5]

As well as Kanchelskis, Royle brought in Craig Short from Derby County for £2.7 million. Short was seen as a long-term successor to Dave Watson, and although his time on Merseyside lasted five years, he struggled to establish himself in the team or prove to supporters that he was a worthy heir to their giant of a captain.

The end of the pre-season also saw the death of former manager Johnny Carey. After leaving the club in 1961, following his 'taxi ride' with John Moores, the Irishman went on to manage Leyton Orient and Nottingham Forest, and eventually retired at the club where his career had begun, Blackburn Rovers. As Evertonians stood to a minute's silence prior to the opening home match of the season, older fans remembered him best in the words of Sir John Moores: 'A nice man, an honourable man, and a good practitioner.'

On the field Everton began the 1995/6 season erratically. A goalless draw at Chelsea, with Ruud Gullit in their team for the first time, and a home defeat against Arsenal were followed by wins against Southampton and Manchester City, then a two-month stretch without a win, including four league defeats on the run. Kanchelskis, who had had his start to the season interrupted by the transfer wrangling, found himself sidelined for six weeks with a shoulder injury sustained against his former club at the start of September. In the Cup Winners' Cup, Everton were dogged by UEFA's three-foreigners rule, which deemed not just Limpar and Amokachi foreigners but the team's Welsh and Scottish contingent too. They beat the Icelandic team KR Reykjavik 6–3 over two legs in unimpressive fashion, but were defeated narrowly by Feyenoord in the next round. In the League Cup, they were humbled 2–4 at home by lowly Millwall.

It was only when a fully restored Andrei Kanchelskis returned to the side in November that Everton began to turn round their unimpressive start to the season. Indeed, if that season belonged to any single player, it was the Ukrainian. His signing had been a genuine coup for Royle. He was a proven international and one of the stars of Manchester United's all-conquering side of the early 1990s, winning the double in 1994. Born in January 1969 in Kirovograd in the USSR, a Ukrainian mining city 600 miles south-west of Moscow, he began his career with Shakhytor Donetsk in the Soviet League, where he became known for his blistering pace and deadly finishing. He had – ironically – been told as a teenager that he was not quick enough to become a professional footballer and reacted to the news by undergoing a ritual of bizarre exercises that involved jumping so that his knees reached his chest. He would repeat this 200 times twice daily. 'I started a routine of jumping exercises, which I continue to this day,' he admitted, on joining Everton. 'It sounds easy but, believe me, it's not!'

In 1991, while he was playing for Donetsk, Manchester United paid an initial £650,000 to export him out of the Ukrainian mining belt where Kanchelskis earned 1000 roubles a month – approximately £10. He joined a United side on the verge of a glut of honours, and during his time at Old Trafford picked up two Premiership winners' medals and an FA Cup. But being part of a squad crammed full of superstars meant that a first-team place was in no way guaranteed. After failing to regain his place in the side after stomach injury had kept him out during the winter of 1995, he made his discontent known to manager Alex Ferguson and transfer to Goodison followed. It was not until November that he scored his first goals for the club, but he did so in such a fashion as to ensure that he would go down in Goodison folklore.

The scene was the hundred-and-fifty-third Merseyside derby, staged at Anfield where Everton were without a league win in a decade. Collymore, who had snubbed Everton just months earlier, was missing from the Liverpool side, who, like their neighbours, had been foundering in the league. Yet it was Kanchelskis, the man Everton bought as second choice to Collymore who seized the day, scoring the two goals that brought Everton a 2–1 victory. The first came after he headed home a Paul Rideout cross. The second came in what was to be typical Kanchelskis style: played through by Anders Limpar, he let fly with a low, hard shot, hit with such venom that it escaped the grasp of David James in the Liverpool goal.

Confidence restored, a Kanchelskis-inspired Everton soared up the table with the Ukrainian at his best when alongside Limpar or Andy Hinchcliffe, who would play him into space with searching diagonal balls from the left. He was equally confident shooting with his left or right foot, and the strength and accuracy of his shots were aptly described by Willie Donachie as 'frightening'. A more terrifying prospect for opposing defenders was Kanchelskis running full pelt at them, and the only genuinely effective way defences found to stop him was by double-marking him, a tactic that gave other forward players more space to play.

If Kanchelskis emerged as the star of the season, the previous campaign's model, Duncan Ferguson, was having a harder time. The opening months of his season were hampered by a hernia problem. He was returning to fitness when he had to go to Scotland to face his long-awaited court case for head-butting the Raith Rovers player John McStay while playing for Rangers in 1994.

'Duncan Disorderly' was the unwelcome, though not entirely undeserved, nickname with which he had arrived at Goodison. At that point the McStay case was in the process of being brought to court, and Ferguson had a 12-match ban pending the outcome of that hearing. He also had a previous conviction for drink-driving and three for assault, and had only narrowly escaped going to prison in September 1993 after attacking a fisherman in a hotel. The McStay case was arguably the least serious of the various charges that had been brought against Ferguson, but certainly the most notorious.

When the case was tried the week after the FA Cup Final victory in May, he was found guilty of assault and jailed for three months. Sheriff Alexander Eccles told Glasgow Sheriff Court that he was jailing Ferguson both 'in the public interest' and to bring home to him that such behaviour would not be tolerated. He added that

Ferguson was in a prominent position and was looked up to by young people. Ferguson left court that day pending the outcome of an appeal. When that came on 11 October, Lord Hope, the Lord Justice General of Scotland, said that the original three-month term could not be ruled 'excessive' and that it would stand. Ferguson was taken to Barlinnie Prison.

The sentence left Ferguson and his club in shock. Joe Royle attacked the decision as 'incredible', adding, 'We are all amazed and stunned, and can't really believe, in a society that seems dedicated to keeping people out of prison, that we are putting away a young man who is in a good job and is no danger to society.' There was a strong sense that an example was being made of Ferguson in an attempt to bring to an end the series of scandals that had rocked the game over the previous 18 months. Perhaps Gordon Taylor, the chief executive of the Professional Footballers' Association, best summed up the incident: 'I wouldn't condone what Duncan did, but I wonder if the actions of the authorities would be the same if this incident had happened in a lower-profile game and had involved a less well-known player.' As it happened, Ferguson was released half-way through his sentence and, a week later, 11,000 Evertonians braved near-Arctic conditions to see him score twice for the reserves against Newcastle United. His 12-match ban was then overturned, enabling him to return to the senior side. He marked his comeback to first-team action in spectacular fashion on the first day of 1996, scoring twice against Wimbledon – the first of which was an exquisite flick, turn and volley into the roof of the Dons' net. However, his efforts were once more curtailed by injury, and again he missed the latter stages of the season, and subsequently Euro '96.

Ferguson's return was not enough for Everton's bid to retain the FA Cup. After scraping through the third round by winning a closely fought replay 3–2 away to Stockport County, they were unable to overcome their fourth-round opponents Port Vale, drawing 2–2 at Goodison. In the replay at Vale Park they were beaten 1–2 by the First Division side.

In the league, though, Kanchelskis' pace had helped Everton piece together some long-lost consistency. A 2–0 home win over Middlesbrough at the start of March made European qualification by way of the UEFA Cup a distinct possibility, and the team continued to make positive strides in subsequent matches. A brilliant hat-trick by the Ukrainian in the penultimate game of the season, away to Sheffield Wednesday, moved him up to fifth in the Premiership scoring chart and put Everton in a good outside position for European qualification. They went into their last game of the 1995/6 season on 5 May, knowing that if they beat Aston Villa, already assured of fourth place, and Arsenal dropped points at home to relegated Bolton, then UEFA Cup qualification was theirs.

A tense capacity crowd filled Goodison, hopeful that the right permutation of results would see Everton in Europe for the second consecutive season, a feat not achieved since the late 1970s. A plethora of bookings, a ragged pitch and countless misdirected passes did little to suggest that either side was worthy of participation in the following year's UEFA Cup, and it was not until the forty-eighth minute that either goalkeeper had a save to make. It was only with the introduction of Limpar on 55 minutes that Everton began to edge the game: the Swede inspired Everton's winner and the game's only goal on 78 minutes. Limpar made a quality cross from the left, which Paul Rideout attempted to overhead-kick. His miscued shot came out to Parkinson who drilled home the winner. The win was not enough because, at Highbury, David Platt and Denis Bergkamp goals saw Arsenal win 2–1 and take the last European place.

There was, nevertheless, a strong feeling that the form that Everton had shown towards the end of the 1995/6 season showed clear potential for greater things. Kanchelskis had proved his undoubted pedigree; much was expected when the talismanic Ferguson was given a clear run in the side; and a promising bunch of youngsters had emerged. Expectations were high for Michael Branch, Jon O'Connor and Tony Grant, who had all broken through to the first-team squad the previous season. It was also felt that a few signings in key areas were still necessary: a striker to partner Ferguson; some finesse for a dogged midfield; and a long-term successor to Neville Southall. Over the summer Gary Ablett, who had been a peripheral figure after the FA Cup victory, was sold to Birmingham. So, too, was Barry Horne, by then 34, in a sale that Royle came to regret. Daniel Amokachi, an Olympic gold-medal winner in Atlanta with Nigeria that summer, was sold to Besiktas; and Vinny Samways, never a favourite with Royle, was sold to Las Palmas of Mallorca. Former England under-21 goalkeeper Paul Gerrard was brought in from Oldham, and Gary Speed signed from Leeds for £3.5 million, but Royle came under some criticism for not being more active in the transfer market. Attempts had been made to secure the signature of England striker Alan Shearer in what would have been a world-record transfer deal. That was said to be more a publicity stunt than a real attempt to sign the Blackburn forward, but other than that, and an attempt to sign Nigel Martyn from Crystal Palace, no real attempts at further signings were made. Yet there was plainly a need to expand the threadbare squad, which now showed a net loss of two players.

The optimism of many fans, however, was not misplaced, initially at least. Newcastle were the visitors to Goodison on the opening day of the 1996/7 season and, complete with the £15 million Shearer, were many pundits' favourites for the Premiership title. Yet it was not the world's most expensive player who stole the headlines but Duncan Ferguson, who provided a virtuoso performance leading the Everton attack. He was central to both goals too, although his name did not appear on the score-sheet. For the first, he got on the end of Steve Watson's weak header back to his goalkeeper, Shaka Hislop. Seeking to rectify his error, Watson pulled Ferguson down as the striker advanced towards goal, and Unsworth swept home the result-ant penalty. Twelve minutes later, Ferguson beat Hislop to a Graham Stuart cross, and Gary Speed stroked home Everton's second. At the other end, Neville Southall, making his seven-hundredth Everton appearance, was as indomitable as when he'd kept goal in Everton's last Championship season, a decade earlier. When Newcastle rallied in the second half, he made a clutch of saves from Shearer and his strike partner Les Ferdinand, keeping a clean sheet as Everton emerged with a 2–0 victory.

Four days later, Everton visited Manchester United to face the double winners. Again, Ferguson was the game's outstanding player, putting Everton into a 2–0 half-time lead against a side unbeaten in 30 home league matches. First, his turn and left-footed shot past Schmeichel had silenced the 55,000 crowd – then a Premiership record – early on; he added a second shortly after, bulleting a header home from Andy Hinchcliffe's cross from the left. In the second half United began to peg Everton back and, lacking the calming experi-ence of the injured Dave Watson, the shots rained in on Southall. With 20 minutes remaining, débutant Jordi Cruyff scored from a header. Then, with just eight minutes on the clock, Denis Irwin drove in a cross looking for Brian McClair, which David Unsworth unwittingly slipped into his own net. It was a harsh outcome to a generally sound Everton display, but most Evertonians would have been happy at the season's start for a return of four points against the Premiership's two best teams.

Everton followed up their initial good form schizophrenically. It was nearly October before they won again in the Premiership, while in the League Cup, their annual embarrassment against lower-league opposition continued. This time Royle put out a full-strength side in both legs of the second-round tie with York City, but Everton still contrived to lose 4–3 on aggregate, drawing 1–1 in the first leg and losing the second 2–3 at Bootham Crescent.

Many had expected Kanchelskis' end-of-season form from the previous campaign to carry over into that summer's European Championships and on into Everton's 1996/7 challenge. Yet besides giving Paolo Maldini a torrid time in the first half of Russia's match against Italy, Kanchelskis and Russia were generally disappointing. The rumour mill ground out stories that he was set to move to either Inter Milan or Fiorentina, which he had denied on the eve of the 1996/7 season: 'I am a loyal person,' he said, 'and Everton have been loyal to me. I have another three years of my contract to run and I am very happy here.' The gossip was clearly unsettling him, though, and his form dipped. At first his below-par performances were blamed on fatigue after Euro '96, but as the season progressed he continued to miss chances that he would have put away a year earlier, or took shots from impossible angles when a simple pass would have easily set up a team-mate. It was becoming increasingly evident that he was not the same player who had set Goodison alight just months earlier. Antagonism with his fellow players also became more and more noticeable. After Kanchelskis scored against Sheffield Wednesday in September not one of his team-mates ran to congratulate him. 'We think the publicity about him going abroad has disrupted him a little bit,' said Donachie. 'Once your concentration and attention goes elsewhere it is hard to get it back on track.'

Much had been expected of Duncan Ferguson too. He had spent the summer of 1996 resting, and it looked to have paid off after his displays in the first two games of the 1996/7 season, against Newcastle and Manchester United. Against Newcastle, Joe Royle described the Scot's display as 'awesome'. 'The bigger the reputation of the opposition, the more he's up for it,' explained Ferguson's Scotland team-mate Gary McAllister. 'He acquires that strut as if he's saying, "You might be Bruce or Pallister, but now Fergie's arrived." It turns him on.' However the problems of old came back when he was sent off at Blackburn in mid-September for the use of 'industrial language', and he then had to undergo further surgery, this time on his knee. Suddenly the striker's pedigree was put under the microscope, and it was pointed out that in his first two years at Goodison he had missed half of the games because of either injury, suspension or his custodial sentence. Fans also saw that the highest standard of football was played when Ferguson was not in the side, when there was less of a temptation to play a long, hopeful ball for him to get on the end of.

With Ferguson's latest absence, Royle sought to strengthen his team again. At the end of October, the young Middlesbrough forward Nick Barmby, upset at losing his place in the starting line-up to the Brazilian international, Juninho, requested a transfer. Barmby was a highly promising deep-lying forward who, by the age of 22, had played alongside some of the world's leading strikers, the likes of Gary Lineker, Jürgen Klinsmann, Fabrizio Ravanelli, Alan Shearer and Teddy Sheringham, all benefiting from his youthful enthusiasm. The news of his imminent departure from the Riverside Stadium sent Premiership teams into a scurry, but after he was linked with Liverpool, Manchester United and Blackburn, he signed for Everton for a club record £5.5 million. Royle saw him as the ideal man to kick-start Everton's flagging season, and in his second game, adding artistry to a forward line full of power and pace, he inspired Everton to their biggest victory in 20 years, beating Southampton 7–1. After the match the new signing picked up the man-of-the-match award and was in no doubt that it was 'the best performance I've ever played in'. He enthused, 'I love it here, I love the club, and the fans are just the best.' The words were to have a particularly hollow sound later, but for then Goodison had found a new star. Moreover, the win provided a fitting tribute to Tommy Lawton, who had died in Nottingham just days earlier aged 77.

By Christmas 1996 Everton had risen to seventh and it was hoped that if Kanchelskis' indifferent form could be overcome, coupled with the arrival of Barmby and the efforts of a fully fit Ferguson, then a strong run could be put together and the previous year's position bettered. Few could have foretold how Everton's season was going to unravel.

The turning-point arguably came a few days before Christmas when Everton played out a dull 0–0 draw with Leeds at Goodison. Andy Hinchcliffe, who had, just months earlier, made his England début and was showing signs that he was developing into one of the country's most complete defenders, made an innocuous-looking slip. After treatment, he struggled on, but was obviously in pain and had to be substituted. 'No one realized the scale of the problem until the surgeon had operated,' said Hinchcliffe. 'Then suddenly I wake up on Christmas Eve with my cruciate and a cartilage in a bottle beside my bed.' The injury kept him out for nearly a year.

Forty-eight hours later, on Boxing Day, Everton fell to a 2–4 defeat away at Middlesbrough. Two days after that they lost 1–3 at Wimbledon, then on New Year's Day 0–2 at home to lowly Black-burn. The run of defeats extended into 1997, with losses against Sheffield Wednesday, Arsenal and Newcastle United. The Newcastle game, a 1–4 reversal, was a record sixth straight defeat in the league, although Everton had reached their nadir a few days earlier when they went out of the FA Cup, losing 1–3 at Goodison to Bradford City who were at the bottom end of the First Division. The lowest point came when the veteran Chris Waddle sent a 40-yard lob over the head of a bemused Neville Southall.

The writing was – literally – on the wall for Joe Royle. Days after the Bradford humiliation, a disgruntled fan daubed the legend 'Royle Out' on the Bellefield walls. He spoke for a small but growing minority of Everton's support, fef up with the manager's ineffective tactics and obtuse running of the club. There was poverty of imagination in the Everton attack, other than a long ball played on to the head of Ferguson. A typical attack consisted of Unsworth hurtling up the left flank until he reached a 45-degree angle with the penalty area, where a hopeful ball would be lumbered in in the usually vain hope that Ferguson would come near it. The flat-footedness of the defence was exposed time and again. Kanchelskis was impotent and Limpar criminally shunned. Even when Everton were at their most wretched, Royle refused to introduce Limpar to the field of play. Indeed, at a time when Everton most needed the Swede's sparkle, Royle sold him to Birmingham City for £100,000.

Questions were not just being asked about his tactics, but about

Royle's running of the team in general. Fans were up in arms over the suggestion that he had bid to sign Carlton Palmer, perhaps the most uncultured player to turn out for England, while his signing of Claus Thomsen from Ipswich Town attracted equal amounts of incredulity. Thomsen possessed an unfortunate gait and looked more like an ungainly teenager than an experienced Danish international, while plodding around the Everton midfield to little real effect. Evertonians will probably best remember him for an own goal he scored in the following April's derby match, and his only goal for the club a year later – an overhead kick against Derby County executed with all the finesse of a 20-stone ballet dancer, which left the hapless midfielder injured. Not only were Royle's transfer forays becoming more and more bizarre, but after a spat with the *Liverpool Echo* journalist Phil McNulty, who had been one of his most ardent critics – not always without justification – he refused to speak to the press. It was a bad move, and rather than decreasing attention or criticism, it magnified it.

Few supporters were surprised when Kanchelskis left for Fiorentina in an £8 million deal at the end of January. He had been virtually non-existent in the club's worst run of results for 25 years and most agreed that the time was right for the Russian to go. His form had been indifferent all season, and his team-mates made little secret of their ambivalence towards him. There were rumours of gambling debts and gangland links (later hinted at by Alex Ferguson), none of which were proved, but it added to the perception of an unsound and unstable team member. His spell in Italy was short-lived and he returned to Britain 18 months later in a £5.5 million switch to Glasgow Rangers. Evertonians' last memory of him was the stray pass that set up Chris Waddle to score for Bradford City in the FA Cup débâcle. That summed up Kanchelskis' time at Goodison: untouchable when he was really flying, missing when the contest didn't suit him.

Royle dropped Neville Southall for the Newcastle game, the first time the Welshman had suffered such an indignity in some 15 years. The appalling run came to an abrupt end in the game after that, when Everton beat Nottingham Forest 2–0 at the start of February, but the manner in which they played continued to lack style, it betrayed the fine traditions of the School of Science and was plagued by the continual whiff of farce. For instance, they threw away a two-goal lead at Southampton, conceding two goals in as many minutes, the second of which was a spectacular diving header by Craig Short into the back of his own net.

The manager's attempts to sign West Ham's centre back, Slaven Bilic, were put on hold until the end of the season after the Croatian revealed that he wished to help the Eastenders' relegation fight. Frustrated, Royle re-entered the transfer market on deadline day at the end of March and sought to re-sign Barry Horne from Birmingham and bring in two Norwegians, Tore Andre Flo and Claus Eftevaag. It was a deal too far.

Royle had long wanted to bring in Flo from SK Brann to bolster his attack for £3 million. As part of the deal his team-mate Eftevaag would follow him to Merseyside. Flo was in Saudi Arabia with the Norway squad when he heard of Everton's attempts to sign him. The day before, FIFA, football's world governing body, had decided that the Bosman ruling, which entitled an out-of-contract player to a free transfer, was to be extended to include players from non-EU countries. That would enable him, Flo realized, to make a lucrative transfer at the end of the season (and Everton to sign him without a transfer fee if they so chose – that they wouldn't wait showed an extraordinary lack of foresight on Royle's part), so he pulled out of the deal. On hearing this, Royle still went ahead with the Eftevaag deal. While the pedigree of Flo was not in doubt, the long-term wisdom of signing the other Norwegian – described by his manager a week earlier as playing like 'an old man' – was more questionable. So, too, was that of bringing Horne back at a net loss of £350,000. It smacked of panic buying, and Johnson pulled the plug. Furious at his chairman's lack of confidence, Royle resigned.

Few were surprised at Royle's departure, but the timing and cause came as a shock. It left Everton managerless with just six weeks of the season left, and with the spectre of another relegation fight facing them. Dave Watson was appointed caretaker manager and he steered the team to safety including, satisfyingly, a draw in the derby match that spelt the end of Liverpool's Championship challenge.

The abdication of Royle had been oft-debated during his traumatic final three months as manager. 'I think when he came in, Royle was definitely the right man at the right time,' opined Peter Mills, 'but he had the wrong chairman and over time his limitations began to show.' It was clear that his was a fading star, and the necessary progression from the Dogs of War back to the School of Science never came about. All too often his Everton team looked clueless, with single-faceted attacks from Kanchelskis' pace or Ferguson's head. Just months into his Everton career, Nick Barmby – football craftsman that he was – was already becoming an outcast on the field, watching forlornly as long ball after long ball was hoofed over his diminutive shoulders. The staunch refusal to play Limpar, or to move for someone of his ilk, prompted fury among purists, while it became evident that the likes of Carlton Palmer or Claus Thomsen were Royle's favoured players: solid, physically powerful, unspectacular. His later refusal to speak to the press revealed a side to his personality that was far removed from Genial Big Joe: it was as short-sighted as it was puerile.

In fairness to Royle, he had only a single full season in charge, in which he led Everton to the brink of European competition, and in the season of his arrival he had been both hero and saviour. The FA Cup victory was all his. But most Evertonians – that most astute breed of football fan – realized that for the club to move on to the big stage, the top four and Europe, with all its rewards, they needed a different man in charge. A new 65,000-seater stadium was already being discussed and it seemed that their chairman had finances in a Moores-like abundance that would underwrite future success. All that Everton needed was a world-class manager, and that was exactly what Peter Johnson promised the ever-expectant fans.

◊

As was so often the case during Johnson's time at Goodison, he proved unable to match his lofty aspirations with a tangible outcome. His search for a 'world-class' replacement for Joe Royle turned into a three-month farce during which he was snubbed by Europe's great and good. At the outset it ought to be said in his favour that he spent much of his excruciatingly long search in pursuit of Bobby Robson. Robson had twice turned down the Everton job in the past and was the current Barcelona boss. In an incredible slight, the Spanish club's board had appointed – mid-season – the Ajax coach, Louis Van Gaal, to take over from an incredulous Robson at the season's end. Stunned by the lack of confidence shown, he made it known that he wanted to leave Barcelona, but as he hadn't been sacked and apparently didn't favour walking away from an £850,000 salary, a question mark hung over his head. That took some six weeks to resolve, but Robson ended up staying at the Nou Camp in the capacity of general manager, and Johnson was left to continue his search.

Over the following month Christian Daum, George Graham, Dave Jones, Joe Kinnear, Jürgen Klinsmann, Martin O'Neill, Bryan Robson, Arigo Sacchi, Wim Van Hanegem and John Toshack were all linked with or offered the vacant job. Eventually, on 15 June, it emerged that Johnson was talking with Andy Gray, now a presenter on Sky TV, with a view to his being the next Everton manager. It was rumoured that he was to form a 'dream ticket' with Howard Kendall, who would act as general manager. Most Evertonians were thrilled by the prospect, despite Gray's lack of experience. The talks rumbled on for more than a week, and it seemed little more than a formality that Gray would rejoin the club after a gap of 12 years. He even indicated that he wanted to make the Aston Villa striker Dwight Yorke his first signing. Less clear was Kendall's role, although he, too, was interviewed by Johnson.

As Gray appeared set to sign, he shocked everybody by making a U-turn and sticking with Sky. 'In my heart, I wanted to manager Everton,' he said. 'In many ways it would have been the realization of a dream. But increasingly over the weekend my head had been telling me different things. Maybe I got a little carried away with all the speculation, and to take the job then let the supporters down would have been too much to bear.'

Johnson was livid. 'We have been nothing other than the totally wronged party in this episode,' he raged. 'What has happened has shocked me. You can gather I'm upset.' Fans were equally miffed, more so as news broke that Gray had signed a lucrative new contract with Sky on the back of the collapse of the Everton talks. Their fury was also directed at Johnson, who was blamed for protracting the search and leaving the club still managerless just days before pre-season training was due to commence. 'I am aghast that the man has behaved like this,' he protested. 'It is quite difficult to believe and take in.' Twenty-four hours later, desperate and frustrated, Johnson turned to the man who knew Everton best, and for the third time Howard Kendall was appointed manager.

〇

AFTER LEAVING Goodison so unexpectedly at the end of 1993 Kendall had had a brief spell in charge of the Greek club Xanthi before he returned to Britain in January 1995 as manager of Notts County. The rot and decay at the bottom end of the First Division were no real stage for the man who, at that point, was still the most successful English manager in the game. He won the Anglo-Italian Cup with his new team, but was sacked after just 10 weeks in charge. The pretext for his dismissal was the damaging accusation that Kendall encouraged a drink culture, which was bringing the Meadow Lane club into disrepute. Perhaps Kendall's biggest crime was that he was from a different age of managers, unattuned to the new vogue for fitness coaches and nutritionists (although one would hardly have expected Nottingham's ramshackle second team to be either). His favoured alternative to fining a player was making the accused pay for his team-mates on a night out, and it was naturally mere coincidence that 'El Kel's' favoured haunt, Mr Ho's Chinese restaurant in Waterloo, went to the wall not long after he left Everton for a fourth time. Building team spirit is one thing, damaging accusations another. They came unsubstantiated and without proof. Kendall, who should have sued, maintained a dignified silence and took up the manager's job at Sheffield United the following December. In 18 months he led them from the bottom of the First Division to within a match of the Premiership, the 1997 play-off final, which they lost 1–2 to Crystal Palace.

If people could understand Kendall's return to Goodison in 1990 as his leaving a 'love affair' with Manchester City to return to his 'marriage' to Everton, few could fathom his return seven years later when he was not even fourth or fifth choice for the vacant manager's job. Maybe it was unrequited love that prompted it. When Johnson asked him what salary would bring him to Goodison, Kendall apparently replied, 'All I want to do is manage Everton.' With him came Viv Busby, his assistant at Sheffield United, as well as Adrian Heath, who left the manager's job at Burnley to become Kendall's assistant at Goodison. Their arrivals bolstered the coaching staff after the inevitable departure of Willie Donachie, but also of Jimmy Gabriel, who had left Goodison at the end of the previous season to pursue a coaching career in the United States. The man whose association with the club spanned over four decades left with little fanfare, a quiet departure for one of Goodison's finest and most diligent servants.

Had Johnson got a Sacchi or a Robson he might have shown a little more care and interest in his Everton hobby-horse, but after his last-gasp appointment of Kendall he discarded his toy. The funds to sign a Dino Baggio or Les Ferdinand did not appear to be available, and Kendall was left to scrape around the bargain basement, to trade David Unsworth for West Ham's Danny Williamson, and bringing in the unknown John Oster and Gareth Farrelly, as well as the undistinguished trier Tony Thomas from Tranmere Rovers. True, they had Bilic, a deal brokered by Royle and completed by Johnson while he scraped around for a new manager, but the Croatian's time at the club proved a farce.

The season began with the fans understandably muted and without much hope. A banner unfurled at the opening fixture against Crystal Palace reminded the chairman of his questionable priorities: 'A hamper is for Christmas, Goodison is for life.'

The pessimism that greeted the 1997/8 season was not without foundation. None of the signings made any real impact, and the team played with a lack of distinction. The sole pluses were the emergence of Michael Ball and Danny Cadamarteri. Dave Watson had introduced both teenagers to first-team action at the end of the previous season, but Kendall established them in the senior squad. Ball was a stylish left back who showed a cool maturity and composure that belied his years. The dreadlocked Cadamarteri exploded on to the scene with a flurry of goals, most notably against Liverpool in October when he robbed the Reds defender Bjorn Tore Kvarme, ran 40 yards and let fly with a rasping shot that sealed a 2–0 victory. That goal was the highlight of an Everton career that went rapidly downhill thereafter. He lost some of the swagger that had marked his exciting arrival in the first team and became a mere bit player. After he was found guilty of punching a woman in the face outside a nightclub in September 2001, he was released by Everton and tried later to pick up the pieces of his career with his hometown club, Bradford City.

The emergence of Ball and Cadamarteri might have papered over some of the cracks, but Everton seemed to be teetering perpetually on the brink of crisis. Prior to the derby win, 20,000 leaflets had been distributed by fans calling for Johnson's head. He was not the only one under pressure. Four days earlier, Everton had been dumped out of the League Cup, losing 1–4 to Coventry City. After the match Kendall had become embroiled in an argument with Craig Short, as the Everton players trooped off the field without applauding their visiting fans. It continued inside the dressing room when Kendall demanded that his players go back out on the pitch for an impromptu training session. They refused. Outright mutiny was only averted when they finally relented.

By November 1997 Everton were bottom of the Premiership. When Spurs arrived at Goodison at the end of the month, both sides came into the game having suffered four successive defeats. In a dire game, with the pitch ringed for most of its duration by stewards seeking to prevent a demonstration against Johnson, Everton lost 0–2 and were left four points adrift at the bottom of the table. After the match, 2000 supporters remained inside the ground, protesting at the chairman's running of the club.

That match also marked Neville Southall's seven-hundred-and-fiftieth game in goal for Everton. It was his last too, a most inauspicious end to the distinguished career of the club's greatest servant. Swansea City had been at the top of the league when Southall had made his début for Everton on 17 October 1981. Everton beat Ipswich 2–1 and he was listed as Neville Southman in the programme. Later that season he likened his début to a visit to the dentist and, with a hint of the perfectionism to come, added, 'I was disappointed with my all-round performance.' Southall had been standing in for first-choice keeper Jim Arnold, who had been 'on edge', according to Howard Kendall. 'I felt it was time for Jim to take a break,' he added. 'How long that break will be depends on Neville Southall.' Sixteen years and two League Championships, two FA Cups, one European Cup Winners' Cup and the Football Writers' Player of the Year award later, Southall, aged 39, bowed out as Everton's number one, uncompromising, unorthodox and unkempt as ever. When once asked how he would describe himself he famously replied, 'I don't fucking know.' Pat Nevin called him 'the classic eccentric with a complex character'. To an outsider he seemed a mass of contradictions. He was a man who trained religiously, whose idiosyncrasies and indifference to the press cultivated the image of the former bin man – sullen and withdrawn;

happier in domestic bliss with his wife and daughter than living it up with his team-mates. After the 1995 FA Cup Final Southall simply got into his car and drove home to Llandudno. Yet there was another side to the goalkeeper that few saw. For one, he was a committed helper of charities. For another, almost everybody who had played with him had been the butt of one of his practical jokes. Once, in the late eighties when playing in a friendly at Bellefield, he got bored with the lack of action and was seen lying across his own crossbar with all the lazy indolence of a lion. He was still perceived by many as a sad player: hair plastered to his forehead, socks rolled round his ankles, overheating in layer upon layer of clothing as he rocked between the goalposts while a patently inferior defence once again left him humiliated. But then, as the finest goalkeeper of his generation might just say, 'So fucking what?' Either way he was, and still is, sorely missed.

A month later Southall moved to Southend United. That season he also played for Stoke City. In his place came Thomas Mhyre, an £800,000 signing from Norway's Viking Stavanger. Paul Gerrard, who had seldom inspired confidence in his intermittent first-team appearances since arriving from Oldham, was overlooked. Kendall had been sufficiently impressed with his new signing to put him straight into the starting line-up for the away game at Leeds. Without a league win at Elland Road since 1951, few people gave them a chance. However, an accomplished performance from the Norwegian, including a fine point-blank save from Rod Wallace, saw them hang on for a point in a goalless draw. The run that followed lifted Everton clear of the relegation zone and won the keeper widespread plaudits. 'I've been really impressed so far,' Mervyn Day, Everton's goalkeeping coach told the *Evertonian* newspaper. 'If things go according to plan,' he added, 'he will have been very much worth the money.'

Off the pitch, matters in the boardroom – not least for Johnson – were going from bad to worse. His once-mighty business empire was on the decline, with Park Foods' losses up 19 per cent to £6.2 million. DJ Spuddles, his much hyped and oft-mocked 'revolutionary' flavoured potato snack, proved an embarrassing flop for the group, with half-yearly sales of £87,500 set against start-up costs of nearly £12 million. In another example of Johnson's ambition overreaching his ability to bring returns, he launched into production of the new snack food with some considerable zeal but without having any contacts in place to sell it to retailers. Perhaps he would have been better using the money to buy Alan Shearer. At the Annual General Meeting of Everton shareholders, days after Mhyre's début at Leeds, Johnson went on the offensive, stating that he had spent more money than any other Premiership chairman. His argument was persuasive but flawed. Since 1994 Everton had spent a net outlay of £26.7 million on players, Liverpool £20.7 million and Manchester United just £400,000, but he was missing the point. These clubs had the same laudable aims as Everton – namely the Championship and European success – but also had a strategy in place to attain them. Johnson's leadership of Everton was inconsistent and haphazard, he didn't even have a chief executive – a role he had sought to create when he arrived at the club but which was still to be filled more than three years later. As the shareholders' representative, Norman Dainty, said, 'If your businesses had been run like this club, they would have been bankrupt years ago.'

A prime example of Johnson's lax running of Everton was the £4.5 million signing of Bilic. The deal had been agreed by Royle, but should not have been allowed to go through until it had the approval of the incoming manager. Johnson went ahead and completed the deal anyway. In the event Bilic played a smattering of games that were dogged by injury, indiscipline and inconsistency. He eventually left Goodison on a free transfer, the £4.5 million written off. That, with Bilic's ruinously expensive wages, cost the club close on £8 million – or a cool £250,000 per game. In fact, the only thing of note he did in his entire time at Everton was to fake an injury in the World Cup semi-final, which got France's captain, Laurent Blanc, sent off and suspended for his country's victory in the final.

A day after the AGM, the recently installed club captain Gary Speed asked for a transfer. In a drawn-out saga, he got his wish at the end of January when he was sold to Newcastle United for £5.5 million – after he had gone on strike. That same week Andy Hinchcliffe was sold to Sheffield Wednesday in a £2.8 million deal. In little over 12 months Everton had sold three players of international calibre, and essentially replaced them with also-rans. Hinchcliffe's replacement, for instance, was the Manchester United reserve John O'Kane. Of those players of a similar stature left – Ferguson, Bilic and Barmby – only the former, now captain, was living up to his billing. Joe Parkinson and Danny Williamson were both out with long-term injuries. Neither played another game for the club. The squad had an undisguisably threadbare look about it.

Yet some of Kendall's wheeler-dealing reaped dividends. Mickael Madar, a former French international, added some potency to the Everton attack, although he looked every bit a short-term acquisition. The one-time Liverpool bad boy Don Hutchison surprised many by showing genuine quality and emerged as one of Everton's better players in later seasons. Between them this ragbag army of scrappers and journeymen strung together a run of results over January and February that put some distance between them and the bottom of the table. It was certainly not enough to fulfil the once proud motto of '*Nil satis nisi optimum*', or to put any clear light between them and the relegation zone. When they lost the penultimate game of the season 0–4 to champions-elect Arsenal, they plummeted back into the relegation mire. They went into the final game of the season against Coventry needing to get a result better than Bolton, who were away at Chelsea. If Bolton won, Everton were relegated.

By the time 10 May 1998, the season's final day, rolled round there was an air of resignation over Goodison Park. Unlike the Wimbledon game four years earlier, nobody expected to survive. That they did was not down to the efforts of the team, or a moment of inspiration, like Horne's thunderous equalizer. So excruciatingly awful were they that they couldn't even beat a Coventry City side, distinguishable only by their own mediocrity. Everton had fallen far. What Dixie Dean, the seventieth anniversary of whose 60-goal season it was that week, would have thought is anyone's guess. Between all his heirs, they had mustered but 40 goals all term.

Yet the Blues began the Coventry game well. As early as the sixth minute they took the lead. Gareth Farrelly, who had been out of sorts all season, let fly with a shot from 25 yards that nestled into the roof of the Coventry net. Goodison erupted, but the goal failed to settle the team. Coventry took control of the game, with their midfielder George Boateng outstanding, and David Burrows, a pariah in his brief time at Goodison, matching him. Darren Huckerby, Roland Nilsson and Noel Whelan all went close for the visitors. The longer the game went on, the more edgy Evertonians and their team became. Tempers frayed on the pitch, with Ferguson and Ball each squaring up to their midfielder Paul Telfer. Then, with 15 minutes left, a sudden roar, unconnected with events on the pitch, erupted. Chelsea had scored, through their player-manager Gianluca Vialli. Goodison reverberated with the echo of his name.

With five minutes remaining, Cadamateri was played through by Barmby's flick header. He was cleanly tackled by Paul Williams, Coventry's centre half, but the referee, Paul Alcock, inexplicably gave a penalty. With the chance to put Everton into a 2–0 lead, and maybe ensure Premiership survival, Nick Barmby was given the task of taking the penalty. However, he shot poorly, and Marcus Hedman saved.

Four minutes later the stadium was silenced. Burrows surged down the left and, eager to gain his revenge, sent a telling cross in for Dion Dublin, whose header slipped out of Thomas Mhyre's grasp and into the Everton goal.

The crowd bayed for the final whistle to bring an end to this most wretched of seasons. Among the whistles and jeers from the crowd came a second roar, as news came through that Jody Morris had added a second for Chelsea. Moments later came the final whistle at Goodison and the players ran for the dressing room as the crowd stormed on to the pitch, singing and dancing in relief.

The unrestrained joy of Goodison soon turned to anger. Before the Main Stand 10,000 angry fans were calling for Peter Johnson's head. Given what had happened, their fury was understandable.

○

JOHNSON SHOULD HAVE walked away there and then. He had already signalled that he would be receptive to the right offer for the club, although it was not yet formally for sale. But for reasons he alone knows, he had one final meddle in Everton's destiny.

Four weeks after the Coventry game, the board met and backed Johnson in a decision he had made to sack Kendall. The news was leaked to the press and Johnson was meant to meet or phone the manager to tell him that his third reign in charge of his beloved club was over. Embarrassingly for Kendall, he was left to answer speculation about his own future as Johnson flew to France on holiday without saying anything. In fact, it was three more weeks before Kendall was formally told that he was sacked, a shocking position to put any employee in, least of all the greatest manager in the club's history. Moreover, it was an undeserved end for Kendall, an appalling way to treat the man who had answered Johnson's desperate call just a year earlier.

Walter Smith became Kendall's successor and money was suddenly available to 'compete with the best'. While Kendall had been forced to swap Graham Stuart for Mitch Ward, and sign other teams' reserves to replace internationals sold to make ends meet, Smith found himself with an abundance of funds. Olivier Dacourt, John Collins, Marco Materazzi, David Unsworth, Steve Simonsen and Ibrahima Bakayoko were bought for a total of nearly £20 million. Where had all this money come from?

A month into the new season Johnson implied that it had always been there: he just didn't trust Kendall to spend it. It was a terrible slight on the former manager, but more so on the players he had brought in, most of whom were still at the club. 'It would have been totally wrong of me to release the funds last year – and you know that,' he said. 'There was no problem with the cash side, just the quality of the players that came in. Howard Kendall did not have his hands tied. Just before he left he paid out £1.6 million for John Spencer. Doesn't that say it all? Did you want Howard Kendall to spend all the money on the type of players he brought in last season? I think you would have been appalled.'

The reality was somewhat different. The money was no more there for Smith than it had been for Kendall. All that had happened was that the Rangers boss had been allowed to spend a short-term overdraft, which nobody had underwritten and which left a gaping hole in the Everton finances. When that had to be plugged in November, Johnson simply went behind his manager's back and sold Duncan Ferguson to Newcastle United for £8 million. Smith was furious. 'At no time was I consulted about Duncan's transfer,' he said. 'Last week I was made aware by a number of people that attempts were being made by the club to attract offers for Duncan Ferguson. I ignored this because the chairman had indicated to me that there was interest but it did not constitute any kind of transfer. On Monday morning I received the same information and with the rumours going around I felt it necessary to talk to Duncan as his manager. I spoke to him and told him that I felt moves were afoot to try and sell him and that I would speak to the chairman before the game [with Newcastle] to try and clarify the situation. That meeting never took place and, unknown to me, Duncan was transferred to

Newcastle during the match. I stress that at no time was I made aware that Newcastle had made an official bid and, more to the point, that the club had accepted it and Duncan was in talks with a view to a transfer.' Ferguson was said to be devastated by the news, and it took the intervention of Bill Kenwright to avert Smith's resignation.

Forty-eight hours later there was another stunning departure. Peter Johnson resigned his chairmanship of Everton, his dreams in tatters. In his place, Sir Philip Carter returned, and Kenwright was appointed deputy chairman.

Although Johnson did not return to Goodison after the Newcastle game, his Goodison sojourn was not yet over. In fact, it was another year before he relented in his attempts to hold out for a tidy profit, and his heir-apparent Kenwright succeeded him.

The whiff of scandal and farce was still not averted by his departure, when it emerged that Johnson had retained his controlling interest in Tranmere Rovers all along. The FA threatened to suspend both teams from the 1999 FA Cup unless he severed financial ties with one or both clubs. It also placed controls on transfers between the two neighbours and set about investigating Steve Simonson's recent transfer to Everton. Johnson returned to take control of the Tranmere shares he had originally sold to Frank Corfe, who had succeeded him as chairman at Prenton Park in 1994. The two fell out later and although he has never publicly disclosed how he had the right to reclaim them, David Dent, the Football League secretary, said that Johnson referred to a clause, in his original 1994 agreement with Corfe, that enabled him to claim back the shares. Johnson's arrangement to do this seemed to conflict with assurances he had given the league, and as such he was allegedly in breach of the dual-ownership rules for four years. Yet the authorities were unable to act decisively against him, waiting only for him to sell one of the clubs. With no bids accepted for Tranmere, he held out for the Everton sale.[6]

The breakthrough finally came on the eve of the new millennium. Kenwright came to an agreement with Johnson to buy his 23,725 shares in a deal worth £30 million. 'This is a great Christmas present for all Evertonians,' said Kevin Nolan, spokesman for Everton's shareholders. 'The news is fantastic that Peter Johnson is now going. It has taken Bill Kenwright a very long time to get to this stage, but he has the support of all Evertonians.'

The club was back in Blue hands after a gap of six years since the death of Sir John Moores, but what of Peter Johnson? Thirteen months after he had sold his Everton shareholding, Johnson returned to Goodison in his old role as owner of Tranmere Rovers when the two sides met in the FA Cup. Everton were well beaten that day, losing 0–3, and the look of elation on Johnson's face must have been unmistakable. He might have claimed the last laugh, but it was a return to a level – where the exposure was less intense, so too the stakes involved – more in keeping with his abilities.

In 1994 he had set out to restore Everton to greatness and establish them as one of Europe's finest clubs. Few could doubt the sincerity of his intentions, but he lacked the wisdom and imagination to take Everton to that level, or even to have the club function as an effective operation. Everton was run in the same manner an impatient teenager might have adopted when playing the computer game *Championship Manager*. It was despotic, short-sighted and, when Howard Kendall had taken over again as manager, downright nasty. Moreover, in all but one of the seasons Johnson was there, Everton flirted with relegation. Just as his attempts to take Park Foods a stage further and revolutionize the snack market with DJ Spuddles had ended in failure, with a further loss of £7.1 million being posted in 1998 and the share price tumbling, so too did his efforts to take on the world of football by shifting his allegiance from Tranmere to Everton. The name 'Hamperman', and with it the suggestion that he was no more than a small-time operator, plagued Johnson during his time at Goodison, but it was an apt gibe, which he never shook off. He might have had perennial aspirations, some might say pretensions, to move up a level, but lacking the nous to put them into practice, he was always going to be merely 'Hamperman' – no more than the Birkenhead boy made good, perpetually swimming out of his depth.

14

The People's Club

SCOTLAND HAD ALWAYS BEEN one of the main breeding grounds of Goodison's finest sons. From the days of the 'Dumbarton Delights' – Latta, Bell, Boyle and Holt – to the likes of Alec Troup and Jimmy Dunn, the stars of the sixties like Alex Young, and more modern legends, Graeme Sharp and Duncan Ferguson, Everton had almost always boasted some of Scotland's finest among their ranks. Yet as Scotland's fortunes as a footballing nation declined in the later years of the twentieth century, its finest export became not its players but its managers. In nine out of the 10 seasons that had preceded the start of the 1997/8 season, the English League Championship had been won by a Scotsman, and it took a Frenchman, Arsène Wenger, to set about redressing that imbalance. Likewise, in six of those 10 years FA Cup glory was masterminded by a Scot. In August 2001, when the *Observer* listed its 10 greatest club managers of all time, four hailed from north of the border. Just as the Italians provided a plethora of brilliant defenders or the Brazilians an abundance of wing wizards, Scotland seemed destined to be the production line for soccer's great gaffers.

Maybe because of the unhappy memory of Ian Buchan's brief reign as 'head coach' in the 1950s, or perhaps because the chance had never presented itself, Everton had always – despite the flirtation with Andy Gray – resisted the temptation to appoint a Scot to the helm. Come the summer of 1998, when Peter Johnson cast his net into the football wilderness for a replacement for Howard Kendall, Evertonians braced themselves for another managerless eternity. The board's first choice, Manchester United's assistant manager, Brian Kidd, was quickly ruled out of contention by his employers; and rumours linking several other Englishmen to the club – Kevin Keegan, Peter Reid and Ron Atkinson – were soon dismissed. An

Irishman, Martin O'Neill, was but an optimistic thought, and the prospect of a Welshman, John Toshack, too unpalatable, given his past associations.

Then, on 1 July 1998, the club called a press conference. There, the former Glasgow Rangers manager Walter Smith was unveiled as Everton's new boss, and his assistant at Ibrox, Archie Knox, was installed as his number two at Goodison. 'Rangers are the biggest club in Scotland but there's nowhere for us to go after Rangers except to try abroad or England,' said Smith. 'Now we have been given the opportunity here and that's a tremendous motivation for us and we will try to do as well as we can. Archie and me are a good team, that's been proved over the seven years we have been together at Rangers. We hope that continues, and that the success we achieved at Rangers continues. I'm a football man, I know all about Everton's history, and that is what attracted me in the first place when I was approached. Everton's traditions were some of the reasons that I accepted the job. They are a club that can get themselves into a winning position in terms of going for trophies and I intend to help them along in that respect ... It's a big challenge. It's one of the reasons we are both here.'

The appointment was viewed with some optimism by Evertonians, still mindful of the lengthy and embarrassing search for a successor to Joe Royle only a year earlier. Smith's managerial record, albeit within the confines of the two-horse race of modern Scottish football, was hugely impressive. Within four games of succeeding Graeme Souness towards the end of the 1990/91 season, he had won the first of six successive Scottish League Championships, only conceding that trophy in his last season in charge. Success had also come three times in both the Scottish FA and League Cups, but had eluded him on the European stage where, apart from guiding Rangers to the latter stages of the 1993 European Cup, he had failed to make an impression. That ultimately proved to be his undoing at Ibrox, but so far were thoughts of European glory from the minds of Evertonians after a traumatic 1997/8 season, that it was deemed a hurdle to worry about when it happened.

At Ibrox, Smith had spent £45 million on an array of domestic and foreign stars. In the late 1980s, there had been a brief fashion for top English stars – deprived of the chance to play in Europe – to try their luck in Scotland. With the lifting of the post-Heysel ban in

1990 and the influx of serious money into the coffers of English clubs, following the formation of the Premier League in 1992, it had become harder for Scottish clubs to compete, but Smith had succeeded in attracting the likes of Paul Gascoigne, Brian Laudrup, Marco Negri and, of course, Britain's first £4 million player, Duncan Ferguson, in the summer of 1993.

Walter Smith wasted little time in opening the Goodison cheque-book and blowing the (non-existent) transfer funds that Peter Johnson had granted him. First in was the stylish Italian centre back, Marco Materazzi, bought from Perugia for £2.8 million. A tall, confident, ball-playing defender, his signing was testament to Smith's ability at spotting talent unknown beyond British shores.

Similarly unknown was Strasbourg's skilful defensive midfielder, Olivier Dacourt, bought for £3.8 million. Like Materazzi, the Frenchman went on to shine for his national side and the initial signs were that he could fill the void in the heart of the Everton team long left vacant by Peter Reid, and later by the premature demise of the unfortunate Joe Parkinson. He was the star of Everton's 1998 pre-season tour, and correspondents following the team reported his progress enthusiastically. 'He can run, beat people, tackle, pass, block, pull rabbits out of hats, feed the multitudes with a loaf and a few fishes and raise the dead,' noted the *Toffeeweb* website, tongue firmly lodged in cheek.

The arrival of John Collins, who was to be Dacourt's midfield partner, was seen by many as the most important signing in years. At Glasgow Celtic, he had been one of the Scottish League's most elegant performers in the early nineties, before he benefited from a so-called 'Bosman' free transfer in 1996 when he joined AS Monaco. His time there saw him improve as a player, and he was a key influence behind Monaco's march to the 1998 European Cup semi-finals; that summer he had been Scotland's best player at the World Cup Finals. For Everton, his £2.5 million transfer represented a real coup, and for Collins, the main reason behind his decision to join Everton was their new manager: 'I have known him since I was twelve, when he coached me one night a week at Dundee United,' said Collins. 'We go back a long way. I have always been impressed by him. He was manager at Rangers while I was at Celtic, and I believe he can turn things round at Everton after a few poor years.'

Rather less orthodox was the way in which David Unsworth

returned to Goodison Park. He had enjoyed a successful season with West Ham after being horse-traded for Danny Williamson a year earlier. A £3 million deal that took him to Aston Villa was agreed and the transfer went ahead at the end of July, but within days of joining the Birmingham club he learned that his beloved Everton had wished to re-sign him, and he publicly declared that he would never have joined Villa had he known. There then followed a lengthy transfer back to Goodison, protracted by Peter Johnson's attempts to pay Villa less than the £3 million they had paid West Ham. Eventually, a week after the season kicked off, Unsworth made his début, coming on as a half-time substitute in a 0–2 defeat away at Leicester.

Everton's performance that day set the pattern for things to come. They had been uninspiring on the opening day of the 1998/9 season at home to Aston Villa, where they drew 0–0 after Collins missed a penalty, and followed the Leicester defeat with a loss at home to Tottenham. Four draws and a solitary win in September left Evertonians scratching their heads as to what had gone wrong.

The most pressing problem lay in attack. Partly because of a lack of creative drive in the midfield and partly because of the profligacy of the forward line, Everton simply could not score. At Goodison, the problem was at its most acute, with Duncan Ferguson not grabbing the first home-league goal of the season until 31 October.

In an effort to remedy the lack of goals, the Ivory Coast-born striker Ibrahima Bakayoko was signed for £4.5 million from Montpellier. Like Daniel Amokachi before him, his arrival was the subject of much excitement and he kicked off his Everton career in explosive fashion when, on his début against Liverpool, his first-minute header almost brought a goal. That moment of promise aside, Goodison waited for a deluge of goals, but they never came. Bakayoko looked lost in the English game and was continually plagued by rumours that he was not the promising 21-year-old he purported to be but a man 10 years older. A move to Arsenal the previous summer had collapsed at the last minute because, so the story went, tests on his bones revealed him to be 30. Hearsay or not, 20 starts and seven goals later, he returned to France, joining Marseille for a fee of £4 million.[1]

It was not until 23 November 1998 that a desperate Goodison crowd witnessed the first home win of the Smith era, when Michael

Ball's penalty saw off Newcastle, the same day Duncan Ferguson was sold to Newcastle in such controversial circumstances. Although the anger that followed the Ferguson transfer was softened by the news that it had precipitated the end of the ruinously inept chairmanship of Peter Johnson, the year-long takeover saga that ensued (see previous chapter) did nothing but unsettle a struggling team further. Goals were still hard to come by, and Everton had by far the fewest goals-for column in the league, even after an unexpected 5–0 thrashing of Middlesbrough in February, inspired partly by the return to form of Nick Barmby, and by Don Hutchison's successful switch to centre forward.

Both of these players were entering the 18-month-long peaks of their Goodison careers. Previously hampered by the inadequacies of so many of his team-mates, not to mention managerial decisions that left him looking baffled, Smith seemed to harness Barmby's unspent potential, pitching him in an attacking role on the left of Everton's midfield and channelling what little football his highly functional team played through him. It was an inspired piece of management, and one of the few 'footballing' successes of Smith's spell in charge. Hutchison enjoyed a similar renaissance and proved a far more adept centre forward – makeshift though he was – than Bakayoko, and in his favoured central midfield role he was a cut above that other expensive flop, John Collins.

February 1999 also saw fresh blood added to the Everton team. The 18-year-old striker Francis Jeffers, who had become Everton's youngest player since Joe Royle when he had made his bow against Manchester United on Boxing Day 1997, made the step up to the first team and immediately impressed with his pace, finishing and intelligent running off the ball. On his own, he was too inexperienced to shoulder the burden of the Everton attack, but with a more experienced partner up front, he was deadly.

From Heart of Midlothian came the 28-year-old Scottish international centre back, David Weir, for a cut-price fee of £200,000. The highly rated defender – big, strong and powerful in the air – immediately endeared himself to the home faithful with the revelation that he had snubbed Liverpool a year earlier, but beyond that did little to impress during the remainder of the 1998/9 season. Part of his problem was Walter Smith's insistence on playing him at right back. Indeed, the Everton manager's fascination with centre backs often saw four and even five played in the same team. Given his persistence with lumpen centre halves in positions where some pace, agility and creativeness were necessary, it is little wonder that Everton struggled to score goals and often seemed flat-footed at the back. Needless to say, the home faithful were seldom impressed.

They took heart, however, from the FA Cup. Early-round victories over Bristol City, Ipswich Town and Coventry City saw Everton's progression to the quarter-finals for the first time since they had last won it four years earlier and, as in 1995, they were to meet Newcastle United, this time at St James's Park. For more than an hour Everton held their own, with Unsworth's thundering left-footed drive on 57 minutes cancelling out Temuri Ketsbaia's opener, but then Newcastle regained the lead through a shot deflected off Materazzi. Thereafter Everton capitulated. The eventual 4–1 score-line might have flattered Newcastle, but it still meant the end of another season for Everton. With a 2–1 win over Blackburn – including an unlikely double from the mercurial Bakayoko – Everton rose to the safe but meaningless obscurity of fifteenth. With 31 points in the bag – just nine off the 'magical' total of 40, traditionally cited as the safety mark – and 10 games to play, Everton would surely not be threatened again by the spectre of relegation? Would they?

In the time-honoured tradition of the 1990s, they could not let a season pass without flirting with an exit to the First Division, and 1999 was to be no different. After losing their following three matches, including a first defeat to Liverpool in five years, Everton hosted Sheffield Wednesday – the club Smith had snubbed – on Easter Monday, 5 April. Making their home débuts were transfer-deadline signings Scott Gemmill and Kevin Campbell, although neither player inspired much hope.

Gemmill, son of the former Scottish international midfielder Archie, was himself a midfield international, but seemed to lack the same cut and thrust that had so distinguished his father in the 1970s. Tellingly, he was a mere reserve for a Nottingham Forest side who were nine points adrift at the bottom of the table.

The promise Campbell had shown in his early career in Arsenal's successful teams at the start of the nineties had seemingly faded away, and he was regarded by most Evertonians as little more than a journeyman, remembered mostly for a lack of composure in front of goal in his last days at Highbury. More recently, he had been plying his trade in Turkey, after a personally lucrative transfer to Trabson-spor, but had dramatically become available after suffering a public torrent of racist abuse from his chairman, who described him as 'discoloured' and a 'cannibal'. Alerted by this development, Walter Smith had signed him on loan for the rest of the season to fill the void left by Ferguson, and an out-of-sorts Bakayoko.

Although little was expected of either Campbell or Gemmill, neither performed badly in a game that was otherwise marked by a team performance of startling ineptness. Jeffers's twelfth-minute goal – which, *The Times* joked, 'represented something of a Goodison Park goal feast' – was not built upon, even though Sheffield Wednesday boasted a particularly lame team. Then, after the interval, Materazzi and Unsworth combined to commit defensive suicide. First, on 52 minutes, Materazzi's half-hearted clearance found Unsworth, who compounded the Italian's error with a spectacular miskick that presented Benito Carbone with a clear shot on goal, which he dispatched with aplomb. Sixteen minutes later the roles were reversed: Unsworth's limp header made it as far as the Italian, whose appalling backpass allowed Carbone to steal in to grab his, and Wednesday's, second goal. Everton's heads dropped and the remaining quarter of the match was played without fight or spirit – a factor of far more concern than the defensive mistakes. 'The signs are that no one at Goodison Park believes they can drag themselves back from the brink this time,' reported the *Independent*. 'After 45 consecutive seasons of top-flight football,' added *The Times*, 'this could be the year that Everton go down in flames.' Everton now occupied the third relegation spot, having played a game more than fellow strugglers Charlton. Things were not looking good.

Nobody, however, had banked on Kevin Campbell. In the first half of the Sheffield Wednesday débâcle, he had shown some deft touches, and his link-up play with Jeffers had brought a couple of sparkling moments from the youngster. Despite that, he was still thought of as a mere stopgap, and nobody really considered him a sound replacement for Ferguson. The perception of him was still as the rather clumsy, wayward striker, who had lumbered as an under-study to the prolific Ian Wright in George Graham's Arsenal sides of the early nineties. That was unfair: it took no account of Campbell's improvement as a player at both Nottingham Forest and Trabsons-por, or that George Graham had often asked him to fill roles that were incongruous – right-winger being one – with the sort of player he was: a hustling centre forward very much in the tradition of the Everton number nine. Indeed, his movement was good and link-up play excellent, and he possessed a poacher's eye for goal – an instinct not always apparent in Ferguson. If there were any lingering doubts about Campbell, he dispelled them over the final weeks of the season.

Six days after the Sheffield Wednesday game there was another 'six-pointer', this time against Coventry City. For the first 30 minutes, Everton energetically attacked their opponents, displaying the sort of verve that had been so lacking in the previous match. Then, on the half-hour mark, Jeffers, just past the halfway line, threaded the ball through the Coventry defence to Campbell. Ignoring the attentions of a couple of Coventry City defenders, he took it past Hedman and scored from an oblique angle. Everton continued to hold their own, even in the face of some bizarre refereeing, which saw Dacourt pick up his fourteenth yellow card of the season and Materazzi his third red. Finally, two minutes from the end, Everton's perseverance paid off: Barmby beat the Coventry offside trap and his cut-back was expertly turned home by Campbell.

The following Saturday Campbell was at it again, with two first-half goals in a 3–1 victory at Newcastle, Everton's first win at St James's Park since they had last won the title. 'A goalscoring centre forward!' remarked Mark Staniford, editor of the fanzine, *Speke From the Harbour*, 'What's all that about? Duncan Who?'

Everton were five points clear of the third relegation spot going into the meeting with its occupants Charlton Athletic. Knowing that a win would secure survival, Everton took to the task with gusto, Jeffers and Campbell running amok in a 4–1 win. Again Campbell scored a brace, with Jeffers and Hutchison adding their names to the scoresheet. A fortnight later Campbell hit a hat-trick in the 6–0 demolition of West Ham, which took his end-of-season tally to nine goals in nine games, and Everton to the security of fourteenth place. Goodison had a new hero to warm to.

○

WALTER SMITH's first season in charge had been set against the backdrop of the off-the-pitch civil war that had preceded and followed Peter Johnson's acrimonious departure. The effect of that was unquestionably unsettling, but even taking that into account, the team had struggled until the on-loan arrival of Campbell. His transfer was made permanent, at a cost of £3 million, but the financial problems facing the club meant that the summer of 1999 was notable more for departures than arrivals. Materazzi returned to Perugia and Dacourt to Lens in France, for £6 million – a tidy profit on a player who, in a better team and with more discipline, might have become a Goodison legend. Bakayoko was sold, while Craig Short and John Oster departed for Blackburn Rovers and Sunderland respectively. Over the next season other fringe players, such as Gareth Farrelly, John O'Kane, Tony Grant, Michael Branch and Terry Phelan, left with a mere smattering of further appearances between them. In the face of all these exits, only the Welsh international midfielder, Mark Pembridge, bought for £850,000 from Benfica, and the veteran Scottish international, Richard Gough, were acquired, in addition to Campbell.

Cause for optimism became even more muted as the start of the 1999/2000 season neared, when Thomas Mhyre broke his ankle while on international duty with Norway. Then, three days before the new season kicked off, contract negotiations with the brilliant Jeffers exploded into a public spat. Smith dismissed the young player's demands as excessive, and Jeffers apparently asked for a transfer. The quarrel was resolved within a week, but it marked the start of a series of contractual disputes between the Everton manager and his players.

Nevertheless, when the 1999/2000 season opened with a daunting Goodison tie against Manchester United, freshly crowned as European and English champions, such problems were laid to rest. On Smith's instructions the pitch had been narrowed ('That was symbolic,' said Charles Mills junior. 'It said it all about the suffocating negative tactics of Smith's teams') and Everton's wingless wonders gave a rousing performance. Paul Gerrard, previously noted only for his inconsistency in an Everton shirt, put in his best performance for the club, while Richard Gough was a similar colossus at the heart of the Everton defence, along with Dave Watson, providing an aggregate total of nearly 74 years' worth of experience. The result, a 1–1 draw, was no less than Smith's men deserved.

By late September, although Everton had failed to take a point away from home, their excellent form at Goodison had lifted them as high as seventh place. Then came a visit to Anfield.

One of the few sources of solace in a wretched decade had been

Everton's proud record against Liverpool. While they had made themselves difficult to beat and helped transform Goodison into a veritable fortress, Anfield was still one of Everton's less happy hunting grounds: in 30 years, they had won there just three times, and only twice in the previous 15. In the face of such a formidable record, Walter Smith's young heroes provided a stirring performance. Within five minutes they had taken the lead: Barmby played Jeffers through; he looked to be shaping up to shoot, but instead flicked the ball to Campbell, who took one touch before burying it past Sander Westerveld in the Liverpool goal. It was a lead that Everton never looked like conceding and could have added to before the game exploded into controversy in the last 15 minutes and the chances petered out. First, Barmby's through ball played Jeffers into an offside position, but the youngster's momentum kept him going and he clattered into Westerveld, who reacted by grabbing his throat. Jeffers punched the Liverpool goalkeeper (a mere seven inches taller than him) and the referee sent both men off. With Steve Staunton forced to take the goalkeeper's jersey, Liverpool were reduced to nine men when Steven Gerrard was dismissed for a sickening lunge on Campbell, and the dying moments were played out before the referee's whistle heralded the onset of glorious celebrations.

Five days later, Smith was crowned Manager of the Month for September, but as is so often the case, the award proved a poisoned chalice. In fact, it was mid-December before Everton won again, although five of the intervening eight matches ended in a draw. Nevertheless, it was unquestionable that this Everton side were proving more than a cut above anything Goodison had witnessed for some time. Europe, rather than relegation, was the word on everybody's lips, and when they beat third-placed Sunderland 5–0 on Boxing Day they became the third-highest scorers in the division. The goal famine of the previous season was a distant memory.

Indeed, Christmas 1999 was a happy one for Evertonians, with the news emerging that Walter Smith had signed a two-year extension to his contract and that Bill Kenwright's takeover bid had been accepted. 'I cried when I was told we had succeeded,' said Kenwright at the time. 'It has been a very difficult year because there was no guarantee that I would manage it. My mum thinks I'm mad, but I am a very happy man. We have no magic wand, but there is hope for us now.' A league table was also drawn up showing the performance of all the clubs to have experienced top-flight football in the twentieth century. Based on two points for a win (the system that predominated for most of the century) and one for a draw, Everton came out on top. Longevity may have played its part, but there was no question of the club's greatness.

The men who kicked off the twenty-first century with a 2–2 draw at home to Leicester City on 3 January might not have been greats, but among their number was a man who could claim his place amid Goodison's finest. Twelve days later, in another 2–2 draw, this time against Tottenham Hotspur, Dave Watson made his 523rd and last Everton appearance. Injuries and years had taken their toll on Everton's captain, and though he kept his playing registration until May 2001, when he took the manager's job at Tranmere Rovers, he had effectively called time on his playing days a year earlier. Despite winning a Championship medal in his début season, for the majority of his 15-year Everton career he carried lesser men in a succession of poor sides. As utterly dependable stalwarts go – either as pivot of the Everton defence, captain or even caretaker manager – few have come better than Watson. He will not be forgotten.

Two weeks after the Spurs game, Everton met Preston North End in the fifth round of the FA Cup at Goodison. Without an FA Cup win since 1958, and not in the final since 1964, Preston had not progressed so far for 35 years. Yet the Lilywhites were on the up. Although not in possession of a Tom Finney, or even a young Howard Kendall, they went into the game third in the Second Division and full of confidence. In a classic Cup tie Preston battled gamely in a match won by David Unsworth's sixty-fourth minute free kick and sealed in injury time with a strike from Joe-Max Moore, an American international striker Smith had signed shortly before Christmas. 'I'm disappointed we didn't get a draw,' said David Moyes, Preston's confident young manager. 'They took their chances when they came about and we didn't.' Maybe not, but his team's performance meant that *he* had left a lasting impression among the Everton hierarchy.

By the time Everton met Aston Villa at Goodison in the FA Cup quarter-final, they had entered the reckoning for a European place, after wins over Wimbledon and Derby County. Such good form and home advantage should have been critical factors in that stage of the competition, but Smith put out a 3–5–2 formation that set out to defend and failed to rouse the watching crowd. Steve Stone put Villa ahead after a basic goalkeeping error by Mhyre, but after Joe-Max Moore cleverly equalized, Villa should have been there for the taking, even after Carbone had put them ahead on the stroke of half-time with his side's second chance of the game. Yet Everton lacked either the passion or the inventiveness to break down a solid Villa defence in the second half, and lost their chance of reaching the FA Cup Final in one of the most open competitions in years.

The defeat marked a watershed of sorts. It effectively ended Thomas Mhyre's Everton career; he lost his place to Paul Gerrard, then Steve Simonson. Smith was obstinate in his refusal to play him, purposely leaving him out of the side lest he make his eightieth appearance for the club and Everton be subject to a clause in his transfer that would have resulted in a further payment of £300,000 to his former club, Viking Stavanger. True, Everton were deeply in debt, but the exercise was self-defeating. A year earlier Mhyre had been regarded as one of the Premiership's top goalkeepers and spoken of as a successor to Peter Schmeichel at Old Trafford. His confidence was wrecked. A succession of loan moves added to this and, all but out of the Premiership shop window, his market value plummeted. Eventually, 18 months later, he signed for the Turkish side, Besiktas, for £325,000, perhaps a tenth of his market premium.

Don Hutchison was also a victim of Smith's lack of munificence. With Dave Watson's playing days coming to an end, Smith had rewarded Hutchison with the captaincy – in the event of Watson being absent – at the start of the season, a role that by February he was filling on a weekly basis. Not only was he captain, he was, along with Gough and Campbell, one of the team's key men and best performers, already weighing in with five goals that season, mostly from midfield. However, with Hutchison's contract up for renewal in 15 months' time, the club were keen to start contract negotiations lest he move on a lucrative free transfer under the Bosman ruling. Yet on Hutchison's basic salary of £9000 per week, Everton were only prepared to offer him an increase of £750. In ordinary terms he would still be one of the club's middle-ranking earners – even though he was among Everton's star players – but in reality he could have expected to earn up to three times as much, plus a weighty signing-on fee, had he moved on at the end of his contract.

Hutchison misguidedly described the offer as 'a disgrace' and, with the contract negotiations over as far as his manager was concerned, Smith not only placed him on the transfer list but dropped him from the starting line-up for the next seven games. During that run, Everton lost three times, drew twice and won twice, sliding out of contention for a European place. To many Evertonians, although Hutchison's comments about a proposed half-million-pound annual salary were viewed with distaste, the attitude of the Everton management seemed particularly self-destructive: when the injured Kevin Campbell was ruled out for the remainder of the season the veteran Mark Hughes was signed on wages said to be twice Hutchison's, to avoid using Hutchison as an auxiliary centre forward. In 18 games, the 37-year-old scored just once and made little other impact, his presence ahead of Hutchison merely making Smith's thinking all the more baffling, and his inconsistency – as far as money went – more blatant.

Before his cut-price summer move to Sunderland, Hutchison was embroiled in one final piece of controversy. He was recalled for the Good Friday derby meeting with Liverpool, and the match was the usual tense affair. It seemed to be heading for its customary stalemate when, 90 seconds into the two minutes of allocated stoppage time, Sander Westerveld took a free kick quickly. It hit Hutchison in the back as he was walking away, and flew over the Liverpool goalkeeper's head and into the back of his net. 'GOAL!' screamed thirty-five thousand Evertonians. Apparently not.

The next thing they saw was the referee, Graham Poll, picking up the ball and walking off to the dressing room. No goal, he said, claiming that he had already blown for full time. 'The players got excited and confused as they do in derby matches but it was clear in my mind,' Poll told reporters after the match. 'Strange, then,' noted *The Times*, 'that his hands should have been down by his sides as Westerveld took the kick.' Walter Smith was similarly bemused: 'The fourth official put up two minutes on the board, but the ball crossed the line 15 seconds short of that. We have a computer that measures it. I feel the referee has taken the easy way out.' The game might not have had the same importance as the Clive Thomas FA Cup semi-final 23 years earlier, but on the blue side of Merseyside the conclusions were the same: Everton had been robbed of a derby victory by poor refereeing.

○

EVERTON ENDED the 1999/2000 season in thirteenth place, a final position that belied the progress they had made during the campaign. In fact, the last day of the season marked the first time they had dropped out of the top 10 since the previous autumn. Yet at the same time, the final league placing in many ways befitted Smith's Everton team – they always seemed destined to disappoint. The let-down of the FA Cup quarter-final with Aston Villa was a prime example, where, despite enjoying home advantage against a side similarly ranked in the league, Smith opted for a defensive formation, which still managed to concede two soft goals, then proved unable to claw back the deficit.

One man who had had a good season was Nick Barmby. Previously the proverbial square peg in a round hole, Everton's record signing had stayed free of injury and in his attacking, left-sided role weighed in with 10 goals in all competitions and deservedly won the club's Player of the Year award. His form earned him a recall to the England team after a gap of three years and eventually a place in England's European Championship squad, for that summer's finals in Belgium and Holland. Yet, like Don Hutchison's, Barmby's contract was up for renewal in the summer of 2001. Unlike with Hutchison, Walter Smith was prepared to pull out all the stops to keep him – even if it meant meeting his demands and making him the highest paid player in the club's history, on wages of £28,000 per week.

That, apparently, was not enough for Barmby, and he stated his desire to leave Goodison, so that he could complete his dream move . . . to Liverpool.

Not since Dave Hickson had moved to Anfield had a transfer caused such anger. The difference this time was the player's stated desire to leave Goodison for money. As Bill Kenwright, who had written to the England manager, Kevin Keegan, championing Barmby's recall to the national side earlier on in the season, put it: 'To say I was shocked and surprised doesn't begin to describe how I feel about it . . . he had used the six worst words in the English language as far as Everton fans are concerned. He said, "I want to play for Liverpool."' Others were more hostile. Kevin Ratcliffe said, 'His decision to turn down the contract he was offered at Everton – and then the club he signed for – is an example of player power going beyond the pale. Nick has made his own bed now, and it is up to him to lie in it, no matter how uncomfortable it may be.'

Three weeks after announcing he wanted to leave, Barmby signed on the dotted line for Liverpool at a fee of £6 million. Along with the sales of Hutchison (£2.5 million), Mitch Ward (£200,000 to Barnsley) and John Collins, who was reunited with his old Monaco boss Jean Tigana at Fulham for £2.5 million, Everton had an unusually full bank account, which Walter Smith did not hesitate to broach.

He made seven new signings during the summer of 2000 in an effort to improve the fortunes of the Goodison giants. First in were the full backs Alessandro Pistone and Steve Watson, who had been team-mates at Newcastle United, although Watson came via a spell at Aston Villa. Watson, signed for £2.5 million, was a natural contender for the right-back berth, which had proved so difficult to fill adequately ever since the departure of Gary Stevens. It was not easy to decide where to play Pistone – bought for £3 million. Although he had arrived at Newcastle three years earlier as a highly promising 22-year-old, sitting on the fringes of the Italian national team, and he looked accomplished enough in his début season in the North East, questions about his fitness and temperament were often raised. In three years at Newcastle he had played just 61 times in all competitions; while his team-mates had once given him a pig's heart on the premise that he lacked one of his own.

With Collins, Hutchison and Barmby gone, Smith set about restructuring his midfield. He signed SV Hamburg's Danish international midfielder, Thomas Gravesen, for £2.5 million. Nicknamed 'Mad Dog', he came with a reputation as a midfield hardman, but in the cauldron of the English league seemed more an aggressive puppy, and was a more elegant, if not always consistent, player than previously given credit for. Similarly polished but wayward was Sheffield Wednesday's Swedish international right midfielder, Niclas Alexandersson. Lens Ghanaian midfielder, Alex Nyarko, arrived for a hefty £4.5 million, but it was an Englishman and a Scotsman who attracted most excitement

Paul Gascoigne, the most prodigiously talented English footballer of his generation, was signed on a free transfer from Middlesbrough to enormous fanfare. At the age of 33, it represented a 'last new start' for the midfielder whose colossal talents had never been matched with achievements on the pitch due to a combination of self-destructive behaviour and appalling injuries. Oddly, his arrival was widely welcomed. Walter Smith, who was so often unforgiving when dealing with the shortcomings of other players, had shown abundant patience with Gascoigne when he was in his charge at Rangers, and in so doing brought out the best in him. Nevertheless, after two patchy years at Middlesbrough and his acrimonious exit from the England squad in 1998, Goodison Park represented Gascoigne's last-chance saloon. As the *Daily Telegraph* commented: 'He has one final, final chance to restore his tarnished reputation with Everton or forever be consigned to the dustbin of history.'

Finally, two days before the 2000/01 season kicked off, Walter Smith shelled out £3.75 million to bring back Duncan Ferguson from Newcastle. His return brought mixed feelings for Evertonians. On the one hand, he was the darling of the mid-nineties, who had battered defences – notably those of Liverpool and Manchester United – into submission time and again. On the other, after some progress in the way Everton played their football, there was concern that the one-dimensional hoof-it-and-hope tactics of the Royle years might return. Equally, Ferguson had been plagued by injury in his 21 months at Newcastle (as indeed he had in his first spell at Goodison) and, given the emergence of Jeffers and Campbell, who on a game-for-game basis were statistically the most prolific partnership in the Premiership, it was doubtful that Everton needed another big-name striker, much less one on a reported weekly salary of £35,000.

Yet with money spent and fresh blood in the squad, there was renewed optimism going into the 2000/01 season. Even Goodison Park had received a fresh lick of paint. Smith's summer arrivals, bought at a net cost of £7.25 million, were viewed by and large positively, particularly when allied to the experience already present within the squad and the plethora of promising youngsters – Ball, Jeffers and Richard Dunne – who had been establishing themselves over previous seasons. More signings were promised too. Smith had been allowed to go into a transfer deficit in lieu of an impending media deal – worth in the region of £20 million – which would write off the Goodison overdraft and provide more funds to strengthen the squad.

The first day of the new season brought a visit to Elland Road, where Everton celebrated half a century without a league win there by losing again, this time 0–2. Four days later, newly promoted

Charlton were seen off in style, 3–0, with two goals from the returned Ferguson.

Twice, in the next two games, Everton went into two-goal leads, and twice they gave them up, drawing 2–2 with Derby County at Goodison, then losing 2–3 at Spurs. By then – only four games into the new season – they were beset by an injury crisis with Gough, Pistone, Xavier and Ferguson all ruled out with medium-term injuries. Goodison's prodigal son had lasted just two substitute appearances and did not feature again until Christmas.

Plagued by injuries and increasingly by bizarre selections, with negative tactics usually thrown in for good measure, Everton embarked upon a run of just two wins in their next 10 games, which took in a derby defeat and another League Cup humiliation, this time at the hands of Bristol Rovers. Off the pitch, bad news came in October when it emerged that the media deal with NTL had collapsed at the eleventh hour, leaving another gaping chasm in the Goodison finances. Less than two years after Duncan Ferguson had been sold to appease the club's bankers, it seemed probable that more big names would have to go to pay for the previous summer's transfer binge.

Despite all this financial uncertainty fresh plans were revealed by the board to move Everton away from Goodison Park. Peter Johnson had first mooted the possibility during his spell as chairman, but his blueprints had been as sketchy as they were potentially ambitious and had died with his regime. Despite the controversy that they had aroused, when Bill Kenwright took control of the club one of his first acts was to commission a feasibility study assessing the possible expansion of Goodison Park. It concluded that the limitations of an inner-city site were such that the club should seek pastures new. The suggested location for Everton's new home was the Kings Dock area, just south of Liverpool city centre, and the proposals revealed what would have been one of the most advanced and magnificent structures of its kind in the world. It included a seating capacity of 55,000 (including 70 executive boxes and 2750 business seats), a retractable roof and pitch, plus extensive conference facilities. While the main purpose of the stadium was to host Everton's home fixtures, and possibly other major footballing events, it was to double as an entertainment arena with a varying capacity of between 5500 and 24,000. It was to be built in conjunction with public finance and private partners, which would provide Everton with a 49 per cent share of the project.

Everton unquestionably had a good deal. The stadium part of the development was estimated at £155 million, with Everton needing to meet just £30 million of that for their 49 per cent stake, and approximately £35 million was to come from the public sector. The rest of the cost was to be met by private investors and sponsorship and the total cost of the project – which was to include apartments, a cinema complex and a hotel – would top £300 million. Everton were set a number of tough deadlines in providing plans and financial backing over the following thirty months. The success or failure of the planned move – which was pencilled in for 2005 – rested upon their ability to meet those targets.

On the pitch, back-to-back wins over Bradford City and Championship contenders Arsenal and Chelsea brought renewed hope in November, but Everton were unable to will off a jinx that extended as far back as 1990 and win a fourth straight match, losing 0–2 to Sunderland. However, when they met Manchester City – now managed by Joe Royle – on 9 December after City's run of six straight defeats, there was hope that the November resurgence could continue. Walter Smith, as ever, put out an attacking formation, playing four at the back, stringing five across a workmanlike midfield, and playing Campbell as the solitary striker. Everton still conceded five goals against a side in sixteenth place, who ended the season relegated. Subsequent defeats against Charlton, Coventry and Derby plunged Everton towards the drop zone and proved to the fans that the level of spinelessness and negativity was not just a Maine Road aberration. Nevertheless, the nadir of the 2000/01 season was still to come.

On 27 January 2001, Everton met Tranmere Rovers in the fourth round of the FA Cup. This marked the return not only of Peter Johnson to Goodison (though in the event, perhaps wisely, he never showed his face) but also of Paul Rideout, the hero of Everton's last FA Cup triumph. Nobody was expecting an easy game in the first competitive derby between the two sides in more than thirty years, but Tranmere were fourth from bottom in the First Division (and ended the season relegated) and boasted just a solitary away win all season. Moreover, they had never beaten Everton. That all changed on that January afternoon. After some early pressure from the home side, Tranmere took a surprise lead on 21 minutes and Everton capitulated. 'They just fell apart, opened up and played into our hands,' said Rideout, after the game. Further goals came on 34 and 61 minutes, and Everton rarely looked like reducing that deficit. 'About 60 per cent of Everton's players let themselves and the fans down in front of a full house,' added Rideout. 'They should have shown passion and they certainly didn't do that – I really couldn't believe how easy it was at times.'

The problems that Everton – and Walter Smith – found themselves facing were deeper than poor form and results. In the previous decade, supporters had endured the long-ball game, below-standard players, defensive tactics, obstinate management and inexplicable decisions at every level, and suffered it well, in part through loyalty to the club but also because of the players' commitment to it. Success might have been infrequent, but at least Evertonians could hold on to the perception that the players – usually – cared, tried, and even played for love of the club. Sometime, however, during the 2000/01 season, that bond broke, and on 21 April things finally came to a head.

Everton, all but safe from relegation for another year, were playing Arsenal, who still had a mathematical chance of catching Manchester United in the hunt for the title. After Campbell had equalized Freddie Ljungberg's opener, Everton held their own against an Arsenal side who were struggling to find their rhythm. But as soon as half-time had passed, there was the usual surrender. Grimandi headed home from a corner on 55 minutes, and 12 minutes later, Sylvan Wiltord strode through to make it 3–1. Arsenal began to toy with Everton.

For one Evertonian, Stephen Price, it was too much. He climbed over the perimeter fence and stormed on to the pitch. He stripped to the waist and offered to exchange his shirt for Nyarko's. To watching Evertonians, his gesture was clear: that he could do better; and that the Ghanaian – whose languid style had proven ineffective since his arrival – was not worthy of the royal blue shirt. Stewards ushered Price off, but Nyarko was clearly disturbed by the incident. He pleaded with the Everton bench to be substituted and was duly replaced three minutes later, but the incident was not over. After the match he went absent without leave, claiming to be finished with football. Under contract to Everton until 2005, the club tried to sell him when he made it clear that if he were to play football again it would not be at Goodison. He was eventually shipped out on loan to Monaco, then Paris Saint Germain, but walked out of the latter in February 2003, leaving his future in limbo after the French side reneged on a promise to make his move from Everton permanent.

The 2000/01 season ended with Everton in sixteenth place, eight points clear of relegation, but the mood was downbeat. Even Bill Kenwright, so often a fountain of optimism, was moved to admit, 'This season has been miserable. It has been miserable for every Evertonian. Absolutely horrible. I think even more so because we gave Goodison Park a lick of paint, made ten or eleven signings over the summer and there was a lot of joy and expectancy around the club, but we have all failed to live up to that. That is the sadness of it. Everton cannot celebrate avoiding relegation. However, we can be thankful for it and grateful for it.' None of Smith's signings could be described as an unqualified success, plagued as they all were by injury, inconsistency or merely their manager's tactics. Of all of Everton's league games, between them they had started less than half.

With no money to spend and huge debts incurred after the collapse of the NTL deal and the previous summer's transfer splurge, rumours flew around about the sales needed to plug the hole in Everton's finances. The most likely candidates seemed to be Jeffers and the highly talented Ball. Both were nearing the ends of their contracts and set about talks with the Everton management aimed at improving their current deals but, just as they had with Hutchison, the talks broke down over the issue of purported pay demands. The club put it around that each was asking for £30,000 per week, a huge amount in anybody's terms, but not in the context of the other two top earners – Ferguson and Campbell. Had not Duncan Ferguson been given a five-year contract worth some £35,000 per week at the beginning of a season in which he had made just ten starts? And had not Kevin Campbell, at the age of 31, just signed a £30,000 per week deal that would take him up to his thirty-fifth birthday? It was an era in which players' salaries had been inflated out of proportion to their worth, but one in which Ball – who had just been capped by England and crowned the Everton Player of the Year – and Jeffers legitimately felt aggrieved and undervalued. Eventually they were sold: the left back to Glasgow Rangers for £5.75 million, the striker to Arsenal for £8 million.

The Celtic centre back Alan Stubbs arrived at Goodison on a free transfer and the Polish-born Canadian international striker, Tomasz Radzinski, for £4.5 million from Anderlecht. For Stubbs, at the age of 29, his transfer to Everton represented a 'dream move'. Born in Kirkby, the lifelong Evertonian had first risen to prominence at Bolton Wanderers. Although he was tipped repeatedly for international honours and a transfer to Goodison, neither materialized. A successful five-year spell at Celtic was interrupted by a cancer scare before his move to Everton, where he replaced Richard Gough, who had retired to the United States. 'I know I've always dreamed of playing for Everton and this is my last chance to do so,' said Stubbs, on completing the transfer. 'I simply cannot wait to pull on the Everton jersey for the first time. I know it is going to be the best feeling I've ever had in football.'

Radzinski's background was a little less steeped in the lore of Everton Football Club. Born in Poznan, Poland, in 1973, he was whisked out of the Communist state by his parents at the age of 13 for a new life, first in Germany and then in Canada, where he got his first taste of professional football with Toronto Rockets. A return to Europe with the Belgian side Germinal Ekeren, then a switch to Anderlecht, saw him prosper at a higher level. After he had scored five goals in 12 Champions League appearances in the 2000/01 season, Walter Smith was convinced that this slight, speedy player was the man to fill the gap left by Jeffers. Yet come the start of the 2001/02 season, Radzinski was missing from the Everton squad through injury, and it was to be the end of September before he made his full début. Thereafter he was playing catch-up with his fitness, and it was nearly a year before Evertonians saw him at his peak.

Even with the Canadian in the side, Everton struggled to look like anything other than a lower mid-table side. Tom Mills, who with his sister Lucy, had carried on the Goodison tradition set them by their father Charles since the mid-nineties, found Smith's tactical rationale often unfathomable: 'He kept playing 3–5–2 with all these centre backs. But what's the point of using wing backs if you have the narrowest pitch in the country?' Injuries also played a part, with

Ferguson once more an early victim and Campbell – who had been appointed Everton's first black captain at the season's start – joining him in the treatment room. Things got so bad in December that Steve Watson was deployed as an emergency centre forward.

A miserable Christmas, with straight defeats at Leeds and Sunderland, at home to Manchester United and – worst of all – 0–3 to Charlton, left Evertonians fearing that the club was about to go into freefall. When they lost their fifth consecutive game, on New Year's Day to Middlesbrough, they had slid to thirteenth place, just four points clear of the drop zone. Even Walter Smith was feeling the pressure and had intimated a couple of days earlier that he might have had enough. 'This season I'm starting to feel a bit of frustration. I just don't really feel we are getting any better,' he told the *Daily Telegraph*. 'This is my fourth season, and I need to see that we are improving. Managers are no different to anyone else. I need the motivation.'

The crunch game that would decide Walter Smith's future came on 5 January 2002, against Stoke City in the third round of the FA Cup. Almost eighteen years to the day earlier, Howard Kendall had taken a similarly beleaguered team to the Potteries for a tie that proved the catalyst for much future success. Some eternally optimistic souls banked on a similar turnaround, but most were braced for the worst. Even *Match of the Day*'s cameras were on hand to capture the potential upset in the offing: Everton were up against a Stoke side at the top of the Second Division on a damp, misty day with high winds: the circumstances seemed ideal for an upset. Indeed, the way Everton set out, with their dull, error-bound, flaccid football, it looked like Stoke were in with a chance. But, turgid though the Blues' display might have been, it was enough to contain Stoke, and in the second half they improved and began to put the Second Division side under pressure. On 63 minutes, Ferguson was fouled on the edge of the Stoke area; the resultant free kick was tapped to Stubbs and he curled the ball into the back of the Stoke City net to send six thousand Evertonians wild and Everton into the fourth-round draw. 'The most important thing at Everton this week was not what happened off the pitch, but what happened on it and we are delighted to have won,' said Smith, after the game.

Yet Evertonians had spent nearly fifteen years waiting and watching for 'another Stoke' or a Kevin Brock backpass that would act as the prompt for a change in fortunes. False dawn had followed false dawn, and those who believed that Stoke 2002 could be that turning-point were disappointed again. While Everton stuttered through the next two rounds of the FA Cup, against Leyton Orient and Crewe Alexandra, there was no discernible upturn in league form, despite the arrivals of the midfielders Lee Carsley and Tobias Linderoth, plus the extravagantly gifted French winger David Ginola on a free transfer from Aston Villa. If the signings of Linderoth and Carsley were made with a view to strengthening a threadbare squad, the arrival of an out-of-sorts Ginola was a signal of desperation. When Everton met Middlesbrough in the FA Cup quarter-final on 10 March, they had won just one league fixture since the Stoke match and stood a mere point above the relegation zone.

The performance in the Middlesbrough tie was to typify the sort of football to which Evertonians had been subjected during the majority of Smith's three and a half years in charge. They started well and held the Teessiders at bay for the best part of thirty minutes, but a comedy of errors led to a first goal, which thereafter opened the floodgates. A long clearance from Paul Ince was well covered by the advancing Steve Simonsen, but Pistone inexplicably intervened to head over his own goalkeeper and Noel Whelan was on hand to tap in a simple opener. Two minutes later, the tie was all but over. Everton were caught on break, Alan Boksic hit the bar, and Sylvian Nemeth followed up to head in off the post. Everton were in disarray, and a mix-up between Gascoigne and Stubbs allowed Greening to run through the middle unopposed. He played the ball to Boksic, whose shot was parried by Simonsen, but Ince was there to tap in a simple rebound and make it three goals in seven minutes. This was not an Everton side with the spirit to turn round such a deficit, and although further breaches were avoided in the second half, they were out of the FA Cup in the most miserable fashion. 'Surely now Bill Kenwright will act to end the suffering and dispense with the incompetent Walter Smith?' pondered the *Toffeeweb* website. 'No, he won't; Walter will stay until the end of the season, if not the end of his contract.'

Yet, like Joe Royle five years earlier, the writing was on the wall for the Smith regime. When he arrived for training at Bellefield the next morning, 'Smith Out' had been plastered over one of its walls. 'All the criticism comes with the territory and you just have to accept it,' he said. 'When you are going through a spell like this, criticism is always there, especially at a club like Everton where expectations will always be greater than at other clubs in similar positions to ourselves. I'll be soldiering on. I have done before and I will do it again.'

Yet even Bill Kenwright had had enough of the managerial reign of a man he described as a 'close friend'. Following a board meeting 48 hours after the defeat, it was announced that Walter Smith's term of office had ended.

When the news finally came, it seemed like a release for every Evertonian. The standard of football had become abysmal, with results to match; the tactics were inconsistent and one-dimensional; the standard of fitness, organization and enthusiasm of the squad was low. Smith's dealings with players were often inconsistent, and grudges were seemingly held against certain individuals, even to the detriment of the team. 'I think anybody in management – no matter what your profession – should be able to recognize talent and have the guts to try and harness it. Smith didn't want to do that,' recalled Charles Mills junior. Some of the 70 transfer dealings in which he was involved had been made with a degree of foresight; others, such as the Nyarko deal, seemed to have been naïvely undertaken. His preference for grizzled veterans, none of whom, with the exception of Richard Gough, had been a success, was a step back, given the prevalence of highly talented youngsters in reserve. 'He always brought in older players,' said Tom Mills. 'How many games did Ginola play? How many has Ferguson played?' Everton had won the FA Youth Cup three months before Smith became manager, but out of that crop, only Francis Jeffers established himself in the first team. Yet the biggest indictment of the Smith years was that his players lacked soul when they wore the famous blue and white colours. There was no passion and no heart.

On the other hand, there was also a sense that he had done well in difficult circumstances. He had shown patience in the face of Peter Johnson's meddlesome running of the club, and been instrumental in helping to oust him. Even in the face of extreme adversity, he had conducted himself with dignity and proven a worthy ambassador to a club that often verged on being a laughing-stock. Given the context of all the off-the-pitch acrimony – takeover battles, crippling debts, lack of transfer funds – he had done well just to ensure its survival. 'It was the tactics that did it for me,' said Charles Mills junior, 'but you do wonder, if he hadn't played that way, would they have gone down?' Indeed, you only had to look at the club he had turned down to take charge at Goodison, Sheffield Wednesday, who teetered on the brink of relegation to the Second Division and bankruptcy at the time of his sacking, and ponder what might have been. Perhaps Walter Smith was a man for the time: dour, stubborn, but a survivor. In the end, he had done just about enough, but there was no sense of progress. 'Walter Smith brought a stability and dignity to Everton when it desperately needed it most,' said Kenwright, when he announced his decision. His epitaph was generous, but nonetheless fitting.

Everton's board moved quickly to appoint a successor to Smith. A shortlist of five was drawn up, and 24 hours after Smith's dismissal, Kenwright had a midnight rendezvous with one of them in a motorway service station. Within minutes of meeting the candidate, Kenwright knew that he had found the man for the job. 'He said the word "win" about seven times in the first sentence,' Kenwright said later of David Moyes. 'There was a real energy and desire to learn. He told me about how he was a coach when he was 22. I said, "Why? Did you want to be a coach?" And he said, "No, I wanted to be a better footballer." We talked about his desires for the football team and at the end he said, "But more than anything, I want to win. I want to have players with me who want to win." It was a very good first few hours together.'

As a player David Moyes had underachieved. He had been a promising Celtic centre half in the early 1980s with a Championship medal in his trophy cabinet, and had just begun to establish himself in the first team when a section of the Parkhead crowd turned against him. He was just 20, and decided to move on. He was offered a trial by Arsenal and Sunderland, but rejected both. A move to Manchester City fell through, and Moyes found himself starting a tour of the English lower leagues. 'It sounds daft to say I turned down a move to Arsenal and went to Cambridge, but I did,' he joked later. 'It just didn't work out for me.'[2] Three years with Cambridge were followed by two at Bristol City, a move to Shrewsbury Town in 1987, then a return to Scotland with Dunfermline in August 1990. From Fife he moved to Preston North End in September 1993, via a few weeks at Hamilton Academicals. At Deepdale he finally settled, becoming captain and later assistant manager under Gary Peters. When Peters resigned at the end of 1997, Moyes – then 34 – was the surprise man for the job. If there were questions about his level of experience, his coaching qualifications were impeccable and he became the first manager in England to hold all of the UEFA coaching badges.

Moyes transformed Preston from a side who were seventeenth in the Second Division in January 1998 to the First Division play-off finalists who lost to Bolton at the end of the 2000/01 season. His achievements at Deepdale added to his reputation among other top managers, many of whom knew him from his playing days, when he would write and ask to watch their training sessions, a request deemed so out of the ordinary that they almost always said yes. On meeting him, they were invariably struck by his single-mindedness and willingness to learn. One of those individuals was Sir Alex Ferguson, who even asked Moyes to become his assistant in 1998 – an offer he turned down so that he could concentrate on Preston.

When the call came from Goodison, Preston North End were rather less enthusiastic about their brilliant young manager taking up the Goodison reins than Kenwright, and demanded £3 million in compensation for his services. Eventually they settled on a sum closer to £1 million, with bonuses payable if Everton retained their Premiership status that season and the next.

At teatime on 14 March 2002 – just 96 hours after the end of the Middlesbrough farce – a press conference was called at which David Moyes was introduced as Everton's thirteenth manager.

'I had a meeting with Walter who I respect greatly,' Moyes told the assembled journalists. 'I was sorry to see him leave the club – he was a very good manager and an honourable man. I asked him if it was a good club to join and he could not speak highly enough of it . . . The Everton supporters deserve a good side. I am from a city [Glasgow] that is not unlike Liverpool. I am joining the people's football club. The majority of people you meet on the street are Everton fans. It is a fantastic opportunity, something you dream about. I said yes right away as it is such a big club. I want to win and I am sure the supporters want to win . . . I want the players to know what it is like to win again, and I want the supporters to know what it is like to win. We will try and play a brand of football that the people will enjoy, but when it comes down to it, winning is the thing I want to do.'

His statement of intent won over Evertonians and he set about keeping his promise. A day's training was scant preparation for the visit of Fulham, but it was enough to instil the belief in his charges that they could win. Yet on walking into the Bellefield dressing room, he saw how big the step up from Preston actually was. 'David Ginola, Duncan Ferguson and Paul Gascoigne, some of the biggest names in football,' he said later. 'They were sitting on the bench, looking for direction. I thought, "Jesus Christ. What do I do here?" And then I thought I'd just better do what got me there in the first place. They seemed to think it was OK, what I did, after a while.'[3]

Moyes had an immediate impact on the futures of each of these three individuals. One of his first acts as Everton manager was to let Gascoigne leave for Burnley after 20 months at Goodison, which had been hampered by injury and a spell in rehab. It was tragic to witness this once extraordinary player attempt tricks he was no longer able physically to pull off; but on other occasions, usually against lower-league opposition, there were glimpses of the Gazza of old. Sadly, though, Goodison was no poorer without him. Likewise David Ginola, another of Smith's white elephants, followed him soon after, with only another substitute appearance to add to the two starts and two substitute appearances he had made.

The third man, Duncan Ferguson, enjoyed a brief renaissance under his fellow Scot. He was restored as captain, a position he had last held in the death throes of the Kendall era, for the Fulham game and put in a performance that brought back memories of his mid-nineties heyday. 'Duncan's an influence,' Moyes said, explaining the decision. 'We need to get him back thinking: "This is my club." It was a bit of psychology. We needed a rallying cry.'

Evertonians turning up early to the Fulham match saw straight away the contrast in styles between Moyes and his predecessor. Fifty minutes prior to kick-off, Everton's new manager was on the pitch warming his players up. This would have been inconceivable under Smith. As Lucy Mills put it, 'He was on the pitch in his tracksuit and trainers, running with the players. It was completely different to Walter Smith, who used to just sit there in his suit and shout at the players.'

Once play got under way it took just 27 seconds for the Moyes revolution to kick in. Alessandro Pistone's throw in was knocked back to the edge of the area by Thomas Gravesen, where David Unsworth met the ball and pummelled a left-foot volley beyond Edwin van der Sar in the Fulham goal. It was the signal for unrestrained delight among a crowd without a home-league goal in a month. Ferguson added a second on 12 minutes, and not even the sending-off of Thomas Gravesen, a man described by the *Guardian* as being as 'hare-brained as he is hairless', after only 28 minutes could sour the party. 'What's my philosophy?' grinned Moyes, after a 2–1 win. 'Winning is important, but wanting to win is more important. If I can instil that into my players, we'll be successful.'

Moyes steered his new team to safety with a further three victories in the last eight games of the 2001/02 season, lifting Everton to fifteenth place. Yet it was not that he had secured Everton's Premiership place that made him an instant messiah on the blue side of Merseyside, but the way in which he had done it. The ultra-defensive mindset of the Smith years had been forgotten overnight. Suddenly Everton had become a team who played, and attacked, without fear. Players who had been previously consistent only in failing to deliver were suddenly performing almost at their peak, and their games quickly took on additional dimensions: the sight of Pistone, for instance, overlapping and sending in a cross from the by-line would have been unheard of under Smith. Suddenly it was *de rigueur*. Everton became a team not frightened to test their opponents, no matter who they might be: on the last day of the season, they played Champions Arsenal, at Highbury, where the Gunners had a formidable reputation. Yet Moyes's men tested them until the end, and could count themselves slightly unfortunate to end up losing 3–4. 'Offensively, the Moyes revolution is pláin for all to see: a team that couldn't score goals has been banging them in for fun since he arrived, but defensively everything seems to have gone to hell in a handbasket,' wrote Lyndon Lloyd on the *Toffeeweb* website after that game. 'If he can solve that conundrum, next season is going to be very interesting.'

Moyes knew when he took over that he would have scant financial resources at his disposal, in the short term at least. Everton had restructured their debt with a £25 million loan from the American Investment Bank, Bear Stearns, shortly before Smith's departure. The new money was raised through a deal that gave the bank a charge over cash from season-ticket sales for the following 20 years. But after the cost of new training facilities and a youth academy, plus more than £4 million for Linderoth, Carsley and Ginola, had been met, just £5 million was available for Moyes. Nevertheless, they were funds he was to use well, and use imaginatively.

His first signing as Everton supremo was the 21-year-old Nigerian international defender Joseph Yobo, who had just starred for his country in that summer's World Cup in Japan and South Korea. The tall, elegant defender was signed for £5 million, with Everton paying £1 million up front to Marseille to acquire his services for a season, with an option to pay the balance if they sought to make the transfer permanent. The Brazilian midfielder Juliano Rodrigo came on a similar deal. He was signed on a season-long loan for £1.2 million with a further £3 million to his Brazilian club, Botofaga, should Everton wish to keep him after a season. Sadly, after just four substitute outings, Rodrigo snapped his cruciate ligament and never again played for Everton.

Moyes's squad also received a further boost in numbers from an unexpected source. Everton became the first team in Europe to establish sponsorship links with China after they officially unveiled communications firm Keijan as the new shirt sponsors in a two-year deal. While they had signed more lucrative deals in the past, this one was seen as a way of tapping into the potentially lucrative football-mad Chinese market. The other part of the deal involved year-long loans for the Chinese international defender Li Weifang, from Shenzhen Pingan, and the midfielder Li Tie – dubbed the 'Chinese Beckham' on account of his incredible popularity in the Far East – from Liaoning Fushen.

The new Everton manager had also spent much of the summer attempting to bring in a new goalkeeper. Paul Gerrard, who had played less than a hundred games in his six years at the club, had rarely held the confidence of any of his managers or the supporters, while Steve Simonsen, who had been promoted to first-team duty by Smith during the 2001/02 season, was dropped shortly after Moyes arrived. After lengthy negotiations to sign Derby County's Estonian international goalkeeper, Mart Poom, broke down, Moyes turned his attention to the 24-year-old Arsenal and sometime England goal-keeper, Richard Wright.

Having moved to Highbury a year earlier in a £6 million deal from Ipswich Town, then played a part in the Gunners League and FA Cup double, Wright was being groomed to succeed David Seaman for club and country. Few gave Moyes any chance of signing him, even when his £3.5 million bid was accepted. As well as having to persuade Wright to take a salary cut (to fit in with the Goodison pay structure), Moyes also had to talk him into forgoing the glamour of the Champions League and the upper echelons of the Premiership for the comparatively unfashionable Goodison. 'I want to get that Saturday feeling into the club,' Moyes told him, when he met Wright to discuss the transfer. 'That is, when you can take your family out for a meal on a Saturday night on a high because you've had a great victory, or you are absolutely shattered because you've done everything you can but you've failed.' Inspired, Wright signed.

And then there was Rooney. During the final days of the Walter Smith regime, there had been excited whispers about an Everton-mad schoolboy prodigy by the name of Wayne Rooney, who was shining – and scoring freely – in Everton's junior sides. Those who had seen him described in awestruck terms a boy with the technique of a Brazilian, lightning speed, and the bullish strength and physique of a man. They described his imperious touch, his acceleration, and his preference for *Roy of the Rovers* shots, which he would rain in with unerring accuracy whenever he caught a glimpse of the goal. But most of all they were taken by how naturally football came to the wonder kid. There was nothing manufactured about Rooney's talent: it was raw, instinctive and God-given. Even Walter Smith had tried to include the 16-year-old in one of his squads, only to be told by Premiership officials that he couldn't as Rooney was still at school.

He had announced his arrival to Evertonians in April 2002, when Everton had played in the FA Youth Cup semi-final against Tottenham. Rooney had already put Everton in front with an early goal but, on 38 minutes, made the killer blow. From 35 yards outside the Tottenham penalty area, he took a free kick, but scuffed the shot. The ball hit a Spurs defender, and bounced back to Rooney. Taking two steps forward, he hit a shot on the half-volley, which screamed into the top right-hand corner of the Tottenham net. The crowd rose to applaud an extraordinary goal, while the watching Aston Villa manager, Graham Taylor, later described it as the best he had seen all season.

Mindful that he had something special on his hands, Moyes included Rooney, now out of school, in his first-team squad to face Southampton at the end of April 2002, although he never made it off the substitutes' bench. He was then named in the pre-season squad that toured Austria and Scotland, and Moyes was duly rewarded with hat-tricks against SC Weiz and Queens Park and further goals against SC Bruck and Hibernian. 'A lot of people have heard about him now and I don't think he'll disappoint,' said David Unsworth, on the eve of the 2002/03 season. 'The biggest leap for any young player is going from boys' football to the men's game, but Wayne looks like he is going to bypass every level and go straight in . . . He's quick, skilful, strong and nasty, something I like and hope he doesn't lose, and it's hard not to get excited about how far he might go.'[4]

Come the opening day of the new Premiership season, with Everton celebrating their hundredth season of top-flight football, Rooney was a surprise débutant, lining up alongside Richard Wright and Li Tie to face Tottenham at Goodison. By his own standards, his first outing for the first team was quiet, although he neatly set up Mark Pembridge for Everton's first goal in a 2–2 draw, and was substituted on 67 minutes. Nevertheless, noted the *Observer*, the teenager 'revealed hope for the future'.

Moyes, however, was keen to shield him from over-exposure both on and off the field, refused to allow him to speak to the press and used him sparingly over subsequent weeks. By the middle of October, Rooney had made three starts and seven substitute appearances, plundering his first goals against Wrexham in the League Cup. It had been a good start and his performances had begun to attract notice on the national stage.

While Rooney's cameo appearances had added a much-needed injection of flair to the Everton team, as a unit they looked more cohesive, fitter and more willing to fight than in previous seasons. The standard of performances was not always matched by the results that they deserved in the early stages of the new season, and elementary defensive errors had cost them dearly on several occasions. The return of Joseph Yobo at the end of September from an injury he had suffered during the pre-season provided a boost to the back four, and he was soon thrilling Goodison with his composure on the ball and his distribution, not to mention his defending. 'He had a look of T. G. Jones about him,' said Charles Mills. 'He is outstanding. In the fifty years since TG left, I don't think I've seen anybody quite like him. Cool as you like, he never once looks flustered. For me, it was him that was the outstanding presence in many of those early games, not Rooney.'

On 19 October Arsenal were the visitors to Goodison Park. Unbeaten in their previous 29 league matches, their manager Arsène Wenger had, during the week that preceded his team's meeting on Merseyside, talked of the possibility of his double winners lasting the entire season without being beaten. It was a measure of how good his team was that nobody mocked the suggestion.

When battle commenced it was Everton who had the better of the early exchanges, but yet again they were let down by poor defending on seven minutes when Ljungberg put Arsenal in front after they had failed to clear. That was against the run of play, and 14 minutes later, Everton got the equalizer they deserved. Gravesen laid the ball off for Carsley, who rattled the post with a rasping shot, and the ball then fell kindly to Radzinski on the edge of the penalty area. He beat two defenders and hit the ball past Seaman to equalize. The game ebbed and flowed from one end to the other, and Wenger tried to step up the pressure by adding Francis Jeffers to the fray on 71 minutes. Yet it was not him, but the young star who had replaced Jeffers as Evertonians' source of hope for the future who broke the deadlock.

With 10 minutes to go Rooney replaced Radzinski. Seconds remained when he killed a high, awkward Gravesen pass 35 yards from goal. He spun around, cut inside and unleashed a curling, teasing shot from 30 yards that beat Seaman, crashed down off the bottom of the crossbar and over the line. Goodison erupted. In all its history it had seen few better goals and seldom in such dramatic fashion, or against such mighty opposition. 'Remember the name,' yelled the ITV commentator, Clive Tyldesley, struggling to make himself audible above the tumult, 'WAYNE ROONEY!'

'We were beaten by a special goal from a special talent,' said a magnanimous Arsène Wenger afterwards. 'You don't have to be a connoisseur to see that. He has everything you need for a top-class striker. I haven't seen a better striker under the age of twenty since I've been in England. He's a great prospect for English football.' The goal catapulted Rooney to national fame and his was the name on everybody's lips. 'I've been watching Everton since 1957,' said Charles Mills junior, 'and I have never seen a player as good as that. I've seen Duncan Edwards, I've seen Pele play live, I've seen Eusebio. George Best. Law, Dalglish, Keegan. He's got the two great gifts: his first touch is immaculate; and he has the vision to see things.' His father, who had seen Dean and Lawton, put him on the same level: 'Is he better than Lawton? Yes, I think he could be.' 'Wayne has got everything you look for in a top-class player,' said Graeme Sharp. 'It's not just his goals, it's his all-round awareness that catches the eye.' 'If I were his coach,' added George Best, 'I'd have him as the first name on my team sheet week after week.' Paul Gascoigne, with whose natural ability comparisons were inevitably drawn, was moved to say, 'He is a fantastic player and as long as he keeps his head right he will go on to be a great, an unbelievable player.'

Rooney the person was an additional source of interest, despite David Moyes's embargo on his outpourings. There was a certain charm, in such a cynical era, in the boy wonder starring for the club he loved (and for which he was even once a mascot) living with his mum and dad in an ordinary house, in an ordinary street, riding around his neighbourhood on a BMX bike and earning just eighty pounds per week under the terms of his youth contract.

Other Rooney watchers were less enthusiastic. Some tried to portray him as the kid from the wrong side of the tracks, another Gascoigne or Best, just waiting to self-destruct. The suggestions were unfair, without substance and made with a hint of snobbery.

Nevertheless when David Moyes received a call from a concerned member of the public about Rooney a week after the Arsenal game, he feared that some of the more snide prophecies might have been fulfilled. He need not have worried. Not content with being the new King of Goodison, Rooney wanted to prove he was still the lord of his street and he had been spotted having a kickabout on the road outside his house! 'We've got to look after him, and that includes every Evertonian. If you see him out on the street then send him home,' said a relieved but perplexed Moyes. 'I remember Sir Alex Ferguson used to offer a hundred pounds to anyone who'd tell him where his young stars were and I'm thinking of doing the same.'

Rooney's goal set Everton on a seven-match winning streak, which even ended the 51-year-long Elland Road jinx. Inevitably, it was Rooney who scored the winner. 'I am banging my head against a wall to explain how Wayne Rooney scored that goal,' said an awestruck Lucas Radebe, whom the youngster had turned and beaten when scoring the only goal of the match.

Yet it would be wrong to describe the Everton of autumn 2002 as being merely the Wayne Rooney show. His performances were

still often 20-minute cameos, usually in place of the impressive
Radzinski, who would accept the arrival of his replacement gra-
ciously. 'His technique, ability and vision are amazing for someone
his age,' he told the *Guardian*. 'I signed my first professional contract
at seventeen, too, but I ought to check his passport to make sure
he really is that young.'[5] The Canadian's forward partner, Kevin
Campbell, whom many had written off at the season's start, looked
fitter and sharper than he had done in nearly three years, and
shouldered the burden of leading the forward line well, particularly
since Ferguson was off injured again.

Although Li Weifang returned to China having played just one
game, Li Tie was to prove doubters wrong: a graceful, technically
gifted player, with an eye for a good pass, he was one of the surprise
heroes of Everton's 2002/03 season, and started three-quarters of the
fixtures, despite having played continuously for more than a calendar
year.

At the back, Yobo and Wright were not the only new stars: Tony
Hibbert, a quick, powerful right back, and an FA Youth Cup winner
four years earlier, had played a few games under Smith, but established himself in the first team, not once looking out of place in the
step up.

Within eight months of taking over at Goodison, David Moyes,
with hardly any resources and practically the same squad of players,
had turned Everton from a team of no-hopers into Champions
League contenders. By Christmas they were fourth, and ahead of a
Liverpool side who in the previous summer had spent twice Everton's
transfer budget on a single player and since used him as a reserve. It
was a stupendous achievement and a tribute to Moyes's dedication
to training and scouting his opponents. 'He's always prepared,' said
Tomasz Radzinski. 'He arrives on Monday morning with the whole
training mapped out for the week; he knows everything about our
next opponents and their specific weaknesses and what we need to
do. That means that training every week is different, and if you enjoy
training, you enjoy games. The results just follow.'[6]

In his dealings with the players, there were none of the disputes
that had marred the Smith era. Here was a manager who cared for
and nurtured his players, and they responded to his loyalty by giving
their everything for him. 'I'm a psychologist in everything I do,'
Moyes once explained. 'I have to be. The players need motivating at

all times. They've got to be happy.' His players were forthright in how much they enjoyed working with him. 'He has injected enthusiasm,' said Radzinski. 'You can have a bad day, but as long as you show courage and the will to fight, you'll have done well for him.'

Everton were over-performing against better and more expensively assembled sides. Cynics waited for slip-ups, but even when they came – a 1–4 battering by Chelsea in the quarter-finals of the League Cup, a 1–2 defeat at Shrewsbury in the FA Cup – Moyes's side had the resilience to pick themselves up and continue their progress in the league. The FA Cup débâcle, which possibly represented the worst defeat in the club's history (Shrewsbury finished the season bottom of the Football League), was soon compensated by the double fillip of Yobo's transfer being made permanent, and Rooney signing a three-and-a-half-year professional contract. 'This is a dream come true for me,' said Rooney. 'I never wanted to go to another club, and playing for Everton means a lot to me. It's difficult to put into words, but running out to "Z Cars" is simply the best feeling in my life. I was nine when I first came to the club – and there's been a lot of people who've helped me along the way, especially Colin Harvey who has been brilliant for me. The fans have also been great ever since I started playing. It's gone better than I thought it would have. It's been brilliant.'

A month later, on 12 February, Rooney made his England début against Australia, the youngest player ever to turn out for his country.

Everton, meanwhile, were still pushing for a Champions League place. A brilliant last-minute goal from Radzinski saw off Southampton's challenge in a 2–1 win on 22 February; just six minutes from the end they had been 0–1 down. It was one of seven times when Everton came from behind to win during the 2002/03 season, testament to the battling qualities Moyes had instilled in his team, if not to some of the defensive weaknesses that were still present.

As Everton approached their final 10 games of the season, though, the threadbare nature of the squad was exposed. They were fifth after the Southampton win, level on points with a Chelsea team that had cost more than £70 million to assemble. Ahead were similarly expensive and extensive Newcastle and Arsenal squads, and a Manchester United side that included a player who had cost as much as the entire Everton squad. Five points below them was a Liverpool side managed by a man who had spent £105 million on players in three years. Injuries, fatigue and suspensions all worked against Everton when they were pitted against these opponents. When they succumbed to a 1–2 defeat to Liverpool on 19 April, their Champions League hopes were all but ended. 'At the start of the season if anyone had said we'd be in this position, still with a chance to reach the Champions League and the UEFA Cup, we'd have taken that,' Moyes said, after the game. 'People are talking as if that's the norm now. It's great they're thinking like that. We're hurting because we lost to our local rivals, but they set out to qualify for the Champions League and we set out to avoid relegation. There's a huge financial gap between us.'

Lack of cash had also led to the collapse of the proposed move to the Kings Dock. As work on the plans progressed, costs spiralled, and it became clear that Everton was struggling to raise its share of the funding. A boardroom rift over how to pay for the stadium also hampered developments: Everton simply did not have enough to cover an increase in costs of some £38 million. They put forth a compromise bid, consisting of a 55,000-seat stadium, minus the sliding roof and pitch, with a 10,000-seat arena for conferences and concerts built alongside it. The regeneration company who had originally backed Everton rejected the new plans. Everton will remain at Goodison Park for the foreseeable future.

On the pitch, with four games left, Europe was still the priority but, lacking the resources to rejig his tired squad, Moyes's men fell to a 1–4 defeat against Chelsea on the Monday after the derby game, and only beat Aston Villa with a last-minute Rooney goal the next Saturday. Then came a 0–2 defeat away at Fulham, which left Everton in sixth place, still in line for a UEFA Cup place but needing to win their last game of the season against newly crowned champions Manchester United at Goodison Park. Everton started the day sixth – they had occupied a place in the top six since November – with Blackburn Rovers two points and a place behind them.

Interest from supporters of both Everton and Manchester United had been enormous in the build-up to the game. Until Arsenal's unexpected home defeat against Leeds a week earlier, the match had been billed as a potential title decider, with Everton playing the role of kingmaker. Even with the 2003 Premiership title in the bag, United obviously wanted to end the season on a high and reward their travelling supporters – some of whom had paid up to £250 for a black-market ticket – with a victory. Nevertheless, the onus was on Everton to win, and their energetic start was rewarded on eight minutes when Gary Naysmith and Lee Carsley played a short corner and the Irishman swung in a cross, which Campbell headed power-fully home: 1–0, but 83 minutes still to play.

It was a free-flowing end-to-end encounter, and testament to the improvement Everton had undergone in 14 months under Moyes that they continued to hold their own against a deadly Manchester United attack. The buzzing presence of Wayne Rooney was a constant threat, and so, too, was United's awesome Dutch striker Ruud Van Nistlerooy. Both men were profligate in their finishing, though, and otherwise came up against some inspired goalkeeping. Campbell was replaced by Ferguson on 40 minutes, due to injury. Three minutes later, United gained a free kick 30 yards from goal. David Beckham shaped up, and scored. Honours even, and with Blackburn leading Spurs 2–0 in their game, the Blues had suddenly slipped out of the European reckoning.

Everton continued to press in the second half, but for once the huge weight of expectation resting on Rooney's square shoulders seemed too heavy. He spurned a treble of gilt-edged opportunities, one of which, from point-blank range, even fooled a hasty electronic scoreboard into awarding a goal. At the other end, Richard Wright was performing heroics against Van Nistlerooy and, even more spectacularly, against Beckham. With the game drawing to its con-clusion, and Blackburn in an unassailable 4–0 lead at Spurs, a piece of luck was needed to decide Everton's European fate. Eventually, on 79 minutes, United got some of the latter: Van Nistlerooy was debatably fouled by Alan Stubbs; the referee, Mike Riley (who had already awarded United *six* penalties that season), pointed to the spot; Everton's players protested and the crowd howled; Van Nistlerooy kept his composure, stepped up and scored; Everton's European dreams were over.

'There are winners and losers,' sighed a disconsolate David Moyes, at the end. 'This has been a good season for Everton but there's no consoling us. We just didn't have enough to get over the finishing line.'

In the context of 125 years of Everton history, seventh place hardly ranked with Everton's best showings. But given the previous dozen years of sterile mediocrity it represented real progress. 'Ultimately,' wrote *When Skies Are Grey*'s Mark O'Brien, 'you get what you deserve, and we came a little short of quality when it mattered most. That doesn't change the fact that this has been the most entertaining season for years – and for that all Evertonians are grateful to Moyes, his staff and the players.'

Three days after the Manchester United defeat, Moyes was named as the League Managers' Association Manager of the Year. It was a fitting reward and some personal consolation in the midst of the week's disappointments. 'I believe he's destined to be a great Everton manager,' said Bill Kenwright. 'And I'm convinced he will become one of the greatest managers in the world.'

Expectations have risen in tandem with the progress of Everton under David Moyes. For him to be one of the great ones he will need time, money and the dedication of his players, fans and board. He might not have another Dean, Young or Ball, but he has Richard Wright, Joseph Yobo and Wayne Rooney, three men whose names might well register in a future chapter of Everton success. If Moyes can add a couple more stars to their number and continue getting the best out of the rest, he might one day fulfil his vice-chairman's prophecy. Nevertheless, the task of making Everton great again is one of the stiffest to face any individual who has been involved with the club. But, then, the motto upon which Everton Football Club was built has always placed a stern challenge in the hands of those who have run it: '*Nil satis nisi optimum*' – 'Nothing but the best is good enough.'

Notes

1: From St Domingo's to the Football League

1. Thomas Keates, *History of Everton Football Club*, Desert Island Books, 1997, p. 10.
2. Ibid., p. 15.
3. Ibid.
4. Ibid., p. 28.
5. Quoted in Simon Inglis, *League Football and the Men Who Made It*, Collins Willow, 1988, p. 11

2: The Split

1. Thomas Keates, *History of Everton Football Club*, Desert Island Books, 1997, p. 40.
2. Quoted in Percy Young, *Football on Merseyside*, Stanley Paul, 1963, p. 33.
3. Ibid., p. 35.
4. *Out of Doors*, 3 December 1892.
5. Young, *Football on Merseyside*, p. 43.

3: Early Stories, Early Glories

1. John Roberts, *Everton: The Official Centenary History*, Granada, 1978, p. 52.
2. David France, *Gwladys Street Hall of Fame*, Skript, 1999, p. 29.

4: Dixieland

1. John Keith, *Dixie Dean: The Inside Story of a Football Icon*, Robson Books, 2001, p. 45.
2. *Liverpool Echo*, 12 March 1938.
3. Ken Rogers, *100 Years of Goodison Glory*, Breedon Books, 1998, p. 72.
4. Keith, *Dixie Dean*, p. 65.
5. Ibid., p. 75.
6. Ibid., p. 79.
7. Ibid., p. 85.
8. Ibid., p. 87.
9. Nick Walsh, *Dixie Dean: The Life of a Goalscoring Legend*, McDonald and Jane's, 1977, p. 51.
10. Keith, *Dixie Dean*, p. 59.
11. Joe Mercer, *The Great Ones*, Oldbourne, 1964, pp. 19–20.
12. Keith, *Dixie Dean*, p. 131.
13. Ibid., p. 135.
14. Mercer, *Great Ones*, p. 23.
15. Rogers, *100 Years*, pp. 71–2.
16. Walsh, *Dixie Dean*, p. 54.
17. Stephen Studd, *Herbert Chapman, Football Emperor*, Peter Owen, 1981, p. 106.
18. Keith, *Dixie Dean*, p. 164.
19. Walsh, *Dixie Dean*, p. 56.
20. Keith, *Dixie Dean*, pp. 177–8.
21. David McVay and Andy Smith, *The Complete Centre Forward, The Life of Tommy Lawton*, Sportsbooks, 2000, p. 48.
22. Rogers, *100 Years*, p. 72.

5: Sagar, Smiler, the Master's Apprentice and the Uncrowned Prince of Wales

1. David McVay and Andy Smith, *The Complete Centre Forward, The Life of Tommy Lawton*, Sportsbooks, 2000, p. 10.
2. Ibid., p. 51. See also Thomas Lawton, *When the Cheering Stopped, The Rise, The Fall*, Golden Eagle, 1973.
3. Ibid., p. 54.
4. Lawton, *When the Cheering Stopped*, p. 45.

6: Hard Times

1. *Liverpool Echo*, 22 October 1951.
2. John Roberts, *Everton: The Official Centenary History*, Granada, 1978, p. 165.
3. *Liverpool Echo*, 27 February 1954.

7: The Golden Vision

1. *Liverpool Echo and Evening Express*, 4 April 1961.
2. Ken Rogers, *Everton Greats*, Sportsprint Publishing, 1989, p. 44.
3. Brian Labone, *Defence at the Top*, Pelham Books, 1968, p. 60.
4. *Liverpool Echo*, 7 October 1961 (after the 1961 Forest game).
5. See Rogan Taylor and Andrew Ward, with John Williams, *Three Sides of the Mersey*, Robson Books, 1993, pp. 113–14.
6. *Liverpool Echo*, 24 October 1962.
7. *Football Echo*, 23 March 1963.
8. George Orr, *Everton in the Sixties: A Golden Era*, Blueblood, 1995, p. 39.
9. Alex Young, *Goals at Goodison*, Pelham Books, 1968, p. 25.
10. *Football Echo*, 7 May 1966.
11. 'Harry Catterick's Secrets', *Liverpool Echo*, 4 May 1978.
12. Ibid.
13. *Liverpool Echo*, 15 August 1966.
14. Alan Ball, *Ball of Fire*, Pelham Books, 1969, p. 50.
15. Labone, *Defence at the Top*, p. 60.
16. Ibid., pp. 58–9.
17. Young, *Goals at Goodison*, p. 85.
18. Ibid., p. 81.

8: The Three Graces

1. *Liverpool Echo*, 2 December 1967.
2. *Daily Post*, 14 August 1969.
3. *Football Echo*, 21 March 1970.
4. *Liverpool Echo*, 2 April 1970.
5. 'Harry Catterick's Secrets', *Liverpool Echo*, 4 May 1978.
6. Ibid.
7. Howard Kendall, *Playing for Everton*, Arthur Barker, 1971, p. 83.
8. *Liverpool Echo*, 21 August 1978.

9: Decline and Fall

1. *Football Echo*, 2 December 1972.
2. *Liverpool Echo*, 7 February 1973.
3. Ibid., 5 February 1972.
4. Ibid., 4 May 1978.
5. *Daily Post*, 20 May 1973.
6. Bill Shankly, *Shankly by Shankly*, Mayflower, 1976, p. 150.
7. Dave Bowler, *Shanks – The Authorized Biography*, Orion, 1996.
8. *The Times*, 14 December 1974.
9. *Liverpool Echo*, 27 March 1975.
10. Robert Allen, *Billy: A Biography of Billy Bingham*, Viking, 1986, p. 168.
11. Duncan McKenzie, *One Step Ahead*, Souvenir Press, 1978, p. 103.
12. *Liverpool Echo*, 11 December 1978.
13. *Football Echo*, 25 August 1979.
14. *Daily Express*, 2 May 1978.
15. *Football Echo*, 3 December 1983.

10: Gray Skies Turn to Blue

1. *The Times*, 7 February 1984.
2. Ibid., 26 March 1984.
3. Ibid., 16 April 1984.
4. Ibid., 29 October 1984.
5. Andy Gray, *Shades of Gray*, MacDonald Queen Anne Press, 1987, p. 174.
6. *The Times*, 29 April 1985.
7. Ibid., 16 May 1985.
8. Gray, *Shades of Gray*, p. 170.
9. Howard Kendall, *Playing for Everton*, Arthur Barker, 1971, p. 103.
10. Howard Kendall and Ian Ross, *Only the Best Is Good Enough*, Mainstream, 1993, p. 156.
11. Gray, *Shades of Gray*, pp. 192–3.

11: The Devastating Impact of Heysel

1. *Daily Mirror*, 30 May 1985.
2. *The Times*, 30 May 1985.
3. Ibid., 4 June 1985.

4. Ibid., 15 May 1985.

5. Howard Kendall and Ian Ross, *Only the Best Is Good Enough*, Mainstream, 1993, p. 151.

6. *The Times*, 23 September 1985.

7. Peter Reid, *Everton Winter, Mexican Summer*, MacDonald Queen Anne Press, 1987, p. 52.

8. *The Times*, 1 February 1986.

9. Ibid., 10 May 1986.

10. Ibid., 12 May 1986.

11. Reid, *Everton Winter*, p. 170.

12. It was later reported that Lineker's transfer fee was £2.8 million. His agent, Jonathon Holmes, said that Everton accepted £2.2 million with cash paid up front.

13. Colin Malam and Gary Lineker, *Strikingly Different*, Stanley Paul, 1993, p. 45.

14. *The Times*, 2 July 1986.

15. Ibid., 8 December 1986.

16. Kendall and Ross, *Only the Best*, p. 191.

17. Ibid., p. 194.

12: The Unbearable Weight of Expectation

1. Tony Cottee, *Claret and Blues*, Independent UK Sports Books, 1995, p. 163.

2. Ibid., p. 168.

3. Interview with the author, November 1995.

4. *Liverpool Daily Post*, 25 January 1989.

5. *WSAG*, issue 3.

6. Rogan Taylor (ed.), *The Day of the Hillsborough Disaster*, Liverpool University Press, 1995, pp. 125–6.

7. Ibid., pp. 127–8.

8. Cottee, *Claret and Blues*, p. 180.

9. Ibid., p. 185.

10. Ibid., p. 172.

11. *WSAG*, issue 8.

12. *Liverpool Daily Post*, 6 November 1989.

13. *WSAG*, issue 8.

14. Ibid.

15. *Guardian*, 2 November 1990.

16. Howard Kendall and Ian Ross, *Only the Best Is Good Enough*, Mainstream, 1993, p. 242.

17. Interview with the author, December 1995.
18. See *WSAG/ Gwladys Sings the Blues*.
19. Alex Fynn and Lynton Guest, *Out of Time: Why Football Isn't Working*, Simon & Schuster, 1994, p. 44.
20. *Independent*, 20 August 1992.
21. Ibid., 16 September 1992.
22. *WSAG*, issue 20.
23. Cottee, *Claret and Blues*, p. 289.

13: Johnson's Odyssey

1. Ken Rogers, *100 Years of Goodison Glory*, Breedon Books, 1998, pp. 62–3.
2. Interview with the author, September 1996.
3. *Independent*, 19 November 1994.
4. Ibid., 8 April 1995.
5. Alex Ferguson, *Managing My Life*, Coronet, 2000, p. 367.
6. *Independent*, 4 November 1999.

14: The People's Club

1. Nevertheless the rumours would not leave Bakayoko. In October 1999, after the African had scored for Marseille against Manchester United at Old Trafford in the European Champions League, reports again surfaced claiming that Everton were conned into paying £4.5 million for a player who was eight years older than he said. The watching French coach Jean-Marie Guillou was quoted as saying, 'Bakayoko must be at least thirty because he was playing in the u-21s ten years ago.'
2. *Observer Sports Monthly*, April 2003.
3. Ibid.
4. *Observer*, 11 August 2002.
5. *Guardian*, 26 October 2002.
6. Ibid.

Bibliography

Allen, Robert, *Billy: A Biography of Billy Bingham*, Viking, 1986.

Ball, Alan, *It's All About a Ball*, W. H. Allen, 1978.

Barwick, Brian, and Sinstard, Gerald, *The Great Derbies: Everton v. Liverpool*, BBC Books, 1988.

Beardsley, Peter, *My Life Story*, Collins Willow, 1995.

Bingham, Billy, *Soccer with the Stars*, Stanley Paul, 1962.

Bowler, Dave, *Shanks – The Authorized Biography*, Orion, 1996.

Cottee, Tony, *Claret and Blues – My Autobiography*, Independent UK Sports Books, 1995.

Davies, Dai, *Never Say Dai*, Siop y Siswrn, 1987.

Ferguson, Alex, *Managing My Life*, Coronet, 2000.

France, David, *Gwladys Street Hall of Fame*, Skript, 1999.

Fynn, Alex, and Guest, Lynton, *Out of Time: Why Football Isn't Working*, Simon & Schuster, 1994.

Geldard, Albert, and Rowlings, John, *The Life and Times of a Professional Footballer*, Countryside Press, 1990.

Gray, Andy, *Shades of Gray*, MacDonald Queen Anne Press, 1987.

Inglis, Simon, *League Football and the Men Who Made It: The Official Centenary History of the Football League, 1888–1988*, Collins Willow, 1988.

James, Gary, *Football with a Smile, The Biography of Joe Mercer*, Polar Print Co., 1993.

Keates, Thomas, *History of Everton Football Club*, Desert Island Books, 1997.

Keith, John, *Dixie Dean: The Inside Story of a Football Icon*, Robson Books, 2001.

Kendall, Howard, *Playing for Everton*, Arthur Barker, 1971.

Kendall, Howard, and Ross, Ian, *Only the Best Is Good Enough*, Mainstream, 1993.

Labone, Brian, *Defence at the Top*, Pelham Books, 1968.

Lawton, Tommy, *Football Is My Business*, Sporting Handbooks, 1946.

Lawton, Tommy, *When the Cheering Stopped, The Rise, The Fall*, Golden Eagle, 1973.

Malam, Colin, and Lineker, Gary, *Strikingly Different*, Stanley Paul, 1993.

McKenzie, Duncan, *One Step Ahead*, Souvenir Press, 1978.

McVay, David, and Smith, Andy, *The Complete Centre Forward, The Life of Tommy Lawton*, Sportsbooks, 2000.

Mercer, Joe, *The Great Ones*, Oldbourne, 1964.

Orr, George, *Everton in the Sixties: A Golden Era*, Blueblood, 1995.

Orr, George, *Everton in the Seventies: Singing the Blues*, Blueblood, 1996.

Orr, George, *Everton in the Eighties; Singing the Blues*, Blueblood, 1998.

Ponting, Ivan, *Everton Player by Player*, Hamlyn, 1998.

Reid, Peter, *Everton Winter, Mexican Summer*, MacDonald Queen Anne Press, 1987.

Roberts, John, *Everton: The Official Centenary History*, Granada, 1978.

Rogers, Ken, *Everton Greats*, Sportsprint Publishing, 1989.

Rogers, Ken, *100 Years of Goodison Glory*, Breedon Books, 1998.

Ross, Ian, and Smailes, Gordon, *Everton: A Complete History*, Breedon Books, 1985.

Shankly, Bill, *Shankly by Shankly*, Mayflower, 1976.

Southall, Neville, with Ric George, *Everton Blues, A Premier League Diary*, B&W Publishing, 1998.

Studd, Stephen, *Herbert Chapman, Football Emperor*, Peter Owen, 1981.

Taylor, Rogan (ed.), *The Day of the Hillsborough Disaster: A Narrative Account*, Liverpool University Press, 1995.

Taylor, Rogan, and Ward, Andrew, with John Williams, *Three Sides of the Mersey, An Oral History of Everton, Liverpool and Tranmere Rovers*, Robson Books, 1993.

Walsh, Nick, *Dixie Dean: The Life of a Goalscoring Legend*, McDonald and Jane's, 1977.

Young, Alex, *Goals at Goodison*, Pelham Books, 1968.

Young, Percy, *Football on Merseyside*, Stanley Paul, 1963.

Index

OTHER PAN BOOKS

AVAILABLE FROM PAN MACMILLAN

PIERLUIGI COLLINA
THE RULES OF THE GAME   0 330 41872 6   £6.99

FRANCIS HODGSON
ONLY THE GOALKEEPER TO BEAT   0 330 35111 7   £6.99

JOE LOVEJOY
BESTIE   0 330 36750 1   £7.99

BOBBY ROBSON
MY AUTOBIOGRAPHY   0 330 36985 7   £6.99

All Pan Macmillan titles can be ordered from our website,
www.panmacmillan.com, or from your local bookshop
and are also available by post from:

Bookpost, PO Box 29, Douglas, Isle of Man IM99 1BQ
Credit cards accepted. For details:
Telephone: 01624 677237
Fax: 01624 670923
E-mail: bookshop@enterprise.net
www.bookpost.co.uk

Free postage and packing in the United Kingdom

Prices shown above were correct at the time of going to press.
Pan Macmillan reserve the right to show new retail prices on covers
which may differ from those previously advertised in the text
or elsewhere.